EH—A

Concise Encyclopedia of
World
History

General Editor
Theodore Rowland-Entwistle,
F.R.G.S.

Contributors
Antony Livesey
Kenneth E. Lowther, M.A.
Martin Schultz, B.Sc.
Stephanie Thompson

Editor
Trisha Pike

Art Director
Graham Marks

Picture Research
Anne-Marie Ehrlich, B.A.
Elly Beintema

SBN 361 03502 0

Produced by Theorem Publishing Ltd., London, for Purnell Books
Copyright © 1977 Purnell and Sons Limited
Published 1977 by Purnell Books,
Berkshire House, Queen Street,
Maidenhead, Berkshire
Reprinted 1978

Printed in Great Britain by Purnell & Sons Ltd., Paulton
(Bristol) and London

Concise Encyclopedia of
World
History

Lionel Munby, M.A.

Purnell

Contents

THE SPREAD OF MAN

The Scale of History

The *Pleistocene* began about one million years ago. This is the most recent geological 'age'. It has been broken up by four distinct Ice Ages—*Gunz, Mindel, Riss,* and *Würm*. In each of these Ice Ages the climate became colder and wetter: the ice pack at the two Poles was enlarged and reached farther across the globe; Africa, for example, became less arid. Between each Ice Age there was a longer, warmer phase and the last three Ice Ages were interrupted by shorter, warmer periods—one each in Mindel and Riss, and two in Würm. We live in the long warm phase which has followed the end of the Würm Ice Age, somewhere around 10,000 years ago.

An animal able to use tools certainly existed before the beginning of the Pleistocene. And the changes brought about by the Ice Ages helped this animal to learn; he evolved towards humanity. In the warm period between the second and third Ice Ages, recognizably human beings, making fine flint implements, lived in many parts of the world.

The periods into which man's early history has been divided are named after the materials which he used in tool making: Stone, Bronze and Iron Ages. These stages in technical progress are found in the same order all over the world; but although always in the same relationship they were not contemporary everywhere. Australian Aborigines were still in the Stone Age when

Time scale map illustrating man's achievements in writing, building, weaving and other skills between 2500 B.C. and 500 A.D.

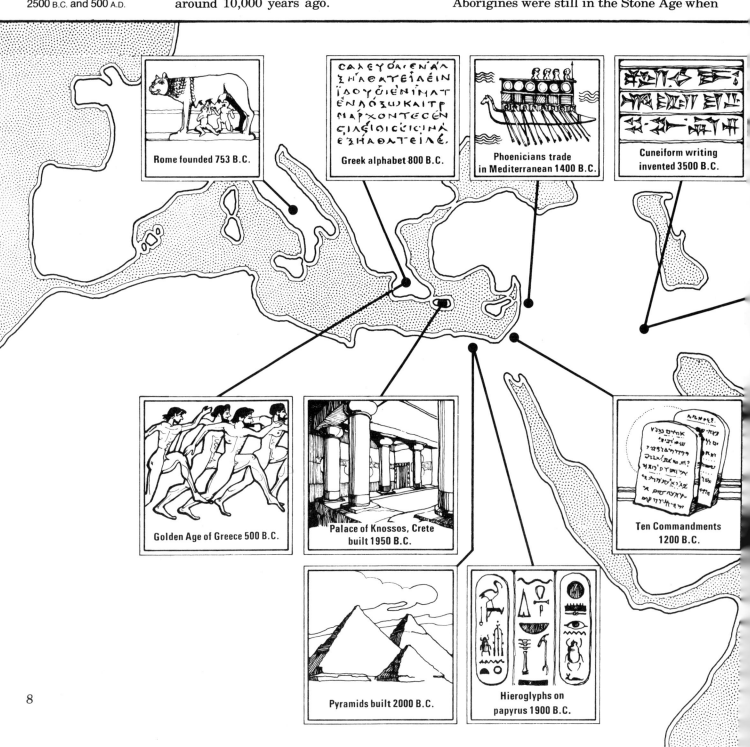

Rome founded 753 B.C.

Greek alphabet 800 B.C.

Phoenicians trade in Mediterranean 1400 B.C.

Cuneiform writing invented 3500 B.C.

Golden Age of Greece 500 B.C.

Palace of Knossos, Crete built 1950 B.C.

Ten Commandments 1200 B.C.

Pyramids built 2000 B.C.

Hieroglyphs on papyrus 1900 B.C.

Captain Cook first met them. Northern Europeans were in the Stone Age when Bronze Age merchants from the Mediterranean began to trade with them. These simple names (Stone, Bronze, Iron) were invented by a Dane, Thomsen, early in the last century. Today, archaeologists (the men and women who uncover the history of the past by exploring and digging in the soil for evidence) divide the history of primitive man into many more periods. The Stone Age has become the *Palaeolithic* (Latin for Old Stone Age) which has Lower, Middle and Upper phases; the *Mesolithic* (Middle Stone Age); and *Neolithic* (New Stone Age).

The Bronze and Iron Ages are identified in each part of the world by names, letters and numbers. The *Minoan* civilization of Crete,

for example (see pp. 30-1), flourished in the Bronze Age. The years in which important events occurred can rarely be known but the order in which they occurred can. So the history of Minoan Crete is divided up into periods of time in accordance with the different types of pottery discovered by the archaeologist. The palace at Knossos was built in the period known as *Middle Minoan I-IIIA,* and it was destroyed in *Late Minoan II.* The *Belgae* (see pp. 24-5), who invaded Britain between 25 and 50 years before Julius Caesar, are identified by archaeologists as Iron Age C.

It is difficult to realize that we have written historical records going back only some 5,000 years, but man has existed for possibly five hundred times as long.

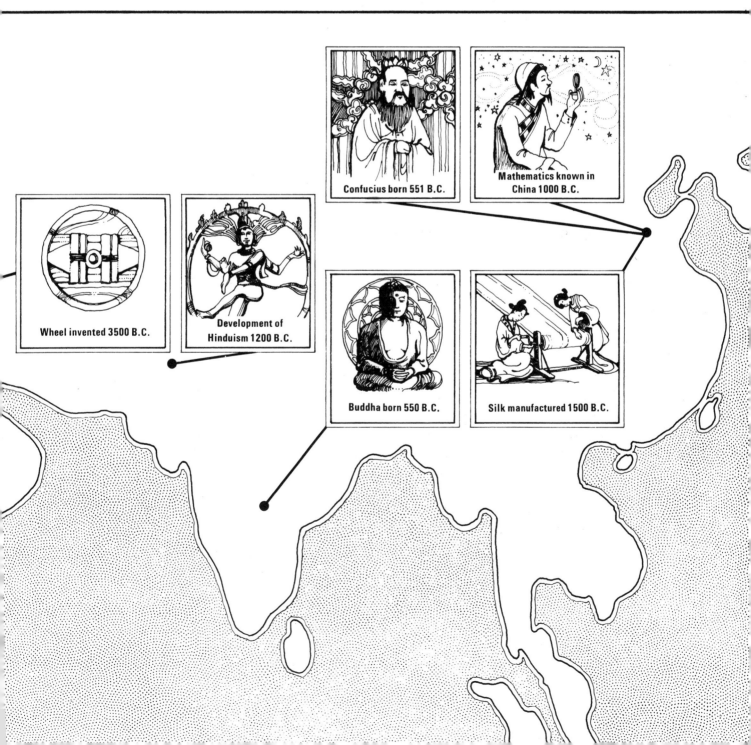

Confucius born 551 B.C.

Mathematics known in China 1000 B.C.

Wheel invented 3500 B.C.

Development of Hinduism 1200 B.C.

Buddha born 550 B.C.

Silk manufactured 1500 B.C.

The Beginnings of Man

People were shocked when naturalist Charles Darwin's new theory of evolution seemed to suggest that man was descended from the apes. For a long time people talked about an ape-man ancestor and looked for the 'missing link' between man and the apes. We now know that men and apes are remote cousins, belonging to different groups within the general family of *hominoids* (man-like apes and men). At a very remote period in the past this family began to divide into *pongids* (apes) and *hominids* (men).

The study of the ancestors of modern man is based on surviving fossils, often only bits of the body. The line dividing primitive hominids from primitive apes is not a sharp or clear one. When the two groups first began to grow apart their differences were less anatomical than mental and these differences cannot easily be identified in a fossil. What distinguished man from his ape-like cousins was his ability to make tools and use speech.

The first change occurred when a common ancestor came down from the trees and began to walk erect. This meant changes in the feet and in the pelvis. Walking upright set the brain at a different angle to the spine and its expansion began. A walking, grunting animal collected and used natural objects, stones and branches, as tools. When this animal began to make the tools which he wanted and to use speech to explain his needs to others of his kind, man appeared.

The changes in physical make-up which made man may have occurred in slightly different forms in many places. It is, however, in East Africa that we have the clearest evidence for this early evolution of man. But even here skulls and other parts of skeletons which have been discovered show several different mixtures. In some the teeth are very human, but the brain very small. Others, with larger brains, still have a bony crest running along the top of the skull, like modern gorillas. Although there were few of these primitive ancestors of man, there were many types. They seem to have moved across the earth and interbred until the number of different, surviving types of men tended to decrease.

From Africa men spread over the Mediterranean into Europe. By the warm period between the *Mindel* and *Riss* Ice Ages (see p. 8) *Pithecanthropus hominids,* who could make flints with thin, delicately formed blades, were living in Europe. The flints of this period are called *Acheulean* and they are found right through the third, or Riss,

Below: Australopithecus, the oldest and most primitive genus of man, appeared in Africa about four million years ago in the pre-Palaeolithic age. He was about 120 cm tall, walked upright and his palate and teeth were more man-like than ape-like. More than three million years later, Neanderthal man, a now extinct species of modern man, appeared in Europe. He had a much larger brain, and the tools he used were more advanced than anything known before.

Right: Early man began making tools from stones picked up off the ground. The hand-held stone tool gave way to stone lodged in a piece of wood and, later, fixed in a deer's antler for greater leverage and strength.

Australopithecus   Neanderthal

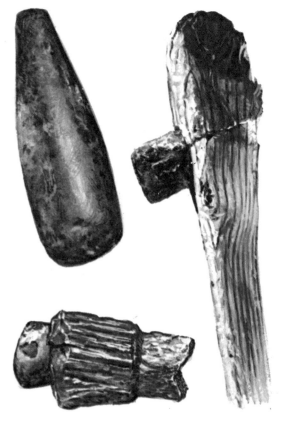

Ice Age. These were *Lower Palaeolithic* cultures (see p. 9). During the warm period between the Riss and *Würm* Ice Ages *Neanderthal* men entered Europe. Their flints (*Mousterian*) were more varied than the Acheulean but they did not use any new materials. The last (Würm) Ice Age seems to have wiped out Neanderthal man and, as it came to an end, *Cro-Magnon* man, *Homo Sapiens*, spread over Europe; this was the *Upper Palaeolithic* period. Men of this period made all kinds of tools, of stone, wood and bone. They were highly artistic and included the cave artists whose magical paintings have been found at Lascaux and other caves in France and Spain.

As the ice finally retreated, man moved northwards and many new groups, with different ways of life, developed. There were mammoth hunters in Moravia about 20,000 B.C. who carved ivory and bone. There were reindeer hunters around Hamburg about 15000 B.C. who used a new weapon, the bow, as well as harpoons. By 9000 B.C. we find men of the *Ahrensburg* culture using the axe. Between 7000 and 5000 B.C. *Maglemose* hunters and fishers spread all over northern Europe, stretching from Poland to the Baltic. They made extensive use of stone and antler tools and were fully acquainted with harpoons. This was a truly *Mesolithic* culture.

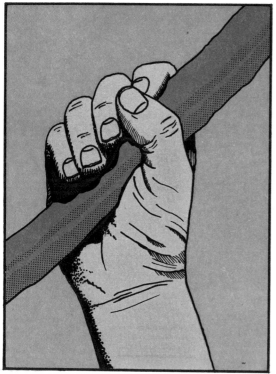

Left: Because man has an opposable thumb, he is not only able to grip objects very strongly, but is also able to make very precise movements with his thumb and forefinger, a movement monkeys cannot do. This enabled man to make the implements which were the basis of our earliest civilizations.

Below: The Upper Palaeolithic age saw the beginnings of man's oldest art form—cave art. One of the most famous examples is at Lascaux in the Dordogne, France. Horses, deer and other animals dominate early cave art. Colours were largely reds, blacks, yellows and browns derived from ochre and other natural mineral colours.

Early Man in Asia and America

Man may have evolved in different parts of the globe more or less at the same time. East Asia has the next best claim after East Africa to be a centre in which man emerged from the *hominoid* family. Fossil remains of the Giant Ape *(Gigantopithecus)*, a near cousin of man, were found in Kwangsi province of China in 1956. In 1964 at Lantian in China the skull of a possible *Australopithecine* was dug up. Much earlier another late Australopithecine was found in Java. Many examples of *Pithecanthropus,* the next stage in man's evolution (see pp. 10-11), came from both Java and Choukoutien near Peking. The bones of 45 men, women and children have been found at this site, with clear evidence that they made and used tools of flint and used fires.

Homo Sapiens emerged from the Pithecanthropus in the late *Pleistocene* and probably somewhere in western Asia. The existing races of mankind represent variants of the species Homo Sapiens which developed as man spread over the globe and settled in different environments. Most of Asia and America was settled by peoples of Mongolian or Mongoloid stock. These yellow-skinned people, some with crinkly, some with straight hair, may have evolved in the

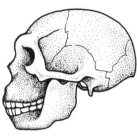

The skulls above show the development of man's predecessors over thousands of years. Australopithecus had a small brain, a massive jaw and dominant eyebrow ridges. Neanderthal man had a smaller jaw and a brain about as large as modern man's.

Above: As man spread across the earth and adapted to new environments, different races developed and within each race there were further variations. This is evident in the features of (from left to right) three types of Mongoloid, Caucasian, Negro and Negrito types.

tropical rain forests of south-east Asia and spread northwards into China and central Asia. Chinese, who vary in their physical appearance as much as do Europeans, are the best known of Mongolian peoples. Turks and Mongols are their nomad cousins. But Mongolian, or proto-Mongolian types, spread much more widely than central and east Asia.

India is inhabited by very mixed peoples.

The aboriginal inhabitants of India were of *Negrito* stock; they survive in the forest tribes, still with an almost Stone Age culture. The earliest invaders, however, were of Mongolian stock; they came across the eastern Himalayas. Mongoloid peoples survive today in Nepal, Bhutan and on the northeast frontier. Dravidians were a mixture of Negrito and Mongoloid peoples. Their great civilization in the Indus valley (see pp. 22-3) was destroyed about 1500 B.C. by Aryan invaders coming in from the north-west. The lighter-skinned Aryans had better weapons and a better knowledge of metals. They may have brought the use of iron to India.

There are no native Americans; man did not originate in America. The American Indians, who inhabited the continent when Europeans first arrived in the late 15th century A.D., were proto-Mongoloid in blood and physical type. That is, they were of the original stock from which the Turks, Mongols and Chinese came. They probably entered America through Alaska near the beginning of the last Ice Age, between 50,000 and 25,000 years ago, when the icecap held so much water that the sea level of the Bering Strait was 90 metres lower than it is today. There would then have been a broad isthmus between Asia and America. Not everyone accepts the argument that man reached America so early. Sandals

The Indians of California lived in dwellings similar to a modern block of flats. The rooms were rectangular, built closely together and often arranged in terraces. An entire village could be housed in what was virtually one building. The awning in the picture above is a modern addition to help in the preservation of the building.

Right: A Navaho Indian shaman, or medicine man, dancing. He is holding a rattle with which he keeps time during tribal chants.

have been found in a cave in Oregon which are some 9,000 years old, which is quite a short time after the melting of the last icecap in northern Wisconsin. All the experts agree that the earliest American Indians had reached what is now the U.S.A. by 12000-10000 B.C.

In a cave near the southernmost tip of South America evidence exists for human occupation as early as c. 6700 B.C. Slowly the invaders had moved southwards and evolved into the peoples we now know as American Indians. They lived in kin groups, knew how to make fire, flint knives and scrapers, and knew how to shape bone tools. They hunted with spears and spear-throwers, and had *shamans* or medicine men. There were three ways of life—hunting, fishing, and gathering nature's crops. The Pueblo Indians of California advanced from this primitive level of savagery towards farming and pottery making. But real civilization was the achievement of the Mayas of Mexico and the Incas of Peru (see pp. 122-5).

Skulls have been found in Ecuador and in part of North America which have archaic features like heavy brow vaults, retreating foreheads and protruding jaws, that are not found in American Indians. They are, however, found in *Australoids* and *Melanesians*. These physically different peoples must have been overwhelmed or assimilated by the American Indians. They too may have come via the Bering Strait or even across the Pacific Ocean.

The inhabitants of the Pacific islands are extraordinarily mixed racially. In the island of New Guinea and the Melanesian islands negro-type peoples predominate, though frizzy-haired pygmies and light brown-skinned peoples are found too. In Polynesia the latter predominate. Settlement of some islands is recorded, by *radio-carbon dating*, as early as 1500-1000 B.C. It is possible that the negroid population and the pygmies came to the Pacific from Africa by way of India, while the brown-skinned peoples may have come from Indo-European areas in central Asia through Malaysia and Indo-China. Boats from the large islands of south-east Asia and from the southern American mainland brought together, in the remotest islands, people of mixed stock, as well as crops and animals from many parts of the world. Only a people with considerable skill in navigation could have reached these islands, yet these people have remained extraordinarily primitive throughout the centuries of their settlement. There were about 800,000 people in the Polynesian islands in 1800 A.D. This population could have grown from roughly 50 people in 800 B.C.

From Savagery to Civilization

Palaeolithic man was a savage; he lived by food-gathering and hunting. Such a way of life set a limit on the numbers of human beings who could live in a given territory. At their maximum density every Australian Aboriginal needed 53 square kilometres to feed himself. North American Indians lived in much more favourable conditions, but there were only 17 of them in every 26 square kilometres. Even Palaeolithic man was gregarious—he liked the company of his kind, and he could speak and so learn by exchanging experiences. But the opportunities for talking and learning were pretty limited when people were so few and had to live so far apart. However, one vital discovery, which finally separated man from the animals, was made by Palaeolithic man. That is fire—a discovery unequalled in importance until man learnt to split the atom, for with fire man could radically change and so control his environment.

Another group of discoveries made it possible for more people to live in a given area. They were agriculture, pottery, and cloth making. The development of these three ways of improving life was probably under-

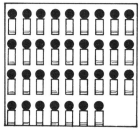

Above: Man's development is closely related to his conditions. The nomadic Australian Aboriginal needed 53 square kilometres to feed one person while the North American Indian, living in more abundant territory, could feed 34 people in the same area of land.

taken by women. This would explain why early peoples worshipped female gods, and in particular a mother goddess. By sowing the seeds of an edible plant and waiting for a new crop to come up and be gathered, human beings were able to ensure their food supplies much better than by gathering natural crops. Emmer wheat was first cultivated by man somewhere on the Russian-Persian-Turkish borders. Yeast and grain produced bread and beer. To store grain and food human beings needed containers which would neither rot nor let in water. Baking clay in a fire produced such pots. By spinning and weaving natural fibres human beings were able to make clothes and free themselves from having to depend on hunting for skins.

Men discovered how to tame animals and breed them for food and milk. Later, animals were used to carry people and loads of goods. Men improved their flint tools, making polished stone axes. The care of animals and tool-making was man's work from the beginning. Not all of these discoveries took place at the same time or in the same place. The *Neolithic*—New Stone Age—is marked by the making of better stone tools. But the most important discovery was of agriculture, which marked the end of the first stage in human history, savagery, and the begin-

ning of barbarism. In the pioneer centres this took place between 8000 and 7000 B.C.

It is remarkable that as early as 7000 B.C. these new discoveries had led men to live together in large groups—cities came into existence. Somewhere in the area between Palestine and Syria in the south-west and the Caspian and the Turkmen and Tadzhik Soviet Republics in the north-east the first city was built. The first of which we know a good deal of is Jericho, which is near the Dead Sea. British archaeologist Kathleen Kenyon's excavations in the 1950s transformed our knowledge of early history.

The period in which Jericho and other towns came into existence was specially favourable, for the last Ice Age and the *Pluvial* (or rainy age) which was its counterpart in Arabia and Africa had just ended. What is today desert was then much wetter and more fertile. At Jericho there is still a spring and around it irrigation ditches. These must have been able to support a much wider area of agriculture in 7000 B.C. The soil is very fertile. So there was a concentration of food available, on which a larger density of people could live. Two quite distinct groups of people lived in early Jericho. The earliest people were in Jericho well before 6800 B.C. They used hog-back bricks in their buildings, built defensive

Below left: No other discovery was as important to the development of man as the use of fire. Through fire, he learnt to control his environment. He could cook food to make it easier to digest, keep himself warm, light up the dark and keep predators at bay.

Below right: Excavations at Jericho in the 1950s led to greater knowledge of early history and man's first towns. Jericho was built about 8,000 years ago with brick dwellings, walls for defence and irrigation for agriculture.

walls round their town and a tower, which Kathleen Kenyon says 'would not disgrace one of the more grandiose medieval castles'. The walls were to protect them from a hostile people, who in the end conquered and occupied Jericho. The houses of these conquerors are marked by polished plaster floors. Wherever they came from, they too were city dwellers before they reached Jericho. So other towns older than Jericho may still be found in the Jordan valley. The pioneer townsmen of both these early levels of occupation in Jericho neither made pots nor had any writing. They were very close to the break-out from Palaeolithic savagery, and yet they had created a town.

The importance of town or city life to human beings is immense. Civilization was the third stage in human history and the word, civilization, comes from the Latin *civis* meaning a town or city. This is no accident, for it is only when large numbers of men and women live closely together that specialization becomes possible. No longer were all men hunters or herdsmen: some could farm, others could trade, and others make tools. There was even enough food for some just to think. The cities in which we know that man took his next jump forward were in Sumeria—Mesopotamia—and the best known is Ur, in southern Iraq.

15

The River Valley Civilizations

The first civilized states in the world appeared in river valleys: in the lush 'Fertile Crescent' of the Nile Valley and Mesopotamia (the land between the Tigris and Euphrates rivers) between 4000 and 3000 B.C., in the Indus valley of Pakistan about 2500 B.C. and in the valley of the Huangho (Yellow) river in China about 2000 B.C. It cannot be an accident that the world's first states all appeared in river valleys of a special kind. These five rivers were all very long and with a large and constant supply of water which flooded in their lower regions.

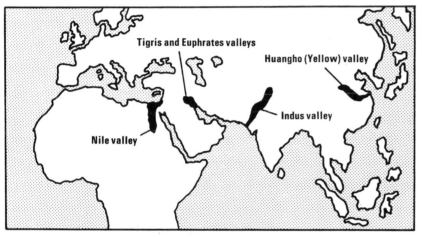

Map of the river valley civilizations showing the Nile valley, the land between the Tigris and Euphrates rivers, the Indus valley in Pakistan and the Huangho valley in China.

Floods are destructive, but if the flood waters can be captured in irrigation systems and the water guided through channels over the surrounding soil it can make possible the growth of rich crops. Floods also bring down fertile soil and deposit it in these river valleys. With water available and the hot climate these river valleys became some of the richest crop-growing soils in the world.

As the climate became drier with the retreat of the ice, following the last Ice Age, the countryside around these river valleys became too dry to sustain life in abundance. Animals and their hunters moved into the marshy flood plains. They found food growing and animals flourishing. It was an ideal area into which to introduce agriculture. But to give security and continuity, the flood waters had to be controlled. This could not be done by the small *Neolithic* village communities nor even by town populations such as those of Jericho. To control the floods and get the full benefit of life in the river valleys, the manpower of many villages had to be united under one controlling power.

So we find god-kings *(Pharaohs)* uniting the whole Nile valley. In the Huangho valley Chinese rulers achieved the same unification. It is no accident that in two different parts of the world a similar problem produced a similar solution. In these two cases flood control had to be along the complete length of the river to be really effective. So in both cases very centralized governments came into existence headed by absolute rulers employing a large number of full-time officials to manage their states. These were totalitarian bureaucratic states, in which for several thousand years a succession of dynasties—family lines of rulers—held power.

In the other two river valleys—Mesopotamia and the Indus—a more localized control of flood waters was sufficient. So in Mesopotamia different cities in succession became rulers of states which covered only parts of the river system. In the Indus valley there was a uniform culture for a thousand years. We do not know its history because no written record is available, but the evidence suggests that here too there were several states. Certainly neither Mesopotamia nor the Indus valley produced long lines of absolute rulers with the total control of their subjects which the rulers of the Nile and Yellow river valleys had.

But in all the river valleys similar developments took place. Mesopotamia was the first, but the others copied its ideas and developed their own versions. The new ideas which men living in cities and organized in states produced were at the heart of what we mean by civilization. A large group of people organizing their daily life had to keep records. To do so writing was invented. The first form of writing was the *pictograph*, from which the *ideograph* developed; then came the *phonograph*, and finally individual letters of an alphabet (see diagram). With the invention of writing history begins in the formal sense, for we have written records of man's activity.

With writing the Mesopotamians invented units of measurements. Without standard measurements, cities and irrigation systems could not be built properly. Standard weights and a balance were necessary with the growing exchange of goods in a more specialized society. Money as a unit of exchange was necessary too. In time metal coins were used, but before this all kinds of goods, the cow in particular, were used. So important did this seem that the cow became a sacred animal to the Indians and the Scythians. The merchants' god was a cow god. To know when the flood waters might be expected men needed some measure of time. They looked to the orderly movements of the sun and moon and stars. Astronomy was, in a sense, the first science and with it the calendar was created.

In these new civilized societies, men soon found better materials for tools and weapons

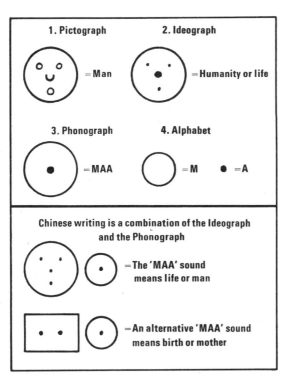

1. Pictograph = Man

2. Ideograph = Humanity or life

3. Phonograph = MAA

4. Alphabet = M ● = A

Chinese writing is a combination of the Ideograph and the Phonograph

= The 'MAA' sound means life or man

= An alternative 'MAA' sound means birth or mother

than stone or wood. They learned with the help of fire to heat natural ores and mould the metal which flowed from them. First copper, then copper combined with tin to make the harder bronze, and much later iron, were smelted. Gold and silver were worked too. *Metallurgy*, the craft of working metals, was not the only technical advance in the river valley. The potter's wheel made it much easier to work clay and make better pots. The wheel was used to help animals move larger loads; the wheeled vehicle was a vital discovery. The plough was developed out of the hoe and this made for better crops.

These discoveries were not made all at once nor known everywhere. The Egyptians in the Nile valley, for example, used the potter's wheel for a thousand years before using wheeled transport, while in primitive Europe, north of the Alps, wheeled transport was in use a long time before the potter's wheel was known.

Mesopotamia

Mesopotamia, the land between the two rivers Tigris and Euphrates, now in the state of Iraq, is the best known centre of the first mature and literate civilization. There were towns long before this emerged in the *fifth millennium* B.C. (see pp. 14-15) and archaeologists are beginning to find evidence of cities outside Mesopotamia with just as early a civilization. Tepe Yahya, on the south of the Iranian plateau, has recently produced tablets with writing which is contemporary with the earliest known writing from Uruk in Mesopotamia. It is in proto-Elamite script. Tepe Yahya seems to have been occupied continuously from c. 4500 B.C. to 200 A.D. Its merchants traded with the Persian Gulf and with countries to the east (see pp. 22-3). This suggests that trade colonies developed over a wide area, not only in the river valleys but also in upland areas, and that they were linked by an advanced trading network. This was a society with writing, keeping organized accounts and archives. Certainly in Mesopotamia it flourished remarkably.

Mesopotamia was an area of many towns —Ur, Lagash, Uruk, Akkad; the area was known as Sumer to its inhabitants. Sumerian cities were centred on a great temple, a *ziggurat* or stepped building, looking rather like a *pyramid* but with a flat top. The ruler

Two objects found in the royal tombs at Ur were the Ram found in the Thicket (right) and the 'Royal Standard' of Ur (below). The 'standard' is a long box decorated with figures of shell and limestone on a blue lapis-lazuli background. On one side scenes of war are shown: on the other peace.

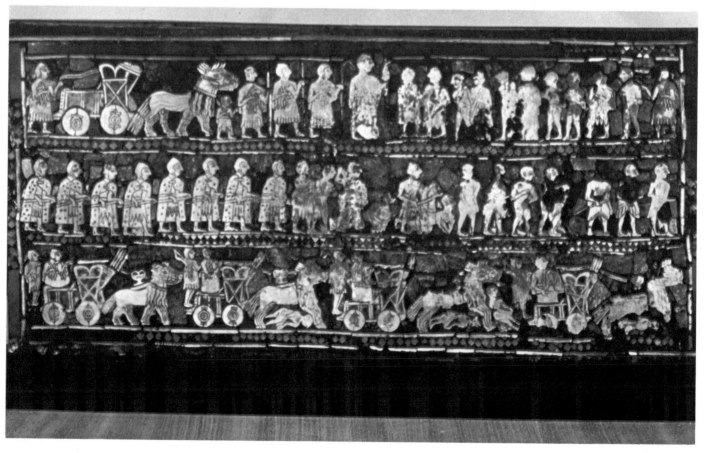

was the god. A secret society of priests controlled each town on behalf of its god. It was they who organized trade and kept the accounts and records of events *(archives)*. In time a 'tenant-farmer' of the god appeared as governor of the city. The governor later became king and his office and title passed to his son. At 'Ur of the Chaldees' the British archaeologist Sir Leonard Woolley excavated the royal tombs, in which household ministers, slaves and soldiers were buried with each royal personage. They had taken sleeping draughts before being buried with the dead ruler. Of all the gold objects found in these tombs the two most interesting, perhaps, are 'The Standard of Ur' and 'The Ram caught in a Thicket', which is so reminiscent of the story of the sacrifice by which Jehovah tested Abraham (Genesis 22). Abraham came from Ur of the Chaldees to the land of Canaan.

One after another the towns of Sumer rose to predominance: first Ur, then Lagash. Civil war between the cities continued until Sargon of Akkad, a Semite, conquered the whole valley and founded an empire which stretched from the 'cedar forest', present-day Lebanon, to the 'mountains of the lower sea', the Persian Gulf. It is difficult to date these events precisely, although we know the order in which they occurred. Sumerian records of dates have to be related to Egyptian ones, which are more precise. There have been many different views of how to do this: for example, Woolley, in 1946 A.D., dated Sargon approximately to 2560 B.C. Another British archaeologist, Grahame Clark, in 1961 A.D., wrote that 'Sargon founded his city of Akkad in c. 2340 B.C.'. Quite recently the *radio carbon* method of dating which seemed to give scientific accuracy to early dates has been found to have substantial errors.

Somewhere between 2180 and 1700 B.C. the empire of Sargon and cities like Ur were overwhelmed by Semitic barbarians. Around 1800 B.C. a new empire arose centred on the Semitic city Babylon. One of its rulers, Hammurabi, drew up a code of law for his people which had a strong influence on the Mosaic Law of the Hebrews. It covered an enormous range of subjects: property, military service, banking, the legal rights of women and children and many other topics. Hammurabi was a poet and scholar and built up an enormous library. Babylonian records were written in *cuneiform* on clay tablets. Cuneiform takes its name from the wedge-shaped marks which the reed *stilus* (pen) made on the clay. Babylonian weights and measures, their currency and their language spread all over the Middle East. Law and order were maintained from Mesopotamia to the Mediterranean. Religion was very important in Babylonia. The priests were wealthy and the King himself claimed to be a god.

After Hammurabi's death various tribes within the Babylonian empire revolted and after the sack of Babylon in c. 1595 B.C. (see pp. 26-7) the Kassites founded a new dynasty. In 1107 B.C. the Assyrians, led by Tiglath-Pileser I, conquered Babylon. They organised a warlike empire which reached the frontiers of Egypt. In 671 B.C. Esarhaddon conquered Egypt; under his son Ashurbanipal the Assyrian empire reached its greatest extent. By 626 B.C. a new Chaldean dynasty had been established in Babylon. This empire reached its peak under Nebuchadrezzar II (605-561 B.C.) who built temples, palaces and the 'hanging gardens of Babylon', one of the seven wonders of the Ancient World. The Chaldeans were skilled mathematicians and astronomers. Their detailed records of the movements of the planets and eclipses were studied and explained by Greek scientists. This empire in turn was conquered by the Medes and Persians. By 539 B.C. the whole of Babylonia was ruled by Cyrus the Great.

The centre point of Sumerian towns was the ziggurat, a flat-topped temple made of mudbrick with burnt brick casing. The temple, built in honour of the town's god, is thought to represent a mountain which the Sumerians of the plains believed was a suitable place for a god to live.

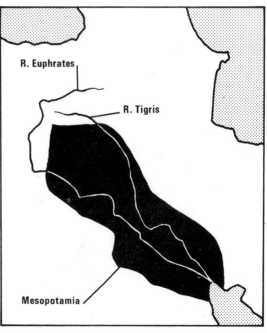

Map of Mesopotamia, the land which saw the first mature civilization of mankind. The inhabitants of the time called their land Sumer: today it is known as the state of Iraq.

R. Euphrates

R. Tigris

Mesopotamia

The Nile Valley

Ancient Egypt was the home of the second oldest civilization in the world. It flourished for 2,000 years, and then declined slowly for nearly another 1,000 years. In its lowest reaches the River Nile flows through desert sands to the Mediterranean Sea. Once a year floods poured down and covered the desert with silt. The Nile valley was wonderfully fertile and it became a refuge for both animals and men. The valley dwellers learned how to grow emmer wheat and flax; they kept sheep and goats, cattle and swine. The earliest communities known to have become farmers are those of the Fayum basin in Lower Egypt; this happened towards the end of the *fifth millennium* B.C. They probably received their knowledge from Palestine, and it spread southwards up the Nile valley into Upper Egypt. From Asia Minor (modern Turkey) came the knowledge of how to make things of copper. Building with sun-dried bricks and pictographic writing may have been learned from Mesopotamia. *Pictographs* are picture writing, in which each symbol is not a letter but a picture of an object or an idea. Egyptian pictographs are called *hieroglyphs*. This mixture of an African way of life with the Bronze Age culture of the Near East produced Egyptian civilization.

The scattered villages of the Nile valley were united by Menes (or Narmer) about 2700 B.C. He was the first *pharaoh* of the first dynasty, or family of rulers. Menes was the first ruler to emerge from the south, Upper Egypt, after uniting its more primi-

tive villages. With their power behind him, he could conquer the more advanced and quarrelling communities of the Nile Delta (Lower Egypt). It seems the country developed very quickly. Six different dynasties ruled a united Egypt from c. 2700 to c. 2180 B.C. This was the Old Kingdom. The unity of Egypt was symbolized in the pharaoh's crowns: the Red Crown was for Lower Egypt, the White Crown for Upper Egypt. In the time of the third dynasty the first *pyramid* was built by Imhotep, the 'Step Pyramid' at Saqqara which is the earliest really large stone building anywhere in the world. Pyramid building technique came to its climax with the Great Pyramid of Khufu at Giza of c. 2590 B.C.

These magnificent buildings and the later royal tombs, cut in the rocks, were tributes to the rulers of united Egypt, the pharaohs. The pharaoh was god and king to his subjects. The word pharaoh means great house, and the household of the pharaoh was the government of the country. The household foretold the arrival of the Nile flood and planned irrigation works, so that the flood waters enriched the largest possible area. The pharaoh's household consisted of priests and *scribes* (men who could write). Artists and craftsmen were employed. Egyptians

The Great Sphinx and the pyramid of Chephren at Giza which were built by the pharaohs of the 4th dynasty in about 2500 B.C. The pyramid at Chephren is one of three guarded by the Sphinx. The others are the Great Pyramid, built by Chephren's father, Khufu, and the pyramid of Mycerinus, built by his son. They were erected in an age which had no elaborate mechanical devices yet achieved extraordinary accuracy in the placement of limestone blocks, some weighing up to 15 tonnes.

were masters of building and carving in stone. They made jewellery, and invented *faïence,* a ceramic of a brilliant blue or green colour. They also discovered a way of making a writing material *(papyrus)* from reeds. Much Egyptian art was for the dead; they were buried with all the things which they would need in the after life.

Many people had their bodies preserved. They were embalmed: a body was drained of fluids, treated with preservatives, covered with bitumen, and then wrapped in linen cloths. This is called a *mummy.* The word comes from an Arabic word *mumiya* which means bitumen, and mumiya comes from a Persian word which means wax. The mummy was placed in a casket on which the dead person's face was painted. We know

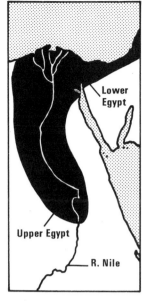

Above: Map of the Nile in Egypt, home of one of the oldest civilizations the world has known.

about the Egyptian religion and its cult of the dead because of this practice and because preservation is good in the dryness of the Egyptian climate.

The god of the dead was Osiris. The Egyptians believed that he had married his sister, Isis, and that he was killed by another god, Seth, and revived by his son, Horus. Horus was the god of sky and rain and ruled over the living. He was also a falcon or hawk god. Many Egyptian gods were half animal. Hathor was a cow-goddess. Ra, or Re, was the sun god of Heliopolis, the city of the sun. When Thebes became the capital of Egypt under the eleventh dynasty, Amun, the local god, became Amun-Re and king of the gods.

The Old Kingdom collapsed but the unity of the Nile valley was restored about 2080 B.C. by the eleventh dynasty. This process was to be repeated several times in the next 2,000 years (see pp. 32-3). The last native pharaoh, Nectanebos, belonged to the 30th dynasty. The special quality of Egypt's contribution to ancient civilizations was the permanence and continuity in her culture. Foreigners came to Egypt and revivified her but they nearly always took away far more than they brought.

Below: The inset shows the internal layout of the tombs of the Great Pyramid of Khufu, Giza.

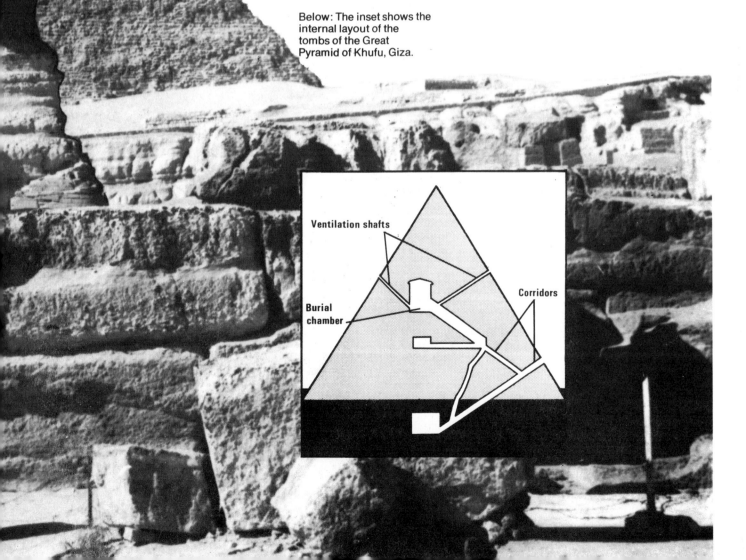

The Indus Valley

The earliest known cities in the Indian subcontinent were in the Indus valley. The two biggest cities are Mohenjo-daro and Harappa in Pakistan. They were 560 kilometres apart, but similar, smaller settlements have been found over a region 1,600 kilometres long. This Indus civilization covered an area larger than any other until the creation of the Roman empire. The two chief cities were inhabited from about 2500 B.C. to about 1500 B.C., but the more southerly towns lasted for several more centuries.

It is extraordinary that we know so little about the people whose civilization this was. Seals with picture writing have been found by archaeologists but so far no one has been able to decipher the writing. So we have to rely on the evidence of archaeology or on the dim light cast by the traditions of Aryan invaders who destroyed the Indus civilization between 1700 and 1500 B.C. The skeletons found in Indus sites are of *proto-Australoids,* people with dark skins and flat noses. They were described in Aryan legends as *Dāsas,* which means despicable enemy, people with black complexions, no noses to speak of, and 'of unintelligible speech'. The Anglo-Saxons invading Britain, 2,000 years later, spoke of the Celtic-speaking natives with the same contempt (see pp. 58-9). Much of the population of southern India today is of this Dravidian physical stock.

These Dravidians created their remarkable civilization quite suddenly. The cities are not as old as those in the Nile valley and Mesopotamia; the idea may have come from Mesopotamia but small towns with walled citadels and square towers of stone and mud-brick existed in the foothills to the west of the Indus valley before the cities were built. The new cities were different from those elsewhere. From the beginning they were planned in regular rectangular blocks of buildings, about 365 by 185 metres, with wide main streets between each block. The buildings were drained and lanes, with street drains, ran between them. Building was in brick, fired in a kiln, not just dried in the sun. Rich men's houses had baths and water tanks. There was a large public swimming bath. Cleanliness had been of great importance in later Indian religions and this bath may have had something to do with their religious beliefs.

There was a state granary in the central citadel at Mohenjo-daro. These citadels had walls with towers surrounding them, but the cities themselves were not fortified. This suggests that the Indus civilization had little to fear from foreign invaders. The citadels contained ritual buildings and

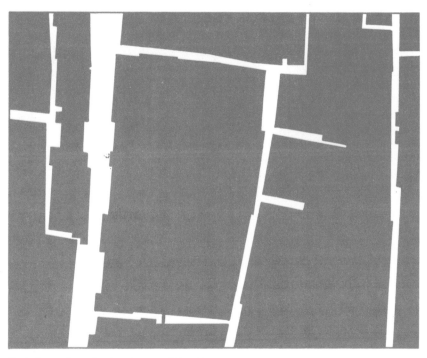

Today's modern city (see layout of New York bottom) has much in common with the well-planned Indus city of 4,000 years ago (top). Both were built on a grid system of regular rectangular blocks of buildings. Between each block wide main streets ran parallel to each other, cut at right angles by smaller streets. The streets were lined with kiln-fired brick houses, many of them two-storeyed, and all of them with flat roofs.

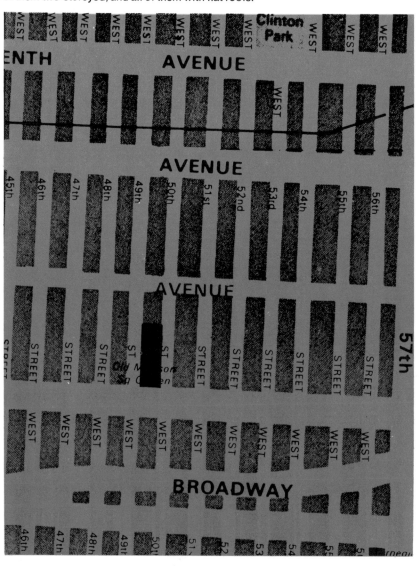

Indus stone bust, possibly of a priest, dating from before 2000 B.C.

assembly places. But there were neither palaces nor very obvious temples. The impression given by the excavations is of a society very different from that of Pharaonic Egypt; this was not a totalitarian society ruled by a god-king, nor were its rulers so obviously a caste of priests as were those of Sumer. It was a society ruled by a fairly large number of wealthy citizens, traders who had some religious functions perhaps, but the general standard of living was high. The Indus people used bronze and made jewellery of silver, ivory and gold. They could spin and weave cloth and used the potter's wheel. Their sculpture was naturalistic, portraying the human form as it really is, like that of the great age of Classical Greece.

For something like a thousand years the Dravidians' civilization flourished. It seems to have been based on an intelligent use of the fertility produced by the flood waters of the Indus. But the Indus' floods became more serious. There are signs that Mohenjo-daro was flooded several times in its later years. Flood walls were built but the effort of maintaining them may have become too great. One reason why the flooding may have got worse is that trees over a great area were destroyed to bake bricks for buildings. Deforestation led to an increase in the desert area.

How far the Aryan invaders destroyed this civilization and how far it died from exhaustion is not yet clear. Excavation may still teach us a great deal about it. Only in Mohenjo-daro is there evidence of burning and killing—the city may have been stormed. The invaders' primitive huts have been found in the ruins. The earliest Indian literature which survives (see pp. 38-9) was transmitted orally and it portrays the Dravidian civilization of the Indus valley, as the Aryan invaders saw it.

These people were 'indifferent to the gods', that is the Aryan gods. They had no rites, but followed 'strange ordinances'; they did not perform sacrifices, as the Aryans did. They were wealthy people with great stores of gold. The Aryans made slaves of them, just as the Anglo-Saxons did of the Celts in Britain. The word Dāsas, which was the contemptuous Aryan term for their Dravidian enemies, came to mean slave. In exactly the same way the Anglo-Saxon word *wealh* first meant foreigner, then the British Celts, and finally slaves. In German, *waleser* means a foreigner. In English, Wales is the country of the Britons, the foreign enemy to the Anglo-Saxons. A thousand years after the Aryan conquest, Dravidian and Aryan cultures mingled to make a new Indian way of life.

23

Beaker and Battle-axe Folk

The torc, or neck ring, was a characteristic ornament of the Celts. The one above is made of iron: others were made of gold or, less commonly, of bronze.

Neolithic farmers were semi-nomadic. They cleared land and sowed crops. But when the soil was exhausted they moved on and began anew.

The *Maglemosians* who spread over Europe after the last Ice Age retreated (see pp. 10-11) were challenged by new peoples moving in from the Middle East. About 4000 B.C. the climate changed. The warm *Boreal* climate was altered by the rise in ocean levels due to the melting ice. This separated Britain from Europe, and the climate became colder and wetter. Oak and beech woods replaced conifers. Into this changed European scene came the world's first farmers at some time after 4000 B.C. They are called *Neolithic* peoples because they used improved and polished stone tools and they made pottery. Such farmers reached Britain and settled at Windmill Hill, Wiltshire, about 2000 B.C. They were almost vegetarian, practising little hunting and fighting very little among themselves. Some of the *Maglemosians* moved farther north with the retreating icecap—their culture survived among the Lapps and Eskimos. Others became the miners and traders who provided the growing number of tools which the Neolithic farmers needed. Axe 'factories' have been found in the United Kingdom at Antrim, Penmaenmawr, and Great Langdale. Neolithic farmers practised shifting husbandry; they cut down or burned wood-land and sowed crops in the soil, fertilized by the ash. When the crops became poor because the soil was exhausted, they moved on and started again.

The use of bronze had already been discovered in the Middle East (see pp. 16-17). The search for ore led Mediterranean traders through western Europe to Britain and Scandinavia. They have been called the *Megalithic Missionaries*, because they brought a new sun worship with them and persuaded the natives to build circles of great stones (Megalith means large stone) as temples. They also built burial chambers of similar stones, called *barrows*. These tombs and temples are found in Malta, Spain, Brittany and Britain. The most famous stone circle temple in Europe is at Stonehenge. A carving of a Bronze Age dagger from Mycenae in Greece has been found on one of the pillars of Stonehenge.

Bronze weapons are much more effective than stone ones. But bronze was scarce so it was used only by fighting aristocrats. Two such bronze-using warlike groups spread over Europe in a pincer movement. The Beaker Peoples, named after the pottery beakers which they made, spread from Spain northwards to Britain, while the Battle-axe folk moved from the Volga-Caucasus area westwards through Europe (see pp. 26-7). This did not mean a large immigration of peoples, but that small groups of fighting men carved out new lands for themselves and subjugated the Neolithic farming majorities. This was a time of fighting in Europe.

The discovery of iron meant even more warfare. Iron has been called the democratic metal because it was much more common and therefore cheaper than bronze. The knowledge of iron-working came to Europe by way of the Danube. The first iron mines in Europe were at Hallstatt in Austria. They developed between 1000 and 700 B.C. A new tribal aristocracy developed here, in what has been called the *La Tène* period. They united the warring tribes of Europe, spreading their language and culture. These were the *Celts*, who captured Rome in 390 B.C., terrifying the Italians with their fierce appearance. They were big, large-boned people with fair or red hair and blue eyes. From 500 to 200 B.C. Europe, north of the Mediterranean, was Celtic.

Hill forts were built by different groups of Celts to defend their conquered territories. Maiden Castle in Dorset is one of the most remarkable. Waves of Celts entered Britain for centuries. The last important group of arrivals were the *Belgae,* who crossed the Channel sometime between 100 and 75 B.C. They were ruling all south-east Britain

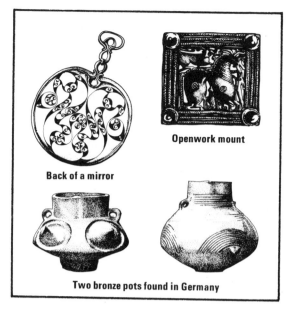

Back of a mirror

Openwork mount

Two bronze pots found in Germany

when Julius Caesar made his attempt at conquest in 55 and 54 B.C. The *Belgae* brought to Britain an effective plough, as well as much improved iron weapons and tools. They began the systematic clearing of the woodlands, so that farming moved down from the lighter downland soils where Neolithic farmers had settled onto the heavier and more fertile soils of the valleys and valley slopes.

It is confusing that today Celtic languages are only spoken by the peoples of the north and west of the British Isles and in Brittany. These are mostly smallish, dark-haired peoples of the older Mediterranean stocks. They learnt their languages from the Celtic invaders and kept them alive when the Celts, in what was to become England, were conquered and absorbed by a physically similar, large-boned, fair-haired people, speaking a Germanic language—Anglo-Saxon.

Top left: Objects of the Bronze Age. An openwork mount, the back of a mirror, and bronze pots.

Successive waves of Celts entered Britain and built hill forts, like Maiden Castle, Dorset (above), to defend themselves and stone temples such as Stonehenge (bottom) mainly for worship.

The Middle East in the Bronze Age

The metal-using peoples of the Middle East lived through some 2,000 years of conflict and change. Both Egypt and Mesopotamia had southern and northern centres of civilization. Just as the Old Kingdom united both parts of Egypt so had Sargon of Akkad and Hammurabi of Babylon united Mesopotamia (see pp. 18-21). Hammurabi's Babylonian empire was the first emergence into civilization of the wandering *Amorites, Semites* of the Arabian deserts. Hammurabi's triumphs occurred in the 18th century B.C. In the 16th century B.C. other Amorites, the *Hyksos,* took power in Egypt for about a century (see pp. 32-3). Hammurabi's empire lasted scarcely 20 years after his death: the Sumerian south of Mesopotamia became independent of the Amorite north, ruled from Babylon. In this break-up of a united Mesopotamia a large part was played by three kingdoms to the east: Elam in the Iranian hills to the east of Ur, the *Kassites* to the north, and Assyria, centred on Assur and Nineveh on the upper Tigris. The *Elamites* were much the same people as those of southern Mesopotamia; the *Assyrians* were Semites like the Babylonians, but the Kassites had new chieftains, who had come from the north, speaking an Indo-European language. On the eastern borders of Mesopotamia in the 18th century B.C. the Semites met the *Indo-Europeans* (see pp. 56-7).

The nomadic expansion which began about 2000 B.C. in the southern Russian steppes is one of the more important of all historical processes. It took peoples speaking Indo-European languages, worshipping a sun god, and using the horse-drawn chariot for transport and the battle-axe as a weapon through much of the known world. As the Battle-axe people they spread through northern and central Europe (see pp. 24-5); as *Aryans* they destroyed the civilization of the Indus valley and laid the basis of new civilizations in India (see pp. 22-3 and 38-9). They came south through the ring of mountains which guards Arabia from the north and east and gave new leadership and new vitality to mountain peoples on the edge of the early river valley civilizations. They took over the rule of the Kassites, and of the *Hurrians* who lived in the mountains from which the Euphrates came; the Indo-European rulers of the Hurrians called themselves *Mitanni.* But most important of all they took over the kingdom of the Hatti in central Asia Minor, and soon ruled almost all Asia Minor as the *Hittites.* The first two

Chariots of (from top to bottom) the Egyptians, the Britons and the Etruscans.

Hittite kings were called Labarnas; the second Labarnas rebuilt the old Hatti capital Hattusas (Boghazköy) and renamed himself Hattusilis (c. 1580 B.C.). His heir Mursilis I (1550-1530 B.C.) conquered Syria and sacked Babylon. When he was murdered the new Hittite empire disintegrated until Telipinus seized the throne about 1525 B.C. and proclaimed a succession law and other laws which gave stability to the state. Only under Suppululiumas (c. 1375-1335 B.C.) did the Hittites expand again, reconquering Syria and finally incorporating the Mitanni as a vassal kingdom. Mursilis II (1334-1306 B.C.) maintained the empire and strengthened its control of Asia Minor. Muwatallis (1306-1282 B.C.) met the Pharaoh Ramesses II at Kadesh in 1285 (see pp. 32-3) in a drawn battle, but the advantages went to the Hittites whose control over Syria was extended. In 1269 B.C. Hattusilis

III (1275-1250 B.C.) made a peace treaty with the Pharaoh Rameses II which brought peace for 70 years. Rameses married a daughter of Hattusilis 13 years after this treaty was made. Within 50 years of the death of Hattusilis III the Hittites were swept away by a southward movement of other Indo-Europeans (see pp. 30-1).

The *Semitic* peoples were expanding too. It was probably during the long reign of Rameses II (1290-1233 B.C.) that Moses led the *Amorite Israelites* out of Egypt into Sinai and then into the land east of the river Jordan. Under Joshua the *Israelites* captured the Canaanite city of Jericho. Only after Joshua's death was Jerusalem taken and the coastal towns occupied. A new Semitic state, Israel, was born.

More immediately important for the Middle East was the rise of the military empire of Assyria. The Amorite kingdoms of Babylon and of Assur occupied the middle Euphrates and the upper Tigris. Babylon, recovered from the Hittite onslaught, drove out the Elamites and reunited southern Mesopotamia. The Assyrians survived a Babylonian attack and began to train armies. In 1116 B.C. Tiglath-Pileser became king of Assyria and let loose the Assyrian armies. He conquered the old Mitanni kingdom, occupying Carchemish, seized Syria and the southern Hittite lands and in 1107 B.C. captured Babylon. The Assyrians now ruled from the Upper to the Lower Sea, from the Mediterranean to the Persian Gulf. Egyptian unity was gone and the first Indo-European intruders had lost their kingdoms. The Assyrians were the major power in the Middle East for about 500 years until they collapsed before the advance of a second wave of Indo-Europeans from the mountains to the east, the Persians (see pp. 42-3).

The horse-drawn chariot revolutionized warfare. It enabled the Aryans to conquer much of the known world. An early Aryan victory was over the Indus valley people (above) who were helpless against such superior force. Their entire civilization was destroyed, their cities were burnt, and their people enslaved by the triumphant conquerors.

DATA DIGEST

Many of the words which are italicized in the previous section are explained more fully in the following data digest. They will help to expand your knowledge of history.

Acheulean. Category of delicate flint tools made by Pithecanthropus hominids of the Lower Palaeolithic cultures who existed from 420,000 to 340,000 years ago.

Ahrensburg. Sometimes known as the Ahrensburg-Lavenstadt Mesolithic culture which occupied the north European plain (stretching from Belgium to Poland) from 8300 to 7500 B.C.

Amorites. A Semitic people who originated in the country named in the bible as Canaan and set up a ruling dynasty in Babylonia in the 18th century B.C.

Aryans. People who speak languages related to a single ancient language. Sanskrit, the language of the Hindu sacred texts, is developed from it as are most of the European languages. Aryans are the same as Indo-Europeans.

Assyrians. People living in the land known as Mesopotamia, whose origin is obscure. They may have come from Sumer. By 1100 B.C. their influence had spread as far as the Mediterranean during what became known as the "First Assyrian Empire".

Australoids. The Australian Aborigines, a basically Caucasoid people.

Australopithecine. Literally the southern ape, it lived more than 500,000 years ago. It stood erect and had a number of human characteristics. Raymond Dart discovered the first fossil skull in southern Africa in 1924. Many other skulls have been found in Africa.

Belgae. A warlike tribe in ancient Gaul which lived roughly in what is now Belgium. Large numbers of Belgae settled in Britain about 75 B.C. and took control of much of southern England. Julius Caesar conquered the Belgae in Gaul in 57 B.C. though occasional uprisings continued for another 30 years.

Boreal. Temperate northern climate.

Celts. The Celts were an Indo-European people who, after 500 B.C., spread over large areas of Europe.

Cro-Magnon. An early type of *Homo sapiens* living between 30,000 and 8000 B.C. Cro-Magnon men created superb cave paintings.

Cuneiform. A form of writing probably invented by the Sumerians and later used by the Babylonians and Assyrians, the Elamites, the Hittites and the Persians. Characters were scratched on clay tablets with a stylus of reed. Each

character might represent a syllable or a whole word. The Latin *cuneus* means a wedge, and the strokes in cuneiform are wedge-shaped.

Elamites. People living in the Sumerian city-state of Elam about 4500 years ago. It was their defeat that later helped to lay the foundations of the Persian empire.

Faïence. Clay earthenware covered with a glaze. The Egyptians produced figurines and ornaments worked by this method.

Günz. A glaciation period of the Pleistocene epoch. It started about 600,000 years ago and lasted about 65,000 years.

Hieroglyphs. Form of picture-writing used by the ancient Egyptians. Each character was used to represent words, syllables or letters.

Hittites. A people who controlled most of Asia Minor from about 1750 to 1200 B.C. They had a sophisticated culture and at their zenith were almost as powerful as Babylon and Egypt.

Homo sapiens. Wise man. The name given to all creatures with a human body and with a brain capacity not less than 1,100 c.c. Modern man is among this group.

Hurrians. The people (known in the Bible as the Horites) who lived in Upper Mesopotamia about 1700 B.C. In 1500 B.C. the small Hurrian principalities formed themselves into the kingdom of Mitanni (see Mitanni).

Hyksos. A Canaanite people, probably Amorites, who ruled Egypt in the Middle Kingdom period for more than 100 years. Their empire included Palestine and Syria. They taught the Egyptians the use of horse-drawn chariots.

Ideograph. A picture representing an idea rather than merely representing an object as a pictograph does. Thus in Chinese a sun and moon together convey the idea of brightness.

Indo-Europeans. People who speak one of a vast range of related languages which derived originally from a single Indo-European language, perhaps spoken 4,000 years ago in the Black Sea area.

Israelites. Another name for the Jews or Hebrews, the descendants of Jacob who was given the name Israel.

Kassites. An Indo-European people

who invaded Babylonia from Persia in the 18th century B.C. and kept control of the area for 600 years.

La Tène. Iron Age culture dating from 450 B.C. to 1 A.D. and located in various regions in western Europe.

Late Minoan II. Bronze Age culture which evolved out of the Middle Minoan period, from 1550 B.C. to 1100 B.C. on the island of Crete. This period was notable for the destruction of the Palace of Knossos.

Lower Palaeolithic. The earliest of the three periods of the Old Stone Age. It began about 1,000,000 years ago and lasted about 300,000 years.

Maglemose. Mesolithic axe culture which spread all over northern Europe from 7500 to 5550 B.C..

Melanesians. Negroid people of the Pacific islands, found mainly in New Guinea, New Caledonia, Fiji, the New Hebrides and the Solomon Islands.

Mesolithic. The Mesolithic period, or Middle Stone Age, started about 8000 B.C. and lasted about 2,000 years.

Middle Minoan I-IIIA. Cretan culture which saw the flowering of the Minoan civilization and the building of the great Palace of Knossos. The culture lasted from 2200 B.C. to 1550 B.C.

Mindel. A glaciation period of the Pleistocene epoch. It started about 470,000 years ago and lasted for over 150,000 years.

Minoan. Name of a Bronze Age people who lived on the island of Crete in the Aegean Sea for 3,000 years. During this time they reached a very high level of civilization. They were called Minoan after the legendary King Minos who created a sea empire stretching across the Mediterranean.

Mitanni. Kingdom of Mitanni, formed in 1500 B.C. by the merging of all the principalities established in Mesopotamia by the Hurrian people. Eventually the kingdom was overrun by the Egyptians and later pillaged by the Assyrians.

Neanderthal. This early type of man lived about 50,000 years ago. The first fossil was discovered in 1856 near Dusseldorf. Others have been found in Africa and Asia.

Negrito. Negritos are a pygmy people, similar to the pygmies of Africa, who are found in East Asia, particularly the

Andaman Islands, the Philippines and the Malay Peninsula.

Neolithic. The Neolithic period, or New Stone Age, started about 6000 B.C. and lasted for 3,000 years.

Palaeolithic. The Palaeolithic period, or Old Stone Age, started about 1,000,000 years ago and lasted until very nearly 8000 B.C.

Pharaoh. The title of the Egyptian kings which came into use with the ascendance of Tuthmosis II to the throne in 1504 B.C. (New Kingdom).

Phonograph. A symbol representing a spoken sound, a predecessor of the alphabet.

Pictograph. A picture of an object which is used as a symbol of that object. Pictographs were the earliest form of writing. Ideographs developed from them.

Pithecanthropus erectus. Java man, discovered in Java by Eugene Dubois in 1891. One of the three sub-species of *Homo erectus,* he lived about 500,000 years ago.

Pleistocene. The best-known and most recent Ice Age. It started about 1,000,000 years ago and ended about 8000 B.C. During this period ice covered large areas of Europe, America and parts of Asia. There were four periods of glacier formation—Günz, Mindel, Riss and Würm. During the Pleistocene epoch the elephant, camel, horse and man himself appeared on the Earth.

Pluvial. Pluvial periods were the equivalent of glacial periods in areas periodically covered with ice during the Pleistocene epoch. In these pluvial periods arid areas such as Africa and parts of America and Asia experienced an increase in vegetation and the formation of lakes.

Pyramid. Huge stone or brick structures which were built to immortalize the pharaohs of ancient Egypt and also to serve as their tombs. Pyramids were also built in Mesopotamia and, in Mexico, by the Aztecs.

Radio carbon dating. This is a method of discovering the age of a fossil or artifact by determining the amount of carbon 14 still remaining in its structure. However, it is not very accurate.

Riss. A glaciation period of the Pleistocene epoch. It started about 230,000 years ago and lasted for something like 55,000 years.

Semites. People who spoke one of the related languages called Semitic because they are presumed to come from a single language—Semitic. Among Semitic peoples are the Arabs,

the Bedouin and the ancient Assyrians, Phoenicians and Hebrews.

Stilus. Ancient writing instrument usually made from reeds. It was used to incise cuneiform texts onto clay tablets. It was later adopted by the Egyptians for scribing hieroglyphic texts on to papyrus.

Upper Palaeolithic. The last of three periods of the Old Stone Age, beginning 50,000 years ago and ending about 8,000 years ago.

Würm. A glaciation period of the Pleistocene epoch. It started roughly 115,000 years ago and lasted for well over 100,000 years.

Ziggurat. Sumerian temple constructed in the form of a flat-topped pyramid in which the sides formed a sort of endless stairway leading from the bottom, round the walls and up to the top.

The Sphinx (below) with Cheops Pyramid of Giza, Egypt, in the background used as a royal tomb.

ANCIENT CIVILIZATIONS

Crete and the Sea-peoples

Above: A map of the island of Crete in the Mediterranean. The Palace of Knossos, below, was built around a central court with the royal apartments on the right and public rooms for state business on the left. It was built by the Cretans in about 1500 B.C. Right: A colourful fresco painted about 1300 B.C. showing a woman wearing the distinctive and very elegant topless Cretan dress of the time.

The first wave of *Indo-Europeans* which pressed into the Middle East used horses and brought the war chariot with them, but they were bronze users. Iron smelting, which requires great heat compared with bronze, was developed by the *Hittites* (see pp. 26-7). Iron was worked in the Aremian mountains before 2000 B.C., but it was a secret of the Hittites. It became widely available with the fall of the Hittite empire (c. 1200 B.C.), and it was cheap. By 1000 B.C. the knowledge was current among the barbarians from north-east Siberia to Hallstatt in Austria. Cheap iron democratized agriculture, industry and warfare. A second wave of Indo-Europeans, descended from the battle-axe peoples of northern Europe (see pp. 24-5), poured into the countries bordering the eastern Mediterranean.

Their precursors were the *Achaeans*, Indo-Europeans who settled around the Adriatic, at Mycenae and Tiryns and Pylos in Peloponnesus, and on the south-western coast of Asia Minor, Ionia. The Achaeans were the first Greek speakers. Similar Indo-European early arrivals set-tled at Troy in the north-west of Asia Minor. The charioteers of the *steppes* now took to the sea, as merchants and raiders. Between the Achaeans and the settlers at Troy there was fought, probably sometime around 1200 B.C., the earliest war to be immortalized in literature. Homer's great epic poem *The Iliad* tells how the Greeks besieged and captured Troy. Archaeologists have excavated both Mycenae, from which the Greek High King, Agamemnon, sailed, and the Troy which he captured.

The barbarian Achaeans were civilized by the culture of Crete. The island of Crete was the centre of the finest civilization of the early second *millennium* B.C. The Cretans were traders who dominated the seas be-

tween Asia Minor, Greece, Egypt and Syria. They built impressive palace-factories at Knossos and Phaestos, but there were no defences for they feared no invaders since they controlled the seas. The wealth and artistry of the Cretans have been wonders of the modern world ever since the British archaeologist Sir Arthur Evans excavated Knossos in Victorian times. The impact of this civilization on the Achaeans must have been overwhelming. But they learnt quickly, and somewhere between 1480 and 1400 B.C. *Mycenaean Greeks* conquered Crete and occupied it. The earliest Greek alphabet, *Linear B*, was developed from the earlier Cretan alphabet, *Linear A*. For another 200 years the Mycenaeans traded all round the eastern Mediterranean and Cretan-Mycenaean civilization continued to flourish. One of the great legends of the ancient world, that of Theseus, Ariadne and

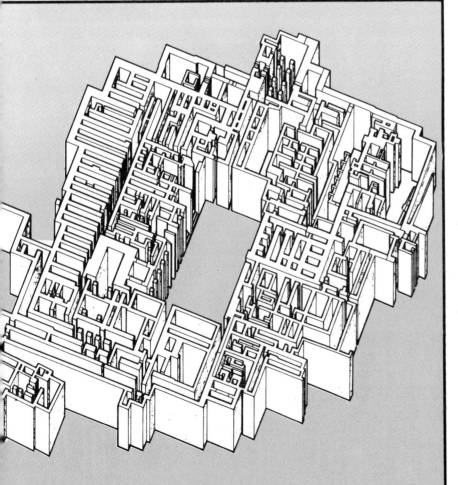

the *Minotaur*, commemorates the Greek conquest of Crete. Theseus was an Athenian prince who chose to become one of the tribute of slaves sent to Minos, king of Crete, to take part in the sacrifices to the bull god of the Cretans. Helped by Minos's daughter, Ariadne, he slew the bull-like Minotaur and the Greek slaves escaped.

By 1200 B.C. Mycenaeans were settling all round the Mediterranean and being reinforced by Indo-European cousins from farther north. Libya to the west of Egypt had an army of northern *mercenaries* which invaded Egypt in the last years of Rameses II's reign in the 1230s. About the same time the Hittite Great King was being attacked from the western coast of Asia Minor by Achaeans or similar peoples (see pp. 26-7). People from the Balkans begin to appear in the sea lanes and in the ports. Gradually a build-up of pressure from these *nomads* took place and civilizations collapsed. Hattusas was sacked and the Hittites lost Asia Minor to a vast host of peoples on the march. The British archaeologist Sir Leonard Woolley has described them as 'not an army but a congeries of peoples; some came by sea, skirting the coast; others marched overland with their women-folk and children, travelling in heavy two-wheeled ox-carts, prepared to settle down in the conquered land'. This they did in Asia Minor where they became known as *Moski* and *Phrygians*. But others pressed on towards Egypt, sacking Carchemish and Aleppo. Their fleet laid Cyprus waste. The Peoples of the Sea, as they were called by the Egyptians, were defeated by Rameses III about 1190 B.C. One group turned back and settled on the Palestine coast, to become known as the *Philistines*. Others moved all over the Mediterranean. The Egyptians record their names: the Pelest who became Philistines; the Teresh may be the *Etruscans* who settled in Italy; Shardana became *Sardinians*; the Shekelesh who, as *Sikels*, settled Sicily; the *Danaans* who settled in Greece. These latter may be the peoples whom we know in Greek history as *Dorians* (see pp. 44-5). Certainly mainland Achaean Greece was overrun and its cities sacked by iron-using Dorian warriors, who spoke or adopted Greek as their language, although it took them centuries to develop once again to the level of civilization reached at Knossos and Mycenae. The mass migration of iron-using Indo-Europeans about 1200 B.C. finally destroyed the bronze age power structure of the Middle East (see pp. 26-7). But the migrants provided the vitality from which new centres of civilization were to spring up all round the Mediterranean, in Greece, Italy, and North Africa (Carthage).

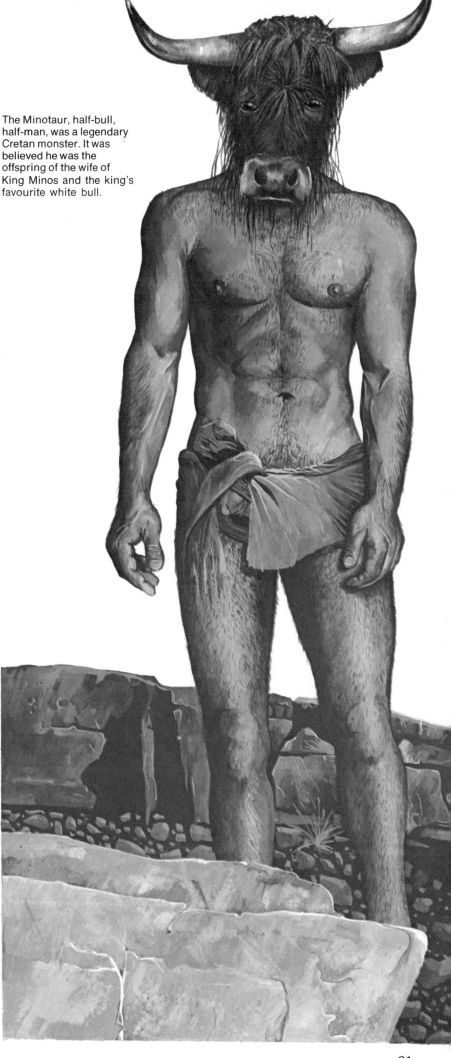

The Minotaur, half-bull, half-man, was a legendary Cretan monster. It was believed he was the offspring of the wife of King Minos and the king's favourite white bull.

Dynastic Egypt

The history of *Pharaonic Egypt* is in three periods; the *Old Kingdom* (see pp. 20-1) which lasted until the end of the sixth dynasty in about 2180 B.C.; the *Middle Kingdom*, covering the 11th to 13th dynasties, from about 2080 B.C. to 1640 B.C.; and the *New Kingdom*, from 1570 B.C. to 1075 B.C., covering the 18th to 20th dynasties. Between these periods and after 1075 B.C. Egypt was either divided among local *potentates* or conquered by foreigners. But in the years of the three 'Kingdoms' Egypt was united as was no other state of these early times, and was powerful and self-assured at home and abroad.

Egypt's unity had brought her foreign influence. There were trading and military contacts with Africa to the south and west, and penetration into Palestine. Egyptian armies fought successfully as far north as Carmel and an Egyptian temple was built at Byblos in the Lebanon. The unity of the Nile valley, achieved by Menes, reached its height under the fourth and fifth dynasties. Under the fifth and sixth dynasties it began to decay. Provincial governorships became hereditary. The last pharaoh to rule all Egypt, even nominally, was Phiops II. He reigned for 90 years and was about 100 years of age when he died.

After years of fighting, Menthu-hotep, prince of Thebes in Upper Egypt, reunited Egypt about 2080 B.C. He founded the 11th

Above: The finest funeral mask ever found belonged to an Egyptian king, Tutankhamun, who reigned for about nine years from 1361 B.C. The mask is made of beaten gold inlaid with precious stones and coloured glass paste. Although Tutankhamun was not a very significant king, the discovery of his tomb in 1922 is considered the world's most exciting archaeological discovery. Found by British archaeologist Howard Carter, the tomb was almost completely intact and full of treasures.

Left: Rameses II reigned as king of Egypt for 57 years. He had more than 100 children and many wives, of whom his favourite was Nefertari. He constructed Egypt's biggest buildings and statues. He built the famous rock temples at Abu Simbel which were moved in 1966 to save them from the rising waters of the dammed Nile.

dynasty, which ruled Egypt from Thebes. Under the 12th dynasty the capital moved to the junction between Upper and Lower Egypt, some 32 kilometres south of Memphis. This dynasty had long-lived and powerful rulers: Sesostris I reigned for 45 years, undertook important irrigation works in the Fayum, and helped restore the borders of Egypt. The Sudan to the south was conquered and 'The Walls of the Prince', a string of forts, was built along the Arabian frontier. Sesostris built a new temple at Heliopolis and restored buildings all over Egypt. Ammenemes III reigned for 50 years and his reign was marked by building on an immense scale.

Many *Asiatic Semites* settled in Egypt during the Middle Kingdom. The Biblical story of Joseph is an indication. Under the 13th dynasty these Semites reached positions of importance in government and, as the pharaohs became ineffective and the unity of Egypt disintegrated again, they set up their own state in Lower Egypt. This was the *Hyksos* kingdom. Hyksos means 'rulers of uplands', wandering Semites. The Hyksos kings adopted Egyptian titles and religion, but kept their own names; one was called Jacob-El. By about 1570 B.C. Ahmosis, Count of Thebes, had reunited the country. His elder brother and father fought the Hyksos before him. They founded one of Egypt's greatest dynasties, the 18th, which lasted for over 250 years.

The Hyksos brought new ideas and new technology into Egypt. The Egyptian bronze age proper began at this time; horse-drawn

chariots were first used in warfare and new weapon designs invented; the olive, the pomegranate, and hump-backed bulls were imported and new musical instruments appeared. The New Kingdom lasted for 500 years. The 18th dynasty set a pattern of Egyptian interference in Palestine and Syria. Under Tuthmosis III, a great warrior who reigned for 54 years, Egyptian power reached the Euphrates. By the reign of Amenophis III, king for 39 years, the whole of Nubia and Kush was Egyptianized. This empire was nearly lost by Amenophis IV (Akhenaten). He introduced the worship of a single god, *Aten* the sun, and built a new capital at Tell-el-Amarna. Akhenaten was a poet—his hymns are remarkably like some of the *Psalms*—and a pacifist. He believed in realistic rather than formal art, so we have sculpture which shows his distorted head and the beauty of Nefertiti, one of his wives.

During the reign of the boy-king Tutankhamun, Akhenaten's successor, the priests of Amun regained power and restored the old gods. Possibly because of his comparative unimportance, Tutankhamun's tomb escaped robbery and when discovered in

Egyptian aristocrats filled their leisure hours with music, games and banquets. Servants were taught to play instruments like the harp (above, left). Senet (top) was a popular game and (below) the sort of toy the child of a well-to-do household would have enjoyed.

1922 contained the greatest of treasure finds in Egypt. The 18th dynasty came to an end when a general, Haremhab, followed Tutankhamun. Sethos I and Rameses II of the 19th dynasty restored much of Egypt's imperial splendour. Rameses II scarcely avoided defeat by the *Hittites* in a great battle at Kadesh in 1285 B.C.; he reigned for 57 years. Rameses III, the first great king of the 20th dynasty, managed to defeat the incursion of the sea-peoples (see pp. 30-1). The power of the pharaohs was fading as new kingdoms and new peoples appeared in the Middle East (see pp. 26-7).

The New Kingdom came to an end in 1075 B.C.. Many of the dynasties which followed were founded by foreign conquerors. The 25th dynasty came from Kush in the south. Assyrians, Persians and Greeks ruled Egypt in turn. The last Egyptian pharaoh died in 341 B.C. About 20 years later, the period of the Ptolemaic dynasty begins. It was a time of peace and decline. The last well-known Egyptian ruler was Cleopatra VII (50-30 B.C.), the descendant of one of Alexander the Great's generals (see pp. 46-7); she ruled as joint pharaoh successively with her two brothers and her son.

Right: The Egyptian queen, Cleopatra VII, who ruled jointly with her brother, Ptolemy XIII, from 50 to 30 B.C. Her legendary beauty won her many admirers, including Julius Caesar and, later, Mark Antony, one of Caesar's principal heirs. She is said to have killed herself by pressing an asp (a small poisonous snake) to her breast.

Chinese River Valleys

In the north and west, China is cut off from the rest of Asia by mountains. From these flow two great rivers, the Huangho (Yellow) river in the north and the Yangtse in the south. The south of China is a great plain, the west mountainous and desert. It was in these river valleys, in particular in the Yellow river valley, that Chinese civilization developed. The Huangho floods regularly, but a Chinese archaeologist has pointed out that 'the floods that brought destruction were at the same time a blessing. To them should be attributed the credit for the broad fertile fields which made possible the growth of the *Neolithic* population who introduced agriculture.' (see pp. 16-17). Ordinary Neolithic villages covered between 5,850 and 21,740 square metres, but in the Huangho valley villages of 125,420 (Chi-chi-ping) and 200,670 (Yang-shao-tsun) square metres have been found. They were nearly towns.

There is no evidence for the slow evolution of an agricultural economy in the Yellow

Right: An early form of Chinese currency was 'knife and spade' money —bronze replicas of valuable tools which were exchanged for food and other goods.

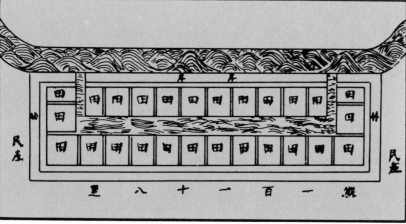

Above: An illustration taken from an early Chinese print showing an irrigation system with the fields shown as squares, and the river above. Chinese rural life followed a rigid feudal system in which the lord ruled his peasants completely. The peasant worked his own field and a central field for the lord. The name of the system 'well field' is taken from the Chinese symbol for 'well' which also resembled the layout of the unit.

Right: Confucius preached a philosophy based on the preservation of traditional rituals and was deified after his death by the Han dynasty.

river valley. The practical knowledge of the Neolithic revolution, crop growing and cattle raising, must have come from the west of Asia. There were two distinct, fully developed agricultural cultures, that of *Lung Shan* in the east, and *Yang Shao* in the centre and north-west. They emerged about 2200 B.C. and continued until bronze users conquered the plains and built cities about 1600-1500 B.C. The Yang Shao settled on the *loess areas* (loam deposited in river valleys) and avoided any upland areas; they cultivated millet and some rice. The Lung Shan settled on low knolls or river terraces and kept tame pigs, goats and cows. This Neolithic farming culture spread southwards into the Yangtse delta.

Quite suddenly an advanced Bronze Age culture entered and united the river valleys.

The *Shang* dynasty emerged about 1750 B.C. and controlled the Yellow river valley from the 16th to the tenth centuries B.C. The first definite date in Chinese history is 1401 B.C., in the middle of this Shang period. But long before then we know, from archaeological evidence, that there were walled cities controlled by men who kept slaves and who used bronze weapons and chariots. As with the earlier Neolithic techniques, there is no evidence for a primitive stage of bronze *metallurgy* in China. The Shang, or their teachers, probably came from the west. But they came quickly to prominence. The quality of Shang bronzes was not yet equalled

anywhere so early and has been rarely surpassed since. Shang potters both discovered how to use a pure white clay (*kaolin*) and invented a hard glaze. Potters and bronze-smiths, like carvers of jade and of bone, were organized in regular workshops in the cities. The rectangular layout which became normal in Chinese cities probably began under the Shang. Writing seems to have begun with marks on bones used for *oracles*. Chinese writing was to remain in *ideographic* form and never develop into an *alphabet* (see pp. 16-17 and 20-1).

In 1122 B.C. the Shangs' slave army rebelled and the barbarian Chou, from upland Shensi, conquered the Yellow river valley. The new King, Wu, distributed *fiefs of land* to members of his family. A social and economic system which was partly *feudal* (see pp. 78-9), but much more closely organized by the state than European feudalism, came into existence. The *well-field system* (see diagram) was at its base, as the manor was in Europe. By 770-475 B.C.—the *Spring and Autumn* period it is called by Chinese historians—the Chinese were using hoes and axes made of iron. The state-controlled reallocation of land ended and private ownership of land by both nobility and peasants began to emerge. The Chou power lessened and from 479 to 221 B.C. there was civil war between small feudal states—the period of *Warring States*, as the Chinese called it. 'Civilized' China was still confined to the two great river valleys. Between the cultivated areas were vast tracks of grassland and forest, *nomad* paradises. The existence of these nomads added to the general insecurity of the valley civilizations.

It was towards the end of the Warring States period that the philosopher Confucius (Kung Fu-tsu) lived (see p. 234). Confucius's teaching, that ruled and ruler alike should each observe the rule of conduct which was fitting for him, was basic to the stability of a feudal society. It paralleled the ideas of *hierarchy* and order in European feudalism. It is no accident that it was in a time of disorder that Confucius's ideas were developed. Iron implements spread; the use of decomposed grass as a fertilizer was discovered. Iron spades made possible the digging of irrigation and transport canals. The peasant became more prosperous and trade and the towns grew, while the nobles and the kings fought their wars, rather as in England during the Wars of the Roses (see pp. 106-7). The logic of events was leading to a united China and this was achieved by the *Chins*, between 221 and 207 B.C. Appropriately we call the Chinese by the name of this dynasty (see pp. 36-7).

Warlords ruled civilians by terror—and dressed to emphasize their power and strength. Their armour was made of layers of rhinoceros hide and they carried swords with long curved blades.

Dynastic China

The *Chin* state, from which China gets her name, was in the north-west, around the Wei river valley. By its military prowess and diplomatic skill the Chin state overcame all rivals and by 221 B.C. the Middle Kingdom (*Chung Kuo*), as the Chinese called their country, was united. The ruler of Chin took the title Chin Shih Huang-ti (First Emperor). During the period in which the Chin rose to supreme power thinkers flourished like Lao-tse, who taught a philosophy of universal love, and Han Fei who argued that, for the monarchy to be strong, it should rely on an official *bureaucracy* and not on the feudal nobility. Han Fei's views were adopted. In the new state all power came from the emperor, the nobility losing their independent power. The centralized bureaucracy, which has been the peculiar mark of Chinese government for 2,000 years, was created. A detailed *census* was taken; a uniform script, but not an *alphabet*, was introduced; weights and measures were standardized; a round coin with a square hole in the middle replaced cruder means of exchange; this was called *cash*. Chin Shih Huang-ti built roads through his empire and a continuous 'ten thousand li' wall in the north to keep out the *nomads*. This was the Great Wall of China. A li is about half a kilometre; the Great Wall is about 2,700 kilometres long, so it never reached the expected length.

The fighting and the new building by the Chin emperor put an intolerable burden on the peasantry. In 209 B.C. the first of the great peasant risings which fill Chinese history occurred. Chen Sheng and Wu Kuang led it and were joined by a noble, Hsiang Yu, and a petty official, Liu Pang. By 206 B.C. Liu Pang had overthrown the Chins; he founded a new dynasty, the greatest and longest lasting in Chinese history, the Han. The Chinese call themselves *Sons of Han*. The Han rulers took over and consolidated the changes introduced by the Chin. Liu Pang, the Emperor Han Kao Tsu (206-195 B.C.) as he became, repealed many of the harsher Chin laws and eased the burdens on the peasants. Under the Chin there had been a deliberate attempt to destroy all records of earlier times, a burning of books. The Han not only stopped this, but sought out all the past records which had escaped destruction. A bureaucratic *civil service* was recruited by examination in the *classics*, not by hereditary right. Under the Emperor Wu Ti (141-87 B.C.) the Han empire reached its greatest heights. Canals were built; one joined the capital, Changan, to the Yellow river. The empire was divided into *pro-*

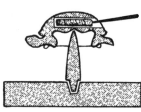

Above: An early Chinese compass which was made about 200 B.C. by setting lode stone, a naturally magnetic iron ore, into a model of a tortoise. By balancing it on a wooden peg, the tortoise was able to rotate freely. The first compasses were used to locate a suitable site for building and it was not until the eleventh century that they were used for navigation.

vinces, prefectures and *districts*, each controlled by imperial officials: the system remained until 1911 A.D. In 124 B.C. an *imperial university* was created for the study of the classics and the training of future government servants.

Wu Ti expanded the boundaries of the Han empire to reach from Mongolia to Indo-China. He began the attack on the Huns which finally drove them westwards (see pp. 56-7). He invaded north Korea and made contact with Japan. He sent his envoy Chang Chien westwards to Parthia and over many years extended the Chinese empire until it almost reached the edge of Roman influence in the Middle East. The *Old Silk Road* was opened along a chain of *oases* defended by Chinese forts. Trading contact was made with the Roman empire. Silk came to Europe, grapes and cloves to China;

The Great Wall of China, built about 2,200 years ago, is one of the world's most remarkable achievements. Some parts of the wall had been built in earlier centuries by the northern city-states to keep out marauding nomads. It was not until the Chin dynasty in the third century B.C., however, that the gigantic task of joining all these walls together was carried out. Millions of peasants worked on the construction of the wall, guarded by 250,000 soldiers. When it was finished, it stretched for 2,700 kilometres and was almost seven metres high.

Below left: A pottery model of one of the 3,500 watchtowers which were built along the Wall.

but the chief Chinese import was horses from central Asia. The Han empire by the first century B.C. covered a greater area than the contemporary Roman empire.

But all this cost too much, as had the earlier Chin expansion. The rich got richer and the peasants poorer: 'the footpaths of the rich ran across every field, and the benefits from streams and mountains were monopolised by them, the poor hadn't enough ground on which to rest the end of an awl'. In 9 A.D. a nephew of one of the empresses, Wang Mang, seized the throne. He attempted to centralize power and wealth, to reduce the private fortunes of the rich and to improve the public provisions and to give the peasants land. The *Red Eyebrow* and *Green Woodsmen* peasant risings threatened the empire and in 23 A.D. Wang was killed. Two years later Kuang

Wu restored the Han dynasty, moving the capital to Loyang.

This restored Han dynasty survived until 220 A.D. The nomads were driven out and General Pan Chao reconquered central Asia. But Han society was degenerating: landlords, court *eunuchs*, and scholars quarrelled over wealth and power. In 184 A.D. the *Yellow Turban* peasant revolt began. The generals who should have put it down set themselves up as *warlords*. The last Han emperor died in 220 A.D., a puppet in the hands of a warlord. From 220 to 589 A.D. China was disunited. This cycle of dynastic unity, collapse and reunification was to be repeated several times. It always began in the same way: the peasants became impoverished, the rich richer, the economy faltered, and the court's effectiveness was destroyed by intrigues.

37

H-C'

Hinduism and the Maurya Empire

India was united by *Hinduism*. Indian society is the product of many races (see pp. 12-13) and many cultures, which have mingled and mixed over centuries. Hinduism emerged from this process and, because it drew on the traditions of the different peoples of India, it could provide them with a common way of life. Most religions have a *prophet* or 'son of God' as their founder. Hinduism, on the other hand, was created by many people over a long period of time.

An Indian 'Dark Age' followed the *Aryan* invasions and the collapse of the Indus civilization (see pp. 22-3). There are 1,000 years of history (about 1500-500 B.C.) on which *archaeology* is only beginning to shed some light and for which oral tradition is the best evidence we have. This is embedded in the immensely rich epic-religious literature

Bathing ghat (or steps) at Benares, India, leading into the Ganges river which is sacred to the Hindus. The Hindus believe that the Ganges once washed the skies but was invited by the gods to descend to cleanse the earth centuries ago. The river is still said to have the power to purify the soul and body.

of India written in the classical language, Sanskrit. The oldest work is the *Rigveda*, which contains over a thousand hymns and is as long as the *Iliad* and the *Odyssey* put together. The earliest of its hymns probably go back to between 1500 and 1400 B.C.; others were added later. The *Brahmanas* are books of *liturgy*, service books for *priests*,

and were probably made up between 800 and 600 B.C.. The *Upanishads* began to be composed about the same time. They were in existence by 600-500 B.C., when the *Buddha* (see pp. 40-1 and 233) based his teaching on them. The *Bhagavad-Gita* dates from between 400 and 200 B.C.; it is part of the *Māhābharata*, one of India's two great epics. The other is the *Rāmāyana*.

From these sources we discover that the Aryan invaders believed in many gods and that these gods were crude. They are rather like the savage gods of the *Celtic* Iron Age in Britain. *Indra* was an Aryan god who later passed into Hinduism and was transformed. Both Celtic and early Indian literatures tell of a band of young heroes, whose cattle raiding is revealing of their way of life. From the *Dravidians*, Hinduism drew *asceticism*, renunciation of the world by holy men, and the holy bathing places. These were quite foreign to the active, warrior Aryans. The two cultures began to mix in the Upanishads—Hinduism was created. The many gods of both earlier traditions are seen as aspects of the one all pervading God (the Brahman). *Monotheism* replaces *polytheism*. The Brahman 'dwells in the heart of all beings', in the words of the Bhagavad-Gita; it is the same as the *Ātman*, which is the Self. The *Supreme Being* shows itself in every soul and there are an infinite number of different paths to the One Infinite. So Hinduism has, naturally, been marked by a deep and sincere respect for all living things.

This new and superior religion, with its own way of life, began to emerge between 1000 and 500 B.C. when new cities were being built in India's second great river valley, the Ganges. From about 500 B.C. the use of iron and coins was spreading. This was the centre of India's second great civilization, the *Maurya* empire, and probably it was here that Hinduism, and later *Buddhism*, were born.

The Mauryan empire was based on slavery (see pp. 22-3), and this policy may have produced the Indian *caste system*, which divides people by their trades into groups which live separate lives. Slavery is not compatible with the fundamental respect for life which is the essence of Hinduism. To justify slavery, no doubt the people of Maurya times developed the idea that everyone had his proper defined place in society. The caste system is only an extremely rigid form of the idea which we find in medieval Christianity (see pp. 74-5).

The Maurya empire was founded by Chandragupta Maurya, who began his conquests between 330 and 320 B.C. When he died in 298 B.C. his kingdom reached from

the Hindu Kush to Bengal. His son, Bindus-ara, advanced southwards into north Mysore. Asoka, Chandragupta's grandson, came to the throne about 268 B.C. and conquered all India except the southern tip and Ceylon. In remorse for the slaughter he had caused, he became a Buddhist and abandoned all further conquests. He adopted the principles of *maitri* (friendliness) and *ahimsā* (non-violence) and carved his remarkable edicts on the rocks. 'Kalinga was conquered by his Sacred and Gracious Majesty—150,000 people were thence carried away captive, 150,000 were there slain, and many times that number died. Thus arose his Sacred Majesty's remorse because the conquest of a country previously unconquered involves the slaughter, death and carrying away captive of the people.' The

One of the most important of the Hindu gods is Ganesi (above) who has the body of a man and the head of an elephant. According to Hindu mythology, Ganesi is the son of Siva, one of the three gods who form the Hindu holy trinity. All the gods were invited to celebrate Ganesi's birth but when Sani (the Hindu equivalent of Satan) looked on the baby, the baby's head turned to ashes. The only head which could be found was that of an elephant and this was immediately placed on the baby's shoulders. Ganesi came to symbolize good fortune and wealth.

king would tolerate no more killing —'should anyone do him wrong, that too must be borne with by His Sacred Majesty, so far as it can possibly be borne with. His Sacred Majesty desires that all animate beings should have security, self-control, peace of mind, and joyousness.'

Megasthenes, a Greek ambassador to Chandragupta's court, described the Mauryan capital, at Pataliputra, as stretching for 15 kilometres along the Ganges. It is reminiscent of the Indus valley cities, but the immediate influence was Persian (see pp. 42-3). Under Asoka this civilization spread throughout India: he built public gardens, hospitals, wells, and roads along which there was provision for shade and water. The Maurya empire lasted, after Asoka's death, until about 185 B.C.

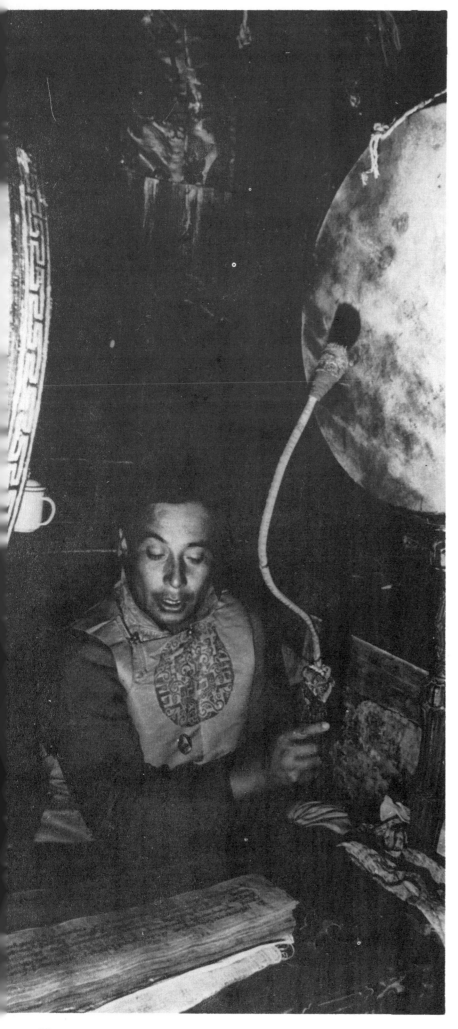

The Spread of Buddhism

Buddhism is an *atheist* religion; it does not accept that there is either a God or an immortal soul in each man. Buddhists believe that all suffering is the result of the selfish desires of the individual, and until these are conquered man cannot escape from the sorrows of life. Once these personal cravings are overcome, spiritual peace, or *Enlightenment*, is achieved. The *Buddha* Siddhartha Gautama showed the Way to Enlightenment.

Siddhartha Gautama was born about 563 B.C. at Lumbini, then in India and now in Nepal (see p. 233). He died about 483 B.C. He was a prince of the *Sakya* clan. One of his later names was *Sakyamuni,* which means Sage of the Sakyas. When a young man, Gautama was revolted by the contrast be-

tween the pleasures he enjoyed as a prince and the suffering which he saw around him. He became a beggar, studying with Hindu sages and practising *asceticism.* When he was 35 years old he achieved Enlightenment and became the Buddha, which means the Enlightened One.

Gautama had been learning the mystical wisdom of the *Upanishads*—the *Dhamma,* or teaching. These were secret teachings of metaphysics or philosophy, of moral ideas intended for the priestly elite. Gautama's life, until he was 35, followed the ideal Hindu model of his time. He broke with Hindu practice when he decided to teach the Dhamma to all mankind. The Buddha did not so much develop a new morality or way of life as purify the best in Hindu religion and lay it before everyone. He lived for another 45 years, until he was 80.

To achieve his aims he founded the

Sangha, a religious order which has spread over the world and still survives. Buddhist monks have two functions: to teach the Dhamma to all and to provide for individuals the best conditions for their personal development towards Enlightenment. On the Buddha's death the first *Council of the Sangha* took place. About 100 years later there was a second Council, at which the first division within Buddhism appeared. This was between the strict 'Doctrine of the Elders', the supporters of the *Hinayana* or *Little Way*, and the supporters of the *Mahayana* or *Great Way*.

The difference between them was very important. The supporters of Hinayana, or *Theravda* as they called themselves, taught that Enlightenment could only come through the strictest observance of the Rules; their Way was hard, a moral philosophy for the few. Asoka, the Mauryan king of India, was converted to Buddhism

Far left: A drummer accompanies the chanting of the scriptures in a Tibetan temple in Nepal.

Left: Buddhist monks gather twice a month to hear the 227 precepts and prohibitions of their religion. Novices must attend daily. In some Asian countries it is compulsory for all young men to spend a period of time in a monastery to learn about their religion.

about 260 B.C.; he called the third Council of the Sangha at Patna. It probably comprised only Theravda supporters. Asoka's behaviour as a Buddhist certainly suggests that he believed in following the Rules, even when they were difficult (see pp. 38-9). In Asoka's reign Buddhism became the established religion of India.

The supporters of the Mahayana taught that potential Enlightenment dwells within and only needs developing. Kanishka, ruler of the *Kushans* (see pp. 92-3), called the fourth Council of the Sangha, of Mahayan supporters, which launched Buddhist missionaries into central Asia. The *Bodhisattva*, the Saviour of Mankind, became the Mahayana ideal. Originally a Bodhisattva was someone whose essential being, or *sattva*, had become perfect wisdom, or *bodhi*, in other words a Buddha in the making. But by the fourth Council the

Mahayana Buddhists had given Bodhisattva a new meaning: someone who dedicated his life to the welfare of mankind, instead of pursuing his own Enlightenment, and by so doing delayed his own entry into *Nirvana*, or nothingness, which was the reward for achieving Enlightenment. This new Mahayana teaching replaced wisdom (*Prajna*) with compassion (*Karuna*) as the Buddhist ideal. Buddhism, ever since, has developed with two wings: one putting the weight on the *Arhat* ideal, that of the human being who, by strenuous effort, achieves his own Enlightenment; the other on the Bodhisattva, who helps others achieve Enlightenment.

Hinayana Buddhism spread into Ceylon about 260-250 B.C. and then into Burma. Mahayana Buddhism spread into Tibet, China and Japan. There is a tradition that Buddhist ideas first reached China early in *Han* times, about 200 B.C. But the first real evidence is that the Emperor Ming-Ti in 61 A.D. sent to India for Buddhist books and teachers. In 520 A.D. an Indian teacher, Bodhidharma, reached China and taught his own, latest development—*Zen Buddhism*. This is almost the exact opposite of Gautama's Way, for it argues that the bars of the intellect must be broken down before the mind can be freed for Enlightenment. It was in this form that Buddhism spread to Japan from the sixth century A.D.

In China Buddhism reached its maximum support under the *Tang* dynasty (620-902 A.D.). But whereas *Hinduism*, and later *Islam*, almost replaced Buddhism in India, its birthplace, Buddhism remained strong in China, Sri Lanka, Burma, Cambodia (the Khmer republic), Laos and Thailand.

Above: In some parts of Tibet and India, Buddhists worship a number of images and many of them date back several centuries. Among the more common images are several different Buddhas, his disciples, saints, and old guardian deities.

Above: Scalp of a Yeti, the legendary monster of the Himalayas who is also known as the Abominable Snowman. This Yeti scalp is in a Tibetan monastery: some disbelievers, however, claim it is the hair of a mountain antelope.

Persia

Persia, or Iran as it is now called, is on a mountain plateau in the shape of a triangle, between the Caspian Sea in the north and the Persian Gulf in the south, Mesopotamia in the west and Afghanistan and the north-west frontier of Pakistan in the east. Iran is a bridge on the lines of communication between Asia and Europe. The oldest of trade routes, the *Old Silk Road* (see pp. 90-1), runs through Iran. This area has seen invaders from north and west and east; in the Persian highlands they have settled and, mingling with their predecessors, produced outstanding civilizations and great empires.

The first known invaders, Indo-European *nomads* (see pp. 26-7), came during the second *millennium* B.C. In Iran they were in touch with the civilization of Mesopotamia and particularly Elam, which had had its own writing as early as *c.* 3200 B.C. The fusion produced dynamic new kingdoms such as that of the *Kassites* who came from Luristan to rule Mesopotamia from 1747 to 1171 B.C. The Iranians arrived at the beginning of the first millennium B.C. There were two groups, the *Persians*, first mentioned in 844 B.C., and the *Medes* in 835 B.C.

The Medes, under Cyaxares, conquered

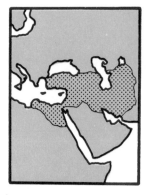

The shaded area on the map above shows the extent of the Persian empire at about 500 B.C.

Below: The skill of their mounted archers enabled the Parthians to halt the Roman advance. They defeated many armies with their famous 'Parthian Shot'. The cavalry would pretend to retreat, encouraging the enemy to follow them. The Parthians would then turn in their saddles and fire arrows onto the pursuing army.

the western half of the Iranian plateau and made Ecbatana the capital. Astyages, son of Cyaxares, was defeated by the Persian Cyrus the Great, his son-in-law, who built the first great Persian empire on the Median foundations. Among other things its priestly *caste*, the *Magi*, were Medes. The Persian royal family called themselves *Achaemenians*. About 700 B.C. Achaemenes had carved himself a little kingdom in Parsumash. Cambyses I married the daughter of Astyages the Median king. Cyrus the Great (559-530 B.C.) was their son. He conquered Asia Minor, Lydia and the Greek cities on the Aegean coast. Then he turned east and built fortified towns on the Oxus and Jaxartes rivers. Babylon fell in 539 B.C. and the captive Jews were sent back to Israel, led by Zerubbabel, in 537 B.C. Cyrus built up his empire as a loose *federation* of different peoples and cultures without a centralizing authority.

This proved fatal to his son, Cambyses, who conquered Egypt and Libya but died on his way home. Darius (522-486 B.C.) restored order; he defeated nine kings in 19 battles over two years. The newly united empire was centrally controlled by Persian *satraps*. Darius created an efficient administration, with travelling inspectors, 'the ears of the

Above: The porch of Xerxes, part of a magnificent complex of palaces and other buildings which were built at Persepolis between 518 and 460 B.C.

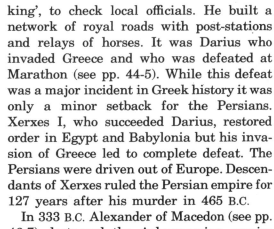

pp. 54-5).

It was the *Parthians*, a Scythian tribe who had settled in the *steppes* between the Caspian and Aral seas, who took over the Persian empire. Mithridates I occupied Iran up to the Euphrates between 160 and 140 B.C. and built a new capital, Ctesiphon, on the Tigris. Phraates II succeeded in 137 B.C. to an empire which stretched from the Euphrates to Herat in Afghanistan. Mithridates II saved his empire from a great wave of Scythian nomads in *c.* 123 B.C. and revived the title *King of Kings*, used by the Achaemenians. The Parthians proved so effective in defence that the expanding Roman empire was stopped at the Euphrates. Armoured heavy cavalry (*cataphracti*) and light cavalry using bows and arrows (*sagitarii*) were more than a match for the Roman legions.

Ardashir, grandson of Sassan, a priest of Fars who claimed descent from the Achaemenians, defeated the Parthian king, Artabanus V, in 224 A.D.; he created a new army and a new Persian state. The Persian *renaissance* was founded on the fusing of *Hellenistic* and Iranian cultures which took place under the Parthians. Ardashir's son, Shapur I, drove eastwards against the *Kushan* kingdom (see pp. 92-3) and put a king subservient to Persia on the throne. Then he turned westwards against the Romans, killing one emperor (Gordian III) and capturing another (Valerian). Later *Sassanian* kings experienced civil war due to the power of the *feudal* nobility. From time to time an outstanding ruler restored order. Shapur II (309-79 A.D.) was such a king; he extended both the eastern and western frontiers. Vahram V (420-38 A.D.) tamed the nobility and defeated *Ephthalite* nomads in the north-east. Chosroes I (531-79 A.D.) finally brought the nobility to heel, rebuilding roads and bridges and whole villages. Chosroes II (590-628 A.D.) came to the throne with *Byzantine* aid but attacked his allies in 610-616 A.D., invading Egypt and besieging Constantinople (Byzantium). A new Byzantine Emperor, Heracles, besieged Ctesiphon and Chosroes was assassinated. A dozen emperors ruled in the next 14 years. The empire was collapsing even as the Arabs conquered it (see pp. 68-9).

Sassanian Persia lasted for 420 years. Its art was carried by *Islam*, its heir, from China to western Europe. Two Sassanian religious teachers, Mani, founder of *Manicheanism*, and Mazdak, who drew equalitarian radical social conclusions from Mani's teaching, had a great influence. Manicheanism explains the world as formed from two warring elements, light and darkness, good and evil.

king', to check local officials. He built a network of royal roads with post-stations and relays of horses. It was Darius who invaded Greece and who was defeated at Marathon (see pp. 44-5). While this defeat was a major incident in Greek history it was only a minor setback for the Persians. Xerxes I, who succeeded Darius, restored order in Egypt and Babylonia but his invasion of Greece led to complete defeat. The Persians were driven out of Europe. Descendants of Xerxes ruled the Persian empire for 127 years after his murder in 465 B.C.

In 333 B.C. Alexander of Macedon (see pp. 46-7) destroyed the Achaemenian empire and replaced it with Greek rulers. By 301 B.C. Seleucus I had created a new Iranian-Macedonian empire which his family ruled for 150 years. The capital was a new city, Antioch, in Syria; several of the *Seleucids* were called Antiochus. New cities on Greek lines were built all over the empire, which flourished economically and culturally but soon broke up politically. Antiochus III (223-187 B.C.) spent eight years reconquering the eastern parts of the empire; Bactria and Parthia had broken away in the mid-third century B.C. But soon the Seleucids ruled only Syria effectively and then they became vassals of the expanding Roman empire (see

43

In 490 B.C. Sparta united with the other Greek states to fight off Persian invaders. The courage and fortitude of her soldiers, like the one illustrated here, became legendary. The symbol on the shield represents Lacedaemon (Sparta).

Right: The Erechtheum on the Acropolis, possibly the most perfect example of the Ionic style. It was begun in 421 B.C. to commemorate the Peace of Nicias and took 15 years to complete.

Classical Greece

The first civilized people of Greece were the *Achaeans* of 2500 B.C. onwards (see pp. 30-1). The Achaeans spoke an Indo-European language, used bronze tools and weapons, made pots and became skilled traders and warriors. Their great stronghold was Mycenae; from here, led by the High King Agamemnon in about 1200 B.C., they set out for the siege of Troy. The story of Trojan wars is told in the epic poem, the *Iliad*. Their dead kings have been found, buried together with their treasures in great beehive tombs, at Mycenae.

From about 1200 B.C. *Dorian* sea raiders preyed on trade and civilization declined. Within a century rough Dorian warriors and farmers settled in Greece. Many of the Achaeans moved to colonies on the coast of

Asia Minor, Ionia. Their civilization survived and in time they built well-planned cities and temples with graceful *Ionic columns*. Their vases were painted with animal patterns, and their trade was extensive. They were influenced by surrounding civilizations but, unlike their neighbours, they established no empires. Each city was independent; some were ruled by the 'best' people, the *aristocrats*; others had *tyrants*, although not always cruel or selfish. Samos had Polycrates, who protected and encouraged poets, artists and craftsmen who could build his palace or his harbour or plan his water supply. Pythagoras grew up there. The Ionians kept their old gods and heroes. Homer told stories of them in the *Iliad* and the *Odyssey*. Miletos was the centre of the pottery trade and the home of the first scientists, Thales and Anaximander. About 600 B.C. this was the most flourishing part of Greece and, from here, civilization, the use of money and the *alphabet* spread to the mainland.

By this time the Dorians were fully settled and city states had grown up. The warrior tradition was strongest in Sparta, where all citizens were, above all, soldiers. Boys left their mothers at seven, to be brought up in state institutions where they underwent intensive training in physical culture and the use of weapons. They became accustomed to hardship and had practically no amusements. At the age of 20 they joined a Spartan *mess*, a group of about 15 young men who lived, slept, fought and played as comrades. No one could marry until he was 30. Each warrior had a farm, which was worked by *Helots* (subject people) to support him.

Athens was a state of farmers and traders. It gradually developed *democratic government.* By the fifth century B.C. every Athenian could speak and vote in the *Assembly*, where decisions were taken; he had the chance of being an *archon* (one of the nine chief magistrates of Athens), for these were chosen by lot; twice in his life he would probably sit for a year on the *People's Council*, which had taken over most of the work of the government. Each time, for a month, his tribe would be in charge; for one day he would be on duty in the *Round House*, the residence of the temporary Prime Minister of Athens. If anyone accused him of a crime he would be judged by a jury of perhaps 500 fellow citizens. Pay was given for these duties, so that even the poorest could take part.

In 490 B.C. Greece faced a crisis: Ionia was conquered by the Persians who invaded Greece. Athens and Plataea faced the invaders alone and defeated them at Marathon. Xerxes sent a larger army in 480 B.C. Themistocles organized an alliance of Athens, Sparta and other states. The Persian navy was damaged at Artemisium and the Spartans fought bravely at Thermopylae until all were killed. The Athenians abandoned their city and occupied the island of Salamis. Here the Greek fleet destroyed the Persian fleet. Xerxes's army was finally defeated at Plataea. This was one of the rare occasions when the Greeks worked together.

Sparta retired from the war; Athens freed the Ionians from the Persians only to make them part of her own empire. This helped Athens' trade and made her wealthy. Money was spent on ships; on temples and public buildings like the *Parthenon*; on open air theatres and drama festivals, where actors, wearing masks to portray emotions and thick-soled shoes to add to their height, first performed the tragedies of Aeschylus, Sophocles and Euripedes. Socrates, the greatest of the *sophists*, challenged accepted ideas on philosophy. Athenian vases were painted with elegant figures. Phidias's statues are lifelike still. But Corinth and Sparta were envious, and Athens' subjects resented the way Athens spent money on herself. After a long war Athens lost her empire and her great days were over by 400 B.C. Many of the leaders whom Athens chose were mob *orators*, not skilled in government; they came and went. Juries worried little about justice: Socrates was condemned to death merely because they did not like his ideas. Plato and Aristotle and other philosophers were his followers; they all thought *democracy* was the worst form of government.

The supremacy of Athens was followed by that of Sparta, and Sparta by that of Thebes; but the Greeks never found a satisfactory way of combining together without rivalry, injustice and resentment. They fell an easy victim to the bigger armies of Philip of Macedon and Alexander (see p. 232).

Above: The Jockey of Artemisium, a bronze sculpture from the second century B.C.

Below: Three classical orders of Greek architecture: 1. Doric; 2. Corinthian; 3. Ionic.

Alexandrian Greece

The squabbling city states of the Greek mainland and Ionia (see pp. 44-5) produced a way of life that has been admired ever since. Between the eighth and the sixth centuries B.C. Greeks settled in colonies over a vast area, from the east coast of the Black Sea and the Crimea to the French and Spanish Mediterranean coasts, Cyrene in North Africa and Naucratis at the mouth of the Nile. These daughter cities retained and spread Greek civilization. The trading economy of the Greeks took them in search of new markets. In the Middle East the old Bronze Age empires had been united by the Persians (see pp. 42-3) but little changed. An opening up of the Persian empire to Greek craftsmen and merchants offered great rewards. The cross-fertilization of the old civilization, developed in the cradle of mankind, with the new Iron Age civilization of

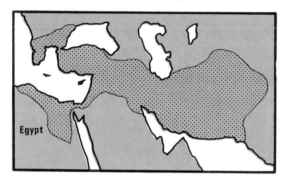

Egypt

Greece, laid the basis for a world empire. Already men were feeling their way towards a single, world union. The achievement of this union was the work of a remarkable young man, Alexander the Great, King of Macedon, in eleven years of unending war (see p. 232).

Philip II of Macedon conquered the Greek mainland between 357 and 338 B.C. He invited Aristotle, the great Athenian *philosopher*, to become tutor to his son, Alexander. In 336 B.C. Philip was assassinated and Alexander became king at the age of 20. He subdued rebellion in mainland Greece and in 334 B.C. crossed the Hellespont to begin the conquest of Persia. This was to be revenge for the Persian attacks of Darius and Xerxes (see pp. 42-3). Alexander's victorious advance was marked by a series of great battles: among them Granicus (334 B.C.), which destroyed the Persian army in Asia Minor, and Issus (333 B.C.), which opened up Syria. Alexander's conquest of Egypt (332-331 B.C.) followed; he was proclaimed king and of divine birth, and he founded the city of Alexandria. In 331 B.C. he crossed the Euphrates and at the battle of Gaugamela once again defeated the Persian Great King; Babylon surrendered to

Left: The shaded area shows the extent of Alexander's empire, achieved in the 13 years of his reign.

Above: The battle of Issus between Alexander the Great of Greece and Darius III of Persia. Alexander had dreamt of invading Persia since he inherited the throne at the age of 20. In 334 B.C., he led 30,000 infantry and 5,000 cavalry into Persia and succeeded first in crushing the powerful Persian navy and then conquering Darius's forces at Issus. Although Darius himself escaped, the Greek forces caught up with him a year later at Hecatompylus. Believing their fight was futile, Darius's men stabbed their king and fled. With Darius dead, Alexander became master of the entire Persian empire.

him. In 330 B.C. he conquered the Persian homeland, capturing Susa, Persepolis and Ecbatana and found Darius, the last *Achaemenian* ruler of Persia, murdered.

Alexander became Great King himself, in order to win Persian support for the introduction of Greek ways. He founded Greek cities all over his expanding empire. By 328 B.C. he had crossed the river Jaxartes (Syr Darya) and founded a city, Alexandria the Ultimate, to mark the boundary of his empire. In 326 B.C. Alexander entered India, crossed the river Indus and defeated Porus at the battle of the Hydaspes. Here two Greek cities were built. In 323 B.C. Alexander the Great died, of a fever, in Babylon aged 33 years. He had conquered and united a larger area of the world than any man before him. He had lived violently, and few men have been both more admired and more hated.

When Alexander died his empire broke up into three and then five parts, but cultural unity was established over an enormous area of the world. Greek became the international language of eastern Europe, western Asia and North Africa. Greek and Babylonian scientific knowledge was blended. The Greeks spread knowledge of

the true distance. About 200 B.C. Aristarchus and Seleucus suggested that the sun rotated round the Earth. *Latitude* was measured against the elevation of the Pole Star; and in 331 B.C. an *eclipse* was used to give standard time in measuring *longitude*. By the second century A.D. the geographer Ptolemy (Claudius Ptolemaeus) had constructed a skeleton map of the globe on a latitude-longitude frame. There were also practical inventions: Archimedes' screw, Ktesibios' pump, and rotary mills driven first by donkey power and then by water power. The Roman empire (see pp. 54-5) was based on the culture of Alexandrian Greece but little use was made of all these advances. The cheapness of slaves meant that inventions which saved labour power were not highly valued.

Babylonian fractions and the decimal point, but neither had a zero sign. This was to come from India. Kings encouraged scientific research, and urged landlords to improve their estates and generals and merchants to improve communications. The Greek cities which spread over Africa and Asia were centres of learning and of trade. At Alexandria in Egypt Ptolemy I built the Museum, a great university and research institute.

The Alexandrian period, opened by Alexander's conquests, produced more understanding of science than man was to achieve again until the 17th century A.D. Euclid (*c.* 323-285 B.C.) systematized geometry and applied it to *optics*. *Conics* was studied in relation to the curve of *artillery projectiles* and the movement of the sun's shadow on a sundial. Archimedes (287-212 B.C.) laid the foundations of mechanics, discovering specific gravity and the principle of the screw. Eratosthenes, director of the Museum (240-220 B.C.), calculated the circumference of the Earth with an error of only four per cent; to do this observations of the Sun's altitude at the summer *solstice* were made from Alexandria and from the Tropic of Cancer. Hipparchus estimated the Sun's distance from the Earth but at ·half

Right: A sculpture of Hercules fighting a lion from the fourth century B.C. Hercules, a kind of primitive Superman, was among the most popular of early Greek mythological figures and was loved and admired for his great strength. According to legend, his wife gave him a poisoned shirt to punish him for his infidelities. Desperate with pain, Hercules had himself placed on a funeral pyre but was rescued by the gods who made him immortal.

In the war that broke out between Carthage and Rome in 218 B.C., Hannibal swiftly took the offensive by invading Italy. He marched overland from Spain with a large force of cavalry and elephants and entered Italy after crossing the Alps in the north.

The Roman Republic

The coming of the Romans, perhaps as followers of Aeneas, and the foundation of their stronghold by their first king, Romulus, are legends with some basis in fact. They must have been few in number, surrounded by powerful neighbours—the *Etruscans* to the north, the *Samnites* to the south, and beyond them the Greeks of Sicily and south Italy. Their last king, Tarquin, probably an Etruscan, was expelled in 509 B.C. and Rome became a *republic*. Authority was shared between two *consuls*, appointed for one year only, and (from 366 B.C.) one *praetor*, or judge. They checked each other's power, and were advised by the *Senate*, the council of the heads of the most influential families. In emergencies a *dictator* might be appointed, who could overrule everyone. The votes of the *patricians* counted for more than those of the common people, the *plebeians*. Rome was therefore ruled by its *aristocracy*.

The first problem of the young republic was military. All Romans had to fight (there were very few years of peace), and by 263 B.C. Rome was mistress of Italy. Many stories showing Roman courage, honesty and determination are told about this period by Livy, a historian of the time of Augustus (see p. 232): the legends of Horatius keeping the bridge, of Coriolanus, and of

Camillus. Rome defeated her neighbours, and made them junior partners in the *Roman Confederacy*: they could trade in their own town or at Rome, but not with each other in case they plotted against Rome. They were not heavily taxed but provided troops for Rome's army. Rome secured her position by founding colonies of soldiers and linking them to Rome by roads.

The second great problem was that of the plebeians. Plebeian families were turned out of their three hectares of public land when they were called up for the army and had no one to leave in charge. The plebeians went on strike, left the city and refused to

work. A compromise gave them the right to elect *tribunes* who could veto, or stop, an action of consuls or praetors of which they disapproved. In 450 B.C. 'the customs of ancestors' were written on *Twelve Tables*, which became the basis of Roman justice, and of the laws of many countries.

Carthage controlled much of Sicily and the Romans defeated the Carthaginians in three wars. In the first (264 to 241 B.C.) the Romans built a fleet, checked Carthage's sea power, and conquered Sicily. They took Corsica and Sardinia. In the second (218 to 201 B.C.) they defeated Hannibal, who had invaded Italy by crossing the Alps and persuaded Rome's allies to desert. Scipio conquered Spain and deprived Carthage of the silver and the soldiers she drew from there. Carthage was only a shadow of her former power. After the third war (149-146 B.C.) Carthage was razed to the ground.

With these conquests, and others in Gaul and the east, Rome now had a large empire. There were great changes in Roman society. Even patricians had lived simply, working their estates with a few slaves. Now slaves and corn were imported in quantity. Only large ranches for cattle and sheep, or vineyards worked by huge gangs of slaves,

remained profitable. Small farmers left their land and joined mobs of unemployed in Rome. A new social class appeared, the rich businessmen, who made money as slave contractors, suppliers to the army, or tax collectors; they were called *equites* (knights) because they were expected to serve as cavalry in the army. All classes began to act selfishly. The empire meant more officials and an army to protect and enlarge its borders. A successful provincial *governor*, with an army behind him, could not be rebuked, even by the Senate.

No reformer succeeded in establishing harmony. In 133 B.C. Tiberius Gracchus, a tribune, introduced a law to redistribute the land. It worked well, but the senators attacked and killed him. His brother, Gaius, tried to give more influence to equites by letting them act as judges, but he and his followers were killed, and the equites proved most dishonest as judges. The Italians set up their own republic and declared war on Rome. They were defeated, but were granted citizenship in 89 B.C.; yet bitterness remained. Two generals, Marius and Sulla, struggled for power. Sulla won, reduced the power of the equites but did nothing for the poor. His *reforms* were cancelled. Pompey, Crassus, and Caesar (see p. 233) combined against the Senate. Cicero as consul

(see p. 233)

Left: The Roman Republic was brought to an end by Julius Caesar. After winning the consulship in civil war, Caesar declared himself dictator for life in 46 B.C. But a group of Roman noblemen, angered by Caesar's actions, stabbed him to death in the Senate two years later. Ironically, Caesar's body fell by the statue of Pompey, the ruler he had defeated in civil war.

(63 B.C.) did his best to keep the peace, but in 59 B.C. Caesar as consul used force against the Senate. There was a brief respite while Caesar conquered Gaul and invaded Britain, but he returned with his army to defy Pompey, defeat him in a civil war, and make himself dictator for life. He began a programme of reforms, but was murdered by Brutus and his friends, who thought it wrong that Republican traditions should be so disregarded. Civil war followed, from which Caesar's nephew, Octavian, emerged as the emperor Augustus. The Republic taught the world much about laws and effective government, but it failed in the end to provide justice.

Above: The Oath of the Horatii by the 18th-century French painter, David. The painting shows the Horatii triplets swearing to defend Rome before departing to fight the Curiatii triplets from warring Alba. According to the ancient Roman legend, two of the Horatii brothers were killed. The third pretended to flee and when the Curiatii triplets separated to pursue him, he was able to kill off each brother individually and return to Rome triumphant.

H-D

The Jewish People

The Jews are the descendants of Abraham He became a *nomad* after leaving the city of Ur in about 1800 B.C. (see pp. 18-19). His family settled in Palestine, but in the 17th century B.C. moved to Egypt in search of food. Here they were enslaved. In the 1200s B.C. their descendants were led to freedom by Moses (see pp. 26-7). They spent 40 years wandering in the Sinai desert. Moses gave them laws and, in a unique religion based on the worship of *Jehovah*, he taught them to believe that they were the special people of God. Led by Joshua, they invaded Palestine, defeated the natives and set up a Jewish state. At first they had no kings, but were ruled by military-religious leaders who often saved them from foreign attack and captivity. They were only held together by their religious beliefs.

Their first king, Saul, was chosen at the end of the eleventh century B.C. He was a great military leader, but was unable to defeat the *Philistines*, who were attacking the land. The next king, David, defeated the

Below: A 17th century representation of the Ark doors of the Covenant from Krakow, in Poland. The Ark is of great significance in the Jewish faith since it is the shrine which traditionally houses the tablets of the Jews' sacred laws.

Below right: Moses and the tablets of law, said to have been handed to him by God on Mount Sinai. Around 1200 B.C., Moses led his people out of slavery in Egypt to Israel.

Philistines and united all the Jewish people. He made Jerusalem the religious and political capital of his kingdom. David built a large, rich, powerful empire. The reign of his son, Solomon, was peaceful and the Jews became a powerful trading people. They resented the heavy taxation imposed by Solomon to pay for the building of a temple, and revolted after his death in 931 B.C. The kingdom was then divided into two parts.

Israel, the northern kingdom, was large and prosperous. But during the next 200 years it became poor and weak for its kings were unable to preserve law and order. In 722 B.C. Israel was defeated and absorbed by Assyria. The people lost their freedom. Many were deported to other parts of the Assyrian empire. Judah, the southern kingdom, was small, poor and mountainous. It was less important than Israel and had little contact with the major powers until the eighth century B.C. The Kings of Judah were all descendants of David and Solomon and managed to keep many of the old religious beliefs. It was at this time that much of the *Old Testament* was written.

From 733 B.C. Judah was controlled by Assyria, and later by Babylon, and the people had to pay heavy taxes to their overlords. In 587 B.C. the country was drawn into the Babylonian empire and most of the

people were deported, although they were still allowed to keep their religious beliefs. In 539 B.C., after the Persians had defeated Babylon, a few Jews were allowed to return to Judaea to rebuild the temple at Jerusalem. During the next century many more people returned to join the religious community that had been established, but most remained in exile. Many Jews had remained in Palestine. They married Arabs and were called *Samaritans*. They opposed the returned exiles.

In the fourth century B.C., the Jews were ruled by their religious leader, the *High Priest*. They had greater political freedom and were governed by the law of Moses, as a religious state. *Aramaic* took the place of *Hebrew* as their language, and the remainder of the Old Testament was written. Great stress was placed on the importance of racial and religious purity. After Alexander the Great had defeated the Persian empire (see pp. 46-7) Palestine became a major battleground between the kings of Egypt and Syria. For 100 years the Jews were ruled by Egypt. Then, in 200 B.C., they were conquered by Syria, which ruled them till 128 B.C. So long as they paid their taxes the Jews were allowed religious and political freedom, and remained fairly peaceful. They revolted against Syrian rule in 165 B.C. when the king of Syria interferred with their religious worship. This 'Maccabean' revolt lasted for 40 years and won for the Jews full political and religious freedom. From 128 B.C. the Jewish leaders rapidly spread their control over the neighbouring states of

The famous battle between David and the giant Goliath (above) took place during a war between the Philistines and the Israelites. Each day, the Philistines sent forward the giant to challenge any Israeli combatant. Only David accepted and, armed with a sling and pebbles, killed the massive Goliath. David later became the first ruler of a united Israel and an empire which stretched from the Euphrates in the north-east to the Gulf of Aqaba in the south-east.

Idumea, Samaria and Palestine. They forced their peoples to accept the Jewish religion.

The Romans invaded Palestine 60 years later, and took over Judaea. The people were forced to obey Roman laws and pay Roman taxes but were allowed to keep their religion. The High Priest lost all his power of ruling. For over 100 years the Romans appointed governors for the Jews. The governors were unpopular because they taxed the people heavily and crushed all revolts. It was during this period that Jesus Christ was born in Palestine and founded the Christian religion (see pp. 52-3 and 237). Between 66 and 70 A.D., a massive Roman army was needed to overcome a serious revolt. Many people were slaughtered, and others were sold as slaves to be scattered throughout the Roman empire. In 135 A.D., Jews were forbidden to live in Palestine.

Until the Roman empire became Christian in the fourth century A.D., the Jews were well treated. Throughout the following 1,500 years of Christian rule they were persecuted. The only people who treated them as equals were the Arabs. The Jews managed to survive through the strength of their religious beliefs and their refusal to marry non-Jews. Towards the end of the 19th century A.D. the *Zionist* movement was founded by European Jews. They wanted to make a national Jewish home in Palestine. After the end of *Nazi* persecution when six million Jews were destroyed (see pp. 184-9), Israel was established as a state in 1948 A.D. (located on the Mediterranean and bordered by Egypt, Jordan and Lebanon).

Rise of Christianity

Christianity began with the teachings of Jesus Christ whom the Romans crucified for sedition. The eleven *apostles* whom Jesus Christ (see p. 237) left to carry on his work were at first too scared to leave their house. When it seemed to them, however, that the *Holy Spirit* had given them courage they first preached to the Jews visiting Jerusalem. When the temple *priests* drove them out they moved to Samaria, Antioch, and Damascus, where many Jews lived. Christians were still a sect within the Jewish faith.

The conversion of Saul (Paul) on his way to Damascus to harry the Christians there was a crucial turning point. The Jerusalem Jews would not listen to such a turncoat, so Paul's mission was mainly to Jews and Greeks scattered in various parts of Asia Minor and Greece. He was a highly educated man, one of the few apostles who could argue on equal terms with both Greeks and Jews. It was most important to weld the two groups into one community and to keep them in touch with the Mother Church. At first Peter had his doubts about baptizing *pagans*; some apostles insisted that pagans must be *circumcised* as Jews before they could become Christians. At the *Council of Jerusalem* 48-49 A.D. Paul persuaded the apostles that this was unnecessary; all were equal as Christians, and separate from the Jewish faith. The purpose of St. Paul's letters was to deal with arguments between Greek and Jewish Christians, and to stress the need for unity. It was he who first called the scattered communities or 'ecclesia' the 'body of Christ'.

It did not occur to anyone to record the activities of the other apostles at the time. Very little had been written even about Christ; all teaching was by word of mouth. Only when Paul was in prison in Rome did Luke write the *Acts of the Apostles*, giving Paul's account of the story. Peter went to Rome, leaving James in Jerusalem; James and his successor were beheaded and Peter was *martyred*. When the Church lost its leaders their followers realized that the *gospel* must be written down before argument arose and the eyewitnesses were all dead. All four gospels were written between 50 and 100 A.D. A much later tradition says that Thomas preached to the *Parthians* and was active in India, John went to Asia, Andrew to south Russia, Matthew to Ethiopia, and Bartholomew to India. Nothing is known for certain.

Rome took the lead when Jerusalem was destroyed in 70 A.D. for Rome was the centre of the Empire and roads and sea routes

Early Christian converts in the Roman empire faced cruel persecution. Usually they were excluded from society but as the converts increased in number and refused to swear allegiance to Roman gods, the intensity of persecution increased. It reached its height under Nero, who blamed the great fire in Rome in 64 A.D. on the Christians. Nero had many Christians thrown to the lions in grotesque public spectacles which were watched and cheered by Roman crowds.

Left: The artist Salvador Dali's interpretation of the crucifixion of Jesus Christ.

radiated from there. Christians and Jews from Jerusalem found new homes anywhere where trade was active. The Romans despised both; ugly rumours circulated about 'their human sacrifices and their hatred of the human race'. Riots occurred and the military were prejudiced against them. In 64 A.D. Nero began persecuting Christians because he blamed them for a fire in Rome. Persecution continued spasmodically for the next 250 years, and usually Christians and Jews suffered together. Both were irritating to emperors because they would not conform. The Romans worshipped many gods, but they could not tolerate people who claimed that their god was the only one. Anyone who refused to sacrifice to the emperors must be disloyal. Usually the Romans did not seek Christians out, but executed those who were handed over by local people. Christians took great pride in their unity and their many martyrs; Christianity spread in spite of persecution. There were periods, of up to 30 years, during which Christians lived as ordinary people and not hidden in *catacombs*. They drew up a list of those *scriptures* which were approved and allowed no one to water down the faith. The final persecutions of Severus in the third century A.D., and Galerius, Diocletian's deputy, in 303 A.D., were extremely severe,

but came too late to crush Christianity.

Constantine, the next emperor, declared himself a Christian. *Bishops* now found themselves ruling a community of every race and social class. The *aristocrats* of Rome held aloof and the peasants clung to the old ways (*pagani* is Latin for peasant), so that the conversion was not complete even in the fifth century A.D. But when the Emperor Julian tried to re-establish paganism he received little support. Christian teaching became more sophisticated as Gregory of Nyssa, Gregory of Nazianzus, Basil, Ambrose of Milan and Augustine of Hippo showed how Christianity could absorb the ideas of Greek and Roman *philosophy*. Disagreements arose over how to describe the *Trinity*, or the nature of Christ as God and Man. Everyone, from *monks* downward, took sides and the Roman world was split. The authority of the emperor and the bishops was needed to settle the quarrels. The bishop of Rome was usually supported by the emperor of the West, so that his authority grew at the expense of the other bishops. Leo the Great, in the fifth century A.D., claimed to be Head of the Church. Gregory the Great, in the sixth century A.D., took over some of the functions of the emperors in the West and sent Christian missions to the *barbarians*.

The Roman Empire—27 B.C. to 476 A.D.

Octavius Caesar, nephew of Julius Caesar, was the first Roman emperor. *Caesar* has become an international word for emperor; kaiser and tsar (or czar) are both forms of Caesar. In 27 B.C., four years after the battle of Actium, the *Senate* called to power Octavius, and gave him the title of Augustus (the majestic) because this victory ended the civil wars which had nearly destroyed the *Roman Republic* (see pp. 48-9 and 232). Augustus died in 14 A.D. The next four emperors were all related to him. Tiberius (14-37 A.D.) was competent but became increasingly tyrannical. Caligula (37-41 A.D.) was both mad and cruel. Claudius (41-54 A.D.) was a much better person but weak. In 43 A.D. he undertook the final Roman conquest of Britain. Claudius was poisoned by his wife Agrippina so that her son Nero might become emperor (54-68 A.D.). Nero was cruel and half insane. In 64 A.D. there was a great fire at Rome, which the emperor blamed on the Christians. In 68 A.D. the army finally revolted and Nero committed suicide.

The Caesar family fixed the frontiers of the Roman empire along the Rhine and Danube. After a military disaster in the forests of Germany, expansion beyond these rivers was halted. A military establishment of *legions* and more lightly armed auxiliaries, stationed in permanent forts, preserved the frontiers most at risk. The empire was ruled by the emperor's servants; they

The Roman villa, like the one above, offered its owner a luxurious lifestyle of elegant dinners, fine furniture and works of art.

Right: Mosaic of a shepherd from a Roman villa.

Below: The Romans took their fine style of architecture with them throughout the empire and when they left, their buildings, such as this amphitheatre in the old Phoenician town of Leptis Magna, remained.

came from all social backgrounds including slaves, but the Senate remained the nominal ruler. Augustus's peace produced a flourishing literature. Virgil (70-19 B.C.) wrote his *Aeneid*, a poem on the foundation of Rome, for Augustus. Livy (59 B.C.-17 A.D.) wrote a *History of Rome* under Augustus's patronage. Tacitus (*c.* 60-*c.* 118 A.D.) wrote two further histories of the early emperors, *Histories* and *Annals*, which bring out more clearly than any other early writing the cruelty and madness which absolute political power can produce in rulers of men.

Vespasian was of lowly origin and became emperor (69-79 A.D.) after a civil war and was succeeded by his sons Titus (79-81 A.D.) and Domitian (81-96 A.D.). The empire had more peace than under the later Caesars although Domitian, who tried unsuccessfully to expand the empire, punished his opponents savagely. The *Praetorian Guard*, the emperor's bodyguard, had chosen most of the emperors since Augustus's death. In

Algeria and from Spain to Persia. Roman roads and *viaducts*, Roman *amphitheatres* and temples, triumphal arches, frontier walls and *legionary forts* still stand in ruins as evidence of the might of an empire which died 1,500 years ago.

Hadrian set up a council of wise men to advise the emperor; they were paid for their work, and the Senate became unimportant. In 161 A.D. Marcus Aurelius, an outstanding *philosopher*, became emperor. He wanted peace but he had to spend most of his reign fighting; his wars cost a great deal of money and they weakened the empire. Marcus Aurelius defeated all his enemies but he died before he could make the empire strong again. The Roman empire was never again quite as well ruled. There were frequent civil wars and revolts, and no less than four emperors in the twelve years to 192 A.D. The Praetorian Guard were making emperors again; they even sold the office to Julianus. Septimius Severus restored order in 193 A.D., and destroyed the Praetorian Guard. But neither the Senate nor the army liked a strong emperor and in 217 A.D. civil war began again. There were over 20 emperors in the next 65 years. The government of the empire became less efficient and more expensive; robbery and piracy increased and barbarian tribes crossed the frontiers (see pp. 58-9). Gaul, Spain and Britain at different times became independent of the central government; the Persians invaded Mesopotamia and Dacia was conquered by the *Goths*.

In 270 A.D. the new emperor, Aurelian, began to bring back peace and order. This work was carried on by Diocletian (284-305 A.D.), who divided the empire into four parts, and chose three other emperors to help him; each emperor ruled one part of the empire. The two most important were called *Augusti*, the other two Caesars. Diocletian was emperor for 20 years. The provinces were made smaller and the governors given less power, to stop them rebelling.

After Diocletian retired in 305 A.D. civil war returned. By 324 A.D. Constantine (305-337 A.D.) had defeated all his enemies and won the support of the Christians. In 313 A.D. he gave them freedom of worship and on his deathbed he was *baptized*. Constantine built a city, later called Constantinople, on the straits between the Black Sea and the Adriatic in 330 A.D. In 364 A.D. the empire was divided into two parts, a Greek eastern empire ruled from Constantinople and a Latin western empire ruled from Rome. Within 100 years, Rome was sacked by *Vandals*; by 476 A.D. the western empire had broken up into independent kingdoms (see pp. 58-9 and 62-3).

96 A.D. they agreed to let the Senate choose for the future. A silver age followed under five emperors: Nerva (96-8 A.D.), Trajan (98-117 A.D.), Hadrian (117-138 A.D.), Antoninus Pius (138-161 A.D.) whose reign was so peaceful that it was said to be empty of events, and Marcus Aurelius (161-180 A.D.). Trajan, a great conqueror and road builder, added Dacia and Mesopotamia to the empire. Hadrian travelled around the empire putting up buildings in places as far apart as Athens and St. Albans. He built walls on the frontiers. Because of emperors like these the Roman empire left its mark on the landscape of Europe and the Mediterranean countries, from northern Britain to

The Praetorian Guard were the personal bodyguards to the emperor. As such, they enjoyed enormous power and even on some occasions overruled the Senate on the appointment of new emperors, such as Claudius. In 96 A.D., they agreed to let the Senate decide in the future.

The Nomadic Explosion— The Huns

In addition to the growth of centres of civilization and their spread outwards to create states and empires, there was another great formative force in world history. In certain areas of the world, in *steppes* and on the edge of deserts, primitive men never learnt to grow crops or settle in cities. Instead they lived by taming great herds of animals; camels in the African and Arab deserts, horses and cattle in the steppes and deserts of central Asia. These people became *nomads* or wanderers, for they moved with their herds of animals looking for water and grazing grounds as the seasons changed; and they moved from market to market to sell their animals and buy the produce of the towns. So the nomads sometimes became the

The Kazakhs of south-east Russia lived a nomadic life for centuries until 1917. Their tents, called yurts, were made of wood and reeds. In winter, cattle skins were stretched over the frames for warmth. Cattle also provided them with clothing and food and sometimes even transport.

merchants and traders who exchanged the produce of one civilization with that of another. The *camel caravan* through the Arabian and central Asian deserts is one of the oldest trading ventures in the world. Such caravans came to Ur of the Chaldees and they were still crossing the deserts in the 20th century A.D.

Nomadic life depended on the weather. If their feeding grounds and wells, the *oases* in the deserts, dried out because the climate got warmer the nomads had to move on. If the climate got wetter and there was more fodder for animals, their herds grew and more people could be fed. A sharp population growth produced changes in their way of life and these sometimes led to an expansionist, aggressive policy. Herodotus, the first Greek historian, described what could happen: 'groups of tribes of different origins and

occupations had been brought together through the overlordship of a warlike "royal tribe"', which led the new nomad 'nation' into battle against other nomads and then against the settled civilizations. Throughout history this process was repeated until civilization grew too strong and the nomads too few and weak to attack it.

The first known example of a nomad explosion is in the eruption of Indo-Europeans, from somewhere in the area of the Caucasus and Caspian sea, in the second *millennium* B.C. They conquered Europe, Arabia and north India. As *Aryans* they invaded India (see pp. 38-9); as *Medes, Persians*, and *Hittites* they invaded Asia Minor and Arabia (see pp. 30-1); as *Dorians* they invaded Greece (see pp. 44-5); and they were the *Italic tribes* which invaded Etruscan Italy (see pp. 48-9). The *Celtic tribes* who dominated central and northern Europe (see pp. 24-5) were united by a royal tribe and they too were Indo-Europeans. The collapse of the Celts and the emergence of the Germans in northern Europe was also explained

by Herodotus, when the royal tribe suffered reverses [as the Celts did from the Romans], 'then the nation fell apart, and new groupings and names incorporated the heterogeneous populaces'. The 'Germans' were very much the same peoples as the 'Celts', but new royal tribes speaking a different branch of the basic Indo-European language now united them for expansion (see pp. 58-9).

The next nomadic groups to range over central Asia and attack the civilizations around them were the *Scyths* and the *Huns*. The Scyths were centred in the lands to the north of the Black Sea; they were skilled horsemen. As the *Sakas*, they invaded and conquered northern India in about 90 B.C. (see pp. 92-3). With the emergence of the Huns, known to the Chinese as *Hsiung-Nu*, began a process which was repeated until the *Mongols* appeared in the 13th century A.D. (see pp. 84-5 and 98-9). Nomad eruptions either broke through the walls of civilization or were driven away. Three areas were affected: China, India and Europe.

It was the strength of the *Han* empire (see

The sacking of a Roman villa by the Huns about A.D 450. The nomadic Huns were briefly united under Attila and destroyed much of the Roman civilization. When Attila died in 453 A.D., the Huns again returned to their tribal groups.

pp. 36-7) which forced the Hsiung-Nu westwards and southwards. They were driven from China by Han Emperor Wu in 127-119 B.C.; they returned to make successive attacks and were finally defeated in 73-91 A.D. Turning westwards the Huns drove other nomads, the *Kushans*, into India about 50 A.D. (see pp. 92-3). Slowly they moved into Europe; their pressure on the semi-nomadic German tribes made these attack the Roman empire more and more frequently. From about 400 A.D. the western Roman empire began to collapse and Germanic tribesmen settled all over its former territory.

In 450 A.D. one group of Huns invaded and devastated north-west India (see pp. 92-3), and another group led by Attila attacked the Roman empire. They levied *tribute* and damaged much of Roman civilization in the area now Austria and Yugoslavia. When Attila died this group of Hun tribes broke up, just as Herodotus explained, and the Huns were absorbed by other nomads moving into Europe.

The Barbarian Invasions

In 249 A.D. an officer in the Roman army named Gaius Trajanus Decius, following precedents already well established, led the army under his command away from guarding the Danube frontier and marched on Rome, where he became emperor by killing Philip the Arabian near Verona. While he was absent from the frontier the *Goths* swarmed down into south-eastern Europe. Although there had been other incidents like this along the border, the force of this Gothic intrusion was a significant point in the decline of the Roman empire.

What the Roman frontier along the Rhine/Danube rivers had done was to dam the flow of peoples from central Europe southwards towards the better climate of the Mediterranean area. It is known that the Goths who broke into the Balkans in 249 A.D. were themselves being forced southwards by the *Alans*, a nomadic people from Asia. As soon as Rome weakened, it was only a question of time before the *barbarians* forced their way through the frontiers of the Roman empire.

In 256 A.D. Shapur, King of a new Persian empire, overran Syria and recaptured Antioch. But this year is better known for the devastating force with which the *Franks* broke into European history by taking the other end of the Rhine/Danube frontier. The Franks were a coalition of tribes living along the lower reaches of the Rhine and who had always been bitterly opposed to the Roman presence. Despite the temporary restoration of the Rhine/Danube frontier, the Franks extended their influence in the third century A.D. through eastern and central Gaul, even into north-eastern Spain.

By this time, the Roman world was becoming used to insecurity as an everyday ingredient of life. Yet it was scarcely 100 years since, by military and diplomatic means, the Romans had so dominated the western world as to achieve what is called the *Pax Romana*. Quite why the Roman empire should have crumbled as it did is not easily explained. Some historians look as far back into Roman history as the first emperor, Augustus, who set limits to military expenditure. Other historians consider that Christianity effectively softened the aggressive instincts of the Romans, a process which is attributed by some writers, oversimply, to decadence.

The decline of Roman power is not considered simply as uncivilized barbarians overrunning an effete Roman empire. The Frankish invasion is looked upon more as a

Tall, blond Saxons invaded Roman Britain in 367 A.D. They came from outside the Roman empire—the coast stretching from Jutland to the mouth of the River Rhine—and brought with them a different way of life. In the next three centuries they populated and tamed much of England replacing the great forests with well-tended fields and villages. In turn, the Saxons were influenced by their new country and by 600 A.D. most of them were converted to Christianity.

period when the Frankish and Roman civilizations fused together, for the two cultures had been in active contact with one another ever since Caesar's invasions of Gaul (now France) and, indeed, for several centuries before that. 'France' was later to become perhaps the most important area of surviving Roman culture.

The arrival of the *Saxons* on the east coast of Britain is another example of fusion. At first they were pirates, whose raids led to the building of the Saxon-shore forts in the last quarter of the third century A.D. Later, in 367 A.D., they are recorded as co-operating with the *Picts* and *Scots* in the invasion of

Roman Britain. The permanent Saxon settlement in Britain may have begun as early as 380 A.D. when a peaceful settlement of allied *mercenary* troops and their families took place at the village of West Stow in Suffolk. Saxons were already co-existing with Romans in Britain well before the Roman abandonment of the province.

In many parts of the Roman empire, however, the barbarian invasions were both massive and violent. In about 272 A.D. the Goths had divided themselves into *Ostrogoths* (Eastern Goths), who had settled in Pannonia and Moesia, and *Visigoths* (Western Goths). Under the leadership of Aluric, the Visigoths crossed the Danube again in 408 A.D. and demanded a *tribute* from the citizens of Rome; in 410 A.D. Aluric returned and *sacked* the city, before retiring westwards into Aquitania.

The fall of the western Roman empire had been hastened by its division (see pp. 54-5). The western half slowly bled to death, although it was still capable, with the help of the Goths of Aquitaine, of beating off the invasion by the *Huns* into Gaul in 451 A.D. The Huns (see pp. 56-7) had been allowed to settle in Thrace in 376 A.D. by the Roman emperor Valens. One of their first feats had

been to destroy the monarchy of the Ostrogoths. The influence of the Huns in western Europe did not long outlast the death of their leader Attila in 453 A.D., one year after Pope Leo the Great is said to have dissuaded him from sacking Rome. Attacking by sea, the *Vandals* plundered Rome so thoroughly in 455 A.D. that it was half destroyed. Like the Goths, the Vandals were a confederacy of Germanic tribes finding new vigour at the time of Rome's decline. In 409 A.D. they had crossed Germany and France to invade Spain and then the various *Romanized* regions and countries of northern Africa.

The eastern *Byzantine* empire, however, survived (see pp. 70-3). In the sixth century A.D., under the emperor Justinian, the Romans reconquered many of the provinces bordering on the western Mediterranean. After Justinian's death in 565 A.D. these were lost again following military successes by the Visigoths in Spain, the *Lombardic* tribes in Italy and the *Slavic* nations in the Balkans.

Left: Valentinian I was elected emperor of the western Roman empire in 364 A.D. He was a cruel ruler but an efficient soldier and defended the west against the barbarians.

Below: A Visigoth soldier.

DATA DIGEST

Many of the words which are italicized in the previous section are explained more fully in the following data digest. They will help to expand your knowledge of history.

THE RISE AND FALL OF BABYLONIA AND ASSYRIA

Sumerians gain dominance in Lower Mesopotamia 3200-2360 B.C.
Pictograph tablets dating from 3000 B.C.

Akkadian Dynasty 2360-2180 B.C.
Sargon of Akkad established strong centralized government and extended his empire to the Persian Gulf, Elam, Persia, Upper Mesopotamia and Syria.

Sargon's grandson Naramsin brought Akkad to the height of its influence. The arts flowered and fine buildings were constructed.

Akkad fell to invaders from the Zagros.

Sumerian Renaissance. Third Dynasty of Ur 2060-1950 B.C.
Urnammu of Ur restored Sumerian supremacy. He controlled Assyria, Elam and north-western Mesopotamia. His code of laws was a predecessor of Hammurabi's great code.

Under the rule of Ibbisin Amorite invaders overran Sumer and Akkad. Elam rose against Ur and the city was destroyed and Ibbisin captured.

The third dynasty saw the peak of Sumerian literature but its cities and buildings did not survive.

Rise to power of Babylonia. First Dynasty of Babylon 1830-1531 B.C.
The founder of the dynasty was Summuabum but the towering figure of the period was Hammurabi (1711-1669 B.C.). The evidence for his reign is plentiful since many thousands of tablets have survived. Hammurabi expanded Babylon's power over a wide area, taking Elam, Isin, Larsa and Mari. His famous law code regulated the empire's administration.

About 1531 B.C. the Hittite king Mursilis destroyed Babylon and the Kassites took control of the area.

Middle Assyrian Empire 1356-1078 B.C.
After 400 years of domination in Upper Mesopotamia by the Hurrians, who eventually united to form the kingdom of Mitanni, Suppiluliumas, king of the Hittites, made some inroads into the area. Mitanni's power was finally destroyed by Assurubalit I of Assyria, which began to expand rapidly.

Shalmaneser I occupied the territory of the Hurrians and Hittites and drove westwards.

In the twelfth century Tiglath-Pileser I led a series of brilliant campaigns and the Assyrian empire reached its height with the Phoenicians paying tribute.

Babylon fell to the Assyrians in 1107 B.C.

The New Assyrian Empire 935-612 B.C.
After a total decline Ashurnasirpal II revived Assyrian power. His son Shalmaneser III levied tribute over a wide area and led several campaigns against states to the West.

Tiglath-Pileser III made vassals of Syria and Palestine and proclaimed himself king of Babylon in 729 B.C.

Sennacherib established his capital at Nineveh. During his reign (705-682 B.C.) Babylonia rebelled and the city of Babylon was sacked. Under his son Esarhaddon it was rebuilt in splendour. Assyria had the advantage in several battles fought against Egypt.

This success was driven home by Assurbanipal who took both Memphis and Thebes. He collected a vast library of tablets many of which have survived.

After Assyria's power quickly declined, Babylonia and Assyria were taken over by the Chaldeans.

Amphitheatre. Arena surrounded by rows of seats rising in tiers. The most famous is the Colosseum in Rome.

Aramaic. A Semitic language that was the popular language in Palestine at the time of Christ.

Archaeology. The study of past cultures from traces left by them, such as tools, buildings, bones, pottery.

Aristocracy. A system of government in which the nobles, literally the 'best people', are the rulers.

Asceticism. Renouncing bodily gratification and living an austere life.

Baptise. The Christian ceremony of adult baptism signifies that a person has accepted the Christian faith. In early times, he would also receive a new, 'Christian' name.

Barbarians. In Roman eyes all people who spoke neither Latin nor Greek were barbarians.

Bureaucracy. A system relying on a centralized administration manned by many officials.

Camel caravan. Line of camels carrying goods for trading. These convoys travel across the desert over age-old routes determined by the location of oases.

Catacombs. Underground passage systems in which early Christians buried their dead, held secret religious services and sometimes sheltered from persecution.

Celtic. The Celts were an Indo-European people who after 500 B.C. spread over large areas of western Europe. Gaelic and Welsh are Celtic languages.

Census. An official count of population and various related statistics.

Conics. The geometry of the cone and its sections.

Democratic government. Form of government in which all decisions are taken by the decision of the people as a whole or of elected representatives.

Dorians. Iron age invaders who brought a new dark age to Greece.

Dravidians. A people who lived in India before the Aryan invasions.

Eclipse. The hiding of a heavenly body as a result of its being obscured by another heavenly body or its shadow. The most spectacular eclipses are of the sun and the moon.

Etruscans. The civilization that preceded that of the Romans in Italy.

Federation. A league of independent states with a centralized government.

Fiefs of land. Under a feudal system a lord granted land known as a fief to his vassal in return for an oath of fealty and a promise of various services.

Goths. A powerful German tribe which in the 3rd century A.D. began to harass Rome's frontiers. They sacked Rome in 410 and later overran Spain, much of Gaul and Italy.

Hebrew. The ancient language of the Jews, now the language of Israel.

Helots. Subject people of the Spartans. They were the original Achaean and Ionian inhabitants of Laconia.

Hierarchy. A system of government or administration in which everyone is carefully placed in certain grades, each grade being a step upwards to or downwards from the top position.

Hinduism. The main religion of India.

Hittites. People who established a powerful empire based on Anatolia between about 1700 and 1200 B.C.

Holy Spirit. Christians believe that the Holy Spirit, the third member of the Trinity, descended on the apostles after Christ's death.

Islam. The religion of the Muslims also known as Mohammedanism. It is based on the teachings of Muhammad who lived from about 570 to 632 A.D.

Legionary forts. Fortresses built by the Romans to guard provincial frontiers. They were built at first of earth and timber and later mainly of masonry.

Legions. The main units of the Roman army. During the imperial period there were between 25 and 30 legions, each comprising about 5,000 infantry and 120 mounted soldiers.

Linear A. Complex script representing consonant-vowel signs. It was in use during the Minoan cultural period.

Linear B. Very early classical Greek script which was in use some 500 years before Homer wrote his epic poems.

Lombards. A Germanic people who set up a kingdom in northern Italy in the 6th century A.D.

Martyred. A martyr is someone who makes an extreme sacrifice, perhaps of his life, rather than go against what he believes to be right.

Mercenaries. Soldiers hired to fight for a foreign country.

Monks. Men who take vows of poverty, chastity and obedience. They generally live with other monks in monasteries and devote themselves to religious studies and duties.

Monotheism. Belief in only one god.

Mycenaean Greeks. An Indo-European people who entered Greece about 2000 B.C. and gained control of much of the Mediterranean area including Crete.

Nomads. Members of a wandering people, such as the Bedouin.

Old Testament. The 24 books that make up the Hebrew Bible and form the first part of the Christian Bible.

Oracles. The replies given by a god, generally through a priest or priestess, to questions asked of him. The term is also used for the shrine where the oracular process was carried out.

Pagan. Strictly means neither Christian, Jew nor Muslim, but is often used to mean non-Christian.

Parthenon. The Doric temple dedicated to Athena which dominates the Acropolis at Athens. The building was begun in 447 B.C. Much of it was seriously damaged when gunpowder the Turks stored there exploded in 1687.

Pax Romana. Literally, Roman peace.

People's Council. The Boule in Athens, which consisted of 500 members who were elected by lot to serve for a year. It was the main administrative and legislative organ of the state.

Phrygians. People who left Thrace in the Aegean migration and settled in Anatolia. They founded a dynasty and empire in 1000 B.C.

Picts. A Scottish people who made many raids over the border during the Roman occupation of Britain and later fought the Anglo-Saxons.

Potentates. Princes.

Praetorian Guard. The personal guard of the emperors of ancient Rome. The praetorians became extremely powerful and were able to create or depose emperors.

Prophet. One who proclaims a religious message, such as Muhammad or Buddha.

Republic. A system of government in which the head of state is not a hereditary position. In most republics the head of state is an elected president and the legislative body is an elected assembly.

Romanized. Romanization was the process by which Rome introduced the Roman way of life into its empire.

Satraps. Governors of the provinces of the Persian empire. Some were appointed and some inherited office.

Saxons. A Germanic people who first raided and then invaded Britain along with Jutes and Angles.

Scots. A Celtic people who came to Scotland from Ireland.

Slavs. Indo-European people who lived in south-eastern Poland and northern Ukraine and migrated into other parts of eastern Europe, including Russia, between 200 and 500 A.D.

Tyrants. Originally, this was the title given to those absolute rulers who seized power in Greek and Sicilian cities mainly during the 7th and 6th centuries B.C.

Vandals. A German people who moved from the Baltic area into Hungary in the late 2nd century A.D. They overran much of the Mediterranean area including parts of northern Africa, and in 455 sacked Rome. The Roman general Belisarius crushed them in 533.

ROMAN EMPERORS	
Emperor	**Reign**
Augustus	27 B.C.-A.D. 14
Tiberius	14-37
Caligula	37-41
Claudius	41-54
Nero	54-68
Galba	68-69
Otho	69
Vitellius	69
Vespasian	69-79
Titus	79-81
Domitian	81-96
Nerva	96-98
Trajan	98-117
Hadrian	117-138
Antoninus Pius	138-161
Marcus Aurelius	161-180
Commodus	180-192
Pertinax	193
Didius Julianus	193
Septimius Severus	193-211
Caracalla	211-217
Macrinus	217-218
Elagabalus	218-222
Severus Alexander	222-235
Maximinus Thrax	235-238
Gordian I	238
Gordian II	238
Gordian III	238-244
Philippus	244-249
Decius	249-251
Gallus	251-253
Aemilian	253
Valerian	253-260
Gallienus	260-268
Claudius II	268-270
Aurelian	270-275
Tacitus	275-276
Florian	276
Probus	276-282
Carus	282-283
Numerian (E)	283-284
Carinus (W)	283-285
Diocletian (E)	284-305
Maximian (W)	286-305
Constantius I (W)	305-306
Galerius (E)	305-311
Severus (E)	306-307
Maxentius (W)	306-312
Maximinus (W)	308-313
Lincinius (E)	311-324
Constantine I the Great	311-337
Constantius II	337-360
Julian	360-363
Jovian	363-364
Valentinian I (W)	364-375
Valens (E)	364-378
Gratian (W)	375-383
Valentinian II (W)	375-392
Theodosius I	378-395
Emperors of the West	
Honorius	395-423
Johannes	424
Valentinian III	425-455
Petronius	455
Avitus	455-456
Majorian	457-461
Libius Severus	461-465
Anthemius	467-472
Olybrius	472
Glycerius	473-474
Julius Nepos	473-475
Romulus Augustulus	475-476
W: West Roman Empire. E: East Roman Empire	

THE FEUDAL WORLD

Barbarian Kingdoms

Between the collapse in the fifth century of the western half of the Roman empire and the two unsuccessful attacks on Byzantium by the *Muslims* in 674-80 and 717-18, the world saw the emergence of several *barbarian* regimes.

Moving down from their homeland on the Prussian coast of the Baltic Sea, the *Goths* arrived on the coast of the Black Sea early in the third century. In 272, Emperor Aurelian conceded to them the whole of Dacia. They split into two groups, the *Ostrogoths* and the *Visigoths*. The Ostrogoths (Eastern Goths) invaded Italy and took possession of the whole peninsula under their king, Theodoric the Great, in 493. The Ostrogothic kingdom in Italy survived only until 553, when Italy was recovered for Byzantium by Emperor Justinian's general, Narses.

The Visigoths (Western Goths), who had sacked Rome in 410, established a kingdom with Toulouse as its capital. From this base they invaded Spain but their regime there was weak and easily succumbed to *Arab-Berber* invaders in 711.

The Germanic confederacy of tribes known as the *Vandals* began to move southwards through Germany and Gaul in 409. After subjugating the *Alani* in Spain, the Vandals built an empire from the remnants of the Roman empire in Spain and northern Africa. Their influence in Spain is still reflected in the name Andalusia. Under their brilliant leader, Genseric, they attacked Italy by sea from Africa in 455 and so ravaged the city of Rome that their reputation for doing damage survives today in the meaning of the word 'vandal'. Their kingdom in Africa was re-annexed to the Byzantine empire in 535 after defeat at the hands of Belisarius, the greatest of Justinian's generals.

The Italian peninsula was in extreme chaos after the Gothic wars. The vacuum was quickly filled by another group of barbarians invading from the north, the *Lombards*. They speedily captured a great part of Italy but a defeat at the hands of a *Carolingian*, Pepin the Short, in the mideighth century was followed by their total annexation to the Frankish kingdom by Charlemagne in the 770s.

Charlemagne, the great leader of the Franks, built an empire which restored most of Rome's western empire. A warrior, scholar and administrator, Charlemagne championed Christianity against the heathens and in 800 A.D. was crowned Roman emperor by Pope Leo III.

Another great confederacy of Germanic tribes, the *Franks,* first broke into history about 240, when they encountered the resistance of Rome in their attempt to settle in Gaul. A Frankish kingdom was extensively, if precariously, established by the time of King Clovis in 496. By the eighth century, political control had passed from Clovis's *Merovingian* dynasty to the mayors of the palace. In 751 Pepin the Short, whose father, Charles Martell, had defeated Muslim raiders between Poitiers and Tours in 733, displaced the Merovingians and established the Carolingian dynasty. Charlemagne (Carolus Magnus) built a Frankish empire which included all of Rome's western empire except southern Italy, England, most of Spain and Venice; but it included many lands in Germany which had never been subject to Roman rule. In 800 Pope Leo III crowned Charlemagne 'Roman Emperor'. The title proved to be an empty one, however, although it lasted for 1,000 years (see pp. 82-3), and the empire created by Charlemagne's personal skills quickly disintegrated after his death in 814.

over the others. All except Wessex succumbed to the Danish invaders and it was from the far western marshes of Wessex that its king, Alfred the Great, rallied the English. Under his son, Edward the Elder, and his grandson, Athelstan, the *Danelaw* was conquered and England came into existence as a united kingdom.

The fusion of Roman traditions and the society created in the Roman empire with those of different groups of invading barbarians laid the basis for the nations of modern Europe (see The Commercial and the Industrial Revolution). Even in areas never conquered by Rome, such as Germany and Scandinavia, the influence of Roman civilization, its law and language, has been great. Two parts of Europe have retained the Roman name and a language close to Latin: Romania, which was the frontier province of Dacia, and an area of Switzerland in which Romansch is spoken. French, Spanish and Italian are also descended from Latin.

The Alfred Jewel (below) is one of the rare pieces of jewellery which survives from the reign of Alfred the Great. It was found in Athelney, Somerset, in England, where Alfred took refuge from the Danes. Made of rock crystal over enamel set in gold, it bears the inscription around its sides 'Alfred had me made'.

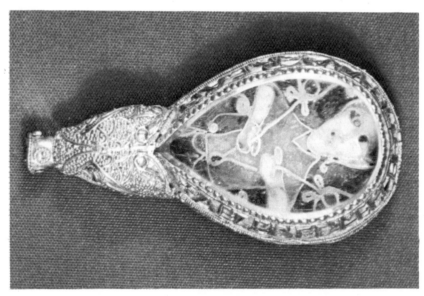

Roman Britain was invaded by groups of barbarians who came from the sea coast areas of modern Denmark and Holland. In the island they drove the surviving Romano-Britons steadily westwards; these Celtic speakers survived, with a distinct culture, in Cornwall and Wales; un-Romanized Britons survived in northern Scotland. But in the area from Devon to the Forth-Clyde a group of seven barbarian kingdoms emerged in which the Germanic dialects were spoken. This became Anglo-Saxon from which the English language slowly grew. This *heptarchy* lasted until Danish invasions (see pp. 64-5) destroyed some of the seven kingdoms. In the sixth to eighth centuries the king of one kingdom was accepted by the others as *Bretwalda,* or Briton ruler. The three most important kingdoms were Northumbria, which extended from the Humber to the Forth; Mercia, which reached from the Humber to the Upper Thames and from the Welsh frontier to the fenland of eastern England; and Wessex, which extended from London to Somerset and Devon. One after another these kingdoms became dominant

Map of the Barbarian kingdoms in 511 A.D. The fall of the Roman Empire made it possible for confederacies of German tribes to conquer and rule much of Europe.

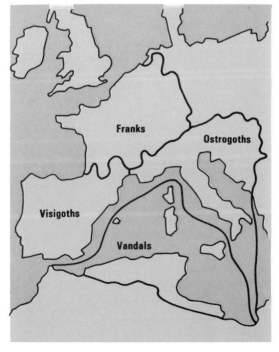

Franks

Ostrogoths

Visigoths

Vandals

The Vikings

The *Vikings,* or Northmen as other Europeans called them, came from the modern countries of Denmark, Norway and Sweden. Their farming land was poor and often overpopulated. So the Northmen took to fishing and developed seaworthy boats. The ships of the Viking Age were the best in Europe, *clinker* built with good sails and keels. Their sailors learnt to find their way over incredible distances by sea. As pressure on space in their homelands grew, they took to trading and raiding. Viking was the name given to the Northmen, or Norsemen, when they became raiders and pirates. Viking raids spread farther and farther from their homeland in Scandinavia. The Vikings became explorers and then they began to settle in distant parts of the world, from North America to central Russia. The Viking Age was from c. 780 to 1070. Over these 300 years or so Vikings moved and settled overseas.

During the ninth century Vikings, mainly from Denmark and Norway, raided all round the coasts of the British Isles and along the *seaboard* of Europe from the Flemish coasts to those of Italy and Sicily; they even reached North Africa. They sailed up the rivers of Europe, the Thames, Rhine, Seine and Rhône, wintering in great camps near the river mouths. A Viking camp has been excavated at Trelleborg in Denmark; it reveals the military order which existed. The Vikings took their measurements and some aspects of their fortifications from the Romans. When the Vikings began to settle they carved great feudal *fiefs* (see pp. 78-9) out of other people's lands. In 886 Alfred, King of Wessex in England, had to accept Viking rule in the *Danelaw,* the area of

A model of one of five Viking trading boats which were found in the harbour of Skuldelev, near Roskilde, Denmark. The ships are believed to have been sunk in the 11th century to block the harbour. Made of pine or oak, these small cargo boats had sails reinforced with rope.

eastern England over which the law of the Danes was enforced. In 911 Charles the Simple, King of France, granted the Norsemen land in northern France, which became the Duchy of Normandy. There were Viking kingdoms at Dublin and at York, and Viking earls of the western isles (Hebrides, Orkneys and Shetlands); there was a Norman kingdom of Sicily and Naples.

In 890 Othere of Halgoland sailed round the North Cape into the White Sea as far as modern Archangel. He told Alfred the Great about his voyage and Alfred recorded it. Wulfstan, a Dane, told Alfred of the extraordinary movement of the Swedish Vikings through Russia. They sailed from the eastern Baltic up the rivers Neva and Dvina and settled round the towns and villages which they found. Novgorod they called Holmgarth, meaning island enclosure; Kiev they called Koenugarth, meaning boat enclosure. In 914 they reached the Caspian Sea. Between 860 and 914 they attacked Constantinople, which they called Mikligarth, meaning great enclosure. These Vikings were called *Varangians,* or confederates. The Byzantine emperor (see pp. 70-3) recruited a *Varangian Guard* from among them. Some Varangians reached Athens where a marble lion in the harbour has an

Below: The Vinland Map shows the outline of North America (Vinland) on the far left of the map. This map is said to date back to medieval times. Although the authenticity of the map is doubted, the discovery of North America by the Vikings is not.

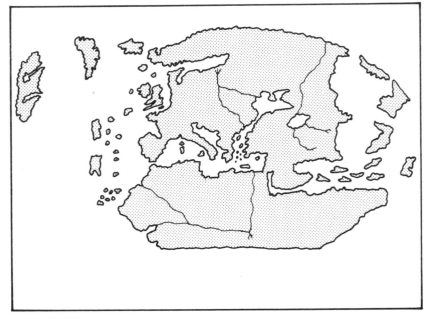

inscription in *runes* (Swedish lettering). Among the famous recruits to this Varangian Guard were Harold Hardrada, later King of Norway, and many English *thegns* who fled from their Norman conquerors after 1066. The earlier word for these Vikings was *Rus*; in time this name was given to the Slav as well as the Viking inhabitants. The name 'Russia' probably means 'the land of the Swedes'.

In 867 Vikings from the Faröe islands reached Iceland. They began to settle there from 874, bringing their own parliament with them, the *Althing*, and a 'speaker to speak a single law'. From Iceland Vikings crossed the ocean to Greenland. Erik the Red, an outlaw, explored the country between 982 and 985 and returned with settlers in 986. In the same year Bjarne sighted land beyond Greenland, probably Cape Cod. In 1000 Leif, son of Erik the Red, explored the North American coast, perhaps between Maryland and Newfoundland. The Vikings called this land Vinland. In 1024 Torfinn Karlsevne may have travelled as far south as North Carolina. The settlement in Greenland survived until the 14th century and contacts between the Greenland Vikings and North America continued for almost as long.

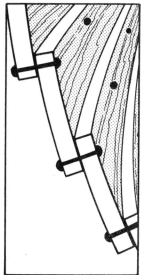

Diagram showing the clinker method of boat-building used by the Vikings. The planks were built up, each with the lower edge slightly overlapping and nailed on to the plank below.

The Vikings were *pagans*, believing in many gods as did other primitive Indo-European peoples. There are parallels between the gods of the Vikings and those of the *Aryans* in India, the Greeks, the Romans, and the Celts. The Vikings considered that the world was a round disc, surrounded by an ocean. In the middle of *Midgard*, the world of men, was the 'greatest and best of all trees', *Yggdrasill*—the World Ash; at its foot was *Asgard*, the home of the gods; beneath its roots were the wells of Fate and Wisdom, guarded by the *Norns* who looked after the destiny of men. *Woden* or Odin was lord of *Valhalla*—the hall of the slain; he lived there with his wolves and ravens. Warriors killed in battle joined the gods to feast there. Wednesday is Woden's (Odin's) day. *Thor*, the peasant god, was armed with an invincible hammer and controlled the thunder. Thursday is his day. *Frey* and his sister *Freya* were fertility gods. Friday is the day of the goddess *Frigg*, Woden's wife.

Viking life was celebrated in prose and poetry, much of it composed in Iceland. Works like the *Vinland Sagas*, the *Edda*, and the *Njals Saga* are some of the greatest works of European literature; they reflect the bare world of sea and mountain.

H-E

Muhammad

At the beginning of the seventh century the Arabian peninsula was a comparatively poor area peopled by wandering tribes, who kept flocks of goats, sheep and camels. There was little farming but much feuding and raiding. Only two cities along the main trade route, Yathrib (now Medina) and Mecca, were of any importance. Mecca was regarded as a holy place and many pilgrims came to visit its chief shrine, the *Kaaba,* but it was in no sense a capital city.

The Arabs worshipped many gods. The Kaaba shrine held an image of the *Koreish* tribal god, Hobal, and other tribal images, but especially it contained the black Stone of Mecca, built into its walls and believed to have been brought from Paradise by the Angel Gabriel. Confused versions of the Jewish and Christian religions were also made the basis of their beliefs.

By 630, however, Arabia had been dramatically unified and filled with a crusading zeal which was to result in the establishment of a huge, world empire. This amazing change had its origins in the teachings and conquests of a great prophet, Muhammad (Mohammed), who still has millions of followers—*Mohammedans, Moslems* or *Muslims.*

Muhammad was born about 570. His father, Abdallah, of the Koreish tribe, died before Muhammad was born. His mother died when he was seven years old. Muhammad lived with his grandfather and later with his uncle, Abu Talib. Most historians agree that the child was an epileptic, sad and introverted. As a boy he had almost no learning and herded sheep and camels. However, his grandfather had been the keeper of the Kaaba and the Holy Well at Mecca, and this meant contact with pilgrims and holy men. When Muhammad was 26 years old, a wealthy widow of 41 called Khadija married him and he lived peacefully as her partner in running a produce store.

Muhammad was interested in religious ideas and influenced by a group known as *Hanifites* ('devoted' or 'dedicated'). These men taught the idea of complete submission to the will of the One God Allah, rejecting all idol worship and living simply and meditating. In 610 Muhammad went with his wife to a cave at Mount Hira to meditate. Here he saw visions and went into states of religious ecstasy. Later, he declared that the Angel Gabriel had appeared to him and told him that he was now the one true prophet of God. Muhammad formulated the simple doctrine which was to form the core of his creed: 'There is no God but Allah (God) and Muhammad is the prophet (or apostle) of God.' Muhammad embodied the Hanifite beliefs in a fierce, uncompromising *mono-*

A 16th century Turkish miniature portraying Muhammad and his soldiers before the Battle of Uhud, the second great battle between the Muslims and the non-believers. Muhammad is veiled—his face is never allowed to be shown—and water springs from his hands.

theism, rejected all images and confused versions of *Judaism* and *Christianity.* Muhammad often went into states of ecstasy and claimed further revelations. These were collected and became the Muslim holy book, the *Koran.*

After converting a few people in secret, Muhammad began to preach with eloquence and passion. He tried to convert Mecca, condemning idol-worship, and asserting that the faithful would go to Paradise but unbelievers would suffer torments in Hell. The traditional keepers of the holy place of the Koreish tribe were angry. But this only inspired Muhammad to preach with more conviction than ever. The people of Mecca finally besieged Muhammad in the house of a rich patron, hoping to starve him to death because they dared not actually shed blood in the Holy City. Muhammad evaded them by claiming that a revelation had shown him that the various goddesses of Mecca were also worthy of reverence. Once free he recanted, saying that this revelation was from the Evil One. Religious persecution was revived and, after the death of his wife and his uncle, Muhammad managed to escape to Yathrib which was later renamed in his honour, Medina, the 'city of the

Above: Muhammad and his followers believed they had Allah's authority to spread Islam by force and to execute those who did not believe. From Medina, Muhammad sent out groups of fighters to raid caravans bound for Mecca and in 630, he occupied Mecca and declared it the Muslim Holy City.

Left: Pages of the Koran, the sacred book of Islam which is said to be the actual word of God passed on through the prophet Muhammad.

prophet'. This retreat or flight is of great importance to Muslims; it is called the *Hegira* and took place on 22nd September, 622. It is from this time that the Muslim year is now reckoned, i.e. 622 A.D. is AH 1.

Muhammad's religion became known as *Islam,* meaning 'surrender to God's will'. The crusading zeal of its followers began soon after the prophet's flight. From a visionary and preacher, Muhammad became a soldier, statesman, lawmaker and virtually a king. He was soon claiming Allah's authority for using force in spreading the new creed, and for the execution of all unbelievers. He caused the first *mosque,* or Muslim place of prayer, to be built and produced a code of laws, which obliged Muslims, among other things, to make ritual washings, pray five times each day, and give up all wines and spirits, pork and tobacco. He sanctioned *polygamy,* but abolished the practice of *infanticide.* The call to prayers went out daily from the *minaret,* or tower, of the mosque. Friday was established as the sacred day of the week. The annual 30 days' fast known as *Ramadan* was also urged on all true Muslims.

Rallying his followers to arms, Muhammad began to attack caravans on their way to Mecca. Medina became rich with the spoils of these raids and in 629, or AH 8, he took an army of some 10,000 men and conquered Mecca. Mecca then became the Muslim Holy City, and prayers were directed to Mecca instead of Jerusalem. Arabia was virtually united under Muhammad's rule. The end of his life was marked by a succession of victories, notably over a confederation of hostile tribes. He died of a fever in Medina in his early 60s and was buried there on 7th June, 632.

The Spread of the Arabs

After Muhammad's death his father-in-law, Abu Bekr, was chosen as his successor, or *Caliph*. In the two years of his rule Abu Bekr crushed all remaining resistance to *Islam* in southern Arabia, and continued Muhammad's process of expansion. He sent forces into Syria and Persia. Abu Bekr was succeeded in 634 by Omar. Under this second Caliph, Syria and Palestine were conquered and the Persians routed at Kadessia in 637; by 643 the Persian empire was occupied (see pp. 42-3).

The attack on the Byzantine empire (see pp. 70-3) began with the invasion of Egypt in 639. Omar sent a force of some 4,000 men and within three years they completely dominated the country. The Arab forces were, at first, comparatively tolerant of other nations and religions, provided they received tributes and the spoils of war. In 646, however, the city of Alexandria rose against Arab domination and the revolt was

Arabic numerals (right) originated in India and were adopted by Arabian scholars about 800 A.D. They were introduced into Europe soon after.

Below: The dhow, one of civilization's oldest sailing vessels, is still used in parts of the Arab world today. Once a trading boat, it is now mainly used for fishing.

ruthlessly suppressed. The great museum and library at Alexandria was dispersed and many valuable books lost, while the docks, arsenals and shipbuilding yards became the basis of Arab sea power. Key islands in the Mediterranean, such as Cyprus and Rhodes, fell to the Arab invaders in 649 and 653. Constantinople was finally besieged in 673-8, but the Arab attack was repulsed. However, Arab maritime expansion continued throughout the Mediterranean, along the Red Sea and the African coast and into central Asia.

Rivalries and intrigue within Islam led to the assassination of Omar in 644. In 656 Omar's successor, Othman, was killed by Muhammad's cousin and son-in-law, Ali. Ali held that the caliphate should pass, on the hereditary principle, to members of the Prophet's family. He also preached a return to the strict interpretation of the *Koran*, and held that a great deal of the traditional teaching which had grown up in association with the Muslim religion should be abolished. This resulted in civil strife and eventually Islam split into two main sects,

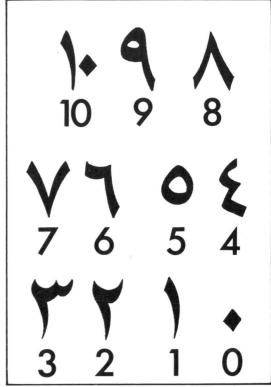

the *Sunnis* who chose the Caliph from the Prophet's tribe, the *Koreish*, and the *Shiahs* who recognized only Ali and his heirs as qualified for the caliphate.

Islam's internal disputes scarcely checked the great wave of Arab expansion: the fiery zeal of the Arabs could not be contained. Their armies swept through north Africa to the Straits of Gibraltar and in 711 into Spain. At the other end of their empire they set up a state in north-west India in 712.

culture and learning. Once the Arab empire had been established there followed, in the wake of military conquest, the spread of a great deal of valuable learning and many highly civilizing influences. The arts and sciences of Greece, Persia and India were preserved and dispersed. Much learning which might have been lost was revived and brought to Europe. Our numerals and the decimal system are Arabic, as is rhymed poetry; alchemy and chemistry, the star names Algol and Aldebrand, are Arabic words. The Arabs took a reasonably tolerant and realistic view of life, encouraged trade and brought new life into a world which had been intellectually and socially stagnant too long. Europe owes much to the scholars and enlightened rulers in Baghdad, Cairo and Córdoba, whose universities and administrations maintained and fostered the arts and sciences of the ancients. Arab traders brought silk, cotton, coffee, lemons, oranges, carpets, muslin, *damascene* steel and gunpowder into Europe. Harun-al-Rashid the Just had a library of 600,000 volumes; he reigned over a brilliant and dazzling court from 786 to 809 at Baghdad. The capital had been moved from Damascus. The full grandeur of the caliphate reached its peak under Harun and Mamun the Great (813-833).

Decay and continual strife within the high courts of Islam followed, several dynasties claiming local power. By the eleventh and twelfth centuries the dominant Muslim power in the Middle East was Turkish, and *Christendom* had begun to challenge the occupation of Palestine by a series of *Crusades* (see pp. 76-7 and 98-9).

Arab advance continued into France, until they were defeated at Poitiers in 732. This battle and a second failure to take Constantinople in 718 saved Europe.

Broadly speaking, the great Muslim advance had three phases. From 632 until the mid eighth century the initial impetus spread the religion, and Arab domination, to Persia, Syria, North Africa, Spain, Sicily, the key islands of the Mediterranean and to central Asia and north-west India. Then, from about 1000 up until the end of the 15th century Turkish tribes and other converts spread Islam through Asia, and past Constantinople into the Balkans (see pp. 94-9 and 166-7). The Byzantine capital finally fell in 1453.

The third aspect of Islam's advance was peaceful, through trade and the spread of

Above: An Arab horseman engages a Spanish knight in mortal combat. By 700 A.D. the Arabs had swept through Europe and were in control of most of the Mediterranean countries. They were halted in 732 A.D. at the Battle of Poitiers, in France, and their second failure to take Constantinople saved Europe from complete Arab domination.

The Eastern Roman Empire

The Byzantine empire had its origin in 330 when the Roman Emperor Constantine made the ancient city of Byzantium his capital, renaming it Constantinople. It ended in 1453 when Constantinople was taken by the Turks (see pp. 166-7). The empire combined the Roman traditions of law and government with the Greek culture of Asia Minor and the moral values of the Christian religion.

Constantine established his 'new Rome' because it secured the north-eastern and eastern frontiers of Rome and also because he felt drawn to the cultivated way of life of the *Hellenic* east. His three sons succeeded him and in turn consolidated the strong centralized government he had set up, based on an *autocratic* emperor and a Christian society. In 395 the Roman empire was divided into independent eastern and western parts, Arcadius becoming the first emperor of the eastern Roman empire and some historians regard that year as the beginning of the Byzantine era.

During the long reign of Theodosius II (408-450) the east enjoyed a period of peace, apart from important religious controversies which exacerbated rivalries among *ecclesiastical* centres. Constantinople was strongly fortified and a university founded there became the most important seat of learning in the empire. The well-known *Codex Theodosianus* was a *codification* of Roman law incorporating the *edicts* of the emperors from Constantine onwards.

The defeat of Attila's *Huns* at the Catalaunian Fields in 450 gave only

Below: St. Sophia, today the metropolitan museum of Istanbul, is an outstanding example of Byzantine architecture. Rebuilt by Justinian between 532 and 537, it was the greatest domed church of eastern Christianity. After the Turkish conquest, it was turned into a Muslim mosque but most of its beautiful mosaics were preserved.

temporary relief to the western Roman empire, which finally collapsed in 476. The eastern empire was rent by political and religious divisions and it needed a strong emperor like Justinian (527-565) to provide stability and confidence. His policies were aimed at the restoration of the old Roman frontiers and the expulsion of the *barbarian* invaders. Justinian was a man of great learning and outstanding intellect; he commissioned another great codification of the law and supervised the building of the beautiful church of Santa Sophia. Under the command of Belisarius and, later, Narses his armies reconquered Africa, Italy and much of Spain. But towards the end of his reign Justinian became embroiled in religious controversy, the *exchequer* was almost bankrupt in spite of excessive taxation, and he died detested by most of his subjects.

In the early seventh century the empire's security was seriously threatened by the

Persians who gained control of almost all the Near East and also Egypt, important for its grain supplies. Despite threats from the barbarian *Avars* and *Bulgars,* the Emperor Heraclius I (610-641) invaded Persia and forced it to make peace. Heraclius reorganized both the army and the civil administration of the empire and so established the basis of the future power of Byzantium.

A new power now arose which constituted an even more severe threat to the empire's existence. Arab forces occupied Palestine, Syria, Egypt and Armenia in an apparently irresistible advance. Each year from 673 to 678 an Arab fleet besieged Constantinople. In the last year in one of history's crucial confrontations the Arabs suffered such heavy losses that they gave up their attempts to overthrow the capital.

Byzantium had been successful in war but the late seventh century was a period of cultural decline. The nature of the empire had undergone great changes. The Greek language and way of life had completely replaced the Roman character of the earlier years, and the Church had acquired considerable power compared with that of the *secular* authorities. The decline continued in the eighth century partly because of a renewed threat from outside as the Arabs again unsuccessfully besieged Constantinople in 717 and 718, but perhaps more seriously because of an internal conflict known as the *iconoclastic* controversy. The emperors Leo III, Constantine V, Leo IV and Leo V were the main iconoclastic leaders, forbidding the production or veneration of images of Christ in spite of riots in Greece and total opposition in Italy and elsewhere. In persecutions images were smashed, monasteries were closed and icon worshippers were imprisoned and tortured. The veneration of images was finally legalized in 843.

Above: An early 6th century mosaic of the Byzantine Emperor, Justinian and his nobles from the church of San Vitale, Ravenna. In keeping with the style of the times, the emperor is represented in saintly guise with a halo encircling his head.

71

The Medieval Byzantine Empire

The second period of the Byzantine empire began with the accession of Basil I (867-886), whose *Macedonian* dynasty occupied the throne for nearly 200 years. Of Justinian's empire little was left—only most of Asia Minor, Greece and parts of southern

Below: St. George, the legendary knight who became the patron saint of England. He was already worshipped in the Middle East when the Crusaders heard of him and brought back to Europe and England in particular the famous story of how St. George slew the dragon.

Italy. But Basil I waged a fairly successful holding action against the Arabs in the west and extended Byzantine influence eastwards into Armenia and the area of the upper Euphrates. Perhaps more important, the empire recovered its confidence, prosperity and splendour and became once more a centre of the arts and sciences. Constantinople was a trading centre to which merchants came from many countries.

In 913 Byzantium became involved in a disastrous war with the *Bulgarians*. Symeon of Bulgaria invaded Thrace and Macedonia and threatened Constantinople. The regency government then in power was forced to agree to humiliating terms under which Symeon's daughter was to marry the young Emperor Constantine VII while Symeon was to be crowned Emperor of Bulgaria. This agreement was revoked by the Byzantines and a protracted war ended with Symeon's death in 927.

The late tenth century saw a resurgence of Byzantine influence. In 961 an expedition took Crete, which had belonged to the Arabs for nearly 150 years. In 965 Cilicia and Cyprus were similarly retaken and four years later Antioch, the wealthy capital of Syria, also fell. The power of Byzantium reached its height in the reign of Basil II

Right: Constantinople fought off Saracen attacks from the sea during siege of 673 by the use of "Greek fire", an inflammable substance which caught fire on contact with water. Bronze tubes which emitted jets of Greek fire were set into the walls of the city and swiftly destroyed a great number of the attackers' ships.

(975-1025). He was an outstanding statesman and an inspiring leader. He sealed an alliance with Russia by marrying his sister to the prince of Kiev, but his greatest success, fulfilling a long-held ambition, was final and decisive victory over the Bulgarians in 1014. He blinded all the captives, said to number 14,000 and sent them back to their ruler. His political settlement of Bulgaria was less ruthless and the Church there was allowed a considerable degree of independence. Basil was also active in the east, annexing large areas of Armenia. At his death the Byzantine empire stretched from the Danube to the Euphrates and from the Adriatic to Armenia.

The *Golden Age* came to an abrupt end with Basil's death. Although there was temporary peace abroad, at home economic and social institutions began to crumble. Under the Empress Zoë (1028-1050) the *feudal* land-owning aristocracy gained control and by punitive taxes and other methods largely ruined the smallholders and peasants. The army relied more and more on *mercenaries* and meanwhile a new enemy was sweeping through the empire. The *Seljuk Turks* seized Armenia and Cilicia and then marched into Asia Minor (see pp. 98-9). In 1071 at Mantzikert the Byzantine army was annihilated, Emperor Romanus IV was taken prisoner and most of Asia Minor was lost. A peace treaty broke down and the Turks continued their march of conquest. Almost simultaneously the *Normans* occupied southern Italy and a revolt broke out in the Balkans.

A period of civil war ensued of which Venice took advantage by gaining control of the whole of Asia Minor. The only general and politician of any proven ability that Byzantium possessed was Alexius Comnenus, and after three days of violence in Constantinople he was crowned emperor in 1081. He succeeded in warding off threats from the Normans and from the *Patzinaks*, a Balkan people, by shrewd alliances. But he did not welcome the *First Crusade* which threatened his position as champion of *Christendom* in the east although, as a result of it, the empire did receive some territory in Asia Minor (see pp. 76-7).

Byzantine power continued to diminish under attacks from the Normans. But it was the *Venetians* who dealt the crushing blow. Alexius had granted Venice valuable privileges in the empire but had several times tried to end the unwelcome connection. In 1203 Venice persuaded the forces of the *Fourth Crusade* to uphold the Church of Rome by marching against Constantinople. The city fell after desperate resistance and the crusaders installed Baldwin of Flanders as emperor in 1204.

The Medieval Church

For centuries the Church, which had the only schools, supplied kings and princes with the able men they needed to assist government. Rich men gave lands to the Church in exchange for prayers for their souls, and so in the end the Church became immensely rich. By the end of the twelfth century, although the Church had long supplied a priest for virtually every parish, many of the poor, especially in the growing towns, had little to do with it. In spite of the *Crusades* (see pp. 76-7) most peoples outside the old Roman empire's boundaries were not Christians. At the same time the Church at home was faced by the first mass defection from it, the *Albigensian Heresy* in southern Europe. The Albigensians were crushed by a so-called Crusade but the challenge of the time was met more by a new movement, the founding of the *Friars*.

The *Franciscan* Friars, followers of St. Francis, living as beggars, made their especial appeal to the poor. The *Dominicans,* followers of St. Dominic, tackled foreign missions as well as the conversion of the *heretics* at home. The *Inquisition* used torture to extract confessions as a method of converting heretics at home. But on the other hand, since in the end, heretics could only be won over by argument, the friars pursued education until they provided practically all the great teachers at the universities. But as with most monastic orders, success attracted gifts, and they too became wealthy and lax.

In the 14th century, after the *Black Death,* when good leadership from the pope was often missing, and rivals struggled for that office, fresh reform movements started which could neither be kept inside the Church nor crushed as heresy. Among such were the followers of Jan Hus in Bohemia (see pp. 108-9) and John Wycliffe in England. In spite of the efforts of the reformers within the Church, at the end of the Middle Ages the splits began which finally destroyed the unity of the Church in the West in the *Protestant Reformation* (see pp. 114-15). So the West lost its common faith as it lost its common language, Latin, an inheritance from the old Roman empire. But in every European country the *medieval* Church left behind it a twin heritage. Everywhere there were, and still are, parish priests and local churches or chapels in which local people worship, and the priest is part of the local society. More generally we can say that many of the ideals of European society are based on those taught by the Christian Church in the Middle Ages. When the Roman empire in the West fell,

Below: Though harsh by modern standards, the life of a monk during the Middle Ages was eagerly sought after by men who wished for quiet repose in which to study and work. While Europe reverted to barbarism after the fall of Rome, the monasteries remained the sole source of learning until the end of the Dark Ages.

the Christian Church nevertheless survived over much of Europe. It could return to those countries from which the *barbarians* had driven it. In keeping itself alive, the Church also preserved much from the wreckage of the Roman empire.

Education, learning, and respect for what was good in civilized life survived the barbarianization of Europe and the *Dark Ages,* chiefly in the monasteries. When St. Benedict founded his monastery at Monte Cassino in Italy in 529 and wrote his rule for

its conduct, he deliberately created a place where the old virtues could be saved and a Christian life lived in a world that was brutal and corrupt. Most of the later monastic orders based their rules more or less on his pattern. Even rougher types of monastery helped in this: in the crude stone cells of the more primitive Irish monasteries Greek was studied and the art of illuminating manuscripts developed at a time when learning was wiped out from the rest of the British Isles. The great monastic buildings of western Europe, even when in ruins, show by their scale and quality something of the importance they had for the men of the *Middle Ages.* As with the parish church, so often the oldest and finest building in a village, they symbolize how the Church became the central part of life.

The idea of the *diocese,* the area in which a bishop ruled the local church, was taken from the late Roman empire. Sometimes the bishop carried on when local government collapsed, and his rule became the only government in some areas. From the first the bishops recognized that the Bishop of Rome, the Pope, was in a vague way their leader. The bishops of the eastern empire were not prepared to concede more than this, and so there developed a split which cut off the eastern Orthodox branch of the Church from the Roman Catholics of the West. In the late sixth century Pope Gregory the Great began the task of converting the rest of Europe, and the churches founded by his missionaries acknowledged Roman rule from the start. The Pope built up his claim to be the highest authority to be called on to settle disputes, and so became the effective head of the Church in the West. In the end even the Celtic Church, which had been isolated for so long, was absorbed by Rome.

Above: View of the monastery at Monte Cassino, near Naples, in Italy. Here, in the 6th century A.D., Saint Benedict wrote his Rule of Conduct for the monks and founded the order which has survived to the present day. The monastery was also the scene of fierce fighting during the Seeond World War.

75

The Crusades

In 1095, at Clermont in France, Pope Urban II called for a 'war of the cross' against the Turks. The aim of this *Crusade* was to liberate the city of Jerusalem. For many years Christians had made pilgrimages and no place was more sacred than the Holy City, where Jesus had lived and died. In 1076 the *Seljuk Turks* captured Jerusalem (see pp. 98-9) and it was no longer safe to go into Palestine. Many advantages were promised by the Church to the Crusaders, including a full pardon for all sins and a firm reassurance that those who died in battle would go straight to Heaven. About 20,000 poor peasants set off, led by a preacher called Peter the Hermit. The nobles remained behind to arrange for their estates to be managed, and also to organize a more conventional army.

There were many motives behind the Crusade. If Constantinople fell to the Turks Europe itself was in peril. The Emperor Alexius made an urgent appeal for aid and the pope was ready to help. Apart from saving Europe, the pope wanted to re-establish his authority over the eastern Orthodox Church. Nobles and princes, especially younger sons, hoped for new lands, as did ordinary men who looked for opportunities ordinarily denied them by *feudal* society (see pp. 78-9).

The Peoples' Crusade which followed Peter the Hermit had no organization and few resources, and thousands soon died from hunger and sickness. Some did reach Constantinople, but at Nicea the Turks massacred all but a handful of them. In 1097, the main army reached Constantinople. It consisted of some 60,000-80,000 knights and foot soldiers, led by Godfrey of Bouillon and his brother Baldwin, Raymond of Toulouse and Bohemond of Taranto. The Crusaders did not realize that their advance towards Jerusalem would take them through more than 1,600 kilometres of hostile and barren land. They had to fight many battles on the way, spend months in capturing towns, like Antioch, only to find themselves once more surrounded by Turkish armies. They suffered from heat, disease, and lack of food and water. They were baffled by the Turkish tactics of avoiding direct attack: arrows shot from horseback inflicted great losses, especially of horses; heavy chain-mail and armour hampered them. But the army did reach Jerusalem after two years and it re-took the Holy City.

Many of the soldiers settled in four Crusader states: the County of Edessa, the Principality of Antioch, the County of Tripoli, and the Kingdom of Jerusalem.

Although fervent idealism prompted young European Christians to join the Crusades to the Holy Land, few were prepared for the hardships they encountered. Thousands died on the way of starvation; thousands more died in battles against the Muslims who fought fiercely to keep control of the Holy Land. Noblemen, peasants and even children joined Crusades; they were promised a pardon for all their sins and immediate entry into heaven if they died in battle.

They built castles, based on new ideas of warfare, which were almost impregnable. Their ruins can be seen to this day, and castles at Harlech and Caernarvon, in Wales, were influenced by them. By 1144 the Muslims had re-taken the County of Edessa in the north. The Second Crusade of 1147 was despatched from Europe but it was a fiasco. The Muslims found unity under a truly great leader in Sultan Saladin. In 1187 he defeated the Crusaders in a battle at Hittin and recaptured Jerusalem. By 1189, less than a century after the first Crusaders' triumph, only three cities remained of the Crusader states. Europe was stirred into a third great attempt to capture the Holy Land and secure Jerusalem.

The Third Crusade was a combined effort by the Emperor Frederick I (Barbarossa) of Germany, Philip II of France, and Richard I of England. The Germans turned back when the Emperor died in Cilicia but Philip and Richard reached the Holy Land by sea, landing at Acre in 1191 and recapturing the city. But soon the two leaders quarrelled and Philip withdrew, leaving Richard to organise and lead the Crusade.

Richard 'The Lionheart' and Saladin treated each other with respect. Richard came within several kilometres of Jerusalem but his forces were by then too small to make a successful assault and he retreated. He had managed to save the Crusader states, and made a pact with Saladin which enabled pilgrims to visit the Holy City freely.

At the beginning of the 13th century what remained of the crusading spirit was des-

troyed by the Fourth Crusade (1202-4). This turned into an expedition for plunder which sacked and looted Constantinople itself. Other Crusades were planned. The most ill-advised of all was the Children's Crusade (1212), inspired by a French shepherd boy called Stephen. He had seen a vision that the Holy Land would be saved by innocent children. Thousands followed him to Marseilles. Two men offered to take them in ships but sold them into slavery in Africa. This Crusade inspired the well-known legend of the Pied Piper of Hamelin.

There were four further Crusades in the 13th century. One, the sixth, did temporarily recapture Jerusalem but only for a short time. The Crusader states were finally overthrown and the last cities fell in 1289 (Tripoli) and 1291 (Acre). Contact with the East, made in the Crusades, brought to

Left: A twelfth-century German sculpture of the Knights Templar, one of several military orders which emerged during the Crusades.

Above: Crusader Castle at Sidon, Lebanon. The Crusaders built many castles in the Holy Land. The designs were copied and used throughout the western world.

Europe knowledge of important Arab achievements (see pp. 68-9).

The Crusades saw the rise of military orders, the *Knights Templars, Knights Hospitallers* (Knights of St. John), and the *Teutonic Knights*. Their members were soldiers who took vows like monks and dedicated their lives to the defence of the Holy Land. They wore tunics over their armour marked with a red cross (Templars) or a black cross (Hospitallers). The Knights Templars were ruthlessly repressed by the Church. The Knights Hospitallers eventually settled in Malta but their order finally collapsed when Napoleon Bonaparte captured the island in 1798. All that remains of it is their emblem, used today by the *St. John Ambulance Brigade*. The Teutonic Knights went back to Germany to attack the Slavs and expand German territory.

Feudal Society

The usual way in which governments have come to raise the money with which to pay their armed forces and essential public servants is by some system of taxation. Faced with the same problem, the *Carolingian* kings of the eighth and ninth centuries (see pp. 62-3) devised a system based not on taxation but on the performance of public duties by individuals in return for certain privileges granted by the king. The persons who received the privileges and concessions, be they knights or public administrators, took an oath of personal loyalty to the king. The most usual concession was of a landed estate previously held directly by the king or confiscated from the Church. The estate remained in the hands of the knight or public official only as long as he performed the duties which were specified at the time the concession was granted. Charlemagne, for example, organized the local government of his kingdom by granting privileges to 300 counts, each one of whom was the king's *vassal* and bound to him by an oath of personal loyalty.

The Treaty of Verdun in 843 divided the Carolingian empire into three sections ruled by Charlemagne's three grandsons. Even after the partition, the new kingdoms were huge and unwieldy, so that government passed, in effect, to the great landed nobles created by this system of personal loyalty to the king. An important result of the collapse of empire was that estates originally granted in return for some public function became hereditary and were not returned to the king at the time of death. The successor to the estate now performed his public duties not because of loyalty to the king, but because the estate he had inherited gave him authority. The new lords then created their own vassals, so that eventually everyone from the serf up to the king was bound by a pyramid of personal loyalties and obligations. The Church also took part in this system. A quiet nunnery in the most remote part of rural England would probably have owed its economic survival to the estate or manor which it held by payment of a knight's fee. No one expected the Prioress to take her place on the battlefield equipped like a knight, but she was obliged to pay the appropriate fee into the royal funds in return for the nunnery's privileges as a landlord. Like a knight, she was the king's vassal. This was feudalism.

The manorial system developed as the economic side of feudalism. The number of persons who actually held property by payment of a knight's fee were only a minute fraction of the total population. Most mano-

Above: A feudal feast with a servant playing the harp while her master and his wife eat.

Above right: A page from the Domesday Book. This book recorded the survey ordered by William I of the economic resources of England. Because of the thoroughness of the book it became possible to implement direct taxation by the king.

Left: The rigid structure of the feudal society is shown in this illustration. At the top is the king, followed by his bishops and barons. Next come the warrior knights, then the freemen such as merchants and traders. At the bottom of the pyramid are the serfs.

rial lords controlled their various freehold and 'customary' tenants by lengthening the chain of obligations. The mutual obligation between, for example, a small freeholder and his lord would be that in return for the money-rent, the lord would protect the tenant's title to occupy the property.

Probably the largest proportion of the population in feudal times were the customary tenancies: they are known by a wide variety of different terms, such as *villein, serf, native, bondman* and *peasant.* A customary tenant would probably owe a wide variety of rents ranging from so many days work per week without pay on the lord's estate to half a dozen eggs at Easter. He (or she) was obliged to perform the duties and services that were customary for that particular property or, sometimes, for that size of smallholding. The lord controlled his villeins by means of the manorial court. Unlike the freeholders, who could take the lord to higher courts, the villein had no redress against his lord higher than the manorial court. The exploitation of the peasant did not end with the demands of his manorial landlord. The local Church, also,

might demand ten per cent of his produce—one parish priest in 14th century England even demanded the tenth son of a local villein as *tithe* (one-tenth).

The classes of society mentioned, by reason of their tenure and obligations, fitted into the system. Modern research, however, is uncovering a whole new class of landless people who barely enter the records of the feudal system at all. It is becoming clear that even the peasant with two hectares was in a privileged position. Little is known of the quite considerable pool of casual workers, although 'a scarcity of labourers' is occasionally recorded in manorial documents the year after a bad harvest.

The defence of feudalism and the manorial system usually begins with the recognition that it helped Europe survive. Our understanding of feudal society is far from complete. Much that appears grim and repressive may in fact be attributed to legal jargon at a local level. Even the peasant notoriously 'tied to the soil' may have received some benefits. Nevertheless, feudal society was organized principally for the benefit of the few at the top of the pyramid.

Peasants' Revolts

Population in western Europe had been increasing for 300 years or more by the end of the 13th century. The available land could not provide enough food for all, except in very good years when there was a bumper harvest. The peasants had grown steadily poorer. They could not leave their manors without the lords' permission, yet had been made to do more work and pay heavier rents for their lands. By this time even the law courts treated *villeins* as if they and their families and all their property simply belonged to their lord.

In the 14th century much of this changed.

ants' revolts in most countries. Often the struggles of the peasants became involved in other movements and in the end the peasants were left, abandoned by their allies, to pay the price. In France, the revolt in 1358 called the *Jacquerie* came after defeat in war against the English and their own hostile countrymen. The civil war halted long enough for the revolt to be suppressed and 20,000 peasants were put to death.

North Italy and the Low Countries were centres of cloth-making. The industry was organized on a very great scale in towns that were exceptionally large by the standards of the *Middle Ages*. Here the workers were, if anything, worse off than the peasants. In

Above: Wat Tyler being executed by Richard II's troops. Wat Tyler and John Ball led the rural revolt of 1381 against the ruling powers. Possibly as many as 100,000 peasants from the south and east of England marched on London. Archbishop Sudbury was murdered, as were London lawyers and officials. Houses were burnt and the Tower was seized. But with the death of Wat Tyler the rebellion was put down.

Famines, the *Black Death* and other plagues, and wars in Europe, killed off large numbers of people. Lords now discovered that they could not easily find tenants when their villeins died. Free peasants who wanted land could easily find it. Rents were low, and men who worked for wages could get more because of the shortage. Some lords tried to solve this by forcing their villeins to do more work for them. This encouraged the peasants in some places to band together in resistance, and from time to time there were local revolts. Villeins began to run away in increasing numbers to escape their burdens, or to take advantage of the opportunities for a better life in the towns and elsewhere.

During the 14th century there were peas-

Germany the peasants' revolts which began in the 14th century continued to flare up from time to time during the next 200 years (see pp. 108-9).

The great peasants' revolt of 1381 in England took place in the most industrialized and most thickly populated parts of the country, particularly East Anglia and Kent. The risings were provoked by attempts to collect a *Poll Tax*. This took as much from a poor man as a rich one. The hatred of the peasantry was directed particularly against their rulers and the tax-collectors, but the peasants also often burned the records of the lords of the manor in an attempt to get rid of their *bondage* by destroying all trace of it. As in continental

Europe, at the same time many people in the towns rose against their lords. In Cambridge the townsmen launched an attack on the university.

It is not known how the revolt was organized. In England travelling agitators went from town to town and village to village. Captured peasants who were questioned often spoke of a 'Great Society', but it is not certain what they meant. Some of the *Lollard* preachers (followers of John Wycliffe) stirred up revolt in their sermons. In Kent one of these, John Ball, had asked: 'When Adam delved and Eve span Who was then the gentleman?' The peasants claimed to be supporting the boy king, Richard II, against evil advisers. The king met the peasants and promised to give them most of what they wanted; but much of this was revoked when the soldiers began to put the peasants down. For the moment at least, the peasants had lost.

But time was on their side. In the next century the royal courts began gradually to protect them against their lords. It was still

Above: In 1358 the peasants of Ile de France and Picardy rebelled against the war taxes levied on them. This uprising, known as the Jacquerie, was quelled in three weeks by Charles the Bad, king of Navarre whose men massacred 20,000 peasant men, women and children.

possible as late as 1549 for East Anglian peasants in revolt to ask, 'That all bond men may be free, as Christ made all men free by his precious blood shedding'. By this time very little remained to be done to make all Englishmen free before the law. But in many places in eastern Europe this freedom did not come until after the middle of the 19th century.

Peasant revolts were essentially revolts against *feudal* society (see pp. 78-9) but they continued to be an important element in social revolution until the 20th century. In England there was an element of peasant revolt in the *Civil War* of the 17th century. The French Revolution (see pp. 158-9) began as a peasant revolt, though it was town-dwellers who carried it forward. In the Russian revolution (see pp. 178-9) a revolt of the peasants was fundamental to the *Bolsheviks'* success. The Communist victory in China was a 20th century peasants' revolt (see pp. 198-9). Since the poor are still in the majority, peasants' revolts lie behind many modern *guerilla* movements (see pp. 228-9).

Pope Against Emperor

In the eighth century, when Pope Stephen II's power in Italy was in danger both from the emperor in Constantinople and from the *Lombards* in the north, he called in Pepin the Short, ruler of the *Franks* (see pp. 62-3), to protect him. Pepin's successor, Charlemagne, was crowned emperor by Pope Leo III in order to gain a permanent protector. So the Holy Roman empire was born.

The empire was revived in the tenth century with Otto the Great. He had saved Christianity from the Hungarian invaders at the battle of Lechfeld, and had become master of Italy as well as Germany. In 962 he was proclaimed emperor. Under him rather than under the pope, the Abbots of Cluny led a movement which reformed and revived the Church. After this, perhaps the most important reform in the Church in the whole of the *Middle Ages*, emperors could easily insist that by right and by duty they were responsible for guarding its welfare. But the pope, who crowned the emperor, and who presumably would refuse to crown anyone falsely claiming the title, could also treat the emperor as his spiritual son and watch over his conduct. Both of them could claim to be the final authority. As there was no clear division as to where each should take the lead, a strong emperor faced with a strong pope could easily begin a quarrel. The emperor might feel it his duty to save the Church from a corrupt pope, and the pope his duty to withdraw recognition from an ungodly emperor. If the election of either was disputed the other would intervene. To complicate matters further, the pope ruled states in central Italy which, in theory, was the heart of the empire. Throughout the empire the great men of the Church, abbots and bishops, were important lords with great estates over which the emperor was certainly the overlord. In the beliefs of the time the world was governed by two swords, the one held by the emperor and the other by the pope.

In the eleventh century another move was made to purify the Church, this time by the popes. They were determined to get rid of all control of the Church by laymen. In 1073 the fiercely reforming monk, Hildebrand, was elected pope as Gregory VII. A quarrel broke out over the right to *invest*, that is to give an abbot or a bishop the badges of his office. When Emperor Henry IV refused to give up this right, Gregory *excommunicated* him and declared him deposed. Rebellion at home during the struggle forced Henry to give way for the moment. He appeared as a penitent, barefoot in the snow, at the gate of the castle at Canossa where the pope was

The rich regalia of the Holy Roman empire. It was used for coronations in the later period of the empire's turbulent history.

staying. He knew full well that the pope was duty-bound to take him in and give him absolution. As soon as he was strong enough he took up the quarrel again. When Gregory again excommunicated him Henry elected an *anti-pope*, captured Rome with his army and drove Gregory out to die in exile. Under the next pope, Urban II, a rebellion by his own son drove the emperor into flight, where he, in his turn, died. A compromise was finally agreed between the two sides at Worms in 1122.

Under the *Hohenstaufen* family of emperors the quarrel broke out again. Frederick I Barbarossa used the power of his armies in Italy to force the pope to crown him. Rebellion, defeat on the battlefield, and plague in his armies forced him to give in, and at Venice in 1177 he held the pope's stirrup to show his obedience. A few years later Frederick had recovered his power again. It appeared as if he would control all

Italy and the pope as well, but in 1189 he set out on the Third Crusade and was drowned while crossing a river in 1190. The years of rebellions and civil wars that followed seriously weakened the empire.

Other countries, especially France, were now more important than the empire. It was against these that Pope Innocent III tried to make good his claim that the pope was the supreme ruler of the world. Even King John of England became his *vassal*. The last great Hohenstaufen emperor, Frederick II, began the struggle once more against Gregory IX and Innocent IV. The pattern was very much like that of his grandfather, Barbarossa. A compromise made in a time of weakness was followed by recovery and renewal of the quarrel. Almost at the point of complete success the pope succeeded in shaking

The Holy Roman Emperor Frederick Barbarossa's submission to Pope Alexander III at Venice in 1177, as seen by the Italian artist Spinello Aretino. Barbarossa later regained his power and challenged the pope again but died before the conflict could be resolved.

Frederick's authority. Frederick suffered serious defeats and died in 1250.

The pope now appeared victor, and the power of the Hohenstaufen was broken. But in fact the papal claims had been discredited by all the trickery used and, when Boniface VIII tried to assert his claims against Philip the Fair of France, he lost. The result of this *medieval* civil war was that the pope lost the respect of many people and his authority over lay princes and kings, and the *Reformation* (see pp. 114-5) became possible. The empire ceased to have any reality and became in effect just one of several European nation states (see pp. 102-9). But it was only in 1806 under pressure from Napoleon I that the *Habsburg* Austrian emperor finally abandoned his claim to the title of Holy Roman emperor.

The Mongols

The most formidable of all the nomad explosions in central Asia (see pp. 56-7) was that of the *Mongols* in the 13th century. Mongolian peoples were found in the area between Manchuria and the Black Sea. Scyths, Huns and Turks were all mongols, but the people who bear the name in history were first united by Temujin who was proclaimed Genghis (or Jenghiz) Khan, 'emperor within the seas' and ruler of the *nomads* on the river Onon in 1206, at a *kurultai* or tribal parliament. The effect of the Mongol eruption was once and for all to end nomadism as a threat to civilization and to link Chinese and European civilizations together for a brief but vitally important moment in time (see pp. 90-1).

Temujin was born in 1155; he was an orphan and became an outlaw, but he

Kublai Khan, the most able grandson of the great Genghis Khan, was elected the Great Khan in 1260. He expanded the empire left to him by his father and grandfather and ruled all China from 1279. He established Peking as his winter capital and brought food there by a massive extension of the Grand Canal system. Under Kublai, the Mongols continued their quest for victory in other parts of Asia, including Japan, Vietnam and Burma. Kublai died in 1294 after ruling his empire for 34 years.

gathered his own band of followers and became recognized as khan of the local Mongols. He was 50 when he was accepted as overlord of the tribes. He immediately set about conquering the world from his remote camp at Karakorum. He had already perfected the nomad tactics of cavalry fighting, shooting from horseback and exploiting speed and mobility to the full. On the move, the Mongols lived off *kumys* (fermented mare's milk). Genghis had among his followers the man who eventually proved to be the world's greatest cavalry commander, Subatai. Many of his sons and followers were to become brilliant field commanders. The Mongols, as they advanced, captured and made use of men with skills from every nation. Craftsmen, physicians, merchants,

When Genghis Khan (above) was born, the nomadic Mongol tribes were scattered over a great area and lacked even a common name. Genghis Khan united and organized them in the most powerful force in Eurasia. His nomad warriors were able to cover huge distances —in a three-day period in Hungary they covered 432 kilometres—and won vast territories in central Asia.

diplomats, and soldiers joined them. So their armies and their knowledge of the world grew together.

Between 1211 and 1216 the Mongols invaded Korea and north China, capturing Peking. In 1217 they occupied central Asia as far as Tibet. In 1219-22 they conquered the central Asian *Khwarizmian* empire (see pp. 98-9), devastating Samarkand and Bokhara. In 1221-24 Subatai raided Europe in a great sweep along the north of the Black Sea up to Kiev. Genghis died in 1227 and all the armies and their leaders came back to Karakorum to choose the next Kakhan (great ruler). Ogodai, Genghis's third son, was chosen and ruled from 1229-41. Jagatai, the second son, was given the central Asian kingdoms as his own. Juji, the eldest son, was already dead, but his son Batu was left the expanding western frontier region.

Batu and Subatai were sent by the kurultai to conquer Europe and allowed 18 years to accomplish the task. The campaign lasted from 1236 to 1242 and was ended because of Ogodai's death. Once again the armies went back to Karakorum to choose an heir. In 1237-38 the Volga was crossed; north Russia was conquered and Moscow burnt. In 1240 Kiev was taken and south Russia subdued. In 1241 three Mongol columns entered Europe. Kaidu swept along the Baltic coast into Poland and Prussia and then turned south into Bohemia. Batu and Subatai forced the Carpathian passes and destroyed the Hungarian army in front of Budapest.

Kadan rode along the Black Sea coast and up the Danube to Budapest. In 1242 Kadan raided through Bulgaria and Yugoslavia to the Adriatic coast, and the Mongol armies turned back undefeated.

When Ogodai died his son Kuyuk succeeded him, but Kuyuk died in 1248. Mangu, eldest son of Genghis's fourth son, Tule, was then chosen as Kakhan. He sent Hulagu, his youngest brother, to destroy the caliphate (see pp. 98-9). Baghdad was burnt in 1258, and Asia Minor and northern Arabia conquered for the Mongols. But in 1258 a Mongol army had the rare experience of being defeated by the Sultan of Egypt, whose troops used early firearms. His name was Bandukdar and to this day in British army slang a rifle is called a 'bandook'. In 1257-59 Mangu and his second brother, Kublai, completed the conquest of northern China. This had been ordered by the same kurultai in the year 1235 which had planned the conquest of Europe.

When Mangu died in 1259 Kublai succeeded him, but he was no longer merely Kakhan; he was the *Son of Heaven*, a Chinese emperor. Kublai was the last of the Kakhans and the first of the *Yuan* dynasty of Chinese emperors. He completed the conquest of China by 1279 and added Indochina and Burma to his empire. He tried to conquer Japan and Malaysia but he failed in sea warfare. It was Kublai whom Marco Polo visited (see pp. 90-1). The Yuan dynasty lasted in China until 1368. The Mongol empire in central Asia, the *Ilkhan* empire, founded by Hulagu, lasted until 1335; it stretched from the river Indus in India to the Mediterranean coast and from Samarkand and Bokhara to Mesopotamia. Batu's armies settled in the Russian steppes between the Ural mountains and the Black Sea. This *Golden Horde* terrorized the Russian cities. Russia won some independence in 1380 but the Golden Horde was not finally destroyed until 1502.

The existence of these new Mongol empires brought peace to central Asia for a century. *Caravans* moved between China and Europe and a great impact was made on European society by the ideas and inventions of the Chinese, such as gunpowder and, perhaps most dramatically of all, that of printing.

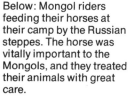

Below: Mongol riders feeding their horses at their camp by the Russian steppes. The horse was vitally important to the Mongols, and they treated their animals with great care.

Tang and Sung China

The China which the *Mongols* attacked and conquered had a long history behind it. The great *Han* dynasty had collapsed by 220 (see pp. 36-7). Two long-lasting dynasties ruled China before Kublai Khan founded the Mongol, *Yuan*, dynasty in 1260, and there were also long periods of disunity and civil war. For 350 years after the fall of Han, China was disunited. There were two important developments in this period: nomad *Hu* settled in the Yellow river valley; and landlords fleeing from the unsettled north came to the Yangtse valley and opened it up. They built dykes along the coast and introduced water control systems on the rivers and lakes.

By 577 north China was reunited and the *nomad* settlers were absorbed. In 581 Wan Ti proclaimed the *Sui* dynasty and in 589 he began the conquest of south China, where cultivation and civilization had been expanding into former wilderness. China was once more united. During the centuries

Above: A bronze figure of a cart pulled by oxen, dating from the Tang dynasty.

of disunity, pessimism and pursuit of the pleasures of wine and poetry had dominated Chinese culture. *Buddhism* (see pp. 40-1) entered China at this time and developed quite new beliefs. For intellectuals *Zen Buddhism* showed the way through meditation. For the peasant masses *Kwan Yin*, a mercy goddess, offered help in reaching the Pure Land, a kind of Buddhist heaven which took the place of *Nirvana* or nothingness.

To preserve Chinese unity the Sui built the Grand Canal uniting the Yellow river

Gunpowder was first made by the Chinese in the seventh century by combining saltpetre, sulphur and charcoal. It was originally used for firework displays on great public occasions and known as "fire trees" or "flame blossoms". It was not until the eleventh century that it was used for explosive weapons.

and the Yangtse. China's new strength and wealth brought diplomatic visitors from Japan, Siam and the far west. But the cost of the wars and of construction works such as the Grand Canal was too much for the peasants to bear. In 617 Li Yuan, a high ranking officer, rebelled against the Sui and founded a new dynasty, the *Tang*.

Li Yuan soon resigned and handed over power to his son, Li Shih-min. As the Emperor Tai Tsung, Li Shih-min based his government on an understanding of the peasants' position. Some of his sayings are remarkable for a ruler living over 1,300 years ago: 'The ruler is like a boat and the people are like the water. While the water floats the boat, it may also overwhelm it', and 'the emperor likes to have a palace built, but the people do not like building it. The emperor craves the flesh pots, but the people hate doing labour service', and again, 'an emperor collecting too heavy taxes from the people is like a man eating his own flesh. When the flesh is eaten up the man dies'. The Tang dynasty practised policies based on these ideas for a long time. There were limitations on taxes and a policy of equalizing land holdings was followed. To prevent the growth of a powerful aristocracy, a competitive examination system was introduced for public office. This was an extension of the Han system.

The Tang empire included Korea and reached the frontiers of Persia in the west. Nomads, like the Turks and *Uighurs,* were driven westwards. But by the middle of the eighth century decay began. The land equalization system ceased and landlord power increased. The frontier defences weakened; a *Tartar* general, An Lu-shan, rebelled in 755 and the rebellion was not put down until 763. Oppressive taxes were introduced with the inevitable result: a warlord in the Yellow river valley, Chu Wen, deposed the last Tang emperor in 907.

Under the Tangs, China had enjoyed an economic and cultural renaissance. Commerce expanded on land and by sea; handicrafts improved; cities grew. Two schools of Chinese painting were created; the manufacture of porcelain spread widely. Printing, first by inking inscribed stones and later by inking wood blocks, was discovered and spread knowledge of a developing literature. This was a great age of poetry.

For 60 years China was disunited: in the northern Yellow river valley there were five dynasties. In 960 a general, Chao Kuang Yin, seized power and founded the *Sung* dynasty, which lasted for 300 years. He ended warlordism and peasant indebtedness. The Sungs ruled by force; their standing army grew in a century from 378,000 to 1,162,000. It was rigidly controlled from the *Court* and this often made it ineffective on the frontiers. The *barbarian* nomads began to settle in China again. In 1004 the *Kitans* were pacified by a huge tribute. Then the *Kins* were used to destroy the Kitans, which they achieved by 1122 but took north China in exchange for their services. In 1226-27 the Sung allied with the Mongols to destroy the Kins, but this last alliance proved fatal. In 1276 the Sung capital was captured and in 1279 the last Sung emperor died.

Below: A magistrates' examination in eighth century China. The examination system, established by the Tang dynasty, required years of classical study before the student sat for his examination. The "chin-shih" degree allowed him to enter various sections of the civil service and was the world's first true civil service merit system.

There was one attempt to reform the Sung system of government between 1068 and 1076 under a prime minister, Wang An-shih. A national budget was drawn up with a large saving in expenditure; a nation-wide land survey and tax assessment was undertaken; the army was cut down to one-third of its size and thereafter comprised crack troops with a home-guard territorial army system (Pao-chia) in support. Loans were offered to peasant farmers when the 'green sprouts' were showing. Money payments replaced compulsory labour services and the privileged, who had been freed from labour services, were again made liable. But the reforms were not carried out effectively.

Under the Sung, Chinese culture became backward looking. It was a great age of encyclopedias embodying past knowledge—and many academies were founded to preserve traditional skills. Nevertheless, there were advances in porcelain and in romantic poetry and drama. In printing movable type was invented, the compass first employed in navigation, and gunpowder introduced.

Korea, Tibet and Japan

Korea stretches out south of Manchuria; to the south lies Kyushu, one of the four main islands of Japan. The other islands are Shikoku, Honshu and Hokkaido. Korea and Japan are close to each other. Tibet is far away, to the south-west of China, between China and India. But Chinese civilization was a formative influence on all three countries and throughout their histories China has been of supreme importance to them. Chinese immigrants are said to have entered Korea in 1122 B.C.; the Chinese called the country 'Chosen' or 'Land of the Morning Calm'. Korean records show that from 57 B.C. to 668 A.D. there were three kingdoms. In 935 A.D. Wang Kien united the country and his family ruled for many centuries. The Koreans became *Buddhists* and copied Chinese art and literature; Chinese design boxes and mirrors have been found in ancient Korean tombs.

Tibetan history begins in the seventh century A.D. when the country was ruled by noble families who were always at war with each other. The art of writing and the Buddhist religion were introduced in the seventh and eighth centuries by two great kings. The first *Lama*, abbot of a Tibetan Buddhist monastery, is recorded in 764.

The first people of Japan were probably the Ainu, some of whom survive to this day. But from a very early time Chinese settlers and influence were strong in the country, and particularly so in the very early centuries A.D.

Chinese writing came to Japan about 400 and Buddhism in about 552. Buddhism was transformed in Japan, where it merged with the native *Shintoism,* a code of conduct rather than a religion. In 741 a Japanese alphabet was created out of the Chinese characters. Many Koreans and Chinese artisans settled in Japan and introduced their crafts. Influenced by *Tang* China, Japanese culture flourished in the *Heian* period (749-1185). The power of the divine emperor was limited by the *Fujiwara* family, who really ruled in his name. Two rival clans, the *Taira* and the *Minamoto,* fought one another as the power of the Fujiwaras lessened. In 1185 Yoritomo Minamoto won a great sea battle in the Shimonoseki straits. The emperor rewarded him with the title of 'Barbarian-subduing great general', in Japanese Sei-i tai-shogun. *Shoguns,* or *generalissimos,* ruled Japan in the name of successive emperors until 1867, with one rather brief interlude.

In 1274 and 1281 the Chinese Mongol ruler, Kublai Khan, tried to invade Japan; he had an army of 150,000 men in 800 Korean ships. His defeat restored the prestige of the emperors, and in 1333 Emperor Go Daigo was able to destroy the ruling *Hojo* family. The Hojo had taken power out of the hands of the Minamotos. But in 1339 Ashikaga, one of the Minamoto family, restored their shogunate and it lasted until the year 1573.

The Mongols were more successful in Korea, which they occupied in 1231 and ruled until 1364, when a Korean general, Yi Songgye, drove them out. In 1392 he made himself king and founded a dynasty which lasted until 1910 when the Japanese conquered Korea. Much was learnt from China about astronomy, geology, history and agriculture. In 1592 Korea was occupied by the Japanese as a base for attacks on China. In 1627 the *Manchu* rulers of China brought Korea under their control.

Kublai Khan was converted by a Tibetan Lama and he made his converter ruler of Tibet. As a result two rival chief Lamas appeared: the yellow-robed *Dalai Lama,* and the red-robed *Panchen Lama.* The quarrels between their supporters gave the Mongols, and later the Chinese under the Manchus, power over Tibet. From the 17th century until the British penetrated Tibet from India in the 20th century, Tibet was in effect a Chinese colony or sphere of influence. In 1951 the Chinese Communists restored Chinese control, using the Panchen Lama.

Below: A Korean water bottle from the 12th century. It is made of clay with a green glaze.

The Dalai Lama (right) is believed by his followers to be the spiritual leader of the Tibetan people. The Dalai Lama is said to be the reincarnation of Chenresi, the Being of Compassion, and many other Lamas, especially those serving as heads of monasteries, are also thought to be the reincarnations of higher beings.

The Dalai Lama fled to India.

In the late 16th and early 17th centuries dramatic events took place in Japan. In the 1540s the first Europeans, the Portuguese, reached Japan, bringing the smooth-bore musket and the Christian religion. The Japanese took to the first but rejected the second. By 1578 a nobleman, Nobunaga, had made himself dominant in Japan by exploiting the musket. He was opposed to Buddhism and so welcomed the Jesuit missionaries. Nobunaga was killed in 1582 and was succeeded by Hideyoshi, who launched Japan on the invasion of Korea and attacks on China. The effect of these wars was to

remove from Japan the quarrelsome and aggressive feudal warriors, the *Daimyo*.

Hideyoshi reorganized the government of Japan. He died in 1598 and Ieyasu, a Minamoto, succeeded him and in 1603 became shogun. The office remained in his family—the *Tokugawa* shogunate—until 1867. Ieyasu retired in 1605; it was he and his successor, Hidetada, who decided to root Christianity out of Japan because they feared that the quarrels between the Protestant Dutch and English and the Roman Catholic Portuguese and Spanish would encourage a revival of civil war led by the Daimyo. In fact in 1637 a great rising at Shimabara was supported by the Christians. By 1639 all foreigners were expelled from Japan except for one Dutch 'factory', or trading post, at Deshima, a small island in Nagasaki harbour.

Under the Tokugawa shogunate Japan enjoyed the benefits of splendid isolation. One writer wrote: 'The Japanese lived in peace—except for local peasant risings —with themselves, and with the world, for two and a half centuries—a record that most nations, reviewing their own history over a similar period, must surely envy'. The peace was rudely interrupted by the Americans and Russians (see pp. 194-5), but it did give Japan the opportunity to develop economically and lay the foundations for industrialization (see pp. 150-1).

An early Japanese silk painting depicting the Dutch at leisure in their trading post at Nagasaki in the seventeenth century. In an upstairs room, traders enjoy a drink together while downstairs others play an early form of billiards. During Japan's years of isolation, the Dutch settlement's only contact with the outside world was the annual visit of one of their East Indies' trading vessels which called in at Nagasaki.

Marco Polo and Ibn Battuta

Medieval Europeans believed that 'they alone constituted the civilized world. Even Alexander the Great did not suspect the existence of China.' The eruption of the *Mongols* (see pp. 84-5) into 13th century Europe enlarged the European horizons and introduced Europeans to parts of the world of which they had never heard. A family of Venetian merchants, the Polos, visited China in the last half of the 13th century and the youngest of them, Marco Polo, produced an account of his visit.

Mediterranean trade had expanded with

Right: The embarkation of Marco Polo. Travelling with his father and his uncle, Marco Polo spent 17 years in China and eastern Asia. His book about what he had seen opened the eyes of Europeans to the world outside their own boundaries, though many dismissed his stories as pure fantasies.

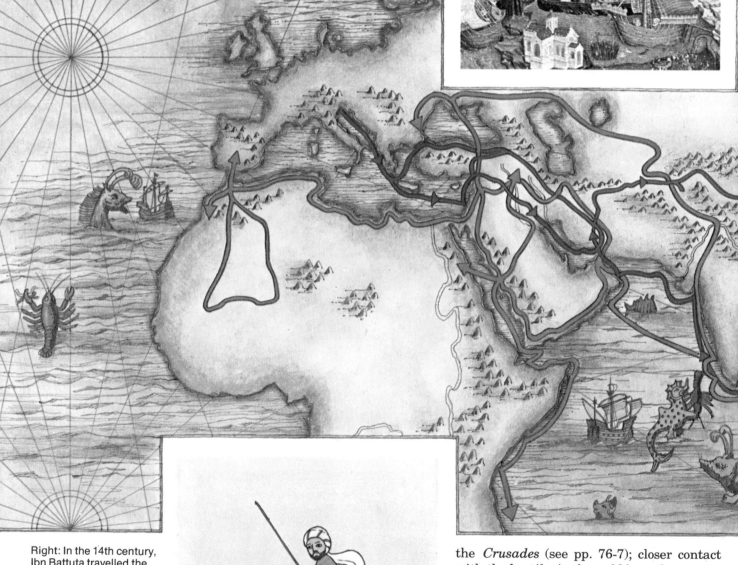

Right: In the 14th century, Ibn Battuta travelled the whole of the Muslim world and, like Marco Polo, told Europe about it through his writings. Battuta travelled as far as Java to the south-east, through China, India and Arabia and down the north-east coast of Africa.

the *Crusades* (see pp. 76-7); closer contact with the hostile Arab world brought greater geographical knowledge. In 1245 the pope sent a *Franciscan friar,* John of Pian del Carpine, to seek a Mongol alliance against the *Islamic* world which blocked Christian Europe on the south and east. Carpine reached Karakorum in 1246. St. Louis (King Louis IX of France) sent William de Rubruquis on a similar mission; he was in Karakorum from December 1253 to July

1254. There were three great historical trade routes between the Mediterranean and China. The Egyptian–Red Sea route through the Indian Ocean was closed to Europeans by the *Muslims*; the Sultan of Egypt had even defeated the Mongols. The other two routes were opened up by the Mongol conquests; they were through the Levant (Syrian-Lebanon-Palestine coast) to the Persian Gulf and then by sea to India and onwards; and the Old Silk Road from the Black Sea through central Asia north of the Hindu Kush and Pamir mountains. Both Carpine and de Rubruquis travelled on the Old Silk Road, though they approached it from different directions: Carpine through

Map showing the routes taken by Marco Polo (red) and Ibn Battuta (green) during their travels in the 13th and 14th centuries.

central Russia and de Rubruquis from Constantinople.

The peace established by the Mongol conquests lasted from 1264 to 1368; a merchants' 'guide book' of the period actually claimed that 'from Tana (on the sea of Azov) to Cathay is perfectly safe, whether by day or by night, according to what merchants say who have used' the route. This has, probably, never been true since. In 1260 two *Venetian* merchants, the brothers Niccolo

and Maffeo Polo, left for China. They got back to Europe in 1269. Kublai Khan had sent them back to bring missionaries; like most Mongols, he encouraged all religions. In 1271 the Polos began their second journey to China, taking Niccolo's young son Marco. They travelled from Acre on the Levant coast through Asia Minor and then along the Old Silk Road. The Polos spent 17 years in China. Marco became a great favourite of Kublai Khan; he learnt many languages, travelled over the Mongol empire for Kublai and was even governor of a Chinese city. He visited Tibet and Burma.

The Polos began their return journey escorting a Mongol princess as a bride from China to Kublai's great-nephew in Persia. At Marco's suggestion they travelled by the sea route, along the coasts of Indo-China, Java, Ceylon (now Sri-Lanka) and Baluchistan. In 1295 the Polos got back to Venice. By an irony of fate Marco was then captured by the *Genoese* in a sea battle with Venetians. It was while in prison that he dictated his experiences. The effect on Europeans of reading Marco Polo's adventures was disbelief. He described the use of coal and of paper money in China, but oddly never mentions printing or the *Great Wall of China*.

Many other merchants and missionaries followed the Polos to India and China, but none wrote of their travels in the same way. One of them, a Franciscan friar, Giovanni de Marignolli, who travelled from Avignon to China and back between 1338 and 1353, commented that 'God willed not that men should be able to sail round the world'. It was in fact the closing of these routes between Europe and Asia, following the collapse of the Mongol empires, that stimulated the Portuguese to find a sea route to Asia, round Africa, and Columbus to look for a sea route across the Atlantic (see pp. 118-21).

Christian Europe faced a hostile Arab-Turkish Islamic world to its south. This civilization had its own Marco Polo in the 14th century. Ibn Battuta, born in Tangier in 1304 (died in 1368), travelled through the whole Muslim world and visited China and wrote of his journeys. He travelled from North Africa to Mecca, Baghdad, Persia and Mesopotamia in 1325. From 1327 to 1330 he returned to Mecca, visited the Yemen and Aden, travelled down the east African coast, and then through Turkey to Constantinople, across the Black Sea and central Asia to India. For eight years he worked for the 'Slave Kings' of Delhi (see pp. 94-5), and was made a *Qadi*, a magistrate. He described *suttee* (a *Hindu* custom by which the widow was burnt alongside her dead husband).

India after the Mauryas

For 1,200 years after the break-up of the *Mauryan* empire there was a *Hindu* revival which finally drove *Buddhism* from its homeland. The main division in India throughout these centuries was between north and south. The *Sunga* dynasty came to power in the Ganges valley in 185 B.C. and lasted until 72 B.C. They were persecutors of the Buddhists. The Indus valley, in much the same period, was conquered by two waves of invaders. The first (135 B.C. to 90 B.C.) were Greeks from one of the successor kingdoms of Alexander the Great (see pp. 46-7). They were followed (90 B.C. to 50 A.D.) by *Scyths* (see pp. 56-7) or *Sakas*.

The Indus and Ganges valleys were once again reunited by a third wave of invaders. They entered north-west India in about 50 A.D. and then occupied the Ganges. This *Kushan* empire lasted from about 50 A.D., until the second or third centuries A.D. It stretched from the Ganges through the Indus valley into Persia and Central Asia. Under the Kushans there was a Buddhist revival and an artistic *renaissance* in India. In Mathura, on a tributary of the Ganges, a native Indian style developed and it was here that artists first found the way to show in sculpture the inner contentment and

repose of the Buddha. The fully open eyes, round and full cheeks, and ample mouth with a slight smile have become the typical representation of the Buddha.

Southern India was united by the *Andrhas* about 100 B.C. Their rule lasted until 225 A.D. and both Hinduism and Buddhism seem at first to have flourished side by side. The Andrha kingdom experienced the beginning of seaborne trade between southern India and the world. On the west coast the links were with the Arab and Roman world. Roman trading posts and many hoards of Roman coins have been found on both coasts of southern India. This trade link brought Christianity into India. St. Thomas was the supposed pioneer missionary. But foreign influence was much less penetrating than in northern India. The south was an area in which the purely Indian cultural tradition was at its strongest. So it is not surprising that the east coast trade with Malaya, Indonesia and China was to lead to the spread of Hinduism into south-east Asia (see pp. 96-7).

About the year 320 A.D. the political structure of India changed both in the south and in the north. In the south the *Pallavas* replaced the Andrhas. About 900 the *Cholas* took over from the Pallavas. Under these two dynasties the Hindu religion revived and, coinciding with the Chola defeat of the Pallavas, Hinduism experienced an intellectual revolution. Hinduism ousted Buddhism and became the universal Indian faith. The Pallava dynasty was based on trade with the east and it planted Hindu communities in

Above: This intricately-carved gateway dates from 35 B.C. and is the entrance to the Great Stupa at Sanchi, central India, a symbolic mound built by early Indian Buddhists representing the heavens and the earth.

Left: An 11th-century marble carving of a Jain goddess from a temple at Mount Abu, Rajasthan.

Right: The Iron Pillar at Qutb Minar, Delhi, was made about 300 A.D. but has never rusted.

Malaya and Indonesia. The Chola empire extended into Ceylon and Burma.

In the north, from about 320 a new Indian dynasty of *Guptas* expanded its power from a Ganges base and drove out the Kushans. It united north India and reached farther south than any previous rulers since the empire founded by Chandragupta Maurya. But the Guptas, unlike the Mauryas, did not seriously try to incorporate southern India into their dominions.

The dynasty was Hindu but Buddhism still survived in many parts of India. A travelling Chinese monk, Fa-Hien, found many Buddhist monasteries. The basis of this new empire seems to have been the development of a kind of feudalism in India (see pp. 78-9). Aristocratic landlords became important. There were provinces ruled by governors and, in each province, districts with administrators and some kind of representative councils. In the villages, the age-old village council government survived. Fa-Hien compared this government with China's and found it much less *bureaucratic*. There was no serfdom and no registration of the population. 'Those who want to go away may go away.' He noted the effects of religion on food and drink provision. The people 'do not keep pigs or fowls, there are no dealings in cattle, no butchers' shops or distilleries in their market places'. There were inns on the main roads where food was provided for travellers, and there were free hospitals in the great cities.

In about 450 Skandagupta defeated *Hun* invaders (see pp. 56-7), but by 465 the Huns had conquered and devastated the northwest. By 500 they had reached the Punjab. In 530 Yasodharman defeated the Huns and revived the Gupta empire, but it did not last beyond his lifetime. Northern India broke up into many kingdoms. Hinduism spread at the expense of Buddhism. Between 605 and 647 Harsha-Vardhana built up an empire in north-west India. He was, probably, the last Indian ruler to support Buddhism. During his reign another Chinese, Hsuang-Chuang, visited India and made similar comments to those of Fa-Hien. The higher *castes* led a simple and frugal life with great emphasis on cleanliness; their chief extravagance was jewellery. He describes the town walls as built of brick, but most houses were still made of wood or *wattle.* Monks gave widespread primary education and there were universities in existence. It was under the Guptas that Indian civilization penetrated into Nepal and Tibet.

After Harsha's death a number of successor kingdoms rose and fell in the north until about 1000, when Muslim invaders threatened the country (see pp. 94-5).

The Slave Kings of India

By the year 1000 the sub-continent of India was becoming solidly *Hindu* in religion and culture but divided among many warring kingdoms. India was becoming *feudal;* one sign of this was the rise of the *Rajput* class. They were probably descendants of the *Huns,* or of peoples brought to India by the Huns, and they were absorbed into Hindu society as *kshatriya* (warriors). *Buddhism,* with its belief in non-violence and *asceticism,* was unsuited to the warlike and self-indulgent tastes of a feudal India and it vanished from the country. However, *Jainism,* a Hindu asceticism which also taught non-violence, did survive in western India.

The Turkish kingdoms which arose in central Asia began to look to India as a source both of loot and culture. Mahmud of Ghazni in Afghanistan raided north-western India from 997 to 1030, destroying temples and taking away much wealth, but building, at Ghazni, a library and museum for his captured treasures. This was India's first real contact with *Muslims.* Muhammad of Ghuri followed to conquer, not to loot. By 1182 Sind had accepted his rule; in 1185 he conquered Lahore and in 1192 he defeated the Rajputs. Muhammad became sultan, or king, of Delhi. His kingdom of Ghuri did not long survive his death, but he left a general,

Qutb-ud-din, who had once been a slave, and in 1206 Qutb-ud-din founded a dynasty, known after its founder as the dynasty of the *Slave.*

The Delhi sultans pursued the aim of uniting all India in their empire. They never achieved this; it was left to their Mughal successors (see pp. 138-9). But Delhi became the main power centre and the cultural centre of India. Ibn Battuta (see pp. 90-1) described it in the 1330s as the most magnificent city in the Muslim world. The rulers of Delhi were Turks, Afghans and Persians —all Muslims. But the majority of Muslims in India were converts. From the establishment of the Delhi sultanate, Hindu India has contained a Muslim minority which could not be totally assimilated as Greeks and Huns, for example, had been. But Hinduism not only survived nearly ten centuries of Muslim and Christian rule, it continued as the religion and way of life of the vast majority of Indians.

Different families and some outstanding individuals ruled at Delhi. The *Khaljis* came to power in 1290. Ala-ud-din (1296-1316) raised the sultanate to the highest point of its power. He reorganized the tax system, increasing state revenues and reducing the power of the nobles. He invaded and conquered much of southern India but, before he died, dependent kingdoms and their ruling families were in open rebellion.

Tower of victory at Qutb Minar, Delhi. It was built by Qutb-ud-din, a slave who became a general and ultimately ruler of Lahore.

In 1320 Ghiyas-ud-din Tughluq seized power and founded the Tughluq line of sultans. The second of them tried to move his capital southwards from Delhi to Daulatabad (1327-30) closer to the southern kingdoms which he wished to annex. The move failed, partly because Muhammad, the sultan, tried to compel the whole population of Delhi to move with the court, and partly because the southern kingdoms proved unconquerable. Firuz Shah became sultan in 1351 and ruled for about 30 years, the last of the sultans to have effective power over much of India.

Muhammad's campaigns in the south had provoked resistance and in 1336 a new southern Hindu kingdom, Vijayanagara, was founded, which continued as the dominant power in the south for two centuries. The country was described as 'so well populated that it is impossible in a reasonable space to convey an idea of it'. And Paes said, in 1522, of Vijayanagara, the capital city, that it was 'the best-provided city in the world . . . not like other cities, which often fail of supplies and provisions, for in this everything abounds'.

Tamerlane invaded north India in 1398 and sacked Delhi (see pp. 98-9). His nominee was the founder of a new dynasty of sultans, the *Sayyids* (1414-50). In 1451 Buhlul Lodi, the Afghan governor of a northern province, took power and his dynasty, the *Lodi*, was overthrown by Babur in 1526. Babur, a descendant of Tamerlane, was the first of the *Mughal* emperors who at last reunited India (see pp. 138-9).

The five centuries of the Delhi sultanate, founded by the Slave Kings, was a period of feudal war and anarchy not unlike the similar period in European history. And, as in Europe, it led to the flowering of native languages. Hindu, Bengali, Marathi and Gujrati developed in the north from Sanskrit; while Tamil, Telugu, Malayalam and Kanarese emerged in the south from a *Dravidian* source. Literature and even reformed ideas about religion appeared in the new languages. At the same time trade developed, based particularly on the growth of cotton manufacture, for the trade in cotton clothing came to dominate the whole commercial situation of India by the 16th century. The towns became centres of work; the production of luxury goods was stimulated by the existence of the court at Delhi; its luxurious tastes were copied by other princes and by the nobles. Ibn Battuta describes the road system and postal services of the Tughluq sultans as highly developed. India, though disunited, was advancing in wealth and culture. As in Italy, it was a period of renaissance and renewal.

Below: Shams-ud-din Iltutmish, one of the greatest of the Slave kings, ruled at Delhi from 1211 to 1236.

South-East Asia before the 19th Century

South-East Asia has two main parts. The islands—the Philippines, Timor, North Borneo, Sarawak, Brunei and Indonesia—form one part; the mainland countries—Singapore, Malaysia, Vietnam, Cambodia, Laos, Thailand and Burma—form the other. Their history can be divided roughly into three periods. First people settled and set up different kingdoms. Second, in the 13th century, a new religion, *Islam,* was brought into the area. Third, from the end of the 15th century, Europeans came to trade.

Most of the people of the island group were *Malays* who came from China about 4,000 years ago. Two exceptions to this are the *Sakai* in Malaya and the *Dayaks* of Borneo, who came from earlier people. On the mainland there were *Burmans, Mons, Tai* and *Viet.* They came from the north and liked to settle in the fertile river valleys between forest and mountain.

India and China traded with the area 2,000 years ago (see pp. 92-3). They set up kingdoms and brought in the *Hindu* and *Buddhist* religions. One big kingdom, Funan, was ruled by an Indian prince. Borneo, Java and Sumatra had Chinese settlements. Funan lasted to the seventh century A.D. It was then divided, but brought together again in 802 by a new king, Jayarman II, who called it Cambodia. We can still see the ruins of its capital city, Angkor. In 1219 the people revolted and Cambodia was attacked by the Tai. A smaller Cambodia survived with a capital at Phnom Penh.

In the middle of the ninth century the Burmans and the Mons came to settle in the Irrawaddy valley and that of the Menam Chao Phya. At most times they fought each other. They did unite, however, in the 11th and 12th centuries under the rulers of Pagan, a state in the centre. But when Pagan rule was broken in the 13th century by a *Mongol* invasion from China, the Mons and the Burmans set up separate kingdoms. They were not united again for any length of time until the 17th century. The Viet settled in three places, the Red River, the Mekong delta and Annam. They

Above: The temple of Angkor Wat in Cambodia (Khmer Republic) is the best-preserved example of Khmer architecture.

were controlled by the Chinese for 1,000 years until 906, when they broke away. Even the Mongols (see pp. 84-5) could not conquer the new state in the 13th century. But a single kingdom was not easy to run. From the middle of the 17th century there were two main kingdoms—Tongking in the north, Cochin China in the south. The Tai were in three groups—the *Thai*, the *Shans* and the *Lao*. Their strongest kingdom was Ayudhya, which was developed in the 15th century. It fell in the 18th century but its excellent form of government was taken over by Thailand, with a capital city at Bangkok.

The struggle on the mainland was for land. On the islands it was for trade routes. For instance, Sumatra could control the Malacca Straits. She also wanted the Sunda Straits. So did Java. Several kingdoms formed with the idea of controlling these and other trade routes. By the seventh century the chief commercial centre was the Buddhist state of Sri Vijaya in Sumatra. It

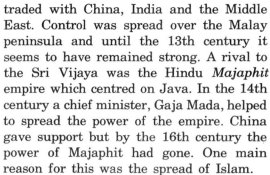

traded with China, India and the Middle East. Control was spread over the Malay peninsula and until the 13th century it seems to have remained strong. A rival to the Sri Vijaya was the Hindu *Majaphit* empire which centred on Java. In the 14th century a chief minister, Gaja Mada, helped to spread the power of the empire. China gave support but by the 16th century the power of Majaphit had gone. One main reason for this was the spread of Islam.

By the 13th century there was a demand for luxuries in Europe like gems, ivory and textiles. Muslim merchants settled in Malacca and their religion spread rapidly from there through Malaya. Malacca became the centre of a new empire guided, in the 15th century, by a most efficient chief minister, Tun Perak. Islam did not spread much farther on the mainland, nor quickly on all the islands. It did provide, however, another cause for rivalry between people who were already divided between Hindu and two of the many forms of the Buddhist religion (see pp. 40-1).

Then came the Europeans. Portugal, Spain, the Netherlands and England all formed East India Companies to develop trade. First the Portuguese took over Malacca in 1511. From there they controlled trade in the islands but they were not successful on the mainland, except for trade from Macao with China. They beat their Spanish rivals and then joined with them against the Dutch. The Dutch set up at Djakarta to protect trade in the islands. In 1641 they took Malacca from the Portuguese. They were helped by quarrels among the native rulers, who often turned to the Europeans for help in exchange for trading rights. In this way the Dutch gained control of Bantam (in Java) during the 17th century.

Europeans did not do very much in the area before the 19th century, except to develop and protect trade. The Spaniards controlled the Philippines and the Dutch were centred on Java. Most Europeans gave attention to Malacca. The French Society of Foreign Missions worked in the area from 1659 onwards. Only in the 19th century did Europe become really interested in taking direct control of countries in which raw materials for their industries could be produced. This is when Britain occupied Burma and Malaya and France marched its way into Indo-China.

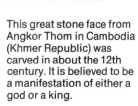

This great stone face from Angkor Thom in Cambodia (Khmer Republic) was carved in about the 12th century. It is believed to be a manifestation of either a god or a king.

The Seljuk Turks and Tamerlane

Very soon after the *Huns* had disintegrated as an effective confederacy of *nomad* tribes (see pp. 56-7), a new grouping of nomads appeared in the steppes of central Asia. These were the *Turks*, whose first recorded activities were in 552 near Lake Baikal in Siberia. They united their neighbours, expanded south-east and south-west and, just like the Huns earlier, divided into an eastern and a western grouping. The eastern Turks attacked the Chinese empire and were driven away between 627 and 629 by strong *Tang* emperors (see pp. 86-7). Their remnants joined with the western Turks, who had entered Persia (Iran) about 620. In 657 some of the western Turkish clans, who had returned to the borders of China, were once again driven away by Tang emperors. The last Chinese defeat of Turkish clans was in 830, when the *Uighurs* were driven westwards by the Tangs.

The strength of the Tang dynasty in China meant that the expansive movements of Turkish nomads were turned westwards and southwards. So a Turkish civilization developed in west central Asia, in the area now occupied by the Soviet central Asiatic republics. The Arabs (see pp. 68-9) conquered this Turkish society temporarily and converted the Turks to *Islam* permanently. When the Turks regained their political independence of the Arabs they emerged as conquerors of their neighbours, introducing Islam wherever they went. In about 1000 Mahmud of Ghazni conquered north India. The Turks had spread through Afghanistan. In 1192 a second Turkish 'Afghan' empire, which was centred on Delhi came into existence (see pp. 94-5).

But the major direction of expansion of the Turks was into Asia Minor and Arabia.

Below left: As the Mongol empire broke up, new leaders determined to establish new empires emerged. One of the most powerful was Tamerlane, shown fighting the Syrians.

Tamerlane made Samarkand, in Russia, his capital. He restored the city, one of the oldest in central Asia, to its former glory with new mosques, palaces and gardens. The rich life-style of his capital, Samarkand, is shown in the illustration below.

In 1071 at the battle of Melasgird the Turks defeated the eastern Roman emperor, the ruler of Byzantium (see pp. 70-3). During the years which followed, up to 1186, the Turks took over the old Arab empire and the *caliphate*. So the head of the Islamic world, the caliph, was a Turk. The greatest military leader of the Turks in this victorious advance was Saladin. The Turkish advance brought Jerusalem and the Holy Places of the Christian religion under the control of a new, militant, Muslim power. Jerusalem was a holy city for Jews and Muslims as well as for Christians; that is the reason it has been fought over so often. So Europeans launched a series of *Crusades* (see pp. 76-7) to reconquer the Holy Land for the Christian powers.

The Turks, who played such an important part in the history of central Asia and

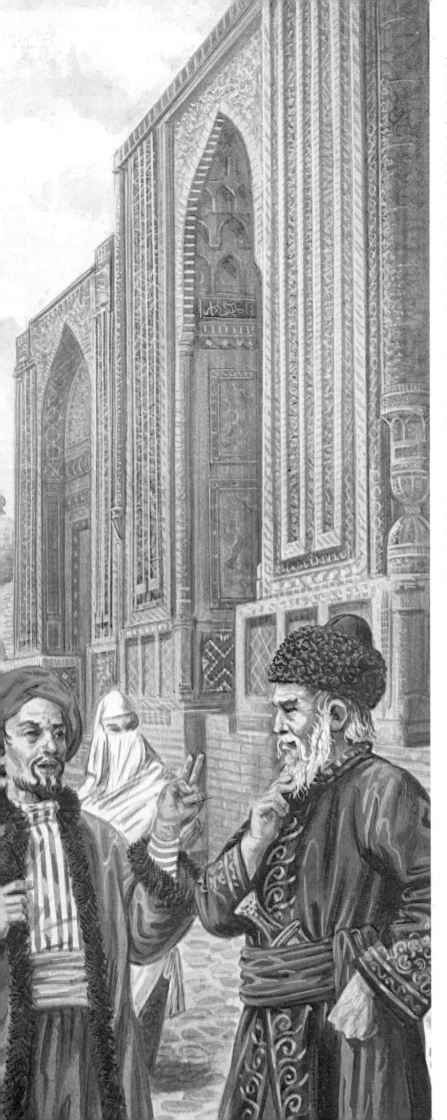

Arabia roughly between 600 and 1200, are known as the *Seljuk Turks*. Their dominions in central Asia and in Arabia became highly civilized. Bokhara and Samarkand were great trading cities, linking Europe and Asia, and centres of Muslim religion and art. In the years 1219-22 the *Mongols* (see pp. 84-5) destroyed this Khwarizmian empire in central Asia; between 1255 and 1258 the Mongols occupied Persia and Arabia. Baghdad was burnt and the caliphate destroyed. In the holocaust which the Mongols caused, a Turkish tribe was driven out of central Asia into Asia Minor. They are called *Ottoman Turks*, and the area in which they settled became Turkey (see pp. 166-7). With the retreat of the Mongols they took over the caliphate.

As the Mongol empire broke up and Mongol power waned, there were attempts in various parts of the Mongol territories to build new empires. One of these was based on the old Seljuk Turkish area of central Asia and it made a considerable impact on Europeans. This was the work of Tamerlane—Timur-i-Lenk. Timur means iron and Lenk lame, for he was lame in both his right arm and leg, but of powerful build and with a chestnut moustache. We know this from the report of the Russian scientists who opened his tomb in Samarkand in 1941 and found his body.

Timur was born in 1336 and died in 1405. In 1366 he seized Samarkand and from then on, leading a new nomad army, he terrorized and conquered the surrounding territories. His first advances were north and east, to the Aral sea and along the north of the Pamirs and Tien Shan mountains. Then in 1381-4 he advanced south towards Herat and Kandahar in Afghanistan. In 1386-8 he campaigned in Azerbaidjan and Persia. In 1391-6 he attacked the Mongol *Golden Horde* in the steppes between the Dnieper and Ural rivers, north of the Caspian sea. In 1398-9 he invaded India, reaching Delhi, and from 1400 he was fighting in Turkey, Georgia and Syria. Timur built up an important empire through ruthless conquests and by continual aggression. His dynasty survived him for a century. His great-great-great-grandson, Babur, conquered India and founded the line of *Mughal* emperors (see pp. 138-9). Samarkand, Timur's capital, became once again a centre of scholarship and science. The first English Astronomer Royal in the 17th century made great use of the astronomical tables worked out in the Observatory of Samarkand, set up by Timur's grandson, Ulugh-beg. Herat, south-west of Samarkand, became, in the 15th century, the centre for the production of Persian miniatures.

DATA DIGEST

Many of the words which are italicized in the previous section are explained more fully in the following data digest. They will help to expand your knowledge of history.

Ainu. Original inhabitants of Japan.

Alani. Russian people who had occupied parts of southern Spain by the fifth century but were conquered by the invading Vandals.

Albigensian Heresy. The Albigenses were a religious sect based in the city of Albi in southern France. They believed that there was a continual struggle between the principles of good and evil and that Jesus had no external reality, but was a kind of angel. They would not eat flesh and insisted on absolute chastity. The Church declared them heretics and a crusade was led against them.

Althing. The parliament of Iceland, the oldest in Europe, was established in 930 by Scandinavian settlers.

Anti-pope. Roman Catholic ecclesiastic elected by a dissident group as pope in opposition to the legitimate pope.

Arab-Berbers. The Berbers are a people inhabiting the western part of North Africa, particularly Algeria, Libya and Morocco. Most speak a Hamitic language though many speak Arabic. Large numbers joined with Arabs in the Islamic invasions in the eighth century though later they fought against the Arabs.

Aryans. Members of a people who spoke languages related to a single ancient language. Sanskrit, the language of the Hindu sacred texts, is developed from it, as are most of the European languages.

Asceticism. Renouncing bodily gratification and living an austere life.

Asgard. The mythological dwelling-place of the Viking gods.

Autocratic. Having absolute power.

Avars. Nomadic people of central Asia who in the sixth and seventh centuries overran southern Russia and the Balkans. They besieged Constantinople unsuccessfully in 626 but remained powerful until defeated by Charlemagne.

Barbarian. To the Romans all people who spoke neither Latin nor Greek were barbarians. More generally it means someone who is uncouth and uncivilized.

Black Death. An epidemic of bubonic plague estimated to have killed one person in every four in Europe during the 14th century.

Bolsheviks. In 1903 the Russian social democratic party split into Bolsheviks, under Lenin, and the more moderate Mensheviks.

Bondage. Condition of servitude.

Bretwalda. Chronicle of the English Saxon kings.

Buddhism. The teachings of Gautama Buddha who lived in India in the fifth century B.C.

Bulgarians. The early Bulgarian empire became extremely powerful under Symeon I and threatened the security of the Byzantine empire. However it was annexed by Basil II in 1018.

Bulgars. A nomadic Asian people who conquered the Slavs of Bulgaria in the seventh century. Later that century the two peoples founded a joint state.

Caliph. The spiritual leader of Islam.

Caravans. Trains of people and pack animals carrying goods for trading and travelling together for security.

Carolingian. Relating to the dynasty of Frankish kings of which Charlemagne was the greatest.

Castes. Social classes, mainly in India.

Christendom. The total area of the world in which Christianity is the recognized religion.

Civil War. War fought between opposing sections or classes of the population within the same country. Civil wars have been fought between different cities, or between nobles, or by nobles against a king and the common people.

Clinker. Clinker-built ships are constructed with overlapping planks for greater strength.

Codification. Systematic collection.

Court. The emperor and his councillors.

Dalai Lama. Spiritual and secular leader of the people of Tibet.

Damascene. An inlay of metal, particularly gold, or other material on steel.

Danelaw. Area of England in which Danish law prevailed. It comprised Northumbria, the eastern and south-eastern Midland and East Anglia.

Dark Ages. The period between the fifth and 11th centuries when western Europe was in decline and learning and the arts were preserved only in monasteries. The Dark Ages were followed by the Middle Ages.

Dominicans. Brotherhood of monks founded in 1220.

Dravidians. People who lived in India before the Aryan invasions.

Edicts. Orders proclaimed by authorities such as monarchs.

Exchequer. The state's financial resources or treasury.

Excommunicate. To cut off from the teachings of the Christian Church.

Feudal. Under a feudal system a lord granted land known as a fief to his vassal in return for an oath of loyalty and the promise of various services.

First Crusade. Launched by the Pope in the 11th century to regain Jerusalem from the Saracens. The crusaders defeated the Turks at Antioch and went on to capture Jerusalem where they created a new kingdom.

Franciscans. Religious order dating from 1224.

Franks. Germanic people who, by the end of the third century, were established in the area of the lower Rhine. They moved into Gaul and became allies of Rome. Clovis I founded the Frankish empire whose greatest ruler was Charlemagne.

Friars. Members of certain religious orders who are allowed more contact with the world than monks. Originally they were allowed to have no possessions of their own. The main orders are Dominicans, Franciscans, Carmelites and Augustinians.

Genoese. Genoa and Venice were rivals in the trade with the East and there were several conflicts during the 13th and 14th centuries.

Golden Age. Period in a country's history when it is at its most powerful and prosperous.

Golden Horde. Batu Khan and his successors were known as the Golden Horde because of their splendid tents.

Goths. A powerful German tribe which in the third century A.D. advanced westwards from the Black Sea area. They split into two groups, the Ostrogoths and the Visigoths.

Guerilla. First used to describe the hit-and-run tactics adopted during the Peninsular War in 1819. Today it has come to refer to the irregular warfare carried on by small groups of people against a superior force of disciplined soldiers.

Guptas. Indian dynasty of 320 A.D.

Han. Ancient Chinese dynasty.

Habsburg. European royal family which provided emperors of Austria almost continuously for more than 600 years.

Heptarchy. Government by seven people or groups.

Heretics. People who opposed the orthodox ideas of the Church.

Hohenstaufen. Family of German princes and kings which was powerful during the 12th and 13th centuries.

Hun. Member of a nomadic Mongoloid tribe originating east of the Volga. Under Attila this tribe was a serious threat to the Roman empire in the fourth and fifth centuries A.D. A combined Roman-Visigoth force defeated the Huns near Chalons-sur-Marne in 451. The following year Attila marched into Italy but did not penetrate to Rome.

Iconoclastic. Opposed to the veneration of images and advocating their destruction.

Infanticide. The killing of new-born children as a social institution.

Judaism. The religion of the Jews.

Kaaba. The most sacred spot in the Islamic world, to which Muslims turn when they pray. It is a building in the Great Mosque at Mecca and encloses a holy Black Stone.

Koreish. The Bedouin tribe to which Muhammad belonged. They grew extremely influential after they became custodians of the Black Stone at Mecca.

Lollards. Followers of John Wycliffe who denounced Roman Catholicism and urged simple worship. Some preached rebellion and the movement was persecuted in the 15th century.

Lombards. A Germanic people who set up a kingdom in northern Italy in the sixth century.

Macedonian. Basil I became emperor in 867 and founded the Macedonian dynasty which ruled the Byzantine empire for 200 years.

Manchu. A people of Manchuria who took Korea and captured Peking in 1644, setting up a ruling dynasty called the Ch'ing.

Mercenaries. Soldiers hired to fight for or in a foreign country.

Merovingian. Relating to the first dynasty of Frankish kings in Gaul. The dynasty was founded by Clovis.

Middle Ages. The period following the Dark Ages, lasting roughly from the 11th to the late 15th century. During this time the economy of western Europe revived and feudalism became the general way of life.

Monotheism. Belief in only one god.

Muslims. Followers of the Islamic religion founded in the seventh century by the prophet Muhammad. Also known as Mohammedans.

Normans. Originally Scandinavian raiders, the Normans had settled in France by the early 10th century. In 1066 William of Normandy took England and at about the same time southern Italy and Sicily also fell to the Normans.

Pagans. Strictly means those who are neither Christian, Jew nor Muslim, but it is often used to mean non-Christians.

Patzinaks. Originally a nomadic people from Russia, they moved westwards and twice threatened Constantinople. Emperor Alexius Comnenus annihilated them at the Battle of Leburnion in 1091.

Poll Tax. Tax levied on all citizens regardless of their wealth. The word 'poll-tax' originally meant 'head-tax', a tax on every 'head' of population levied during the Middle Ages in Europe.

Polygamy. Marriage to more than one partner.

Ramadan. The ninth month of the Muslim year. During this period, Muslims may not eat, drink or smoke between sunrise and sunset.

Renaissance. Rebirth or revival.

Secular. Civil rather than ecclesiastical.

Uighurs. In 744 this partly nomadic people, who were supporters of the Tang dynasty, occupied Mongolia. Then they moved into China.

Vandals. A German people who moved from the Baltic area into Hungary in the late second century A.D. They overran much of the Mediterranean area including parts of northern Africa, and in 455 sacked Rome. The Roman general Belisarius crushed them in 533.

Vassal. In a feudal system a vassal received land from a superior to whom he swore allegiance and rendered various services.

Venetians. Venice was an important trading port as early as the ninth century. It gained control of most of the Dalmatian coast and expanded eastwards particularly in the Levant. After its success against Constantinople in the Fourth Crusade its power increased until it was the premier maritime nation in Europe.

Villein. In a feudal system a serf, bound to his lord though free in other ways.

Islamic soldiers in battle, 624 A.D. as depicted in an Arab print (below).

THE BEGINNINGS OF THE MODERN WORLD

The Unification of Spain

When the Muslims invaded Spain in the eighth century most of the Christians were driven to the mountainous north and west. These Christian communities founded the kingdoms of Astorias (later Léon), Castile, Navarre and Aragon. Some Christians, known as *Mozárabes*, stayed behind under Muslim rule. They grew rich on Muslim trade. They were not persecuted and they learnt much from the more advanced Muslim culture (see pp. 68-9).

In the 11th century Sancho III of Navarre established his power in Léon, Castile and Navarre; his son Ferdinand made the Muslim frontier provinces, Badajoz, Toledo and Seville, pay tribute to him, and he reconquered Coimbra. Portugal and the four Spanish kingdoms each took a sphere of influence beyond the Muslim frontier, which they hoped one day to conquer. Toledo was recovered in 1085; the victories of El Cid in Valencia came a little later. Then the ruler of Morocco led a powerful invasion from Africa: the ground gained was lost and most of the Mozárabes were driven out. This increased bitterness. In the 12th century the Christians advanced again: Toledo became a great cultural centre, and Santiago de Compostella a place of pilgrimage for all Europe. But the Muslims recovered their strength and unity through a third Moroccan invasion, though they did not manage to regain all their lost land.

In the 13th century the Christians united under papal influence, and defeated the Muslims in one battle after another. By 1276 the only Moorish kingdom left in Spain was that of Granada. The crusading order of the Knights Templars helped in the reconquest of Spain. The new areas were difficult to absorb, because they were densely populated with Arabs and Moors from Morocco, and there were no Mozárabes. The Christian rulers were delighted with the luxuries and the trade of Córdoba, Lisbon and Seville, and took a new interest in the sea. But they did not unite in their attempts to gain Gibraltar. Instead they quarrelled among themselves, divided the land among nobles and religious orders, and turned the Muslims into second-class citizens.

In the 15th century Aragon had built up

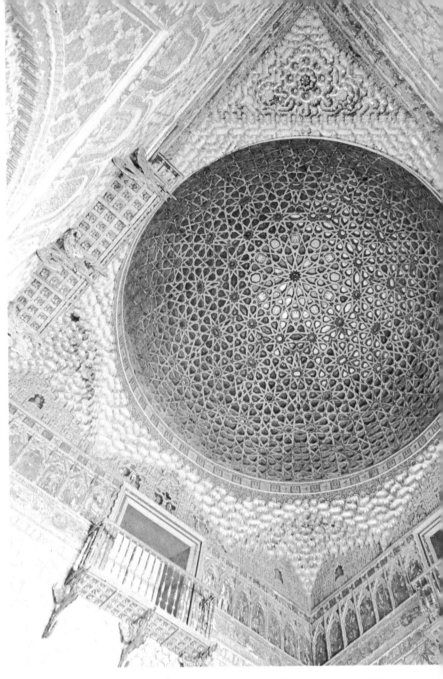

The influence of the Moorish invaders remained in Spain long after the conquerers had themselves been conquered. Above, ceiling and dome in the Alcazar, Seville, shows Hispano-Moorish art at its most elaborate.

her trade in the Mediterranean and became involved in the affairs of France and Italy, but by the end of the century her trade was declining and she needed new opportunities. Henry IV of Castile cared chiefly for luxury, and was unable to control nobles, towns, or religious orders. At his death there was a civil war between the supporters of his daughter, Joanna, and his half-sister Isabella. Isabella was supported by the more responsible Castilians, including Cardinal Jiménez, who arranged her marriage to Ferdinand, the heir of Aragon. His support was vital, for she had to defeat the nobles, supported by Portugal and France. Her marriage united Castile and Aragon, and by 1479 she was secure on the throne. She drastically reduced the power of the nobles. She took away the crown lands they had acquired, and she became head of the religious orders. The *Córtes*, or parliament of Castile, had no power; the council decided on laws and taxes. Royal officials brought

towns under control; royal courts enforced the law; the *Holy Brotherhood* was used as a police force. The Pope gave Isabella control over the Church, which she reformed. Sheep farming, trade and exploration were encouraged. In 1492 Columbus discovered the West Indies, and before the end of the reign new trade was flowing into Seville. Taxes in Castile were so easy to collect and brought in so much money that Ferdinand and Isabella did not have to worry about Aragon; Castile was the centre of their power.

In 1492 Granada was reconquered, and Isabella and Ferdinand had to cope with the problem of Jews and Moors. Under pressure thousands became nominally Christian but in fact practised their old religions; full of resentment, they were ready to revolt or support Moorish pirates or invaders. In 1492 the Jews were expelled, and in 1502 Muslims who would not accept baptism: many valuable craftsmen were thereby lost to Spain. Converts were spied on by the *Inquisi-*

tion, which was under royal control. The Moorish converts remained anti-Catholic and therefore anti-Spanish living in the part of Spain most vulnerable to an Arab invasion. Uniformity was enforced, but the danger remained until all the remaining *Moriscos* (converted Moors) were expelled in 1509. In 1512 Ferdinand annexed Navarre, and the unification of Spain was achieved.

After 1504, when Isabella died, there was a danger that Spain might break apart again, for her son was dead and her weak-minded daughter Joanna, not Ferdinand, was the heir to Castile. Ferdinand remarried, but unfortunately had no children, for these would have been heirs to Aragon. In 1516 Joanna's son Charles, by Philip, the Habsburg Archduke, became king of all Spain as Charles I, and later ruler of the Netherlands, Germany, Austria and much of Italy, as Holy Roman Emperor Charles V. His empire ·became the greatest power in Europe.

Right: The Spanish Inquisition struck terror into the hearts of the country's Muslims and Jews. Those who would not convert to Christianity were expelled: those who did convert were spied upon and often interrogated and tortured by the Inquisition.

The Unification of France—Joan of Arc to Henry IV

France and England had been engaged in a recurring conflict since 1337, when Edward III had claimed the French crown. This lasted until 1453 and came to be called the 'Hundred Years War'. Henry V of England, after the defeat of the French at the battle of Agincourt in 1415, controlled most of northern France, including Paris, as far south as the Loire, and much of Gascony and Guienne in the south-west as well. After his marriage to Catherine, daughter of Charles VI of France (1380-1422), Henry had an additional claim to the French crown. Quarrels between Charles VI and his nobles weakened the French monarchy: the Dukes of Burgundy allied with England.

Henry V's death in 1422 and the succession of an infant, Henry VI, gave the French hope. Charles VI, incompetent and mentally deranged, died in the same year. The *Dauphin* refused to accept the English claim to the crown. In 1428 the Duke of Bedford (regent for his nephew Henry VI) attempted to seize Orléans. It was at this moment that Jeanne d'Arc (Joan of Arc), a peasant girl from Domrémy in Lorraine, persuaded many Frenchmen that she could inspire the French forces to victory. Later a prophecy was attached to her achievements that the

kingdom 'lost through a woman (Charles's mother Isabel) would be redeemed through a woman'. Joan herself had two goals: to raise the siege of Orléans and to see the *Dauphin* crowned as Charles VII in Rheims. Both were achieved, but not long after the coronation Joan was captured, sold to the English, tried and *burnt at the stake* in Rouen in 1431 for witchcraft.

Joan of Arc became an inspiring symbol for the French in their struggle for national unity. Charles VII was reconciled to the Duke of Burgundy in 1435 and was able to recover Paris (1436). He gained the support of the merchants and bankers of the northern French trading centres, and in 1449 the English were forced to withdraw from all France north of the Loire. By 1453 they were also driven from Gascony and Guienne; the greater part of France was now free of English rule.

During the reign of Louis XI (1461-1483), Charles's son, an effective administration was established. A rigorous tax system provided money for an effective army, and communications were improved through a good road system and postal service. Louis had to contend with conspiracies of *feudal*

The Battle of Crécy (above) was the first great victory by Edward III's invading English army over the French. The two sides met east of Crécy, 45 kilometres south of Boulogne. The English were outnumbered three to one but their disciplined lines and their new weapon, the longbow, ensured their victory. The longbow was far superior in range and rapidity to the crossbow (both shown on the right). Its range of 250 metres decimated the French cavalry.

Left: In 1428 Joan of Arc convinced many, including the Dauphin, that she could inspire the French armies to victory. But her enemies saw her as a sorcerer not a saint and, in 1430, she was sold to the English who burnt her at the stake as a witch.

Above: Henry IV with Maria de'Medici by Rubens. Under Henry's reign French unity became possible.

vassals, particularly the Dukes of Burgundy. Provence, Maine and Anjou were added to France but Flanders and Franche-Comte were lost. Louis's successors did little. But the last decades of the 15th century saw France influenced greatly by the *Renaissance* (see pp. 110-13). France's 'renaissance prince' was Francis I (1515-47), who encouraged learning and humanism, brought the great Italian artist and scholar Leonardo da Vinci to France, and more than any other French king of the 16th century enhanced the prestige and power of the French nation. He established a strong central government and built several great royal residences. France extended her interests into northern Italy and rivalled the power of the Habsburg monarchs (see pp. 102-3).

John Calvin, a student in the University of Paris from 1535 to 1553, led an attack on French Roman Catholicism (see pp. 114-15). Francis I had achieved an independent *Gallican* Church and opposed the more extreme demands of the French reformers. Calvin and his followers were forced to flee to Geneva. Nevertheless, the French Calvinists (called *Huguenots*) grew in numbers and influence, many nobles and a large propor-

tion of the merchant classes joined them. The period 1560-1593 was one of factional strife over deep religious differences (see pp. 114-15) because of conflict between the great royal houses of the Guises and the Bourbons. Catherine de' Medici, who had married Francis's son, Henry II, was the virtual ruler from 1559 to 1589. The leader of the Protestant cause was Henry of Navarre, grandson of Francis I and representative of the Bourbons. He was also heir to the crown which he inherited on the assassination of Henry III.

Henry IV came to the throne in 1589. He became a Roman Catholic and was crowned at Chartres. By persuading his opponents that peace was essential to a devastated country, he entered Paris and ended the period of anarchy. The Protestants were assured of religious liberty in the *Edict of Nantes*, 1598. Aided by his able and efficient minister, the Duke of Sully, he established a unified France. In 1610 Henry was assassinated. His Bourbon successors, Louis XIII and Louis XIV (see p. 238), with their ministers Cardinal Richelieu and Cardinal Mazarin, were to make France the strongest single power in Europe and a threat to their nearest neighbour, England.

Right: A Victorian painting of the princes in the Tower of London. The princes, sons of Edward IV, were seized and imprisoned by their uncle, who became Richard III, on their father's death. The fate of the young princes was never fully explained.

When Henry VIII declared himself head of the English Church he confiscated Church property and much of it fell into disrepair, such as (below) the ruined abbey at Whitby, Yorkshire.

The Unification of England under the Tudors

The English kings in the early Middle Ages had been powerful, compared with their barons. Later kings were weaker and this led to the Wars of the Roses. Edward III became a feeble old man, Richard II tried to regain power and roused resentment, particularly that of his cousin Henry Bolingbroke. Richard exiled Henry. While he was abroad Henry's father, John of Gaunt, Duke of Lancaster, died, so Richard took his lands. Henry returned, deposed Richard, and made himself Henry IV. He always had to act cautiously, for he was short of money, and knew his claim to the throne could be challenged by the *Yorkists.* Henry V was more popular because of his victories in the *Hundred Years War,* but he left a young, over-pious and over-submissive son, Henry VI. Government was in the hands of his council of quarrelling barons. Barons, like the Duke of York and the Earl of Warwick, had large numbers of retainers, gentlemen paid to support them in their quarrels. Henry VI could be bullied easily, but not his wife, Margaret of Anjou.

War broke out in 1455. Richard, Duke of York, seized power and ruled in Henry VI's name. Margaret fought on; York was killed and Edward, his son, supported by Warwick, claimed the crown himself. Edward IV ruled well and made himself financially independent by combining crown lands with his own estates. But he refused to be guided by Warwick's advice, and in fury and frustration the earl changed sides, and led the Lancastrians in war in 1471. He was defeated. When Edward died in 1483, leaving two young sons, Edward and Richard, their uncle Richard seized the throne and the two princes disappeared. Perhaps Richard III was a better ruler than young Edward could have been, but in 1485 Henry Tudor, last leader of the Lancastrian faction, invaded with a small army. He was lucky, for some powerful nobles deserted Richard at the last moment, and Richard was killed at the battle of Bosworth. Henry had himself crowned as Henry VII, the first Tudor monarch. He married Elizabeth of York and combined the two badges, the white rose of York and the red rose of Lancaster, which gave to these civil wars their popular name, the Wars of the Roses.

There were several people with strong claims to the throne. Henry faced and defeated three rebellions. If any had had firm support from foreign rulers the Tudors might have lost the throne, but Henry's

Sir Thomas More (left) was Henry VIII's Lord Chancellor but when he refused to recognize the king as head of the Church in England he was tried for treason, found guilty and executed in 1535.

skilful foreign policy prevented this. At first Henry was short of money, but this was remedied by his careful management. He reclaimed all the estates which had been held by both Lancastrian and Yorkist kings, and ensured that all debts were paid. He chose his councillors carefully so that they governed as he directed. He used his council frequently as a court, 'the Court of Star Chamber', and set up similar councils for Wales and the North of England, so that law was better enforced. He tried to establish English rule in Ireland, though this was still a problem for Henry VIII and Elizabeth I. After a period of depression English trade recovered and farming became more profitable. The population increased and England became more prosperous. Henry's government depended on his ability, that of the men he chose to serve him, and his willingness to supervise every detail.

His son Henry VIII became king in 1509, able but less willing to work. He chose capable ministers, Thomas Wolsey and Thomas Cromwell, and left them to manage; they continued Henry VII's work. Cromwell reorganized the *medieval* system of government, laying the foundations of a professional *(bureaucratic)* civil service and creating the modern state machinery, the offices of Secretary of State for example. Henry became anxious because his wife, Catherine of Aragon, gave him no son and heir, and he wanted to replace her. When the Pope refused permission Henry found that the

The strength of a united England reached its climax in the defeat of the Spanish Armada off the coast of England in 1588. The hostilities came about because of religious and personal enmity between Roman Catholic Philip II of Spain and Protestant Elizabeth I of England. Philip's fleet was the greatest the world had ever seen—24 galleons, 40 converted merchantmen, 25 supply hulks and 36 smaller vessels. His armada carried 30,000 men. England's fleet consisted of 21 first-line ships, 40 of the second line and many smaller vessels. The English fleet had only 14,000 men but had twice as many cannon as the Spanish fleet. The English adopted new tactics of trying to outmanoeuvre and sink the enemy rather than attempting to board and take possession.

Pope's authority conflicted with his own. Cromwell suggested he should claim that a king must be master even of the Church in his kingdom. Henry stopped his subjects appealing to the Pope, or sending money; he declared himself head of the Church. This enabled him to remarry, but he did not intend to change the faith or the services of the Church.

The remaining Tudor monarchs were Henry VIII's three children: Edward VI, Mary I and Elizabeth I (see p. 235). As Edward VI was young when he succeeded to the throne, royal power temporarily declined, but the Church of England became Protestant. His successor, Mary I, tried to make England Roman Catholic again, but failed. Elizabeth I, in her turn, declared herself 'Governor' of a moderately Protestant Church. She maintained royal power with skill although she was always short of money, so that she had to listen to *Parliament.* She remained calm in the face of the threat that the French might support Mary Queen of Scots' claim to the English throne, or that Philip II of Spain might invade; when Parliament demanded strong measures over this or the Church she listened, but rarely gave way. Fundamentally, whatever their criticisms, all supported her against foreigners, so England was united as never before. There was rapid population increase, a tremendous growth of cities, the appearance of new industries and a rise in the standard of living.

The Slav Nations

During the 14th century many Europeans began to be conscious of a national as opposed to a feudal loyalty. This new 'nationalism' became effective when royal *autocrats* succeeded in establishing powerful *dynasties*. Successful princely government led to the creation of unified nation states in much of western Europe. However, Italy remained, until the 19th century, divided between the Pope's claim to the loyalty of Italians and the claims of Spanish, French and Austrian princes. Germany was divided too: there were powerful German states like Bavaria and Prussia; and there was a European power, the Austrian (Holy Roman) empire, which was ruled by Germans, although its subjects included Belgians, Italians and Slavs.

National consciousness had long stirred among the Slav peoples but it was not until the late 19th and 20th centuries that independent nation states first came into existence, except in Russia (see pp. 114-15). Eastern Europe's development was behind western Europe's in time, not because of any inherent backwardness of her peoples but because by its geographical situation eastern Europe provided the buffer which protected the Continent from Asiatic nomads.

The nomadic Slav tribes had been converted to Christianity and civilized by the Byzantine culture of the eastern Roman empire. They used a *Cyrillic* (Greek-Russian) alphabet and belonged to the *Orthodox* not the Roman Catholic branch of Christianity. By the early 13th century the kingdom of Bulgaria under the *Asen dynasty*, Bohemia under the *Premyslids*, and *Magyar* Hungary were powerful and cultured states. Serbia had been united in 1169 under a single monarchy which ruled not only Serbia but Bosnia, Dalmatia and Croatia. Under Stephen Dushan (1331-55) this monarchy reached its height. Patriotic, national traditions and legends go back to these very early times. St. Stephen was crowned king of Hungary in 1001 and his crown became a national emblem. St. Wenceslas was King Vaclav, who was murdered in 929, a founder of the Czech Premyslid dynasty.

Two historical forces stopped the development of eastern Europe and kept it backwards for centuries: one came from outside Europe, the other was European. In 1241 a Mongol army (see pp. 84-5) swept through Poland, just when Polish tribes had begun to develop some national cohesion. Poland and Silesia were devastated. Another Mongol army crossed the *Carpathians* and defeated the Hungarian king, Bela IV (1235-70). The land was depopulated and disorganized; Ukrainian fugitives from the Mongols added to the chaos.

The Czechs in the kingdom of Bohemia under Ottakar II (1253-78) benefited most from the devastation left by the Mongols. For a time Ottakar became master of Austria, Styria, Carinthia and the Tyrol. The disintegration of Poland and the decline of Hungary gave the Czech Premyslid dynasty their opportunity. But the effect of the expansion of the Czech kingdom into German lands was to bring German settlers in large numbers into Bohemia; the country became a land of two races with different interests and characters. Poland had already been absorbed in the German *Drang nach Osten* (Drive to the East) which had begun in 1143 when German colonists moved east of the Elbe. The *Teutonic Knights*, founded in the 1190s, conquered Slav territories.

This German cultural and economic penetration into Slav territories was only one aspect of the decisive influence which came from western into eastern Europe.

Above: A drawing of a Teutonic Knight. This order of knights conquered Slav territories in the 12th century.

Below: The Hus monument in Prague, erected to commemorate the Czech nationalist Jan Hus and his religious movement.

108

The disintegration of the newly-established Slav nations was hastened by waves of invading Mongols in the 13th century. First Poland and Silesia were crushed; then Hungary.

Left: 'Good King Wenceslas' (Vaclav in Czech) was murdered in 929 by reactionaries led by his brother.

Another was that of the Roman Church. Hungary belonged to the Orthodox Church but the western influence converted the country to the Roman Church. Hungarian expansion southwards, under Koloman I (1095-1116), brought the Croats into the Roman Church. The Czechs also became Roman Christians. In Poland conflict between the Roman and Orthodox Churches was long lasting. The southern Slavs, except for the Croats, remained Orthodox.

The final disintegration of Slavdom was the consequence of growing feudalism. In Hungary the nobility had extracted the 'Golden Bull' from King Andrew II (1205-35), which gave the nobles liberty and brought anarchy to the kingdom. In Poland the nobility made the kingship elective; there was an end to any strong central power. The southern Slavs finally lost their independence to the Ottoman Turks (see pp. 166-7), who conquered Bulgaria in 1393 and

annexed Serbia in 1459. Romania was fought over through the 15th century and finally absorbed by the Turks. The rest of eastern Europe, from the 15th to the 20th centuries, was a battleground between German states and Russian Tsardom.

Twice only did an independent movement emerge. Poland and Lithuania were united under Jagiello (1386-1434) and became a major power. In Bohemia the religious and social movement led by Jan Hus (1370-1415) produced a revival of Czech national consciousness and became in part a movement against German domination. The *Hussite* peasant armies maintained Czech independence from 1419 to 1434 and began to build a new society, but the German feudal nobility and the Roman Church finally crushed the Hussite movement. Bohemia and Moravia, Hungary, Slovakia and Croatia were all absorbed into the Austrian Habsburg empire. Poland was a divided nation.

Renaissance Art

Realism is the chief characteristic of Renaissance Art. A study of nature and a knowledge of perspective, shading and colour are needed to create a picture which seems to be a window on the world. In the Middle Ages forms of art developed independently in north and south Europe. But whereas the *medieval* artists painted religious subjects, aiming at telling a story and inspiring prayer, the Renaissance artist had greater freedom in his handling of *classical* and religious themes, portraits and landscapes. In the Middle Ages pictures were usually commissioned by the Church, or given to churches. During the Renaissance pictures were just as likely to decorate palaces or civic buildings.

You can see the early use of *perspective* and natural background in the *illuminations* of the Duke of Berry's *Book of Hours* done by the Flemish brothers Limburg in about 1410. In one there are blue sky and a castle behind cornfields with peasants at work; but the proportion is not true and the landscape seems to open only a little way behind the page. There is realism in the carving of the country scenes on *miserere seats* and in the statues of some 12th and 13th century cathedrals. There is shading in the pictures of Giotto di Bondone (c.1266-1337). We have realistic sketches of natural objects by Il Pisanello (before 1395 to after 1455). But in most cases the aim of the picture is still to tell a story; it is not a window on the real world.

The Renaissance gave new impetus to realism in art. Rich merchants like the Medici and Pazzi families of Florence, princes like the Dukes of Milan, popes like Julius II and Leo X, were able to spend huge sums on churches, palaces, pictures and statues; they wanted classical subjects as well as religious ones. The architect Filippo Brunelleschi (1377-1446) measured the ruins of Roman and *Etruscan* buildings to find out how they built huge arches and domes. He used Roman arches and Greek columns and *pediments*, and concentrated on balance and proportion. The dome of Florence Cathedral and the little Pazzi chapel are examples of his work. Other architects followed his lead; but in the north the *Gothic style* survived, and classical ideas only influenced details, until the 17th century.

Brunelleschi worked out the mathematical laws of perspective, and influenced his friends, Masaccio (1401-1428) and Donatello (c.1386-1466). Masaccio painted scenes from the Bible on the walls of the Brancacci chapel in Florence, using perspective and

shading so accurately that the spectator feels that he is witnessing the event. Donatello made statues so full of life and force of character that one half expects them to move. Art flourished as never before, as dozens of sculptors, artists and architects developed these ideas further. The most outstanding were:

Sandro Botticelli (c.1444-1510), a painter of classical themes

Bramante (1444-1514), the original designer of St. Peter's, Rome

Leonardo da Vinci (1452-1519)

Michelangelo Buonarroti (1475-1564)

Raphael (1483-1520)

We can see most clearly the way in which Leonardo tackled his work. In his notebooks

Above: The simple, direct style of Fra Angelico, a Dominican friar, is shown in a scene from the frescoes he painted to decorate the convent of San Marco, Florence.

Below: A scene from the Lives of the Apostles by Masaccio, the first of the great masters of 15th century Florence.

Right, above: The architect Filippo Brunelleschi took his inspiration for the dome of Florence Cathedral from Roman and Etruscan ruins.

Right, below: A detail from Michelangelo's sculpture on the Tomb of Lorenzo de' Medici, his patron.

natural details—hands, grass, old buildings.

In the middle and later 16th century many Italian artists, including Titian and Jacopo Tintoretto, explored the possibilities of brilliant colour, sharp contrasts of light and shade, and exaggerated movement, in paintings of religious and classical themes. El Greco (1541-1614) in Spain combined *Byzantine* and Italian ideas in elongated figures showing human emotion and religious mystery at the same time. In the north of Europe, Hans Holbein the Younger (c. 1497-1543), a German working mostly in the English court, concentrated on portraits. Pieter Brueghel the Elder (c.1525-1569) in Antwerp painted comic peasant scenes. Art flourished most in Antwerp, the centre of the spice and cloth trades, and the home of bankers. Italy was much poorer after a long series of wars (1494-1559). Nearly everywhere artists found fewer patrons, and seemed to be struggling in vain for new inspiration, or merely copying the achievements of the past. Peter Paul Rubens (1577-1640) was the last great painter of Antwerp. He combined all the technical achievements and freedom of the Renaissance in a huge number of works. Then Antwerp declined and Holland became prosperous; the Dutch masters carried on the realistic tradition of the Renaissance.

there are many sketches from life, of the human body, rock forms and natural objects. Leonardo took a thoroughly scientific interest in his subjects. He and his rival, Michelangelo (see p. 240), both dissected bodies in their study of anatomy, but Michelangelo concentrated on the nude figure. His statues became larger than life, and through their weight and tense muscles they express the deepest and most violent emotions. His greatest works were the tomb of Julius II and the ceiling of the Sistine Chapel in the Vatican, but he was also a poet and one of the architects of St. Peter's.

Meanwhile, in the north, Jan van Eyck (c.1366-1440) was painting pictures exact in every detail, with landscape backgrounds which sweep away into the distance. Later painters, such as Jean Fouquet (c.1416-1480) from France and Rogier van der Weyden (c.1399-1464) from the Netherlands, were influenced by the Italians, but the northerners still used their art to tell a story. Their skills in detailed drawing, carving and printing were employed in woodcuts and engravings on copper plates. These provided illustrations for prayer-books and could emphasise religious and political arguments; the greatest exponent of this art was Albrecht Dürer (1471-1528). All his work was based on the accurate study of

111

Right: The sacking of Constantinople in 1204. The Crusaders returned to Venice with a bounty of books and works of art which provided the intellectual stimulus which led to the Italian Renaissance.

The invention of the printing press in the mid-15th century revolutionized the world of learning. The German, Johannes Gutenberg, pioneered the new art of typography with a press which printed from metal types. Printing spread swiftly across Europe and in the next 50 years an estimated nine million books were printed compared with only 60,000-80,000 manuscripts of learning and poetry which existed in the world up to that time.

Renaissance Ideas

Renaissance means rebirth. The term was invented by French and Italian historians to describe the ideas of the 15th and 16th centuries, which they believed sprang from a revival of interest in the classics. Greek and Latin literatures were studied for their own sake. There was a great growth of literature in many languages. There was keen interest in the natural world, and in the life of this world rather than the next. Education received much attention, and a critical attitude was taken to everything, especially religion. Most of these interests were not new, but they had existed in isolation and had produced no dramatic consequences. The combination stimulated changes in every field of human thought.

Greek was rarely studied in the Middle Ages; Latin was the language of scholars. Virgil and Cicero and other Latin writers were carefully studied, but the Fathers of the Church warned scholars to absorb the language only and to despise the *pagan* ideas. The ideas of the Greek philosopher Aristotle, about nature and philosophy, copied and altered by the Muslims, altered

again by Saint Thomas Aquinas, were accepted as gospel truth. But all study was just a preparation for the deeper study of Christian truth.

In the 14th and 15th centuries a trickle of Greek scholars reached Italy by way of Venice or Sicily (see pp. 166-7); a few Italians took endless trouble to learn the language and unearth the manuscripts buried in monastery libraries. The real ideas of the Greeks and the Romans were more stimulating than the distorted versions they had read before, and there were many writers whose works had not been read for years. Accurate texts were produced, and in the 15th and 16th centuries they were printed on the new printing presses and studied in every country of Europe. People knew that *Cicero* wrote letters to his friends and longed for gossip and news when in exile from Rome; politics were his passion, not the cold morality of *About Old Age*. They found that *Catullus* and *Propertius* wrote love poetry. They knew that the Greeks were curious about everything in the world. They read accounts of *Socrates'* persistent questioning of every authority. It stimulated them to imitate, and to find out for themselves. They found patrons to encourage them in the rich

As well as being a gifted artist Leonardo da Vinci was an extensive inventor. Below is a diagram of Leonardo's self-unlocking crane hook. 1. Weight pulling down on the hook secures it. 2. When the load touches the ground and there is no pull on the hook the counter-weight falls down and the hook disengages.

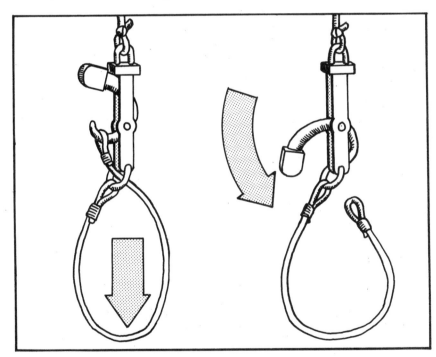

cities of Italy and later in every court of Europe.

Interest was not confined to classical literature. In the 14th century Dante, Petrarch and Boccaccio wrote sonnets and longer poems about life and love, in Italian. Chaucer did likewise, in English. In French there was the *Roman de la Rose*. In the 15th and 16th centuries literature in many languages poured from the printing presses. All human emotions could be expressed in liter-

ature. Cervantes in Spanish described the adventures of a knight, Don Quixote, who took fiction too seriously; Rabelais in France filled his books with a huge variety of characters; Shakespeare's plays show the serious and humorous sides of life and the power of human emotions. Every courtier was expected to 'turn a pretty phrase', to write sonnets and set them to music. The 'vulgar tongue' was now rich and respected.

There were no limits to curiosity about the natural world. The Florentine Leonardo da Vinci (1452-1519) filled his notebooks with sketches of natural objects. He dissected bodies and drew internal organs; he sketched birds' wings and tried to work out how they flew; he designed pumps and guns and engines of all kinds. Very few of his inventions were put to use, but he is important because he insisted that men can find out how nature works and use their knowledge. Nicolaus Copernicus (1473-1543) (see pp. 130-3) questioned whether *Ptolemy* was right in saying that the Sun, planets and stars move around the Earth; some Greeks did not agree with Ptolemy and observation showed that the planets' paths were most intricate. It was simpler to think that the Sun was the centre of the universe.

Education was important, not only for a career in the Church or the law courts, but also for kings and their ministers, for courtiers and gentlemen. The example was set by Vittorino da Feltre, tutor to the Dukes of Mantua and the school at the court of Urbino. Latin and Greek grammar led to a study of classical writings, and the art of argument. Fencing, riding, music and good taste in art were encouraged. Good teachers cared for the moral education of their pupils, and the whole was completed by a study of philosophy. This standard was the subject of Count Baldassare Castiglione's *Book of the Courtier*, which was translated into French and English and reprinted many times. It formed the basis of the good secular education given by *Jesuit* schools in Europe, and influenced the curricula of English *public schools* and French *lycées*.

The new critical attitude had revolutionary results when applied to religion. Desiderius Erasmus (c. 1466-1536) found that the *Vulgate*, the Latin version of the Bible produced by St. Jerome in the fourth century, was inaccurate in many places. He produced an edition of the New Testament with Greek and a correct Latin version side by side, for comparison. He looked forward to the day when the gospels 'might be translated into all tongues of all people, the countryman might sing them at his plough and the weaver at his loom'. His wish was granted in the *Reformation*.

The Reformation

The *Protestant Reformation* was a religious movement which grew out of the concern of many in western Europe in the late 15th century to revive the life of the Church. *Renaissance* scholars, such as Desiderius Erasmus (1466-1536), sought to make available, through studying commentaries and new editions of the *Old* and *New Testaments*, a wider understanding of the scriptures and Christian teaching. Others attacked the authority of the Pope, which they felt limited the freedom of the Church in countries distant from Rome. Still others felt that the Church was corrupt, had concentrated too much wealth in its hands, and that there had been a decline of morality in the various monastic communities and among the clergy.

From the fact that they made a formal 'protest' against both Roman Catholic doctrine and Roman Catholic interpretation of the *scriptures*, they became known as *Protestants*. It is from this movement that most separate Christian Churches originate; non-Roman Christians are known as *Protestants* to this day. The Reformation was one of the most significant upheavals of European history. Like many historical processes the Reformation took years to come about, but the significant departure point came in 1517, when a German Augustinian monk, Martin Luther, nailed to the door of All Saints' Church, Wittenberg, his 'ninety-five theses', in which he set forward his criticisms of the Church. He argued that men and women are 'saved by grace alone' and not by any good work which they do, particularly payments or gifts which they might make to the Church. By this argument

Luther's central doctrine came to be based on the idea that 'Justification (or salvation) is attained by faith alone'.

Martin Luther, who lived from about 1483 to 1546, was the son of a Saxony miner who had hoped that his son might become a lawyer. Luther, however, was of a very religious turn of mind and became a monk and priest. He had a deep consciousness of personal sin. Although the Church taught that by confession and repentance a man could be absolved from his offences, he seems never to have felt that this was enough. He became a lecturer in religion at the University of Wittenberg, and visited Rome in 1510. He was deeply shocked by the seeming irreverence of many Roman priests, and the corruption and luxurious living of the higher officials. In particular, he was shocked by the practice of selling *indulg-*

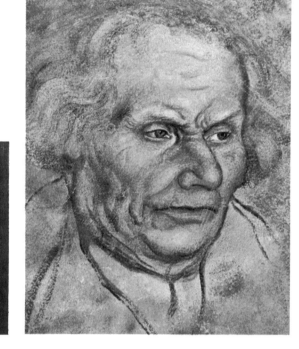

Three men dominated the campaign to reform the Christian Church which swept Europe in the late 15th century. Above: The Dutch philosopher, Desiderius Erasmus, sought to establish a wider understanding of Christian teaching. Above right: Martin Luther saw the corruption of the existing Church and preached a purer form of Christianity and (left) John Calvin, the French scholar who viewed Christianity with a stern simplicity.

ences (automatic pardons for sins) to those who could afford to pay for them. Luther decided that no one, not even the Pope, could forgive sins on this basis. He formed the view that a man was justified, in God's eyes, solely by his faith.

The Pope condemned Luther for heresy but the Elector of Saxony protected him; and other German princes, inspired by nationalism and the desire to have absolute power in their own territories, supported him against both the Pope and the Emperor. Summoned to a trial by the Emperor, Charles V, Luther refused to recant, and made his now famous declaration: 'Here I stand, God help me; I cannot do otherwise.'

A Lutheran Church emerged and Germany became divided. The Lutheran states were forced to defend themselves against the Emperor, who ordered them to abandon

Lutheran teachings. The states formed the *Schmalkaldic League* in 1531, and considerable fighting took place between the Emperor and the Lutheran states. In 1552 the French intervened on the Protestant side to check the power of the Empire. Peace was eventually agreed to in the *Peace of Augsburg* of 1555, which recognized a stalemate and left Germany half Protestant and half Roman Catholic.

Huldreich Zwingli began in 1519, in Zurich, Switzerland, an attack on the institutions of the Church; a separate Protestant movement which came to be called the *Reformed Church*, as distinguished from the Lutheran tradition, was established. Much of Switzerland accepted Zwingli's teachings as did a number of German communities, particularly Strasbourg, Constance and Lindau. An even more famous leader of the Reformed tradition emerged in France. This was John Calvin, a French scholar, who was forced to leave his country in 1534 because of his teachings. Having gone to Basel, he there wrote the *Christian Institutes*, the most influential work of the Protestant Reformation. From 1536 he was established at Geneva, which became the

Charles I cleverly exploited religion to rally support in the civil war that broke out in England in 1642. He appealed to his people as the defender of the established Church against those who wished to impose severe puritanism. The King's supporters were known as Cavaliers, his opponents as Roundheads. The common soldiers of the opposing armies wore very similar uniforms, but the New Model Army (Roundheads) were distinguished by the red garment worn under their armour.

centre of the reformed Churches.

The English Reformation was largely political in its early stages (see pp. 106-7). Only in the 17th century did extreme Protestant ideas become popular, lead to the Civil War and leave behind the *Dissenting* or *Nonconformist* Churches. In Scotland the Reformation occurred late, in 1560. The regent, Mary of Lorraine, and her daughter, the young Queen Mary Stuart, continued to adhere to Roman Catholicism. The Calvinist lords, supported by the ministers, banded together with English help to drive out the French who assisted Mary of Lorraine.

Lutheranism and Calvinism spread, in spite of the Counter Reformation (see pp. 116-17): Lutheranism to the Scandinavian countries, Calvinism to most north-west European countries. In the Netherlands Calvinism won many adherents from the 1530s, but particularly in the 1550s. A defensive league was formed under the leadership of William the Silent, prince of Orange, and from 1566 clashes occurred between the league and Spanish troops, and as the northern provinces became united the conflict intensified. In 1609 the United provinces secured a truce and recognition by Spain.

The Counter Reformation

The counter Reformation was the reform of the Roman Catholic Church in reaction to the Reformation. It sprang from the same roots as the Reformation: the critical attitude to the Church, the wish to think out afresh what Christian beliefs really are, and to teach them more effectively. The first signs can be found in Spain in the late 15th century. Ferdinand and Isabella encouraged Cardinal Jiminez to appoint bishops who would be interested in their *dioceses* and to insist that they looked after them instead of spending all their time on politics. Jiminez encouraged the publication of the Bible and was most generous to the university of Salamanca.

Left: Pope Paul III agreed to reform the Church in Rome. He revived the Inquisition to keep out Protestant ideas and under his auspices the Order of the Jesuits was established.

Everyone agreed that reform was necessary, that good bishops should procure holy priests and train them to teach the people. But both rulers and popes wanted to carry out reform in their own way and to remain in control. The Pope's *Lateran Council* of 1512-1517 attempted reform in Italy, but failed as rulers would not co-operate. In 1516 by a *Concordat*, or agreement, the Pope allowed French kings to choose and control their own clergy. There was talk of a *Council* of the whole Church, but nothing came of

Although the need for reform in the Roman Church was widely accepted, it took 30 years to convene a council of the whole Church—and even then it took place without the French bishops. Despite many problems over the next ten years, the Council of Trent (above) led to sweeping reforms in the Church, defining its doctrine and strengthening discipline.

it. The French kings were at war with Charles V and popes feared he would dominate any Council. Co-operation was impossible while half of Europe had been lost to the Protestants. Catholic action was left very much to individuals.

In 1521 a Spanish knight, Ignatius Loyola, broke his leg. After a period of intense pain Ignatius knew he would never fight again. He lived in poverty, helping beggars and studying at universities in Spain and Paris. With seven friends he formed the 'Company of Jesus' in 1534. They offered themselves to the Pope, who distrusted their enthusiasm. Their first idea, to convert the *Muslims*, was obviously impossible. But in 1540 their rule was approved; they formed a spiritual army ready to go anywhere and do anything the Pope might direct. Their head was a general, and his men vowed to obedience. Francis Xavier went to India and Japan as a missionary; Roberto de Nobili combined Catholic truth with *Hindu* culture, and Matteo Ricci did the same for the *Confucians* of China. Jesuits in Peru and Mexico converted the natives and stood up for their rights. Edmund Campion and Robert Persons risked their lives to minister to the few remaining English Roman Catholics and to convert others. Jesuit schools were most successful, and Jesuit colleges for priests an example for others. Orders of teaching nuns were founded on a similar pattern, so that in every country there were lay Roman Catholics, convinced and well educated, of both sexes, acting as a magnet to the rest.

In Italy small societies of dedicated priests and bishops formed, to discuss ideas and give each other moral support. An example is 'the Oratory' of which Pope Paul IV, who set up the *Index* (a list of forbidden books), was a member. Paul III put his own *Church of Rome* in order and revived the *Inquisition*

(to stamp out Protestant ideas within the Church). He acted by force of law, not persuasion, and had no interest in compromise or peace with Protestants. In 1545 the long awaited *Council of Trent* met, but still without the French bishops. Discussions were guided by the Pope's representatives and ideas put forward by Jesuits and leading reformers were adopted:

1) Luther's idea that the Bible is the only source of Christianity was opposed by saying that truth is found 'both in Scripture and Tradition'. The Church did not abandon traditional practices.

2) Preaching was to give the Church's interpretation of the Bible; there must be a Sunday sermon in every church; priests must be trained for this.

3) Luther's teaching that man is justified by Faith not Works (*prayers, sacraments*, etc.) was opposed.

4) Catholic teaching on sacraments was made clearer.

5) Bishops were to live in their dioceses.

The most important decisions were taken by

Above: Rubens' painting of Ignatius Loyola, the founder of the Jesuits. Loyola became a religious enthusiast while recovering from a severe wound, and determined to become a soldier of the Pope. His small band, called the Company of Jesus, travelled throughout the heathen world as missionaries.

1548, but Charles V withdrew his bishops, so enforcement had to wait until 1562-1563. Then arrangements were made for colleges for priests, *catechisms*, revised prayerbooks, accurate texts and new translations. Greater authority was given to bishops and the Pope.

Co-operation of bishops, rulers and popes was needed to put these laws into practice. Carlo Borromeo, Archbishop of Milan, set an example which other bishops followed. Philip II of Spain accepted most reforms, but not all. Reforms were fairly well enforced in Italy and Austria. French kings refused reform, and the French Church was still awaiting reform at the *French Revolution* in 1789. Popes of the 17th century were energetic. All agreed that the new collegetrained priests were far more successful than the old ones. The Roman Church emerged from the Reformation period stronger than it had been before, but divided from the Protestants by its new *authoritarianism*, which lasted until the *Ecumenical Vatican Council* of 1959.

117

The expansion of trade in the 15th century prompted many courageous voyages of discovery. Vasco da Gama (right) sailed around the Cape of Good Hope and to India in 1498 to bring back spices, jewels and silks.

The fabulous lifestyle of Asia was first recorded in Europe by the Venetian traveller Marco Polo (below). He was taken to central Asia as a young boy by his merchant father. There he was employed by Kublai Khan who sent him on missions to Tibet, Burma, southern China and India. These travels formed the basis of his writings, "The Description of the World", published after his return to Venice in the year 1295.

Right: A map of the world as it was thought to look in c.1490. The shape of Asia is largely guesswork but it shows the seaways to the East as discovered by the Portuguese.

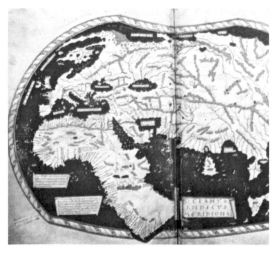

Voyages of Discovery

In the 15th century Europeans knew little of the world beyond the Atlantic and the Mediterranean seas. The maps of the age gave a distorted outline of North Africa and the Near East and hardly even an outline of south-east Asia, the Indies and Cathay (or China) being little more than names. Marco Polo, the Venetian, had returned from a 13th century journey to Cathay with dramatic accounts of the riches of the 'Indies', but little more was known directly of the lands from which came the spices, fine cloths, carpets, *tapestries*, and other luxuries which enriched life (see pp. 90-1). Many knew that the world was round, but ships and *navigational instruments* were too primitive to permit sailing far from land.

One reason the voyages of discovery occurred when they did was the increasingly high cost of eastern goods. Malay traders brought the eastern goods from the Spice Islands, Cathay, and Ceylon to India. The Arab traders who bought them in turn sold them in the eastern Mediterranean to Italian traders, who had exclusive control of the trade routes to Europe. The Turks, after the capture of Constantinople in 1453 (see pp. 166-7), disrupted the Arab trade routes and this combined with the Italian monopoly made costs almost prohibitive. The desire to spread the Christian religion was important. Technical progress also played a part: the *three-masted caravel*, developed in Portugal, allowed greater freedom to manoeuvre and was a sturdier, larger and more seaworthy ship; improvements in navigation instruments, particularly the more precise *directional compass* and the *astrolabe* or *quadrant*, made possible explorations far from land.

The navigation school of Prince Henry the Navigator of Portugal in the mid-15th century encouraged expeditions farther and farther south along the west African coast. Trading posts where European cloths and manufactured goods were exchanged for African ivory, gold and other metals, and, increasingly, slaves, were established. In 1487 Bartholomew Diaz rounded the Cape of Good Hope and nine years later Vasco da Gama voyaged into the Indian Ocean, landing at Calicut in India in 1498. His return with spices, jewels, silks, and tapestries proved the value of a sea route to the east. By the early 15th century the Portuguese had established trading posts and routes to India, the Chinese coast, and the Moluccas.

Six years before Vasco da Gama's voyage, Christopher Columbus (see p. 234) persuaded the Spanish queen, Isabella of Cas-

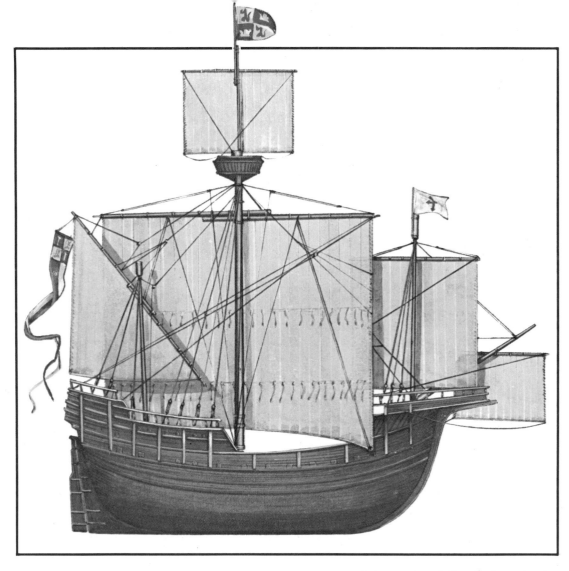

tile (see pp. 102-3), that it might be possible to reach the Indies by sailing west. He sailed from Palos with three ships, the 'Niña', the 'Pinta' and the 'Santa Maria', in August 1492. He sighted an island in the Bahamas on 12th October, landed and claimed it for Spain, and explored the coasts of Cuba and the island he called Hispaniola before returning to Spain. Believing that he had found the Indies he called the natives Indians, but he found none of the riches of the Orient he sought.

Columbus made three more voyages to the *New World*, in 1493, 1498, and 1502. On his third voyage he went ashore on the Venezuelan coast, which he termed an 'Other World'. On his last voyage, 1502-1504, he reached Honduras, sailed south and east along the Central American coast, seeking a channel to the Pacific, having been told of another ocean only a few days' journey across the mountains. Though he had concluded that South America was a new, unknown land, he now thought that beyond the island he was surveying he would find the Chinese coast and that he would not be far from Peking. No *strait* through the *isthmus* could be found, but copper and gold objects in considerable quantities were discovered and this was to lead to the later

conquest of Central and South America by Spanish adventurers (see pp. 126-7).

Other explorers for Spain, particularly Amerigo Vespucci, an Italian merchant, charted the coasts of the Caribbean and established that a new continent had been discovered, but how far north or south it extended was as yet very uncertain. Vespucci explored some 1,600 kilometres of the northern coasts of South America and concluded decisively, 'This land is a whole new world'. His charts were the basis of many early 15th century European maps of the new world. Through his detailed descriptions of the new land his name, and not Columbus's, was given to it.

The northern extent of the new world became known through the voyages of John and Sebastian Cabot, sponsored by Henry VII of England. It is probable that at least the legends of Viking voyages were known (see pp. 64-5). John Cabot surveyed the coast of Nova Scotia, or possibly Newfoundland—the accounts of the voyage are imprecise—in 1497, and then made a second voyage in 1498. He assumed, like Columbus, that he had reached the Far East. His son Sebastian made a more extensive survey of the North American coast, became aware that this was a new continent and searched

In 1492, Christopher Columbus (above) sailed from Spain on his historic voyage to the New World in a 36-metre decked ship, the Santa Maria (left). Two 15-metre caravelles helped to accommodate the 120 men who shared the Genoan sailor's dream that Cathay could be reached by sailing west.
Columbus, also known as Christóbal Colón, claimed new territory for Spain during the voyage but lost the Santa Maria which ran aground in strong winds off Hispaniola at midnight on Christmas Day 1492.

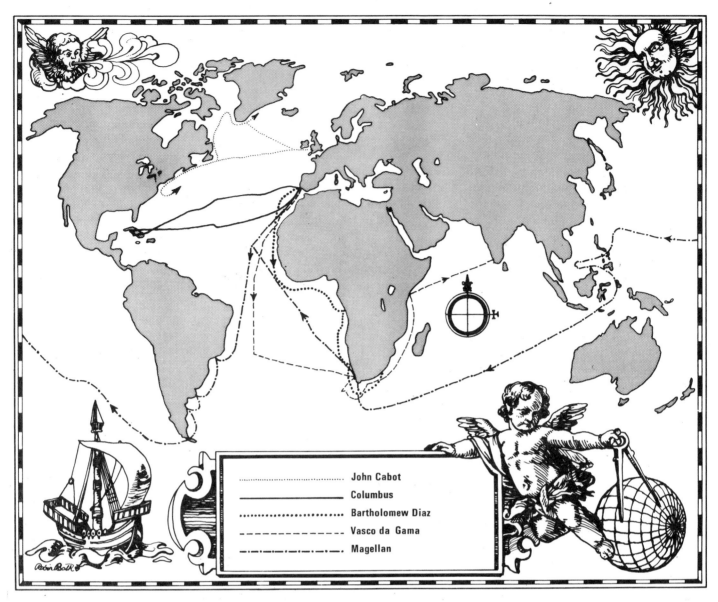

Above: Map showing the great sea voyages of the late 15th and early 16th centuries. In little more than 30 years, Europeans learnt of the vast world which lay outside their own borders.

··	John Cabot
———————————	Columbus
••••••••••••••••••••••••	Bartholomew Diaz
– – – – – – – – –	Vasco da Gama
–·–·–·–·–·–·–·–·–·	Magellan

through the pack-ice of Labrador to seek a 'north-west passage' to the Orient.

Balboa's discovery of the great south sea in 1513 (see pp. 126-7) made it clear that a new world had been found and that China must lie still farther west. The new world was rich enough to satisfy the Spanish *conquistadores*. But many continued to search for a passage around the new world and it was Ferdinand Magellan, the Portuguese explorer, who convinced the Spanish king, Charles I (the emperor Charles V), that it was in the southern *latitudes* that a route could be found. Magellan set sail in September 1519 with five ships, and late in October, in latitudes considerably south of the Cape of Good Hope, found a channel which, by the flow of the tide, convinced him that it was an opening to another sea. After tacking 480 kilometres for 37 days, he reached the South Sea, which he named the Pacific, or Peaceful, Ocean. So it seemed on the day he found it, in contrast to the tempestuous currents and winds of the strait which was to bear his name.

After some 98 days, Magellan's ships reached the Philippine Islands, which he called the Ladrones. On the island of Mactan he was killed in a battle with tribesmen. It was not until September 1522 that the ship 'Victoria', the only one of the five vessels remaining sea-worthy, returned to Seville, having passed through the Moluccas and around the Cape of Good Hope, proving Magellan's theory, and thus Columbus's, that the Far East could be found by the westward passage.

The Spanish laid claim to and controlled the seas of the central and southern Atlantic. So the French, Dutch and English explorers sought, over the next century, a northerly passage and, in the latter part of the century, suitable land for settlement. Giovanni de Verrazano first sighted the Hudson river in 1524 and sailed along the New England coast in the service of Francis I. Jacques Cartier, also commissioned by the French king, crossed the Atlantic in 1534 to seek a passage to the Far East. He surveyed much of the North American coast, and explored the St. Lawrence river as far as the rapids above present-day Montreal. It was

attempted unsuccessfully to plant a colony on the coast of North Carolina in 1584-89. Later, in 1595-96, Raleigh explored the Guiana coast and the Orinoco river, seeking in vain the fabled *El Dorado*—the Land of the Golden Man.

Many men continued to think that the North American continent was a narrow isthmus, as Panama had been found to be. Henry Hudson, sailing for the Dutch in the 'Half Moon', in 1609, ascended the Hudson river 240 kilometres to present-day Albany, and as the river narrowed became convinced that there was no short route to China across the continent. Later in the same year he attempted the northern route and broke through the ice south of Baffin Island into Hudson Bay, and spent the winter of 1609-

Log line and reel

1610 there, frozen in. From this journey he did not return, having been set adrift in a small boat by his mutinous crew. But his charts remained, giving a detailed description of the northern continent. Voyages were followed by successful colonizing expeditions, an English colony being planted at Jamestown in 1607 and a permanent Dutch trading post being established at New Amsterdam in 1624.

Magellan's voyage around the world was not followed up for another 50 years, and then by the English sea captain Sir Francis Drake. Drake's voyage in the 'Golden Hind', 1577-1580, was in part a challenge to the Spanish empire. Drake attacked the hitherto immune Spanish settlements in Peru. He then sailed as far north as San Francisco, claiming the land, New Albion, for England, before sailing west across the central Pacific to the Moluccas. He brought back to England cloves and nutmegs from the Spice Islands and silver taken from the Spanish treasure ships.

Two centuries later, another English captain, James Cook, in three voyages between 1768 and 1779, charted New Zealand and the eastern coast of Australia—the Great Barrier Reef. He crossed and recrossed the south Pacific proving that no very large southern continent existed, and in so doing traversed the Antarctic Circle. He discovered the Hawaiian Islands and, sailing as far north as the Bering Strait, proved that a north-west passage was blocked by ice.

Early compass card

A traverse board

Progress in navigational instruments (above) made extensive sea exploration possible.

not, however, until Samuel de Champlain's expeditions farther up the St. Lawrence to the Great Lakes (1608-15) that France followed up the earlier voyages and began to settle the land.

The Englishman Martin Frobisher made further attempts to find a north-west passage in 1576 and 1577. He surveyed the coasts north of Labrador and west of Greenland, and charted Baffin Island but found his way blocked by ice. Sir Humphrey Gilbert set out to explore and to establish a colony in Newfoundland and Labrador in two voyages, in 1578 and 1583. His efforts, like those of so many others, proved disastrous. Gilbert had a more exalted ideal than those who sought gold or revenge upon the Spanish. His aim was to establish Sir Thomas More's *Utopia* in a world unencumbered by the static institutions of the old world. But shortly after he had put ashore a colony on Newfoundland, Gilbert's small ship, the 'Squirrel', foundered. Gilbert was last seen 'sitting abaft with a book' and shouting through the wind and waves, 'we are as near heaven by sea as by land.' Equally disastrous were the expeditions of Gilbert's brother-in-law, Sir Walter Raleigh, who

Central America— Mayas and Aztecs

Central America was the area in which the first American civilization developed. About the beginning of the Christian era the *Maya* began to build cities in stone in the present-day states of Mexico, Honduras and El Salvador, and in the area between them. This town civilization was based on the development of farming and animal *husbandry*, as was civilization in the *Old World* (see pp.14-17). In the *New World* of America different crops were cultivated—*American beans* and corn, peanuts, *gourds*, *plantains*, *sweet potatoes* and cotton. More than 100 food plants were cultivated by the American Indians. The dog was domesticated, as was the turkey; bees were kept for honey and the *cochineal insect* for dye. But as compared with the old world few animals were domesticated. The Indians of North America were generally farmers, hunters, or fishermen.

Indians had occupied the hot lands of Central America for 3,000 years before their

civilization developed. The inhabitants of what is now Guatemala began to cultivate maize about 1000 B.C. The first stone buildings have been dated at about 350 B.C. and the Mayan civilization began to develop fast. The Maya had a remarkably accurate *calendar* of their own. They traced back the beginning of their history to an event which occurred in 3113 B.C. which they called 4 AHAU 8 CUMHU. This was 3,433 years before the oldest Mayan document which survives, the *Leyden plaque* of 320 A.D. Mayan history is divided into the period of the *Old Empire* from 320 to 987 A.D. and that of the *New Empire* from 987 to the Spanish conquest (see pp.126-7).

Mayan cities contained a temple, a palace, pyramids, a monastery, observatories, and platforms for dancing. There was a *ball court*, in which a religious game, like *handball*, was played. The elbow, fist or hip were used, not the open hand. There were suburbs in which each dwelling was largely an independent farm.

The Maya relied on 'slash and burn' farming. Instead of manuring the ground and

Scenes of human sacrifice such as the one depicted below were common in the Aztec world. Ritual killings centred around Huitzilopochtli, the sun god who the Aztecs believed died every evening to be born the following dawn. The sustenance he needed for his daily struggle to drive away the moon and the stars was human blood. The Aztecs believed they were Huitzilopochtli's chosen people whose job it was to provide him with human blood: in return they would dominate the world.

changing the crops, the forest trees were cut and burnt and the same crop was sown year after year. When the soil was exhausted people had to move on to a fresh part of the forest. So Mayan cities had to keep moving. After 850 A.D. the whole civilization began to decay. The *New Empire* flourished in north Yucatan and was drawn into the orbit of the Aztecs.

Empire is a misleading term, for the Mayans were organized in city-states rather like ancient Greece. A hereditary chief called the *Halach Uinic* was at the head of each city and there was a priest, called *Nacom*, elected for three years. There was an hereditary aristocracy, merchants and a priesthood. Their life was controlled by religion; beautiful temples were at the centre of every city. They worshipped a supreme God, called *Hunab Ku.* Today many of the Mayan cities are hidden deep in the jungle.

Mayan civilization was replaced by that of the *Aztecs* in Mexico. The valley of Mexico was a superb place in which to live. It was over 2,000 metres above sea level, walled in

Below: Aztec mosaic mask made from bands of turquoise and lignite set on a human skull. The mask represents the great god Tescathopica (Smoking Mirror) who the Aztecs believed had been the presiding god of the first stage of the earth's creation.

by high mountains and immensely fertile. The water from the mountains and the lake system made *irrigation* easy. Artificial islands were made on rafts in the lake. Decaying water-plants and dung enriched the soil. There were two or three harvests a year. Many tribes settled around the lake, for there was no need to keep moving as the Maya did in the forests to the south. But the richness of the valley tempted barbarian indians from the north.

For nearly 2,000 years civilizations like the *Olmecs* and the *Teotihuacáns* flourished in different parts of Mexico. They were the oldest civilizations in America. About the tenth century A.D. *Toltecs* from the north occupied the area. In the 13th century civil war weakened the Toltecs and a new wave of invaders entered the valley of Mexico. Among them was a tribe called *Tenochcas.* It was these Tenochcas who were to conquer the other cities and tribes and make their capital, Tenochtitlán (Mexico City), the centre of an empire. The word Aztec is not so much the name of a people as of their civilization and much of this was in existence long before the Tenochcas rose to rule over the area.

The Teotihuacáns were great architects and excellent farmers, cultivating corn, cotton, beans, and Chile peppers. Teotihuacán was a religious centre, the city of the Rain God, *Tláloc*, a strange, spectacle-eyed, tusked creature. Communal dwellings with 50 to 60 rooms each, grouped round patios and linked by passage ways, were found near Teotihuacán. The history of the many later invaders of Mexico is difficult to disentangle since we depend so much on archaeological evidence.

Towns were tribal centres. One tribe or town after another rose to power. The *Tepanecs*, whose city was Azcapotzalco, overthrew the *Texcocans.* The Tepanecs were defeated in their turn by an alliance of the defeated Texcocans with *Tenochtitlán* of the Tenochcas and *Tlacopan.* Texcocan power was restored but only in alliance with the Tenochcas. The ruler who had brought the Tenochcas to the front was Itzcoatl (1428-40). He was succeeded by Montezuma I (1440-69). Montezuma II (1502-20), grandson of Montezuma I, raised the Tenochcas to the supreme position in the valley. Other city-states paid a regular toll of human victims for the mass sacrifices that the Tenochcas practised. It was this cult of sacrifice which helped the Spanish *conqistador* Hernán Cortés overthrow the rule of the Tenochcas, after his invasion in 1519 (see pp.126-7). By allying himself with subject tribes and rival cities Cortés was able to create a Spanish colony.

The Incas

The 'Unique Inca' was the absolute ruler of a great empire on the west coast of South America. This was quite a different society from those in central America (see pp. 122-3). The difference is due to the nature of the land. Rivers flow into the Pacific from the Andes mountains. They flow through deserts. There had to be a central government to control the full length of each river, if the waters were to be properly managed for farming (see pp. 16-17).

Hunting indians were the first to settle in the river valleys. Between 1200 and 800 B.C. corn was cultivated and the first pottery was made. By 500 B.C. much of the area had a similar way of life (*Chavín* culture), which was introduced by the indians from the valley of Mexico (see pp. 122-3). The Peruvians (modern Peru is in the area in which this civilization began to develop) cultivated

over 30 different food plants. They ate guinea-pigs and raised *llamas* and *alpacas* for wool and transport. The Chavín culture covered most of the river valleys of Peru. They seem to have shared a common religion, but there is no evidence of any political unity between the various river valleys as early as this.

For 1,500 years, from 500 B.C. to about 1000 A.D. states rose and fell, new plants

Francisco Pizarro, an almost illiterate Spanish adventurer, conquered the great Inca empire in 1532 with a force of only 180 men. Pizarro's conquest of Peru was made possible when, four years earlier, he had met and won the approval of King Charles of Spain at Toledo (above).

Left: Surviving objects of the lost Inca culture. Far left: A silver beaker in the form of a musician and (right) a figurine of a woman shaped by hammering.

Right: Intermarriage between the Europeans and the indians produced a new breed of South American peasant, the mestizos.

Far right: Machu Picchu, the Inca city the Spanish never discovered. The city was built by the Incas at the height of their empire—about 1500—and lay undiscovered until 1911 when an American expedition stumbled upon it almost 3000 metres up in the Andes. Although it had been deserted for centuries, it was remarkably well-preserved with buildings of fine interlocking masonry, tidy agricultural terraces and a web of paths and staircases. The mist-shrouded peak of Huayna Picchu in the background reaches 5000 metres.

were cultivated, advances were made in weaving, and irrigation was extended, so that the river valleys could feed more people. The details of this period are difficult to unravel, because we have no surviving written history. It is a strange irony that archaeology has provided us with pieces of Peruvian woven cloth from the Chavín and earlier periods, but that archaeologists disagree about the dates of the successors to the Chavín culture by as much as 700 years. The Peruvians were, in fact, quite remarkable weavers and many beautiful examples of their workmanship exist.

Two important cultures which followed the Chavíns have been identified. The first has been called the *Experimental* period, and the second the *Classical*, or *Florescent*, period. Archaeologists disagree as to whether the Experimental period lasted for 200 or 800 years. It was a time of rapid development in irrigation and building techniques and in the introduction of new plants. In the Classical period which followed, the new technical processes were fully developed and highly organized and aggressive states came into existence. Some archaeologists date this period between 300 B.C. and 500 A.D., others between 400 and as late as 900 A.D.

There is agreement, however, that after a breakdown and conflict between the different valleys a new period of Peruvian history opened up about 1000 A.D. and lasted until 1440 A.D. This was the *City-Builder* period. The river valleys were divided between three states, each of which built new capitals. Chimú in the north was the largest state. At this time there may have been some contact across the Pacific with Asia. One sign of this is Peruvian cotton, which is a cross between wild American and cultivated Asiatic cotton. Other signs are the chewable *narcotic drugs* and the making of mosaic patterns out of feathers, both of which were practised in the Andes, Polynesia and South East Asia. The Polynesians, who came from Malaya, reached Easter Island in the 14th century. The *Kon-Tiki voyage* has shown that it was possible to travel from Peru to Easter Island. This small island may have been the meeting point of peoples from Asia and peoples from South America.

Towards the end of the City-Builder period the highland, Andean peoples were united by the Incas. The Incas were a small, militaristic group from the central highlands. They unified Peru and much more of western South America in one of the most extraordinary empires in world history. The Incas were a mountain tribe from Cuzco, a valley over 3,350 metres high in the Andes. In 1438, Pachacuti became their ruler and began to expand his kingdom. By the time his successor and son, Topa Inca, died, in 1493, the Inca empire was nearly 4,800 kilometres from north to south. The Incas became the ruling nobility of all the river valleys; they united the area in a powerful

empire. The state organized the production of food and other goods and their distribution to meet family needs. The Inca rulers gathered hordes of precious metal in their mountain cities. Their buildings, in unmortared stone, are as remarkable as is the situation of their cities, high in the Andes.

The Inca empire fell when attacked by a Spaniard, Francisco Pizarro (see pp. 126-7). At this time two Inca brothers were disputing the succession. Pizarro captured the victor and took over the empire. Indian resistance was weakened by their religious beliefs, for the coming of a white god from overseas was foretold in their legends. The subjects of the Inca obeyed their new Spanish ruler, even when the *Inca Manco* led a revolt in 1535. Spanish firearms were superior to the primitive Indian weapons, and the Inca had lost control of his people. The last claimant to the Inca title, Yupac Amaru, was beheaded in 1571. Descendants of the Inca nobility held important offices in the 18th century, but the mass of indians were simply serfs of the Spanish settlers.

The Conquistadores

On Columbus's first voyage to the new world small quantities of gold were discovered on the island of Hispaniola; copper and gold objects (see pp. 118-21) seemed to promise that abundant precious metals might be found. This led many adventurous and profit-seeking Spaniards to offer their services to explore and settle the new territories. Those who achieved the conquest of the Indian lands in the Caribbean islands and the mainland became known as the *Conquistadores*.

Two of those who sailed with Columbus (see p. 234) and were among the first to seek to extend the Spanish dominions were Alonso de Ojeda and Vicente Yáñez Pinzón. Ojeda, in 1499, explored Guiana and Venezuela and in 1519 attempted to establish a settlement on the north coast of Colombia near present-day Cartagena. His lack of diplomacy and the brutality with which he treated the indians made the expedition a disaster. Pinzón in 1500 surveyed the coast of Brazil, discovering the mouth of the Amazon and Cape San Augustin, but the Spaniards did not follow up his expedition as Brazil was east of the *Pope's Line of Demarcation of 1494* and therefore within the half of the world assigned to Portugal.

The West Indian islands, Hispaniola, Puerto Rico, Cuba, and Jamaica, were by 1510 largely subdued and their deposits of gold exploited by the Spanish captains. Ponce de León 'pacified' Puerto Rico and became its governor, and Diego Velázquez de Cuellar conquered the greater part of the

Above: The Conquistadores, the Spanish soldiers who accompanied Cortés, were a frightening sight to the Aztec warriors. Not only were their firearms more sophisticated than anything the Aztecs had ever seen but their very appearance fulfilled an old Aztec prophecy.

Right: Vasco Nuñez de Balboa, the man who found the Pacific Ocean after hearing about the great sea to the west of Darien on the Panama isthmus. Balboa had to cross some of the most difficult jungle in South America to reach his destination. He caught sight of the sea after 25 days and four days later, with his sword drawn, he waded into the Gulf of San Miguel and took possession of the southern sea and all adjacent lands.

1,130-kilometres-long island of Cuba. The indians initially accepted the Spaniards but, when they came to see the real intention of the intruders, they resisted the seizure of their lands and were eventually exterminated. The islands had limited deposits of precious metals and these were quickly exhausted. The Spaniards began almost immediately to look for further riches elsewhere.

Vasco Núñez de Balboa founded a 'city' at Darien, on the present-day Panama isthmus. Having extracted much of the gold of the region and hearing of another great sea not far distant, he set out in 1513 for the narrowest part of the isthmus. With indian guides and 190 Spaniards he crossed the isthmus through swamps and tropical forest and, reaching hilly ground, he came out on a high rock from which on 25th September 1513 he first surveyed the great south sea. With the news of his discovery he also sent back to the Spanish king pearls from the new ocean and a treasure of gold.

The Yucatán coast was first sighted in 1517 and the rumours of gold and a great city in the interior prompted the governor of Cuba to send an expedition under Hernán Cortés. In February 1519 Cortés landed on the Mexican coast with 650 men. He was able to secure control of the rich Aztec empire which he found in the interior highlands (see pp. 122-3). His success was made possible by the divisions of the Aztec people, their initial hesitation (for they looked upon the Spaniards as visiting deities) and the vacillation of Montezuma, the Aztec chieftain. By the end of 1519 the Spaniards reached Tenochtitlán (Mexico City) and seized Montezuma. Later the Aztecs revolted and Cortés was forced to abandon the city. But with reinforcements and superior weapons and discipline the Spaniards defeated and destroyed the Aztec nation, recapturing the capital in August 1521.

Guatemala was similarly conquered by Pedro de Alvarado in 1524. Spanish control was extended to the north by Panfilo de Narváez, a lieutenant of the governor of Cuba. Narváez, in 1528, explored and secured Florida, and then set out northwards. The eight-year wanderings of his followers led to tales of mythical cities of silver and gold, particularly the 'seven lost cities of Cibola', which inspired others to follow up these explorations. Francisco Vásquez de Coronado led an expedition (1540-42) in which he took possession of New Mexico, north Texas and Kansas, reaching the great bend of Arkansas. Hernando de Soto explored the eastern part of present-day North America, passing from Florida northward through Georgia to North Carolina and westward through Alabama, Mississippi, Arkansas and Louisiana. He was probably the first to see the Mississippi river hundreds of kilometres north of its delta.

The conquest of Peru gained for Spain its brightest jewel and made possible the settlement of the rest of South America. Francisco Pizarro, hearing reports of a rich Inca empire, set out south of Darien in 1531 with 180 men. He crossed the *equator* into Peru

and captured the Inca ruler, Atahualpa, who attempted to buy his life by offering Pizarro a large treasure. Pizarro seized the treasure, but then murdered Atahualpa, and completed the conquest with the capture of Cuzco, the Inca capital. Pizarro ruled from Ecuador to Chile, but in 1541 was executed by his own followers. The viceroyalty of Peru, with its seat of government at Lima, became the richest colony of the Spanish empire, chiefly because of its mineral deposits and particularly the silver mines of Potosi. Rumours of still further riches led to an expedition in which the length of the Amazon River was first discovered and explored.

In 1519 Hernán Cortés founded a little city at Vera Cruz (above) and from here, five months later, he entered Tenochititlán, capital of Mexico. He was welcomed by Montezuma, the Aztec emperor, but Cortés seized the ruler and established a protectorate over Mexico.

Settlement of North America

Three countries were involved in the early European settlement of North America. The Spaniards founded the earliest permanent settlement in 1565 at St Augustine in what is now Florida. Further Spanish colonies secured control of Texas and of California and other areas of the West. But the most important colonizing countries were England and France. Most of the early settlers crossed the Atlantic for economic reasons, but some left their homeland from idealistic motives, such as the desire to practise their own religious faith in peace. In general the English settlements were along the eastern coast of the United States and the French settlements were on the St Lawrence River.

In 1607, 104 colonists landed at Jamestown, Virginia. Sponsored by the *London Company,* the colony nearly foundered disastrously through the ravages of sickness and hostile indians, but was saved by the organizing zeal of Captain John Smith. As the tobacco leaf became popular in Europe the Virginian colonists prospered and within twelve years they had their own representative assembly. In 1620, 102 so-called *Pilgrims,* most of them English Calvinists, sailed from Plymouth in the 'Mayflower' and founded a successful colony at Plymouth, Massachusetts, under the leadership of John Carver and William Bradford. In 1628 and 1630 large numbers of *Puritans* sailed to Massachusetts Bay, and they were followed in the next decade by about 20,000 further colonists who founded many settlements over large areas in Maine, Rhode Island and Connecticut. Massachusetts became a royal colony in 1691.

Some colonies were *proprietary,* that is founded and controlled by rich proprietors, usually noblemen. For example, Lord Baltimore founded a colony north of Chesapeake Bay, Maryland, and much later, in 1681, William Penn founded Pennsylvania as a *Quaker* community. Similarly the Duke of York was granted New Amsterdam by his brother Charles II, and in 1664 he took over the colony without force from Dutch control and renamed it New York. This became a royal province, but Pennsylvania remained under the control of the Penn family. North and South Carolina were also proprietary colonies, while Georgia was founded by the philanthropic James Oglethorpe as a refuge for debtors. Oglethorpe forbade slavery but many negroes were brought to South Carolina to work on the rice *plantations.*

Immigrants sailed to the English colonies from many European countries—Holland, Germany and Sweden as well as Wales and Scotland. They were nearly all Protestants (see pp. 114-15) and life was simple and

Among the early immigrant groups seeking religious freedom in north America were the Quakers led by William Penn, seen here negotiating a treaty with the Indians for land. The treaty led to the establishment of Pennsylvania as a Quaker community in 1681.

The 'Mayflower' which took the first pilgrims to America was just 30 metres long and weighed only 180 tonnes. Bad weather twice forced her to turn back to Plymouth before she completed the voyage. Left: Indians as the new Americans found them.

puritanical with few extremes of wealth or class. By the middle of the 18th century 13 colonies had been established on the eastern coast of North America and more than one-and-a-half million people lived in them. All the colonies had the same type of administration. A governor appointed by the English king or proprietor was advised by a council. A representative assembly passed legislation and levied taxes.

The English settled what is now the eastern United States virtually without opposition, even for the most part from the indigenous indians. In Canada, France also had a free hand at first. In 1608 Samuel de Champlain founded Quebec four years after helping to form a small settlement at Port Royal in Acadia. Montreal was founded in 1642 as a missionary centre. In 1663 France declared Canada a royal province and thousands of settlers crossed the Atlantic.

The initial opposition to the French came from the *Iroquois Indians*. But more serious clashes followed with the English, who were anxious to enjoy the profits of the rich fur trade. The English Hudson Bay Company received its charter in 1670 and conflict between it and French traders was commonplace even after the *Peace of Utrecht* which was supposed to grant Newfoundland, Nova Scotia and the Hudson Bay territory to Britain. The quarrel was settled by the last of the French and Indian Wars in which the British, commanded by General James Wolfe, defeated the French, commanded by the Marquis de Montcalm, in the *Battle of Quebec* in 1759. Four years later France gave up all claims to Canada.

Discovering the Natural World

By the middle of the 16th century European seamen and men of learning had a truer picture of what the globe was like than had any other people in the world, or any of their predecessors, Arabs or Greeks (see pp. 118-21). It is not surprising that geographical exploration led men to explore the heavens. Astronomy, observing and studying the stars, was essential to sailors in the

The Armillary sphere (above) illustrated the difference between the Ptolemaic theory of a central earth and the Copernican theory of a central sun.

15th and 16th centuries. Prince Henry of Portugal had set up an astronomical observatory (see pp. 118-21). New observations led to new questions and new theories. Just as the *Renaissance* had led thinkers to question the authority of Greek and Arab scholars, and the *Reformation* led men to question the authority of the Fathers of the Church (see pp. 112-13 and 114-15), so a new

scientific attitude began to develop: men would only accept ideas which were confirmed by proofs. The authority of past writers was no longer enough. This change did not come easily. Early in the 17th century a *Jesuit* professor was asked to look at the sun spots which could be seen through a *telescope*. He answered: 'My son, it is useless. I have read *Aristotle* through twice, and have not found anything about spots on the Sun. There are no spots on the Sun.' Aristotle was a Greek writer who died in 322 B.C. Francis Bacon, Lord Chancellor of England, living at the very same time as this Jesuit, 'fell into the dislike of the philosophy of Aristotle; not for the worthlessness of the author, but for the unfruitfulness of the way, being a philosophy, only strong for disputations, but barren of the production of works for the benefit of the life of man'.

Perhaps the most important change which occurred anywhere in the world in the 16th and 17th centuries was the shift of opinion from the Jesuit's view to that of Francis Bacon. There took place what has been called the *Scientific Revolution*. This was not the work of one man nor of one country but the total effect of many discoveries by many men. The Renaissance produced a new kind of all-rounder, men whose talents were employed in very different activities, to all of which they brought curiosity and originality. Perhaps the greatest of these was the Italian Leonardo da Vinci (1452-1519), who was an architect, scientist and engineer as well as a painter. He studied human anatomy and the movement of wind and water; he made plans for aeroplanes and tanks. Michelangelo was not only a great sculptor, painter and poet but an expert engineer of fortifications. Leon Battista Alberti, foremost athlete and horseman, was also a composer of music, a painter, architect and author. These three were Italians. The Englishman Sir Walter Raleigh was poet, courtier, politician, sailor, explorer, soldier and author of a *History of the World*. Men like this had open minds, but the real advance of scientific knowledge came neither from the philosophers like Bacon nor from the all-rounders like Leonardo da Vinci.

It is to the men who devoted their lives to the study of particular sciences that we owe new knowledge of the world. Two sciences were particularly important: astronomy and medicine. Four men transformed man's view of the heavens: a Pole, Nicolaus Copernicus (1473-1543); a Dane, Tycho Brahe (1546-1601), who worked in Denmark and Czechoslovakia; a German, Johannes Kepler (1571-1630), who followed Brahe in Czechoslovakia; and greatest of them all, an

Italian, Galileo Galilei (1564-1642). When Copernicus began his work, people followed the teaching of the Greeks that a motionless Earth was at the centre of the universe. Some believed, with Aristotle, that 55 crystal spheres, carrying the Sun, Moon, planets and stars, revolved round the Earth. Others followed *Ptolemy's* more mathematical teaching, which allowed for 80 circular tracks along which the heavenly bodies moved. Copernicus worked out that if one assumed that the Earth turned on its axis and itself revolved with other planets round the Sun, this would make Ptolemy's system

simpler and more sensible. He put forward this interpretation in his book *De Revolutionibus Orbium Coelestium* (about the revolving of heavenly bodies) in 1543.

But Copernicus still assumed that all heavenly bodies moved in circles. It was Kepler who took the decisive step of suggesting that an ellipse fitted the facts better. Kepler used the observations made by Brahe, every night for 20 years, to arrive at his conclusions. Kepler's work required astonishingly complicated mathematical calculations. Galileo Galilei established the Copernican theories as physical fact. In

Above: Joseph Wright of Derby painted Experiment with the Air Pump to illustrate an early experiment showing that animals cannot live without oxygen. In the painting, a scientist comforts weeping children who know that the bird in the jar will die without air.

1609 he heard of the invention of the telescope in Flanders and sent for one. With this new instrument, of which he made many copies himself, the study of astronomy was revolutionized. Galileo commented that 'the Galaxy is nothing else but a mass of innumerable stars planted together in clusters' and that the Moon was 'everywhere full of vast protuberances, deep chasms and sinuosities', not smooth as the Aristotelians believed it should be. Dramatically, it was Galileo who had noticed sun spots.

In 1632 Galileo published his *Dialogue Concerning the Two Chief World Systems—Ptolemaic and Copernican.* He thought that the new pope was sympathetic but the Jesuit influence (see pp. 116-17) was too strong and the *Inquisition* forced Galileo to recant; they used arguments and threats, not torture. For the rest of his life Galileo was a prisoner of the Inquisition, but allowed to study. In 1638 his *The Dialogues on the Two New Sciences* was published in Amsterdam, describing his profound work on motion.

The principle which made possible the telescope also produced the *microscope*. The microscope was developed by Anton van Leeuwenhoek (1632-1723), a draper of Delft in Holland, to reveal further wonders of life.

As man sought to see the stars more clearly, he invented longer and longer telescopes to increase the magnification. The picture above shows the sort of observatory to be found in the 17th century.

The lenses which he made and used must have been as remarkable for their time as was his observation for he first saw and described *protozoa, protophyta* and *bacteria* varying in size from one to thirty thousandths of a millimetre. Leeuwenhoek's lens gave a magnification of up to × 300. His observations and descriptions were unparalleled. His 'little animalcules', as he called them, fascinated and obsessed him: 'But what if one should tell people in the future that there are more animals living in the scum of the teeth than there are men in a whole kingdom.'

The Englishman William Harvey's (1578-1657) discovery of the circulation of the blood established the experimental method in biology just as Galileo's work had in physics. In biology the authority was *Galen* (not Aristotle), a Greek doctor of 131-201 A.D. Andreas Vesalius (1514-64), a Fleming who was Professor of Anatomy in the Italian University of Padua, first challenged Galen's authority. Padua was the foremost university in Europe in the 16th century. Vesalius dissected a great many animals; he designed most modern dissecting instruments and worked out new techniques for dissection. Vesalius showed that Galen had made some 200 anatomical errors; his book,

On the Fabric of the Human Body, was published in the same year as Nicolaus Copernicus's, 1543.

Galen taught that there were two separate blood systems, the *venous* and the *arterial.* Harvey published his theory in 1628; he suggested that the heart acted like a pump which drove two circulations: the right ventricle drove the *pulmonary circulation* through the lungs; the left *ventricle* drove the systemic circulation through the rest of the body. The blood reached the tissues through the arteries and returned to the heart through the veins. Harvey produced a *generalization* (an idea) which fitted all the facts; it took half a century for his theory to become generally accepted. The history of science again and again reveals how difficult it is for grown men to change their ideas. Harvey himself said, very revealingly, that no one over 40 would accept his new theory.

The 17th and early 18th centuries saw many more discoveries and inventions:

Evangelista Torricelli (1608-47), an Italian, in 1643 used a column of mercury in a tube to show that air had weight (the first barometer) and to create a *vacuum.*

Otto von Guericke (1602-86), a German, invented an air-pump with which he created a vacuum in two hollow, metal half spheres which then required two teams, each of

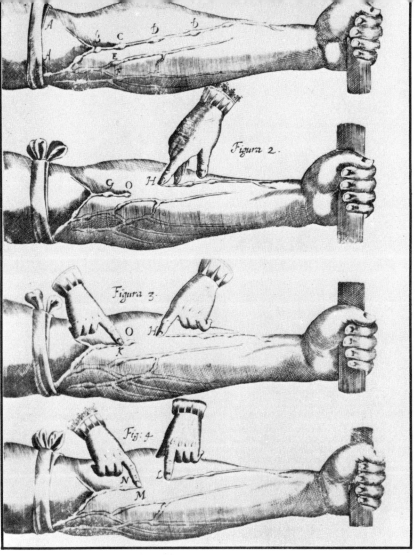

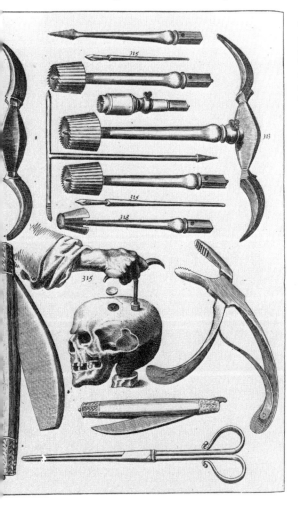

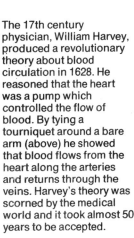

The 17th century physician, William Harvey, produced a revolutionary theory about blood circulation in 1628. He reasoned that the heart was a pump which controlled the flow of blood. By tying a tourniquet around a bare arm (above) he showed that blood flows from the heart along the arteries and returns through the veins. Harvey's theory was scorned by the medical world and it took almost 50 years to be accepted.

Left: A selection of early surgical instruments.

eight horses, to pull them apart.

Blaise Pascal (1623-62), a Frenchman, invented a *calculating machine* and experimentally calculated the weight of air.

Robert Boyle (1627-91), an Anglo-Irishman, built an improved air pump and worked out the first step in the modern physics of gases in his quantitative law.

Between them the scientists had destroyed the *medieval* belief in absolute values and a moral universe. Medieval men estimated; the scientists measured. Medieval men accepted authority; scientists looked to experiment to prove theories. A mechanical universe replaced an organic, moral one. The Englishman Isaac Newton (1642-1727) drew together the work of Galileo, Kepler and many others into general laws of motion, which applied to all motion whether on earth or in the heavens. His genius is shown by his ability to spot in 20 volumes of Kepler's works three vital scientific laws. Newton's *Principia Mathematica* of 1687 has been called 'an event unique in the intellectual history of mankind'. Newton's scientific 'laws' made it possible to predict eclipses and comets in the future, to estimate when they had occurred in the past, and to forecast new natural phenomena. His view of the universe long dominated science.

DATA DIGEST

Many of the words which are italicized in the previous section are explained more fully in the following data digest. They will help to expand your knowledge of history.

Alpaca. South American mammal rather like the llama. It is kept mainly for its wool.

Asen dynasty. Family that ruled during most of the so-called Second Bulgarian Empire in the 13th century. The most loved monarch was John Asen II. The dynasty ended with the deposition of Kaliman II in 1258.

Astrolabe. An instrument by which a navigator was able to measure the angle between the horizon and heavenly bodies.

Byzantine. In art, formality, severity with a lack of realism and a tendency to stylized elongation.

Calendar. Table of months, days and seasons.

Carpathians. A central European mountain range about 900 miles long.

Catechisms. Systems of teaching by question and answer.

Catullus. Roman poet who wrote passionate love poems. He strongly influenced Italian poets of the Renaissance. Lived 84?-54? B.C.

Chavin. The earliest Andean civilization lasting from about 700 to 200 B.C.

Church of Rome. Official title of the Roman Catholic Church.

Cicero. Roman statesman, orator and essayist. His pure style was much admired both at the time and later. Lived 106-43 B.C.

Classical. Related to the style of art and literature of the ancient Greeks and Romans.

Cochineal insect. Insect that feeds on the juice of cacti in Mexico. The dried bodies produce a scarlet dye.

Confucians. Followers of the philosophy and moral teaching of the Chinese sage Confucius.

Crusade. Between the 11th and 14th centuries Christians in Europe undertook nine campaigns known as crusades in an attempt to recover the Holy Land, particularly Jerusalem, from the control of the Saracens.

Cyrillic. The Cyrillic alphabet was derived from the Greek alphabet in the ninth century. It is used by the Russians and other Slav peoples.

Dauphin. The title given to the eldest sons of the kings of France.

Diocese. The territory over which a bishop's jurisdiction extends.

Directional compass. An instrument with a needle that points towards the north magnetic pole. By means of it a sailor can determine in which direction he is travelling.

Dynasty. Line of hereditary rulers.

Edict of Nantes. Henry IV of France issued this edict in 1598. It granted to the Huguenots freedom of conscience and worship, full civil rights and Protestant control over many cities. Louis XIV revoked the edict in 1685.

Feudal vassals. Under the feudal system of the Middle Ages an overlord granted land to vassals, who swore an oath of loyalty to him. The king's vassals were the nobility.

Ghetto. An area of a city reserved for Jews. The segregation was generally compulsory and a night-time curfew was imposed. The earliest ghettoes were established in Spain and Portugal in the 14th century. Other ghettoes were at Frankfurt and Venice. Today there are ghettoes in several American cities.

Gothic style. Applied to the style of architecture in use in western Europe from the 12th to the 15th centuries.

Hindu. Follower of Hinduism, the main religion of India.

Hundred Years War. A recurring conflict between France and England which went on from 1328 to 1453.

Hussite. The Hussite movement was a nationalistic and puritanical movement which opposed feudalism and certain practices of the Roman Catholic Church. It was an early forerunner of the Reformation.

Inquisition. The Inquisition, or Holy Office, was set up by the Roman Catholic Church in the thirteenth century to stamp out heresy. Suspects were tortured and if found guilty fined, imprisoned or sometimes burned. The Spanish Inquisition was a state tribunal instituted by Ferdinand and Isabella in 1478. Tomás de Torquemada was the most notorious of the Grand Inquisitors.

Iroquois Indians. A confederacy of Indian tribes living in the east of the United States and Canada and speaking a similar language.

Irrigation. Watering the land.

Isthmus. Narrow strip of land connecting two large tracts of land.

Jesuit. Member of the Roman Catholic Society of Jesus. They do much educational and missionary work and oppose heretical beliefs. They became very strong and in 1773 the pope suppressed the order. This decision was eventually revoked in 1814.

Knights of St John. An order founded in 1080 to defend a hospital, or hostel, for pilgrims in Jerusalem against the Saracens. The Knights took a prominent part in the crusades. At various times they were forced to move their headquarters from Jerusalem to Cyprus, Rhodes and Malta. They are often known as the Knights Hospitallers.

Kon-Tiki voyage. In 1947 Thor Heyerdahl crossed from Peru to the Tuamotu Islands on a raft called the *Kon-Tiki* in order to prove that the Polynesian islands may have been populated by groups of Incas who journeyed across the Pacific on rafts.

Latitude. Distance from the equator.

Llama. Hoofed animal of the camel family found in South America. It is kept for transport and for its wool and milk.

London Company. Together with the Plymouth Company this corporation received a charter from James I to found colonies in North America. It later became known as the Virginia Company.

Magyar. A people who originated in the Urals region and settled in Hungary at the end of the 9th century.

Manco Inca. Manco Capac, the last of the Inca emperors, turned against his Spanish masters and besieged Cuzco, but Pizarro beat off the attack. Manco Capac continued guerilla warfare until he was treacherously murdered.

Medieval. The Middle Ages.

Mozárabes. Christians who remained in Spain when the Moors occupied the country. They lived in special areas of cities such as Córdoba, Seville and Toledo and paid a tax instead of serving with the Moorish army. They retained their own church hierarchy and rites.

Narcotic drugs. Drugs producing a feeling of well-being and usually drowsiness.

Orthodox. The Orthodox Eastern Church differs from the Roman Catholic Church in not accepting the jurisdiction of the pope. The elaborate ritual was developed in the patriarchate of Constantinople.

Pagan. Strictly means neither Christian, Jew nor Muslim, but is often used to mean non-Christian.

Peace of Utrecht. The treaty signed in 1713 to end the War of the Spanish Succession.

Pediment. Triangular gable decorating a classical building.

Perspective. The technique a painter uses to give an effect of distance and three-dimensional depth to a picture.

Pope's Line of Demarcation. A line laid down by the pope through South America granting Portugal all lands east of it and Spain all lands west of it.

Prayers. Solemn and humble request to a god or gods, or to an object of worship.

Propertius. Roman poet famous for his love poems. Lived 50?-16? B.C.

Protestants. Members of the Christian Churches which severed their links with the Church of Rome and their allegiance to the pope.

Ptolemy. Greco-Egyptian astronomer and geographer who believed the sun, moon and planets revolved round the Earth. Lived in the early 2nd century A.D.

Quaker. Member of the Society of Friends, founded by George Fox in the mid-17th century. Quakers dispensed with priests and ceremonial rites and were frequently persecuted.

Sacraments. Certain rites necessary to the salvation of the soul.

Schmalkaldic League. Founded in 1531 by Protestant states and led by Philip of Hesse and John Frederick I of Saxony. Emperor Charles V defeated the league at the Battle of Mühlberg in 1547.

Socrates. Greek philosopher who followed through the implications of statements to discern their truth or falsehood. He questioned accepted beliefs and was condemned to death for corrupting the youth. Lived 469?-399 B.C.

Strait. Narrow sea passage.

Tapestries. Ornamental textile wall hangings.

Templars. The order of Knights Templars was founded in 1119 to defend the Holy Sepulchre and Christian pilgrims in Jerusalem. They were sometimes called the Poor Knights of the Temple. They fought in the crusades and gained special privileges from the pope and some secular rulers. Pope Clement V abolished the order in 1312.

Teutonic Knights. A German military order founded during the Third Crusade (1189-92). It gained great power and privilege and subdued Prussia and other lands to the east.

Yorkists. Descendants of John of Gaunt's brother Edmund, Duke of York.

EARLY VOYAGES OF DISCOVERY

1487-1488 The Portuguese Bartolomew Diaz was the first European to round the Cape of Good Hope. He sailed far along the eastern coast of Africa.
1492-1504 The Italian Christopher Columbus made four voyages to the Caribbean area. He thought that America was part of the Indies.
1497 John Cabot, an Italian sailing under the English flag, reached the Canadian coast, cruising along either Newfoundland or Nova Scotia.
1497-1498 The Portuguese Vasco da Gama rounded the Cape of Good Hope, continued up the eastern coast of Africa to Mozambique and Mombasa and sailed on to Calicut in India.
1499-1503 The Italian Amerigo Vespucci made voyages to South America and the West Indies on behalf of Spain and Portugal. He established that a new continent had been discovered and America was named after him.
1500-1501 The Portuguese Pedro Cabral landed in Brazil and sailed on to India via the Cape of Good Hope.
1519-1521 The Portuguese Ferdinand Magellan, sailing under the Spanish flag, commanded the first voyage round the world. He died on the voyage, which was completed by Antonio Pigafetta.
1524 Giovanni de Verrazano, an Italian sailing under the French flag, sought the north-west passage.
1526-1530 Sebastian Cabot, an Italian sailing under the Spanish flag, explored the coast of South America to the Rio de la Plata.
1534-1536 The Frenchman Jacques Cartier sailed up the St Lawrence River beyond Montreal.
1576-1578 The Englishman Martin Frobisher searched for the north-west passage, entering Frobisher Bay.
1577-1580 Francis Drake became the first Englishman to sail round the world.
1609-1610 Henry Hudson, an Englishman sailing under the Dutch flag, explored the Hudson River and discovered Hudson Bay.
1616 The Dutchman Dirck Hartog reached western Australia, landing on Hartog Island.
1642-1644 The Dutchman Abel Janszoon Tasman discovered Tasmania, New Zealand, Tonga and Fiji.
1699 The Englishman William Dampier explored the western and north-western coasts of Australia.
1768-1779 The Englishman James Cook in three voyages sailed round New Zealand, explored the south Pacific and discovered Christmas Is. and Hawaii.
1798 The Englishmen George Bass and Matthew Flinders discovered the Bass Strait and sailed round Tasmania.

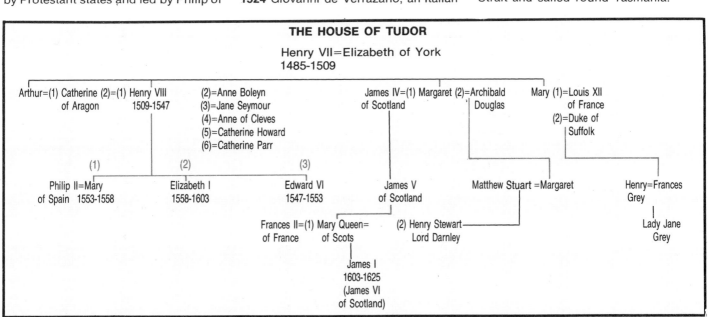

THE HOUSE OF TUDOR

Henry VII=Elizabeth of York
1485-1509

Arthur=(1) Catherine (2)=(1) Henry VIII   (2)=Anne Boleyn   James IV=(1) Margaret (2)=Archibald   Mary (1)=Louis XII
of Aragon   1509-1547   (3)=Jane Seymour   of Scotland   Douglas   of France
(4)=Anne of Cleves   (2)=Duke of
(5)=Catherine Howard   Suffolk
(6)=Catherine Parr

(1)   (2)   (3)

Philip II=Mary   Elizabeth I   Edward VI   James V   Matthew Stuart =Margaret   Henry=Frances
of Spain 1553-1558   1558-1603   1547-1553   of Scotland   Grey

Frances II=(1) Mary Queen=   (2) Henry Stewart   Lady Jane
of France   of Scots   Lord Darnley   Grey

James I
1603-1625
(James VI
of Scotland)

135

THE COMMERCIAL AND INDUSTRIAL REVOLUTION

The Struggle for Markets

The key to Britain's domination of world trade in the 17th, 18th and 19th centuries is to be found in the wording of the *Navigation Act* (1650-1, modified in 1660): '. . . from and after the first day of December one thousand six hundred and sixty, and from thenceforward, no goods or commodities whatsoever shall be imported into or exported out of any lands, islands, plantations or territories to his Majesty belonging or in his possession, or which may hereafter belong unto or be in the possession of his Majesty, his heirs and successors, in Asia, Africa or America, in any other ship or ships, vessel or vessels

economic ends. Supporters of the Navigation Act considered it was 'the wisest of all the commercial regulations of England'.

The commercial aggression contained in the wording of the Act inevitably brought Britain into conflict with her European competitors, some of them already well established in world trading. The *Dutch Wars* (1652-74) allowed England to break into the Dutch monopoly of trade in tobacco, sugar, furs, codfish and slaves: they also allowed Britain to gain a foothold in trade with India and China, and at the same time, by wiping out Dutch competition in manufactured goods, strengthened the English home market. By 1688, British exports had risen by some 400% over the figures for the late 1630s. British shipping tonnage is thought

THE MANER OF THE QUEENES MA.ᵗᶦᵉˢ LANDING AT PORTSMOUTH. DIS EMBARCASÃO DE RAINHA DA GRAN BRETAN. EM PORTSMVIT

Above: The arrival of Catherine of Braganza at Portsmouth. Her marriage to Charles II sealed the Anglo-Portuguese alliance and brought great wealth to England.

whatsoever, but in such ship or vessels as do truly and without fraud belong only to the people of England or Ireland, dominion of Wales or town of Berwick on Tweed, or are built of and belonging to any of the said lands, islands, plantations or territories, as the proprietors and right owners thereof, and whereof the master and three-fourths of the mariners at least are English.'

Perhaps the most important product of this Act was the establishment of an English monopoly of trade between the colonies and England through the insistence on English shipping. It also, in effect, subordinated the colonial economies to the English Parliament, making possible an imperial policy. Accordingly, the British government was soon to show itself amongst the most ready of the colonizing European nations to subordinate all matters of foreign policy to

to have doubled between 1640 and 1680. English merchants entered the Baltic markets in 1673. Trade to Africa on a large scale began in 1698. Russia and Newfoundland became accessible to English merchants in 1699. The American market, particularly, knew no bounds.

The next arena of English military intervention for commercial purposes was Spain, during the war of the *Spanish Succession* between 1701-1714. After the end of the Dutch wars in 1678, the French had become England's greatest rival in world trade. When Louis XIV revealed that he intended excluding English traders from the Spanish empire and throwing it open to French merchants, the English seized Minorca and Gibraltar from Spain to serve as naval bases in the Mediterranean area.

At about the same time the Portuguese

empire was, in effect, acquired by the British by less hostile means. Charles II had married Catherine of Braganza to produce the Anglo-Portuguese Alliance. Catherine brought with her Bombay, Tangier, and the trade with Brazil. At the time, it was considered that the main virtue of the marriage was that it would be 'Good for trade.' The gold of Brazil helped London become the bullion market of the world.

The Seven Years' War (1756-63) and General James Wolfe's defeat of the French in Canada opened up the North American trade with England in fish and furs. The aggressiveness of the British government is illustrated by Wolfe's comment that 'The French fishing in the Gulf of St. Lawrence is, in a great measure, ruined.' Indeed, in the five largest wars of the 18th century, Britain was on the defensive only once.

The British plundering of India in the 18th century has been likened to the treatment of the Aztec and Inca civilizations by the Spanish *conquistadores* in the 16th century (see pp. 126-7). Until the British government began to take a real share of the responsibility for India in the 1770s and 1780s, the *East India Company* had established for itself virtually an 'absolute

After the Navigation Act of 1650, British ships like the First Rate ship (above) dominated the commercial routes of the world. In 50 years, British exports increased by 400 per cent and her shipping tonnage is thought to have doubled.

sovereign power'. Over six million pounds were subsequently alleged to have been distributed amongst the East India Company and its staff in the 1760s when the systematic looting of India reached its peak. Tea imports rose to more than 907,200 kilograms in 1750, an increase of some 40% over the first decade of the 18th century. The profits of the tea and other trades seem largely to have been squandered on social advancement and the acquiring of country estates, but the iron industry of South Wales was largely created by the tea dealers of the Bristol area.

The prize of this systematic commercial and military aggression was world leadership. The cost in terms of human suffering could not be measured: opponents of the British governor of Bengal, Robert Clive, for example, laid at his door 'the late famine in Bengal and the loss of three million inhabitants'. War itself was a major stimulant to industry, however, and combined with the commercial energy and experience gained helped to produce the industrial leadership of Britain in the 19th century. 'The rise of the British economy was based historically, on the conscious and successful application of strength.'

The Mughal Empire

In 1526 Babur, descendant of Tamerlane (see pp. 98-9), defeated the Afghan ruler of Delhi at the battle of Panipat. This was the first step in the foundation of a new Indian empire as powerful as Asoka's (see pp. 38-9) but one which lasted longer. Babur was more Turkish than Mongol; he spoke Turkish, but the dynasty which he founded has come to be called Mughal or Mogul, in India. Babur inherited the little principality of Ferghana, north of Afghanistan, the very area in which Alexander the Great had founded Alexandria the Ultimate, to mark the boundary of his empire (see pp. 46-7). By 1504 Babur had control of Kabul and Kandahar; he created a new state, the nucleus of modern Afghanistan. Then he turned south, invading India in 1523-4 and 1525-6. Victory gave him the two cities in the middle of north India, Delhi and Agra, which became the Mughal capitals. In 1527 Babur defeated the *Rajputs*, the only militarily effective force in north India, at the battle of Kanwaha. When Babur died in 1530 he ruled a loosely knit empire reaching from north Afghanistan to the borders of Bengal.

Far right: The most magnificent surviving example of Mughal architecture is the Taj Mahal, a white marble mausoleum built by the emperor Shah Jahan in memory of his favourite wife, Arjumand Banu Begum. The name by which it is now known is a corruption of Mumtaz Mahal which means 'chosen one of the palace'.

As Babur swept through India, many Indians like the defender of Chanderi, (below) preferred to put their womenfolk to death rather than allow them to fall into the hands of the invading army.

Babur has revealed himself in his *Memoirs*. Jawaharlal Nehru, India's great 20th century ruler, has described him as 'one of the most cultured and delightful persons one could meet.' When Babur died, his son Homayun allowed himself to be driven out of India in 1540 by the *Afghans* led by Sher Khan. Sher Shah, as Sher Khan became, ruled northern India until his death in 1545, laying the foundations of a new administration. This was taken over by Homayun who returned to Delhi in 1556, but died within six months. His son Akbar was only 13 but the restored Mughal empire was saved from anarchy by Akbar's guardian, Bairam Khan.

In 1560 Akbar dismissed Bairam and began to rule himself. His reign lasted until 1605; he was an almost exact contemporary of Queen Elizabeth I of England. By 1605 Akbar ruled effectively all north and most of central India, and south India was being penetrated. Akbar united India. He created a divine mystique around the *Mughal dynasty*, which long outlasted their effective rule. He introduced an effective system of land taxation which the British were to take over. He used *Hindu Rajputs* as his generals and provincial governors. The *jizya*, an

extra tax on non-Muslims, was abolished and Akbar married a Hindu princess. He abandoned *Islam* for a mystical, state religion of his own, but tolerated all. India flourished: the arts and crafts boomed; Persian influence led to the development of a new Mughal school of miniature painting and to a new architectural style. For a century and a half, under Mughal rulers, India, with 100 million inhabitants, had a standard of living slightly higher than that of contemporary Europe. European traders arrived bringing luxury goods and novelties, which they exchanged for cotton goods, which India produced in quantity and of a quality not equalled in Europe until the late 18th century.

Jahangir (1605-27), who succeeded Akbar, was a strange combination of drunkenness and cruelty with great artistic sensibility. He maintained and extended Akbar's empire. Shah Jahan (1627-58), a great architect, built the Taj Mahal as a tomb for his beloved wife Mumtaz Mahal, and the Delhi Fort, reconstructing the Agra Fort. He continued the conquest of south India, but was deposed and imprisoned by his son Aurangzeb.

Aurangzeb (1658-1707) destroyed his brothers, son and nephew in his rise to power. He was no more cruel than most of the Mughals, but more efficient and more statesmanlike. He proved an able administrator, retaining power until his death at the age of 88. Aurangzeb was an orthodox Muslim and he restored the *jizya*, though he did not persecute Hindus. He faced and contained the rebellion of the *Marathas*, Hindus of western India, but he was not able to destroy them; they continued to disturb India until defeated by the East India Company in 1818. Bakadur Singh, Aurangzeb's third son (1707-12), was the last of the great Mughal emperors. By the 1750s the Mughal power was in full decay and India was being torn asunder by rival Indian princes and quarrelling European invaders. Afghanistan became a separate kingdom for the first time in 1747.

The English East India Company had been granted a charter by Queen Elizabeth I in 1600. They acquired *factories* (trading stations) at Bombay, Madras, and Calcutta. During the 18th century the English and French Companies fought for domination of India as allies of quarrelling Indian rulers. The English won and the East India Company became a kind of agent for the British government until the Indian Mutiny of 1857. Britain conquered more and more of India. The Mutiny ended the formal sovereignty of the Mughals. In 1858 Queen Victoria was proclaimed ruler of India.

African History

Modern Africa is divided up into states which were created by European conquerors in the 19th century. Early African history is best understood by forgetting about most of these boundaries and looking at the natural climatic divisions of the continent and at the peoples who inhabit it. North Africa is fringed by a warm, temperate evergreen belt of Mediterranean climate. South of this is tropical desert, the *Sahara*. South again is a wide belt of high grass *savanna*. This was the Sudan, in its ancient usage a much larger area than modern Sudan. South of the Sudan was a forest belt. The savanna extends down the east coast of Africa and there are two westward savanna belts south

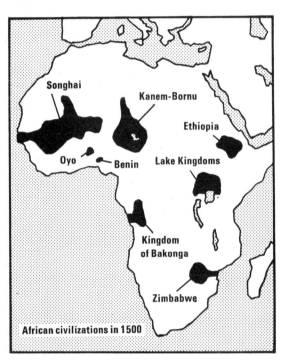

African civilizations in 1500

of the Sudan, between which lie forest belts. The forest extends from the Guinea coast to the Congo basin. The 'Horn' of Africa, Somalia and Ethiopia, consists of mountain forest and grassland fringed with deserts. Deserts fringe the coasts of south Africa.

Man (*Homo sapiens*) probably originated in east Africa (see pp.10-11). Perhaps the Bushmen of the Kalahari desert and the pygmies of the Congo are nearest to these early men. At some time between 8000 and 5000 B.C. negroes evolved in the area of the Sudan-Sahara; the climate then was much wetter. At Tassili in southern Algeria there exist cave paintings of the earliest negroes. The negroes spread over the savanna and forest belts of Africa into virgin lands which they tamed, and in doing so they produced their own civilization. *Hamites*, cousins of the *Semitic* peoples (see pp.50-1 and 66-9), spread from either Arabia or the Horn of

Below: A warrior of the uDloko regiment which was formed by the Zulu king, Mpande, in 1858.

Africa into north Africa (the *Berbers* and *Tuaregs*), and into Egypt, Somalia and Ethiopia. They were pastoral cattle-keepers. Much later, negroes spread into east Africa, mixing with Hamites, to produce the *Bantu*, who conquered much of south Africa just as Europeans began to settle there and expand northwards.

Pharaonic Egypt had regular contact with negro societies to the south, from which much Egyptian wealth came. There are more than 7,000 ancient gold mines far to the south in east Africa. Enki, a Sumerian, visited this area in 2500 B.C. and praised its trees and reeds, its oxen and birds, its silver and gold, its bronze and copper, its human beings. Somewhere between 100 B.C. and Christ's birth this area of negro Africa entered the Iron Age. Meroe on the Nile was the centre of an important negro kingdom. Meroe has been called 'the Birmingham of ancient Africa'. In the western Sudan, in the Nok region of modern Nigeria, where the Niger and Benue rivers meet, a negro culture dating back to the fifth century B.C. was making extensive use of iron. The Pharaohs called iron 'the metal of the south'.

By the early centuries of the Christian era the Sudan-savanna belt was widely settled. Kingdoms rose and fell for a *millennium* and more. Ghana to the north-north-west of the Niger is recorded as in existence by the early ninth century. In the mid-1200s a new empire of *Mali* developed in the same area. Timbuktu became a great cultural centre. These states were *Islamic* and some infiltration of Semitic Arabs and of Hamites had taken place. It was Mali that Ibn Battuta visited (see pp.90-1). In 1464 Sonni Ali, ruler of the Songhai people, began the creation of a new kingdom. In 1591 Moroccan armies from the north captured Gao and Timbuktu and destroyed the Songhai state. These are only a few of the states of the Sudan. Even after their most glorious days, there was much left. When the British explorer, Mungo Park, visited the Bambara capital in 1795 he described 'four distinct towns . . . surrounded by high mud walls' with 30,000 inhabitants. James Richardson, another explorer, wrote of Bornu in 1850 that there were 'villages every quarter of an hour . . . numerous wheatstacks on the plains . . . the whole countryside [was] a succession of cornfields and green hills'.

Farther south, in the Congo region (now Zaire), the *Bushongo* kingdom had a dynasty which in 1680 had already had 98 kings. Their king Shamba Bolongongo, who ruled from about 1600 A.D., is recorded as having abolished his standing army and forbidden the use of the throwing knife. The forest kingdom of *Benin* produced bronzes

Above: The market town of Kano in northern Nigeria. The buildings of sun-dried mud brick are decorated with intricate designs and pinnacles on roof corners.

Below: A 16th century ivory mask of a king of Benin.

and ivories which are world famous. In 1676 a Dutchman said of the capital that it was 24 to 32 kilometres in circumference. The king's court or castle alone was 'quite as large as the town of Harlem'. 'The town has . . . quite straight streets. Each is about 120 feet broad. . . . In each house is to be found a fresh water-well. Indeed the houses are beautifully built'.

East Africa developed a series of trading civilizations and its own language— *Swahili*. The Tanzanian coast is littered with broken pieces of Chinese porcelain from the 10th century onwards. The voyages of Cheng Ho to the east African coast in 1417 and 1431-3 are recorded. He came 'to see safely home the ambassadors of Malindi who had come to Pekin in 1415'. At Zimbabwe and Mapungubwe are the remains of capital cities and a royal burial ground.

Because so little written history of Africa survives, the history of the continent was neglected until independent African states began to look into their past. But today the real history of Africa is slowly being completed from archaeology and folk memory.

The Slave Trade Triangle

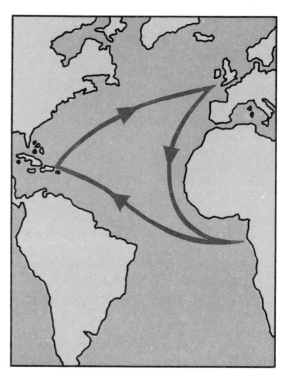

Right: Map showing the slave trade triangle from England to West Africa to the West Indies and back to England.

Slave ships such as the one below owned by Brookes of Liverpool were designed to carry the maximum number of slaves at minimum cost to the slave trader. Africans were packed in cruelly crowded conditions without proper ventilation, no sanitary provisions and little food and water. It is estimated that at least 20 per cent died en route to the West Indies.

Slavery was central to the growing trade which European countries developed with Asia, Africa and America in the 18th century. Trade led to many wars among England, France, Austria, Prussia and Russia over colonies and trading posts outside Europe. England won the wars and took the lion's share of the trade and of the colonies. So her infant industries had an ever-expanding foreign market. This was one important reason why England was the first country to industrialize.

Several European nations had joined in the trade since the Spanish colonised Hispaniola. Between 1619 and 1623 the Dutch had carried about 15,500 negroes to Brazil. Although British seamen like Sir John Hawkins had profited from the trade for some time, Britain did not begin to share in

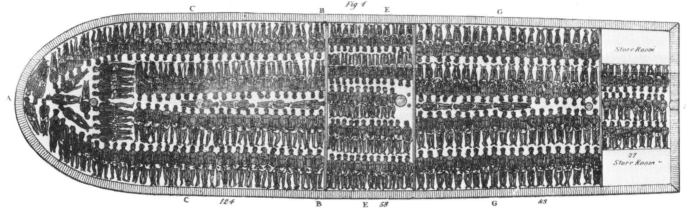

the shame directly until 1620, when the British colony of Virginia first admitted African slaves. No less than 300,000 Africans were taken to British colonies between 1680 and 1720.

The slave trade was triangular: ships sailed from England to west Africa, to the West Indies, and then back to England. On the 11th August 1750 a Liverpool ship, the 'Duke of Argyll', sailed for the west coast of Africa. The master, John Newton, later described the ship as 'very old and crazy, hardly fit to lye in a dock'. She carried iron bars with which to buy black slaves. The slave trade had been in existence for more than 300 years. Slaves were first exported from Africa in 1442, to Portugal. By the time Columbus discovered America (see pp. 118-21), they were being worked in Portugal and Spain. Yet the large-scale expansion of the African slave trade came about almost by chance. Spain had sent some negroes to the colony of Hispaniola, the Caribbean island now divided between Haiti and San Domingo. There, the negroes survived the harsh labour demanded by their Spanish

masters much better than the native *Arawak Indians*. It was to protect this gentle tribe from extinction that the Bishop of Chiapas recommended that more negroes be imported to supply the demand for cheap labour. In 1510, negroes were imported direct from Africa to work in the gold mines of Hispaniola.

On 25th October 1750 the 'Duke of Argyll' took on board the first slaves of its cargo. The *ship's log*, written by Captain Newton, describes later how the trade was conducted: '. . . The traders came on board with the owner of the slave: paid the excessive price of 86 bars which is near £12 sterling . . . But a fine manslave, now there are so many competitors, is near double the price it was formerly. There are such numbers of French vessels, and most of them determined to give any price they are asked, rather than trade should fall into our hands. . . . This day buried a fine woman slave, no. 11, having been ailing for some time . . .'

The 'Duke of Argyll' finally weighed anchor bound, 'by God's permission', for Antigua, on 22nd May 1751. The intervening

months had been spent in expeditions in the long-boats to meet traders and African kings ashore with slaves for sale. Conditions aboard the 'Duke of Argyll' during the voyage to the West Indies are described by Newton: 'Wednesday 12th June . . . Got the slaves up this morn, washed them all with fresh water. They complained so much of cold that was obliged to let them go down again when the rooms were cleaned. Buryed a man slave (no. 84) of a flux . . .'. Probably the conditions on the 'Duke of Argyll' were above average. On occasions, almost one in five negroes died on the voyage. But such was the demand in the *New World* that a slave usually sold for five times his purchase price in Africa. Jamaica, with its sugar plantations, imported 610,000 slaves between 1700 and 1786.

By 13th August the 'Duke of Argyll' was ready to leave for Liverpool, a cargo of Jamaican sugar and *molasses* stowed aboard. Most of the slaves had long since been auctioned off to the *plantation* owners. Part of the money from the sale of the molasses would go to buy more goods to buy

Many African tribes joined the Europeans in slave raids. The Hausa warriors, above, led regular raids on villages in the region of Upper Volta.

more slaves in Africa next season.

Another major export from the West Indies to Europe, and, after 1790, from the southern states of America, was cotton. Much of this cotton was re-exported as cloth to the British colonies, particularly in Africa, where it was used to buy more slaves for the plantations in America to produce more cotton. Altogether the slave trade helped to stimulate the iron trades in Birmingham, the sugar and tobacco trades in Bristol, and the cotton manufacturing industry in Lancashire.

John Newton became a priest and an important *abolitionist*: slavery, he remembered as 'A business at which my heart now shudders'. Slavery was abolished in British possessions in 1807 and the slaves freed in 1833. But the triangular trade was only part of the shame. The Dutch had been taking Indian and Chinese slaves to the East Indies. In 1953 the Iraqi police arrested a man with 50 girls going to slavery in Saudi Arabia. In thinly disguised forms, such as sham adoption and the sale of women in marriage, the ancient trade still survives.

The Industrialization of Britain

Mass production techniques were not new to world history when the *Industrial Revolution* began in 18th century England. The layout of workshops in Athens of the fourth century B.C. suggests that very little was lacking but the moving assembly line.

The first real factory in modern times was built at Derby between 1718 and 1722. This was the silk mill constructed for John and Thomas Lombe and powered by the River Derwent. It was at least five storeys high, equipped with automatic tools and capable of continuous production. The work force of about 300 performed specialized tasks. Silk was not an important branch of industry, however, and it was not until the second half of the 18th century that significant advances were made. The large new Wedgwood pottery factory was opened at Etruria in 1769. The iron works at Coalbrookdale had been extended greatly in 1760. The really large-scale spinning mill at Cromford on the River Derwent was completed by

Richard Arkwright in 1771. For it is with the harnessing of water-power to the large-scale production of iron and particularly cotton that we can begin to talk about the revolution.

There is a formidable range of theories available to explain why the revolution should have started in Britain and why, indeed, it did not happen earlier. In early 18th century England, for example, there had been a *Commercial Revolution* partly caused in turn by the exclusion of *non-Conformists* from the then anti-scientific Oxford and Cambridge Universities. The English gentry are thought to have been less inclined to put all their money into landed estates than their Continental counterparts. These factors produced a financial climate favourable to the capitalistic expansion of industry. But the two elements which are now recognized as being the most important are the stable home market, steadily increasing in size throughout most of the 18th century, and a very active and profitable export trade with the colonies (see pp. 136-7 and 142-3).

As consumers, the labouring class had been virtually ignored before about 1750. It

Spectacular technological progress in the 18th century led to the Industrial Revolution in Britain. The invention of the steam engine by George Stephenson in 1814 transformed transport. 'Locomotion' (below) could travel at eleven kilometres an hour with a load of 91 tonnes.

is at this time that the English working-man apparently began to be less satisfied with a low subsistence income accompanied by a large amount of free time. Instead of retaining his freedom of choice to spend one half of the week in leisure and to double his efforts in the other half, he seems to have become more inclined to forgo his freedom for more material goods earned in factories (see pp. 152-3). After 1700 the climate improved, disastrous harvests were less frequent and so there were more potential consumers. Labour was also kept cheap by the system of the *parish doles*.

The igniting spark of the revolution was undoubtedly the profitability of exporting to a totally under-developed world. Here, the British government was largely responsible. For the advantages enjoyed by Britain stemmed from the willingness of the British to subordinate all matters of foreign policy to basic economic profitability. Wars successfully waged produced a near monopoly of world markets.

Water-power did not in itself bring about the really revolutionary changes at factory level. Some of the early chemical and smelting factories had given a foretaste of things to come. Whereas the mills had previously needed a powerful current or fall of water and so had been built on the more remote reaches of rivers, heavy plant driven by steam could be sited anywhere, preferably alongside the chief arteries of early 19th century industry and trade, the canals. It is with the cheap mass housing on the damp ground alongside the new factories that the industrial slums really began.

Although the quality of human life reached depths previously uncharted in

Little of the increased national wealth found its way to the poor. Above, a London East End couple with their sparse belongings.

Below: Young boys were sent down into the mines alongside their fathers.

British industry, it should nevertheless be remembered that the industrial revolution did not invent child labour, for children had been savagely exploited, often by their own parents, in the longer established cottage industries. Nor should it be assumed that conditions in the slums were necessarily worse than the rural squalor. The population movement, however, was into the slums and not into the countryside. The short lives of the English working-class may not have been appreciably better than their counterparts overseas, the *plantation slaves*.

An even faster industrial growth was produced by the building of the railways. The sheer quantity of metal required produced, in effect, a new heavy industry in iron and steel. The effects on the landscape of the railways were many, but they meant, possibly above all, that cheap building materials could be distributed all over Britain, destroying the traditional local styles of architecture. Unlike the earlier industrialists such as Josiah Wedgwood at Etruria Hall, the new men of industry had their homes well out of sight of their squalid creations.

We can follow the progress of industrialization in various ways: by the inventions which it stimulated and which then advanced production, for example, or by figures for production. Abraham Darby discovered in 1709 how to smelt iron with *coke* made from coal. James Watt's first *steam engines* were made for customers in 1776. Henry Maudslay turned the *lathe* into an instrument for mass production in 1797-1800. In 1802 the export of British cotton surpassed that of wool, which had been the staple export since the Middle Ages.

The Industrialization of America

The *American Civil War* (see pp. 164-5) brought disaster, disorganization and despair to the South but in the North it was followed by an unprecedented industrial boom as vast new markets opened up for shrewd, enterprising and often ruthless businessmen. In the years after the war there was an unparalleled drive to exploit the country's natural resources, to manufacture on a large scale, to expand trade with other countries and to set up conglomerate industrial and investment banking enterprises. To fuel this industrial revolution farming steadily became mechanized and agricultural workers who lost their jobs as a result flocked to the cities to join the immigrants from every country of Europe.

The business boom resulted largely from the growth of a huge national market as Northern manufacturers rushed to satisfy the consumer demand in all areas of the country as they recovered from the traumas of the war. To take advantage of this market a comprehensive network of communications covering the land was necessary, and it was this that caused the remarkable mushroom growth of America's railway system. The Atlantic coast was linked with the Middle West by the New York Central, the Baltimore and Ohio, the Erie and the Pennsylvania systems. The first *transcontinental line* was completed when the Union Pacific linked with the Central Pacific in 1869. Other great railway systems followed, including the Santa Fe, the Northern Pacific and the Southern Pacific. During the 40 years immediately after the Civil War the total distance of railway track in America increased from 48,000 to somewhere nearer 320,000 kilometres.

Similarly, telegraph lines went up with amazing speed linking not only city with city but the nation with other countries, including a cable link under the Atlantic. In 1876 Alexander Graham Bell made the first successful telephone call, the most immediate means of communication of all.

During this period there was a population explosion in the United States. Immigrants swelled the numbers from 31 to 76 million and the big industrial cities such as New York and Chicago became cosmopolitan melting pots devoted to the exploitation of the country's mighty resources—petroleum, copper, iron ore, timber and coal—and of the great new reservoir of cheap labour. This was a period when great fortunes were made and big business dominated what the American writer Mark Twain called the 'Gilded Age'.

Many household names had such uncontrolled power to accumulate wealth that they almost 'enjoyed a licence to print money'. J. P. Morgan built up a banking

The rapid expansion of American industrialization prompted massive immigration to fill the demand for more labour. Large industrial cities such as New York (right) attracted people of all nationalities into its crowded inner districts.

Henry Ford transformed the motor car industry in 1908 with the first mass-produced car. The Model K Ford (below) was constructed on a low-cost assembly line to a standardized design. By 1913, the time required to assemble one car was 5 minutes 56 seconds.

business whose ramifications affected almost every part of the national economy. John D. Rockefeller founded the Standard Oil Company, which within ten years enjoyed a monopoly in refining and transporting petroleum. Rockefeller organized the various corporations which comprised his empire into a trust, a means of centralizing administration and control, pooling *patents* and exerting enormous pressure on other branches of industry and on politicians. Andrew Carnegie similarly emerged as the dominating figure in the steel industry; the Guggenheim family made their fortune in copper and Philip Armour and Gustavus Swift controlled the packing business. All the great industrial magnates set up giant trusts, such as the lead trust, the sugar trust and the tobacco trust. By 1900 more than 5,000 small businesses had been swallowed up by 319 trusts and 2,400 small enterprises were incorporated in 127 utilities. Vast businesses employing millions of workers were controlled by a few men in New York corporation offices. Trust-busting legislation was introduced by some states and also by the federal government, but the conglomerates remained strong and virtually unaffected even when forced to reconstitute themselves in some way. Rockefeller declared, 'The combination is here to stay. Individualism has gone, never to return.'

Manufacturing methods were revolutionized by the rapid spread of the use of electricity for many applications. In the 1890s factories were still dependent on coal and steam and it was here that the new source of energy had its greatest effect. But at first electricity was used mainly for telegraphic and telephonic communication and for illumination. Then it was applied to transport, and electric railways both on and below the surface spread until by 1912 there were 64,000 kilometres of electric track. In the factories the production-line system, which electricity made the most economical method of manufacture, changed the labour situation completely. The demand for skilled workers shrank and machines were manned by an unskilled and often illiterate workforce of immigrants and negroes from the South. The trend was most obvious in the automobile industry, and by 1914 Henry Ford's plants were turning out a quarter of a million cars a year.

The vast wealth accruing from America's industrial revolution in the late 19th century went into the pockets mainly of a few remarkable businessmen and of investors who had put money into their companies. But the working man saw little of the benefits which those who produced the wealth might reasonably have expected. He lived in city slums, worked long hours in dangerous conditions and, as modern machines were installed, was likely to find himself unemployed at a moment's notice. In addition the vast influx of immigrants meant that he had to compete with men who would work for even lower wages under even poorer conditions.

Inevitably for its own protection labour organized into *unions*, generally braving the opposition of the owners and the hostility of the authorities. The *Noble Order of the*

The discovery of oil in America totally changed entire sections of the countryside. The photograph above was taken in 1923 at the Signal Hill field in California and shows the extent to which the oil rigs dominated the landscape.

The vast distances of the American continent were finally conquered with the coming of the railway. Right: Two great companies, the Central Pacific and the Union Pacific, celebrate the completion of a new railway track to Promontory, Utah, in 1869.

Knights of Labor, founded in 1869, was open to all working men. It declared itself against strikes and violence in its efforts to gain an eight-hour day, the abolition of child labour and other reforms. It relied instead on education, political activity and the establishment of *workers' co-operatives*. However, after gaining 700,000 members it became too militant for the taste of the period and its influence declined.

More important and more successful was the *American Federation of Labor,* founded in the 1880s. Its membership was made up of craft unions and had reached 500,000 by 1900. It sought shorter hours and higher wages but preferred to co-operate with owners rather than to confront them. In addition to these large national bodies there were a number of overtly political left-wing workers' organizations which found their main strength among lumber, mining and agricultural workers.

During the last 20 years of the 19th century America suffered about 30,000 strikes. Some involved considerable violence, such as the railway strike in 1877, the *Pullman strike* in 1894 and the so-called *Cripple Creek war* affecting the mines in Colorado. In most cases the owners took extreme measures to break the strikes and could rely on the assistance of the police and government. Eventually and with great difficulty workers achieved the right to organize and to strike. But even so by 1900 working conditions had improved little. Nearly two million children were working in factories and mines and this situation was to remain for many years.

The Industrialization of Japan and Germany

Once Britain had industrialized no other country could continue as before, for there was a model in existence from which to learn and there was capital, skilled labour and *patents* to be borrowed from abroad. Japan's extraordinary march forward from backwardness and isolation to become one of the three or four most productive countries in the world resembled Britain's industrialization in some respects, but in others was totally different. Germany's industrialization was even less like Britain's.

In 1854 the ruling *Shogun* of Japan was forced to accept the ultimatum of the U.S. Commodore Matthew Perry and open Japan's ports to American trade. In the same year a similar agreement was reached with Britain and in the next year with Russia. In 1867 the Emperor Mutsuhito came to the throne and dismissed the Shogun (see pp. 194-5); he had the support of a group of young Japanese *samurai* (nobles), who were determined that their country would not again be humbled by foreigners with superior skills. During Mutsuhito's reign, which lasted until 1912, this group of samurai transformed the country. This is called the Meiji period, from Mutsuhito's adopted reign name.

Japan was able to industrialize because the country already had the requirements for advancement. Like Britain, Japan in the 18th century had gone through a kind of agricultural revolution. There was surplus production from the land, a growth of rural handicrafts and, so, a growth of skilled craftsmen. Japan also had large-scale businesses and thus trading and financial skills. Already in the 18th century the *house of Mitsui* employed over 1,000 people in its shops and practised many modern advertising and sales techniques.

What Japan needed in order to industrialize was a change in her institutions and the creation of railways, roads and ports. These the government provided. By the 1890s Japan had modern machinery of government, schools for all her people, banks and a communications system modelled on those of the west. More than this, the government had taken the agricultural surpluses away from the feudal nobility and used them to finance cotton spinning mills and a silk industry. The export of silk, largely to the U.S.A., played the same part in Japan's advance as the export of cotton did in Britain's (see pp. 144-5).

After centuries of isolation, Japan was forced to industrialize in the late 19th century. With remarkable speed, she established efficient assembly-line factories like the match factory above in Tokyo.

Left: In the late 19th century, Germany built large factories with advanced machinery which led to German domination of European heavy industry.

Around 1900 the government transferred the factories they had built to private ownership; only the railways remained as state property. In 1895 Japan built one steamship of less than 1,000 tonnes; by 1913 50,000 tonnes of shipping were being launched each year. But only between the wars (1920s and 1930s) did Japan's economy move over from one based on *consumer goods* (textiles) production to one based on modern *heavy industry*. This process was accelerated by Japan's military conquests in north China in the 1930s and in south-east Asia in the 1940s. The defeat of Japan in 1945 meant the loss of this empire but the country's economy

met this disaster, with American aid, extraordinarily successfully. Japan began making in large quantities the most advanced products: transistors, radios, watches, cars and ships. Today the country is one of the richest in the world.

Germany in the 1850s was a country of little fairy-book towns, of peasants and *junkers* (feudal nobles), of gild craftsmen and small town professional men. Her experts, visiting the *Great Exhibition* in Britain in 1851, had reported that Germany would never 'be able to reach the level of production of coal and iron currently attained in England'. Germany was divided into many different states until 1871 (see p. 163). The first step forward was the creation of the *Zollverein* (customs union) among the states. This led to the growth of an internal market, the building of railway lines and the creation of an all-German currency. The industry which now developed was heavy industry, producer goods, unlike the early industries of Britain, the U.S.A. or Japan. The result of this was the emergence of the Ruhr to become the greatest centre of industrial activity in western Europe. In the steel industry of the Ruhr German technology jumped from the rear to the front of industrial nations. In 1870 the most powerful furnaces in the Ruhr produced about 250 tonnes of pig iron a week, while the largest British ones produced 550 tonnes. By 1900 the biggest British mills produced only as much as the average German mills.

The Germans developed new industries in the late 19th century, while Britain was content with what she had already. Germany pioneered the new chemical industries; by 1900 she held 90% of the world's market for dye stuffs. She built up the transmission of electricity and the manufacture of electrical equipment. By 1913 her electrical manufacturing industry was twice as big as Britain's and only a little way behind that of the U.S.A. Germany's advance was made possible, like Japan's, by the activity of her government. By 1860, 95% of Germany's railways were publicly owned. From 1878 a *Protective Tariff* sheltered German industry from foreign competition. Anti-Socialist laws hampered working-class opposition and the first state welfare measures kept the workers satisfied. A tradition of paternalism developed.

State education, from the elementary level to great polytechnics and universities, trained technical managers with modern scientific skills and economic expertise. So in Japan and Germany, unlike Britain and the U.S.A., the government was largely responsible for industrialization taking place, though industry was privately owned.

The Industrialization of the Soviet Union

Tzarist Russia had begun to industrialize in the late 19th century. Between 1887 and 1901 and 1909 and 1914 the country's production spurted. This industrialization was like that of Germany's but at a much lower level. By 1914 Russia had developed a new industrial region in the Ukraine; there were some of the largest and most up-to-date factories and the biggest firms in the world, but the national income per head was only one-third of Germany's and one-quarter of Britain's. This was because the vast majority of the population earned their living by the most primitive forms of agriculture.

The First World War (see pp.172-7) was followed by a revolution, civil war and wars of intervention (see pp.178-9). Russia lost most of her new plants; many of her skilled workers and technicians died or fled abroad; valuable territories in which there were some of the more advanced factories became independent (Finland, Poland, the Baltic Republics). It was not until 1926 that the new revolutionary Soviet government had restored the economy to its 1913 level. Meanwhile other countries had advanced further. The new government decided that the only way to catch up was to copy the sensational success of Japan and Germany. That is for the government to take the initiative and to build a heavy industry before meeting consumer demands. In effect this meant people pulling in their belts.

But the *Communists* went farther. Industry was to belong to the state for ever; private enterprise was to be eliminated. To make this change at the same time as asking people to forego improvements in their standard of living meant that the government had to be ruthless and use dictatorial techniques. This was the situation in which Stalin rose to absolute power (see pp.178-9 and 200-1).

Stalin's government succeeded, in roughly ten years of planned industrialization (1929-40), in transforming the Soviet Union from a country with a backward economy into one of the world's major industrial powers. The cost of this forced march into the 20th century was enormous: many people died in exile or *penal colonies*, millions lost their farms and small businesses; human freedoms vanished, secret police arrests of critics and suspected opponents produced an atmosphere of frightened acceptance of official views. But the revolutionary state

Below: Russian peasants working with simple hoes to build the Great Ferghana Canal in 1939.

was made strong enough to survive the ferocious attack of Nazi Germany with much of Europe's industry behind her. In 1913 Russia produced 4.4 million tonnes of steel and 1.9 billion kilowatt hours of electric power. In 1928 the same amount of steel and 5 billion kilowatt hours of electricity were being produced, but by 1940 this had grown to 18.6 million tonnes of steel and 48.3 billion kilowatt hours of electricity. Tractors were being produced in large numbers and when war came the tractor

Below: Peasants working in an agricultural commune in Russia.

factories were soon making tanks.

The transformation of the Russian economy was achieved through state ownership of all industry and planned control of its growth. There have been six *Five Year Plans* (1928-32 inclusive; 1933-7; 1938-42; 1946-50; 1951-55; 1956-60), and then a *Seven Year Plan* (1958-65); a *Fifteen Year Plan* was talked about, but in recent years planning has become much less rigid than in the early days. The early plans only covered a limited number of the main industries and the first Five Year Plan targets were actually achieved in four years. They became goals towards which everyone was encouraged to strive. The Second World War interrupted the third Five Year Plan and there was a gap before peacetime planning could begin again. The wartime destruction was so great that Russia had almost to begin again in 1945. Her electric power production in 1946 was only the same as in 1940 and her steel production less, 13.5 million tonnes. By 1965 steel production had risen to 92.5

Above, right: The first tractors constructed at Chelyabinsk Tractor Factory in 1933, one of the heavy industries established by Stalin during Russia's ten-year industrialization plan.

million tonnes and electric power to 507 billion kilowatt hours.

The planning system meant that the accountants and managers of every factory were in touch with the central planning agency, *Gosplan*. They received a yearly target for the total of goods they must produce, and their wages and salaries were related to their reaching that target. The system was extremely effective in making possible the quick development of particular industries. The Russian space programme is modern evidence of its achievements. But it was a very poor way of meeting the consumer's need for a choice of goods.

Industrialization was made possible by millions of peasants leaving the land to work in factories. Peasant farms were pooled into huge units which could employ an immense number of machines. These *collective farms* did provide the minimum food for a growing town population with less labour, but they were Stalin's least successful economic achievement. Animals were killed by resentful peasants; in 1939 Russia had fewer cattle and sheep than in 1928, before *collectivisation*. The quality of collective farm agriculture was in general very poor and the production of grain per hectare very low. In the last ten years the Soviet government has made big efforts to increase production on its farmlands and to modernise the whole of the *retail trade*. Russian citizens today get better service in the shops than ever before though it still lags a long way behind that in the west.

DATA DIGEST

Many of the words which are italicized in the previous section are explained more fully in the following data digest. They will help to expand your knowledge of history.

Abolitionist. Someone who urged an end to slavery.

Afghans. People of Afghanistan.

Arawak Indians. Indians living on the islands of the Bahamas, Trinidad, Cuba, Jamaica, Hispaniola and Porto Rico. After the arrival of the Spanish they gradually died out.

Bantu. A Negro people that live in most areas of southern Africa. The various groups speak related languages but have different cultural characteristics. In the 19th century several Bantu tribes organized into confederacies such as the Zulu and the Basuto.

Benin. The kingdom of Benin covered roughly the area of modern Nigeria. It was at its most powerful in the 15th century and produced superb sculptures in bronze, brass and ivory.

Berbers. People inhabiting the western part of North Africa, particularly Algeria, Libya and Morocco. Most speak a Hamitic language though many speak Arabic. Considerable numbers of Berbers are nomadic.

Coke. A fuel derived from coal which produces a high quantity of heat and little smoke.

Collective farms. During the 1920s and 1930s small landowners in Russia were foced to give up their land and join a kolkhoz, or collective farm. By 1938 virtually all land was collectivized. The state decreed what and how much was to be grown. In the 1950s the size of the collective farms was greatly increased.

Commercial Revolution. Trade or business revolution.

Communists. Those who believe that all property and all the means of production should be held in common by all the people. Modern Communism dates from 1848 when Karl Marx and Friedrich Engels jointly published the *Communist Manifesto.*

Conquistadores. Expeditionary force of Spanish soldiers who landed in South America and proceeded to colonize the continent in the name of the Spanish throne.

Consumer goods. Goods intended for individual buyers and families, such as food, clothing and washing machines.

Dutch Wars. England fought three wars against Holland in the second half of the 17th century. In the third war (1672-74) England at first allied with Sweden and Holland against Louis XIV's France, but later England and France arranged a joint attack on Holland. The war ended with neither side making appreciable territorial gains.

East India Company. Several European countries established East India companies in the 17th century. The English company suffered from severe competition with the French company as each wooed the various Indian rulers. In 1757 Robert Clive defeated the French at the Battle of Plassey and the English company became supreme in India. In 1858 after the Indian Mutiny control passed to the British government.

Great Exhibition. An exhibition held in the Crystal Palace in Hyde Park in 1851. It demonstrated Britain's technological achievements and scientific expertise. It was the first of its kind.

Hamites. A large group of peoples that moved into Africa from Asia at a very early period. They lived in northern and eastern Africa, many of them being herdsmen.

Heavy Industry. The branch of industry that produces machinery, steam turbines, roller-bearings and other large components that depend mainly on iron and steel and serve other branches of manufacturing industry rather than being sold in shops.

House of Mitsui. One of the oldest of the great family business trusts of Japan. It was particularly powerful in banking under the shoguns.

Industrial revolution. The transformation of England and other countries in the 18th century into industrialized and trading nations.

Islam. The religion of the Muslims, also known as Mohammedanism. It is based on the teachings of Muhammad who lived from about 570 to 632 A.D.

Lathe. A machine tool which can perform many jobs in factories and workshops, such as shaping and turning.

Mali. A country in western Africa. The medieval state of Mali reached its peak of civilization in the 14th century and Timbuktu was a leading centre of learning and culture.

Marathas. Also known as Mahrattas, this people of western India became extremely powerful in the middle of the 18th century, controlling the Deccan and a large part of southern India. The British after several campaigns finally defeated them in 1818.

Memoirs. Record of events observed from a personal point of view.

Millennium. Period of 1,000 years.

Molasses. Syrup obtained from sugar.

Mughal dynasty. The Muslim empire in India that lasted from 1526 to 1857. The name Mughul, or Mogul, comes from Mongol, but the founders of the empire were in fact not Mongols but Turks.

Navigation Acts. Acts of Parliament of 1650 providing that all commerce conducted between England and her colonies would be carried only on British vessels or under the British flag.

New World. The American continent.

Non-Conformists. Protestants in England who would not conform to the articles of faith and the rites of the Church of England.

Parish doles. Payments to the unemployed by the local parish authorities.

Patents. The protection given to inventors to prevent anyone else from copying their work. Patents generally last for 20 years, after which inventions can be used without permission or payment.

Penal colonies. Colonies to which countries sent criminals as a punishment. The best-known was the French colony of Devil's Island in French Guiana. Britain sent criminals to Australia. Many of Russia's penal colonies were in Siberia.

Pharaohnic Egypt. The period during which Egypt was ruled by pharaohs.

Plantation. Estate on which tobacco, cotton, tea or other crops are cultivated.

Protective Tariff. A tax on imports which, by making foreign products more expensive, gives a boost to the home market.

Pullman strike. In May 1894 the workers of the Pullman Company near Chicago struck in protest against a wage cut. The American Railway Union called its members out and the strike spread with several violent incidents. Federal troops broke the strike in August.

Rajputs. Warlike Hindu people of Rajputana, an area in north-western India now in Rajasthan. They were divided into 32 clans. All the clans had been subdued by the Mughul emperors by the early 17th century. Later they expanded into central India but were driven back by the British.

Retail trade. Trade between a shop or stall and a customer. It is the last link in the distribution chain between producers and consumers.

Sahara. The largest desert in the world with an estimated area of more than 3 million square miles. It occupies most of Algeria, Egypt and Libya and large areas of Morocco, Tunisia and Sudan. It also covers parts of Spanish Sahara, Chad, Niger, Mali and Mauritania.

Samurai. Warriors of feudal Japan who served their lord with unswerving loyalty and unquestioning obedience. They prized honour above all and were expected to commit *hara-kiri* (suicide) if they fell into dishonour.

Savanna. Grassland found in tropical and sub-tropical areas, particularly in Africa. The grass grows in clumps and provides good grazing.

Semites. People who were living in and around the lands of Mesopotamia from as early as 2850 B.C. Their descendants possibly included the Akkadians, Assyrians and the Babylonians.

Seven Years' War. From 1756 to 1763 Prussia, Britain and Hanover were ranged against France, Russia, Austria and Sweden. The war spread also to North America and India where Britain made important gains from France. By the end of the war Britain controlled Canada, thanks to James Wolfe's capture of Quebec, and almost the whole of India.

Ship's log. Book recording the daily events during a ship's voyage, including its rate of progress.

Shogun. Between about 1600 and 1867 the shogun was the effective ruler of Japan, the emperor having little power. The shogunate was held at different periods by the three great aristocratic families, the Minamoto, the Ashikaga and the Tokugawa.

Spanish Succession. Charles II of Spain died in 1700 with no children. England, Holland, Austria and Prussia formed a Grand Alliance to prevent the French claimant from succeeding. War broke out in 1702 and the Alliance won victories at Blenheim and Oudenarde. England took Gibraltar and Minorca and fighting also spread to North America. The Peace of Utrecht in 1713 ended the war.

Steam engines. Engines driven by expanding steam produced from a boiler. By the early 19th century they were used for driving machines in factories, for transport on land and sea and many other purposes.

Swahili. A language used by many people in eastern and central Africa as a second language to communicate with

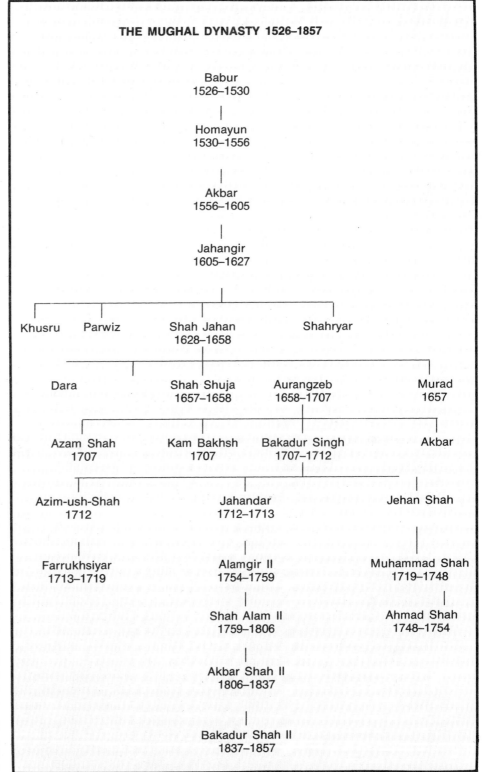

THE MUGHAL DYNASTY 1526–1857

Babur 1526–1530
Homayun 1530–1556
Akbar 1556–1605
Jahangir 1605–1627

Khusru — Parwiz — Shah Jahan 1628–1658 — Shahryar

Dara — Shah Shuja 1657–1658 — Aurangzeb 1658–1707 — Murad 1657

Azam Shah 1707 — Kam Bakhsh 1707 — Bakadur Singh 1707–1712 — Akbar

Azim-ush-Shah 1712 — Jahandar 1712–1713 — Jehan Shah

Farrukhsiyar 1713–1719 — Alamgir II 1754–1759 — Muhammad Shah 1719–1748

Shah Alam II 1759–1806 — Ahmad Shah 1748–1754

Akbar Shah II 1806–1837

Bakadur Shah II 1837–1857

each other. It contains a considerable number of Arabic words.

Tuaregs. A Berber people with a long history and a sophisticated social organization. They live mainly in the Sahara region.

Unions. Trade unions, or labour unions, are organizations for workers that look after the welfare of their members and try to improve their wages, working hours and general conditions.

Viceroy. A governor representing the monarch's authority in a colony or province.

Welfare. Welfare legislation relates to people's health, living conditions and education. The social services, including family allowances, housing, health and recreation, national assistance and compensation for injuries, are all part of the welfare services.

Workers' cooperatives. Associations in which workers contribute to a joint undertaking and then share any profits according to their payments. The most common workers' cooperatives are agricultural. Farmers in a cooperative buy their supplies and market their produce at more favourable terms than if they were on their own.

REVOLUTIONS AND WARS

American War of Independence

This war, fought from 1775 to 1783, began as a struggle between the British government and the people who lived in Britain's 13 colonies along the east coast of North America. Britain had always firmly believed that she should benefit from these colonies. Laws were therefore made restricting the rights of the Americans to trade with other countries and to manufacture what goods they chose. Such laws were disliked by the colonists, many of whom were not even of British origin and felt no loyalty towards a government which was 4,830 kilometres away in Westminster. However, British rule was tolerated because the American colonists were threatened in the west by the French and the Indians and needed the protection of British troops. French power in America was destroyed during the Seven Years War (1756-63) (see pp. 128-9). It was after this that the American colonists began to ask for greater freedom and a larger share in the government of their lands.

Trouble began in 1765 when the British government passed the *Stamp Act*, forcing the colonists to pay stamp duty on newspapers and legal documents. This was done in an attempt to make the colonists contribute more money towards the cost of keeping troops in America. The colonists argued that they must be consulted about any new taxes, using the slogan, 'No taxation without representation', they refused to pay the stamp duty and pulled down the offices of the tax collectors. The Stamp Act was wisely withdrawn, but other ways of raising money were tried, including a tax on tea. This caused further trouble, particularly in Boston where the colonists had a clever leader named Samuel Adams. In 1773 a group of colonists, dressed as Red Indians, boarded two cargo ships and tipped £10,000 of tea

Opposite page: George Washington crossing the Delaware river at night on an expedition against the British during the American War of Independence. The battle of Trenton, fought at dawn on 26 December 1776, resulted in a spectacular victory for the colonists and the capture of 1000 Hessian mercenaries fighting for the British. This battle, and the subsequent one fought at Princeton in January 1777, marked the end of the first campaign of the war.

Below: The Battle of Bunker Hill, 1775, during which the British secured a victory over the colonists' forces but at the loss of one-third of their troops.

Below: Brown Bess, the standard musket of the British army from 1720 to 1790. Many of these flintlocks were captured by the colonists.

into the waters of Boston harbour. As a punishment for the *Boston Tea Party*, the harbour was closed and the people of Massachussetts lost many of their political rights. George III and his Prime Minister, Lord North, insisted on their right to rule over the colonies in all matters. The colonists were determined to resist and began to store arms and to train for war. In 1775 a detachment of British troops came into conflict with some colonial *militiamen* at Lexington. This skirmish was the beginning of the War of Independence.

At first the colonists seemed to have little chance of success. The colonies were not used to co-operating together, their armies were ill-disciplined and ill-armed and many Americans did not support the war. The superior British armies were victorious at the battle of Bunker Hill (1775) and captured New York (1776) and Philadelphia (1777). However, a number of factors helped to improve the prospect for the colonists. In 1775 George Washington (see p. 242), a landowner from Virginia, was chosen to command their armies. He was a good leader who inspired his men to fight well. He avoided pitched battles with the British armies, attacking them instead as they were moving from place to place. In 1776 the *Declaration of Independence* was adopted. This document, written mainly by Thomas Jefferson, declared in stirring language the colonies' intention of breaking completely with Britain. It gave the colonists a great cause to fight for and encouraged Britain's enemies in Europe to send help. Moreover, the British generals, such as William Howe, were both careless and overconfident. They were ill-supported by politicians in Britain, some of whom were sympathetic to the Americans.

The turning point of the war came in 1777. George III sent General John Burgoyne to lead an army south from Canada, join up with General Howe's army at Albany and launch an attack against the New England colonies. The plan completely misfired. Burgoyne's army was constantly attacked by *snipers* as it struggled through swamps and forests. Howe failed to come to his help and, by the time Burgoyne's army reached Saratoga, it was surrounded by a much larger American force. Burgoyne surrendered his army. This victory not only gave hope to the colonists but encouraged France and Spain to declare war on Britain.

Britain now found her possessions in the West Indies and the Mediterranean under attack. Her navy, which had been neglected since the Seven Years War, was unable to keep command of the seas. This fact was important in the *siege* of Yorktown (1781). General Cornwallis, after a successful campaign in Carolina, marched to Yorktown where he hoped a British fleet would come to bring him aid. Washington's army, reinforced with French volunteers, at once *besieged* the town. After several months of waiting, Cornwallis's men sighted sails. To their disappointment it proved to be a French fleet. Realizing the hopelessness of his position, Cornwallis surrendered his army. This ended the fighting in America.

At the *Treaty of Versailles* (1783) Britain recognized the independence of the American colonies. It was fitting that George Washington should be elected the first president of the new nation. It was significant that Frenchmen returned from America determined to gain more liberty in their own land (see pp. 158-9). Britain learned her lesson and henceforward ruled her colonies more sensibly.

157

The French Revolution

One reason for the French Revolution, which began in 1789, was the wide division which existed between the different classes of people in France. The nobility and clergy had kept certain privileges first granted to them in the Middle Ages; for instance, they were exempted from paying many taxes which ordinary people had to pay. The middle classes had grown rich and important, but they were denied any hope of holding high positions in the Government. The peasants were over-burdened with taxes and oppressed by their masters, who had many *feudal rights* over them and could even hunt over their lands (see pp. 78-9).

Another reason for the revolution was a deep dissatisfaction with the way in which France was governed. Due to the work of Cardinal Richelieu and Louis XIV (see p. 238) in the 17th century, the king had become all-powerful. He could choose his own ministers, make his own laws and imprison his opponents. This system worked very badly under a weak king like Louis XVI, who was dominated by his pleasure-loving queen, Marie Antoinette. They lived in the luxurious Palace of Versailles, surrounded by their nobles and caring little for the thoughts, problems and suffering of ordinary French people.

In the 18th century, writers like Montesquieu, Rousseau and Voltaire had pointed out the inequalities and injustices which existed in France. Events, such as the *American War of Independence* (see pp. 156-7), had stirred thoughtful people to demand greater freedom. Sheer poverty and hunger impelled the mass of the French people towards a revolution.

In 1789 a serious financial crisis caused Louis XVI to take the desperate measure of summoning the *States-General.* This was a kind of parliament, which had not met for 150 years. Its meetings were now dominated by the middle-class *delegates* who, with the support of some of the nobles and clergy, proposed all manner of reforms. It soon became clear that nothing useful would be achieved. Meanwhile, the people of Paris, angry at the failure of the States-General and hungry because of the high cost of bread, gathered in the streets. On 14th July, 1789, a violent mob, searching for gunpowder, attacked and seized the *Bastille,* an ancient fortress and prison which stood as a symbol of royal power. Violence quickly spread—the revolution had begun.

For two years the revolution proceeded without too much brutality. The leader dur-

qui ont bravé les menaces d'un détachement de hussards, qui avoit ce traître Bouillé! M. Sauce, Procureur de la Commune, a invité lui et de s'y reposer lui et sa famille Le généreux citoyen de accepté les offres du Roi. disent qu'il devoit tout à sa patrie.

Above: Detail from a contemporary print of the capture of Louis XVI, King of France, and his family. The king, although somewhat more conscientious than his corrupt grandfather, Louis XV, was also less able and less energetic. This fatal combination of stubbornness and indecisiveness made him unable to resist the popular demands for violent change.

ing this early period was the Count of Mirabeau, a moderate man who hoped for peaceful changes. Many of the privileges of the nobles and clergy were taken away and ideas were put forward for limiting the power of the king. Although Louis XVI agreed to all this, he was secretly trying to find ways of preventing these changes. In this he was supported by the nobles and clergy and also by foreign countries such as Austria, birthplace of Marie Antoinette. In the light of these events, many people began to demand that the king should be deposed. They wished to see a *republic* set up and used as their slogan, 'Liberty, Equality, Fraternity'. The king and queen were imprisoned, together with many nobles and clergy. Mirabeau's death (1791) and the outbreak of war with Austria (1792) gave the extremists among the revolutionaries an excuse for violent measures. Louis XVI and Marie Antoinette, along with nobles and clergymen, were put to death on the newly-invented *guillotine.*

Meanwhile, there were quarrels among the revolutionary groups and their leaders. The *Girondins*, or moderate Republicans, were overthrown by the more extreme *Jacobins*. Then the Jacobin leaders quarrelled among themselves and the pleasure-loving but patriotic Danton was defeated by his ruthless rival, Maximilien de Robespierre. Under Robespierre's leadership there was a 'Reign of Terror' in France, during which all opponents were crushed. In the end Robespierre himself was overthrown and executed (1794). For the next few years the French people struggled to find a satisfactory form of government. Then, in 1799, Napoleon Bonaparte (see p. 241), France's most bril-

Far right: The Reign of Terror, during which many thousands of people belonging to the nobility and clergy, together with the royal family, were forced to walk up the steps of the guillotine, a gruesome instrument composed of a sharp blade suspended between two upright pillars. The severed head of each person executed was displayed to the spectators standing in the square. The Terror lasted until the man behind it, Maximilien Robespierre (right) was put to death.

liant general, seized power. As a *dictator,* he was able to give France the strong but fair government which it so desperately needed.

The revolution had brought many changes. Church lands and the estates of nobles were confiscated and shared out. Taxation was made fair and unjust laws were swept away. All men became equal in the eyes of the law and were given some share in deciding how France should be governed. The red, white and blue *Tricolor* became the national flag. The stirring and patriotic song called the *Marseillaise* became the *National Anthem*. However, the French Revolution was of great importance not merely for France but for Europe too. Most foreign governments were horrified at the ideas behind the revolution and many nations went to war with France to resist the spread of these ideas. During these wars, French armies marched through and conquered almost every European country. In this way the French cry for 'Liberty, Equality, Fraternity' was heard in many lands. Sooner or later in the course of the 19th century the movement towards greater freedom which had been felt in France spread throughout Europe.

The Concert of Europe

In 1815, following the final defeat of Napoleon after over 20 years of war, the leaders of the European countries gathered together at a congress in Vienna. The agreement which they made—the 'Concert of Europe'—was an undertaking to settle disputes without recourse to war and to maintain the political structure of Europe, as they themselves established it, against liberal, national, or revolutionary changes. The countries concerned at the beginning were Austria, Russia, Prussia and Britain. Others, not as powerful, came to Vienna to see that they were not treated unfairly, and together with the four members of the concert they made up the Congress. However, each of the leading countries had different ideas of how they should keep the peace.

Austria, although she had been defeated in the earlier battles of the *Napoleonic Wars,* was still powerful, but not rich enough to police Europe on her own. Prince Metternich, the Austrian Chief Minister who dominated the Congress, realized that the cost of the large army which would be needed for such a task would require heavy taxes and if taxes on the ordinary people were too heavy there would be a revolt.

The Russian Tsar, Alexander I, came to the Congress as the leader of a new power in Europe. With an army of 600,000 men, Russia was a leading power. Moreover, the Tsar had shown that he was prepared to use his army in support of his ideas. He had at the same time called a meeting of the other leading powers at Paris. This meeting, known as the *Holy Alliance,* was to form a group of 'Christian rulers to protect the rights of smaller states'—in fact to wage an ideological *Crusade* against the rationalist ideas of the *Enlightenment* and the *Revolution* (see pp. 158-9). Even though Metternich called the Holy Alliance 'a loud nothing', Austria and Prussia joined it. Most European rulers eventually decided to sign the agreement.

Prussia, 'the army which became a state,' having suffered a double shock of defeat by Napoleon in 1806 and French occupation until 1812, badly needed a period of peace in which to rebuild her once-proud army and reform the state. Britain was the richest and economically most advanced country represented at Vienna. She had control of the seas because of her powerful navy. Lord Castlereagh, the Foreign Minister, thought it would be better for trade if there was a lasting peace in Europe. So the four leading powers all wanted a settlement of Europe which would guarantee peace. The price of

Above: Man-of-war at Spithead on the Thames estuary, where a large number of the Royal Navy ships-of-the-line were anchored. At the time of the Congress of Vienna in 1815, Britain's control of the sea was unquestioned.

achieving their harmony was paid by the smaller states.

Russia was allowed to keep Finland (taken from Sweden) and central Poland. In exchange Sweden got Norway from the Danes. Prussia was given parts of the Rhineland and Saxony, while Austria took over some of the Balkan lands and regained control of northern Italy. The Belgians were put under Dutch rule and Britain took Heligoland and the Cape of Good Hope. The small states of Germany (there were 35 of them) were brought together in a *Confederation,* where each state had its own king or prince and sent a delegate to the Confederation. This assembly was largely dominated by Austria.

The Congress most feared France, because this was where the revolution and the war had started. It was, therefore, necessary to

Above: The Congress of Vienna, a gathering of the kings, heads of state and foreign ministers of Europe, in 1815, to undertake to re-establish the rule of 'legitimacy'. The intention was to 'freeze' the continent in a pre-Napoleonic mould which could not be broken by liberal or revolutionary upheavals. The agreement signed in Vienna by Britain, Russia, Austria, Prussia and others remained intact for only 15 years.

Right: Louis XVIII, the gout-ridden king who tried feebly to preserve some of the accomplishments of the Napoleonic era. Within a year he had become widely unpopular with both the nobility and the lower classes. On 20th March 1815 he fled to Belgium on hearing of Napoleon's arrival in France from the island of Elba.

keep France quiet and peaceful, in case another revolt should occur and spread once again through Europe. But by the time the concert of powers held their first meeting on their own after the *Congress of Vienna* (at Aix-la-Chapelle in 1818) France appeared to be peacefully settled under the new King, Louis XVIII, and was admitted to join the concert as an equal partner in a Quintuple Alliance. At this meeting, although there was some disagreements among the powers, they did succeed in carrying out some small reforms.

By the time of the second meeting (at Troppau in 1820) there had been revolts in Spain, Portugal and Naples and, although a further meeting took place in 1821, the powers could not agree among themselves as to what should be done about them. Finally, in 1823, the French, on their own, sent an army into Spain, crushed the revolt and restored the Spanish king to his throne.

By the 1830s the Concert of Europe was no longer a concert, for each country acted as it wanted to and France had had another revolution. Belgium gained independence from Holland in 1831 and unrest was becoming general. The basic mistake which was made by the great powers in 1815 was to arrange the states of Europe without considering the wishes of the ordinary people. The idea of nations coming together to work for peace was to be repeated again and again, however, not only in Europe, but eventually throughout the whole world.

The Unification of Italy

In 1850, Italy was still a collection of separate states ruled by foreign powers. Austria controlled most territory through the occupation of Venice and Lombardy and her influence on the kingdom of Naples and Sicily. The Pope, Pius IX, still ruled the Papal states, with French support. A wave of nationalism was sweeping through these states but until 1850 none of the resulting

Below: Giuseppe Garibaldi, 1807-82, the hero of the movement proclaiming Italian independence and unity. He was loved by his people and admired by foreigners.

revolutions had achieved anything except the expulsion of popular leaders like Mazzini and Giuseppe Garibaldi. However, there was one independent state, Piedmont-Sardinia, which had an Italian king, Victor Emmanuel, and a shrewd Prime Minister, Count Cavour. Both these men were dedicated to unifying Italy, but Cavour realized that a revolt without support from the big powers could not succeed.

The *Crimean War* (1854) gave Cavour his chance to obtain this support. He sent 15,000 Piedmontese troops to the Crimea, where they fought bravely alongside British and French, so that when the *Peace Conference* (1856) was called Cavour attended with his new allies. In this way the problem of Italy was brought to the attention of Britain and France and by 1858 Napoleon III of France had secretly agreed with Cavour to attack Austria; in 1859 the war began. By

Above: King Victor Emmanuel II of Sardinia, who became the first ruler of unified Italy.

Right: Count Camillo Cavour, Italy's outstanding statesman.

July it was over, with a defeated Austria handing Lombardy and the central states to Piedmont-Sardinia. France took Nice and Savoy as her share while Naples, Sicily and the Papal states remained independent.

The next move was in May, 1860. Garibaldi and his *Red Shirts* invaded Sicily, secretly aided by Cavour and not so secretly protected by the British navy. This invasion was successful and was followed by a landing on the mainland in August. On 7th September Garibaldi entered Naples in triumph. However, before he could invade the Papal states, the Piedmontese army advanced and united these states with Italy. The French, who were now no longer favourable to Italian unification, still protected

Rome and the *Vatican*. In this way most of Italy, with the exception of Venice, was united under King Victor Emmanuel. In 1866, the Austrians were defeated by Prussia at Königgratz and in the general confusion the city of Venice was taken by the Italians.

After the defeat of France in 1870, also by the Prussians, and the collapse of the French empire, Italian troops entered Rome and the Pope retired to the Vatican. By 1872, although Cavour was dead and Garibaldi had retired, Italy was united. By using other countries' wars and taking advantage of French and Austrian defeats the Italians had made their dreams of a *Risorgimento,* or Reawakening, come true.

The Unification of Germany

The situation in Germany in the 1860s in many ways resembled that of Italy: a collection of separate states, most of which were under Austrian domination. Even Prussia was split in two, with Brandenberg and Pomerania in the east and Westphalia in the west. This position on two of Germany's natural borders, coupled with economic leadership of the *Zollverein,* or *Customs Union,* made Prussia the natural centre of nationalist activity.

There had been one attempt at unification in 1850, when the King of Prussia had proposed that Bavaria, Württemberg,

Hanover and Saxony should unite with Prussia. But by the *Treaty of Olmütz* Austria had forced him to abandon the idea. However, when in 1861 the new King of Prussia finally came to full power, the shame of Olmütz drove him to an unceasing quest to strengthen the Prussian army. William I was a conservative, but his liberal parliament repeatedly refused to consider any request for an enlargement of the armed forces. In 1862 the king called Otto von Bismarck (see p. 233) to Berlin to be his chief minister. Bismarck was a landowner, a conservative reactionary and, although personally unpopular with the royal family, was intensely loyal to them—and to German unity. His first act as *Minister-Präsident* was to over-rule the parliament; he raised the 39 infantry and ten cavalry regiments the king had called for and eventually brought the parliament under control.

Then, in 1863, the Poles rose in revolt against Russia. Bismarck supported Russia in her attempt to crush the rebellion. This secured the eastern border of Germany and

made sure that Russia would not interfere in any future Prussian campaign against the Austrians. In 1866 there was a dynastic squabble in Schleswig-Holstein. Prussia settled it by going to war with Denmark, defeating her and provoking the Austrians to declare war. In July 1866 the Austrians and the Saxons were defeated at the battle of Königgratz. Having thus secured the southern border, Bismarck annexed Hamburg in 1867 and made the whole of the North Sea and Baltic coast a Prussian domain. By 1869 all the states in Germany, with the exception of Württemberg, Bavaria, Baden and the Palatine, were united under Prussian leadership. When the Franco-Prussian War broke out in 1870 these four states were persuaded to place their armies under Prussian command.

After the French defeat and the fall of Paris, Bismarck brought his king to Paris and had him proclaimed Emperor of Germany *(Kaiser).* Where fine phrases and liberal-democratic revolution had failed, the blood and iron of a reactionary conservative, who was also a shrewd statesman, had succeeded. In Italy the unification had brought all the states together under Rome, the ancient capital; in Germany, unification was achieved by bringing the states under Berlin—a new capital for a new country.

Below: King William I of Prussia being proclaimed Emperor of all Germany at Versailles in France in 1871 after the Franco-Prussian war. The risk of war between Prussia and France had long been growing, but it was the offer of the Spanish throne to a German prince which finally pushed the French into military action against the Germans. The war lasted only six months.

Far right: Otto von Bismarck, Prussian Prime Minister and architect of the brilliant scheme to unify Germany under the aegis of a dominant Prussia. It was largely Bismarck who engineered the circumstances which led to the Franco-Prussian war, the total defeat of the French, the emergence of a powerful German state and the forging of a German empire.

The American Civil War—1861 to 1865

Soldiers of the Civil War. Above: An infantryman in the Union Army of the North and, far right, 'Johnny Reb', a soldier of the Southern Confederate Army.

This war was fought between the Northern and Southern states of the U.S.A. Its causes lay in the differences which had developed between the way of life in the North and that in the South. The southerners were farmers who chiefly grew cotton and tobacco. There were few large towns or industries and rich and poor alike lived from the profit of their farms. The large *plantation* owners used Negro slaves to work on their estates and look after their children (see pp. 142-3). In the North there were many towns where people worked in factories making cloth or iron. Ships crowded at the quaysides of the ports where rich merchants and bankers lived. There were more people in the North and they were generally more prosperous than their fellow-countrymen in the South.

By 1850 it was becoming difficult for *Congress* to pass laws which were fair to people in both North and South. Northerners wanted to protect their industries by putting *customs duties* on foreign goods, but this did not suit the people of the South. The biggest dispute was over slavery. People in the North believed slave-owning was wrong and wished for laws to end it. The southerners saw no evil in slavery and felt they would be ruined if they freed their slaves. As western lands were added to the U.S.A., there were bitter quarrels over whether slavery would be allowed there.

In 1860, Abraham Lincoln (see p. 238), son of a farmer, was elected president of the U.S.A. He belonged to the *Republican Party* which had promised to pass laws to end slavery. Alarmed at this, seven southern states broke away from the U.S.A. in 1861. They chose Jefferson Davis as president, and called themselves the *Confederate States of America*. They were later joined by four more states. Abraham Lincoln, a wise and patient leader, had not intended to force the southerners to free their slaves. As president he had promised to 'preserve, protect and defend' the *Union*. He therefore asked all loyal states to help in ending the Confederacy.

War began when southern troops attacked Fort Sumter in Charlestown harbour on 12th April, 1861. Both sides were hopeful of quick victories and a short war, but it took four years of bitter and bloodthirsty fighting to settle the struggle. Much of the fighting occurred in the areas surrounding the two capital cities of Washington (North) and Richmond (South), separated by only 160 kilometres. At first the initiative was taken by the South, who had brilliant generals in Robert E. Lee and 'Stonewall' Jackson. They led the army of northern Virginia in swift raids up the Shenandoah valley, winning victories at Bull Run and Fredericksburg in 1862. Another victory was achieved at Chancellorsville (1863), but General Jackson was wounded and died shortly afterwards. Later in 1863, Lee led yet another advance up the Shenandoah valley and into Pennsylvania. Here he lost the three-day battle of Gettysburg (1st-3rd July) to a northern army commanded by General Meade. It was a decisive battle, for Lee was never strong enough to advance again.

So far President Lincoln had been ill-served by his generals in the east. Farther west, however, remarkable victories had been won in 1863 at Vicksburg and Chattanooga by General Ulysses S. Grant. He was an energetic and capable commander of the northern armies, which now began to close in on Richmond. Meanwhile General Sherman led a northern army into Georgia and South Carolina, where it destroyed crops, cattle and horses and left behind a devastated land. In 1865 Grant captured

Richmond. General Lee, in order to save the South any further suffering, surrendered to Grant at Appomattox on 9th April.

The North had won the war because it had more men and money than the South. It had the factories needed to make guns and ammunition and a railway system capable of moving supplies rapidly. It had a powerful navy able to blockade the southern ports, making it impossible for southern farmers to export their cotton in exchange for much needed weapons. As the war went on the South became inferior to the North in everything but the courage of its soldiers. A total of 620,000 men lost their lives in the war.

As a result of the war, the eleven Confederate States once again became part of the U.S.A., and so the Union was saved. Laws were passed abolishing slavery and so all Negro slaves were freed. Unfortunately President Lincoln was assassinated five days after the end of the war. Without his tolerance and humanity to restrain them, the northern statesmen would have treated the South as a conquered land. Southerners bitterly resented the new rights given to Negroes, and founded secret societies, such as the *Ku Klux Klan*, to oppose the policies of the Republicans, who remained powerful until 1885.

Below: The battle of Gettysburg. In July 1863 the Union Army of the Potomac under General George Meade checked the advance of the Confederates and resoundingly defeated them in a three-day battle at Gettysburg, Pennsylvania.

The Ottoman Empire

The *Seljuk Turks* had invaded Asia Minor in the eleventh century (see pp. 98-9). After their defeat by Genghis Khan (see p. 237), the Seljuk empire broke up into several smaller states. Sögüt, near the border of the Byzantine empire, was one of the poorest and least important of these Turkish, successor states. In 1288, led by Osman, Sögüt began to attack its neighbours. The *Ottoman Turks* got their name from this leader; their territory grew rapidly and they first invaded Europe in 1345. By 1400 they controlled Asia Minor and had taken over most of the Byzantine empire; their navy dominated the Mediterranean. In 1402 Tamerlane (see pp. 98-9) invaded the Ottoman empire, killing the ruling Sultan and dividing up his lands. But eleven years later the empire was re-established under a new Sultan, Mehmet I.

The Ottoman Turks were *Muslims* but they allowed non-Muslims to live in their lands and they encouraged trade and merchants. Young slaves called *Janissaries* were trained as professional soldiers and formed an elite corps totally loyal to the Sultan. Mehmet I encouraged the development of education. He instigated a religious war against the Greek Orthodox Christians in Byzantium. He captured territory in Europe but gained Constantinople (Byzantium) only in 1453 after a long siege. This was a turning point in European history: the last surviving remnant of the Roman empire in the east (see pp. 70-3) was destroyed.

Greek scholars and artists fled westwards and contributed to the European *Renaissance* (see pp. 110-13).

Constantinople, renamed Istanbul, became the capital of the Ottoman empire and the great cathedral of Santa Sophia in Istanbul became a *mosque*. The empire increased in size until it reached from the Black Sea coast to the Red Sea, including Asia Minor (present-day Turkey), and Arabia (today's Iraq, Syria, Lebanon, Israel and Saudi Arabia). It stretched along the North African coast, including Egypt and countries to the west. In Europe the Turks ruled the Balkan countries, Hungary and Transylvania. In 1571 they were defeated in a sea battle, Lepanto, by the Habsburgs and their advance stopped. They began to lose large areas of land, but there was a revival of Ottoman strength in the late 17th century. A new advance into Europe began: Vienna was nearly captured, but it was saved in 1683 with the help of Jan Sobieski, the Polish king. Villages on the Austrian-Hungarian frontiers experienced generations of threats from the Turks and their fortified churches and village walls can still be seen. The defeat of the Turks before Vienna began their slow retreat from Europe. By 1700 they had lost Hungary and their conquests in the Ukraine.

The Turkish Sultan was also the *Caliph*, the ruler of all Muslims. His huge empire was divided into provinces, each of which had a governor. Government officers, most of whom were Christian slaves, were trained

Below: Battle of Navarino, a painting in oils by Thomas Luny. During the Turkish-Greek war in the 1820s, several European nations attempted to take advantage of the conflict to gain territory at the expense of the Turks. On 20th October 1827 a demonstration of naval might by Britain, France and Russia in support of the Greeks turned into a battle at Navarino in which the Turkish-Egyptian fleet was destroyed.

in a *Palace School.* The Sultan was advised by a council, the *Divan;* the chief adviser was the *Grand Vizier.* After 1654 *Viziers* really ruled the empire. Most of them belonged to the *Kiuprili family* and they tried to reform the government, but in vain. Provincial governors ignored the Sultan's orders; the Janissaries rebelled, killed the Sultan and chose his successor like the *Praetorian Guard* in the Roman empire. The empire grew weaker during the 18th century: more land was lost in wars to Austria and Russia. After 1740 the Sultan allowed foreigners to control Turkish trade and industry and gave them favourable conditions. The Turkish people were still badly treated and they often revolted.

The Sultan Selim III (1789-1807) tried to make changes and improve the government. He was influenced by the ideas of the French Revolution, but his changes were unpopular and unsuccessful. As Turkey weakened in the 19th century, Austria and Russia looked for gains in territory in the Balkans while Britain and France tried to win control of the Middle East. Their quarrels led to sev-

Above: The Favourite of the Harem, an engraving after a painting by Laura Lushington in 1840. Although the print shows the ladies elegantly dressed and not discontented, the Ottoman empire and the Sultan in particular did not hold women in very high esteem, and they were often brutally treated in the harems.

Top right: Abdul-Hamid II, a painting in the Istanbul Museum. Sultan Hamid II, who ruled from 1876 to 1909, instituted extremely repressive measures against the so-called 'Young Turks' whose aim it was to revolutionize Turkey and bring it into the modern world.

eral wars. Gradually the Christian people of the Balkans won their independence from the Ottoman Turks. Greece and Moldavia and Wallachia, two provinces on the Black Sea, rebelled in 1821. Greece's independence was proclaimed in 1822. Byron, the poet, died fighting for it in 1824, and in 1827 a British-led fleet destroyed the Turkish and Egyptian fleets at Navarino. In 1829 the Turks, in the *Treaty of Adrianople,* recognized the independence of Greece, Moldavia and Wallachia and Serbia which had had partial autonomy since 1817. Romania came into existence in 1862 when Turkey accepted the uniting of Moldavia and Wallachia. The *Treaty of Berlin* in 1878 guaranteed Romania's independence and produced two new independent states, Bulgaria and Montenegro. Montenegro, Serbia and other Balkan states were united in 1918 as the state of Yugoslavia.

Turkish protests against the incompetence of their government came to a head with the revolution in 1908, led by the *Young Turks* who came to power and began to change the way Turkey was governed. In the First World War Turkey joined the German side and defeated a British attempt at invasion in the Dardanelles. But an Arab revolt led by British officers, including T. E. Lawrence (Lawrence of Arabia), and supported by a British army from Egypt freed the last parts of the Ottoman empire. By 1920 Turkey was reduced to the original homeland of the Turks, and in 1922 Kemel Pasha proclaimed Turkey a republic. Under Kemel Ataturk (see p. 232), as he called himself later, Turkey was modernized and strengthened.

Russia Before the Revolution

Russian history begins in the sixth century A.D. with the development of organized communities among the eastern *Slavs* on the great plains between the Baltic and the Black Sea. Towns grew up at convenient places on the trading routes linking Scandinavia and Byzantium (Constantinople). Though the Slav invitation to *Rurik* to rule over them (862) is a legend, Norse rule was established (see pp. 64-5) and Rurik's successor, Oleg, made his capital at Kiev, which was to be the chief Russian principality for the next three centuries. Here Christianity was adopted by Vladimir (988). The trading links with Byzantium made it natural to join the eastern *(Greek Orthodox)* branch of the church, to which Russian Christians have belonged ever since. Hence Russia stood outside the unity of medieval Catholic Europe and was not affected by the clash of church and state or by the *Reformation*,

which had such profound effects on the history of Europe (see pp. 74-5, 82-3 and also 114-5).

Another special feature of Russian history was the Mongol (or *Tartar*) invasion (see pp. 84-5). While Alexander Nevsky, Prince of Novgorod, was beating back the Swedes (1240) and the *Teutonic Knights* (1242), the last great invasion from Asia led to the indirect overlordship of the Slavs by the Mongol *Khans* of the *Golden Horde* who exacted tribute for over 250 years. It was during this period that the formerly unimportant town of Moscow grew to prominence. Its rulers gained control of a steadily expanding territory by conquests, purchase, treaty and colonization—generally in co-operation with the Mongols for whom they acted as tribute collectors, but whose over-lordship they were eventually strong enough to reject (1480).

It was a Grand Duke of Moscow, Ivan IV (1533-84), known as the Terrible because of the cruelty and ruthlessness of his rule, who was crowned as the first Tsar in 1547. But the advance of Moscow was not without setbacks. The 'Time of the Troubles' (1584-1613) saw famine, the breakdown of government and the loss of territory on a scale only equalled in the period after the First World War. A national revival, inspired by the church, drove the Poles out of Moscow, and an assembly in 1613 chose Michael Romanov as Tsar: the first of the dynasty which was to rule until the February Revolution, 1917 (see pp. 178-9).

The expansion of Russia was resumed. Peter the Great (1682-1725) (see p. 242) reached Azov in the south, began building St. Petersburg—Russia's 'window on the west'—and, crushing the power of Sweden (Poltava, 1709), acquired a Baltic coastline. Eastwards Russians penetrated to Central Asia and beyond. Catherine II (1762-96) took part in the partitions of Poland (1772, 1793, 1795) which brought Russia's western borders to the new frontiers of Austria and Prussia. In the south the Crimea and the northern coast of the Black Sea were acquired and the Caucasus region pene-trated. During the 19th century the lands of the peoples of Central Asia up to the borders of Persia, Afghanistan and Tibet were acquired, and in the Far East the left bank of the Amur River and the territory of China between the Amur and the Pacific were annexed (1858-1860).

Russia, now a great power of enormous extent, was beset by serious internal prob-lems. Despite forcible attempts at westerni-zation, notably by Peter the Great, Russia was socially, politically and economically backward. *Serfdom* came late to Russia and was still being extended under Catherine. The autocracy of the Tsars, the power of the state bureaucracy and the absence of rep-resentative institutions contrasted with the development of freer institutions in the west. Even Alexander I, under whose rule Russia played a leading part in the war against Napoleon (whose retreat from Mos-cow, 1812, was the prelude to his downfall), and who had previously shown liberal ten-dencies, initiated the reactionary and rep-ressive *Holy Alliance* (see pp. 160-1). On his death in 1825 an unsuccessful revolt by a group of officers (the *Decembrists*) was a warning of storms to come, but at the time

Far left: Ivan the Terrible, who became the first Russian ruler to have himself crowned Tsar, in 1547. Following a conflict with Prince Kurbski of the Boyars, Ivan took a terrible revenge on his opponents and began a reign of extreme brutality. He ravaged Novgorod and massacred half the inhabitants.

Left: Peter the Great. Although ruthless and headstrong, Peter I was intelligent and able. He built St. Petersburg, reorganized the primitive Russian army, constructed a fleet and made a powerful attempt to westernize a very backward Russia.

Above: Students demonstrating in protest at the Tsarist repression in St. Petersburg, 1912.

merely reinforced illiberal trends.

Serfdom was not abolished until 1861, but the rapid growth of population and the reservation of land by crown, church and nobility left a chronic land hunger for the peasantry. Industrialization, often financed by foreign investors, was rapid in the late 19th century and carried out in harsh condi-tions for the workers. Although elected councils began reforms in local government affairs (education, health), central govern-ment remained oppressive and unrepresen-tative. Terrorist groups assassinated many leaders, including Tsar Alexander II (1881).

The defeats of Russia in the war against Japan (1904-1905) precipitated a revolution. Although it failed to overthrow Tsar Nicholas II, who retained the loyalty of the armed forces, he did concede a representa-tive assembly, the *Duma*. Land reform set out to create a class of peasant proprietors. Before the prospects for success of these policies could be judged (though successive clashes between Tsar and Duma did not promise well for development of democratic government), Russia was involved in the Great War. The demands which this put on governments and peoples were too much for the administrative and economic capacities of autocratic, bureaucratic Russia. In Feb-ruary 1917 the Tsar finally abdicated.

The Line-up for War

The causes of the Great War of 1914-1918 are complex and are to be found in events which took place many years before. The war was so terrible and the suffering it caused so widespread that it is difficult to understand how the leaders of the countries which took part could have made the decisions which actually brought it about. If they could have known that the war would last more than four years and cause nine million deaths in battle and many more millions from disease they would have been more ready to use the resources of diplomacy. But at that time most statesmen felt that they had no alternative to acting as they did; to do differently would bring worse consequences for their countries than the

Above: Arrest of Gavrilo Princip, just after he assassinated Archduke Franz Ferdinand, heir to the throne of Austria-Hungary, and his wife Sophie. The Archduke was visiting Sarajevo, capital of the Austrian province of Bosnia. Princip was a member of the Black Hand, a secret society of Serbian nationalists. Austria accused Serbia of organizing the murder, and the act led to full-scale war in Europe a few weeks later.

short war they expected.

To understand this the complicated network of alliances and hostilities which had grown up in the decades before the war must be studied: these relationships ensured that a shock imparted at one point was likely to be transmitted through the whole system and to involve all the powers, even those which had no direct concern with the event which started it all off. It was this situation which meant that the assassination of the heir to the Austro-Hungarian empire, at Sarajevo near the Serbian border on 28th June, 1914, led to a war which within a few weeks would involve nearly all the major European powers.

The basic hostilities in late 19th century Europe were between France and Germany and between Austro-Hungary and Russia.

In addition Italy was in rivalry with France over their imperial ambitions in North Africa, and Britain was in hostility with both France and Russia over imperial disputes in many parts of the world. Franco-German hostility was a sequel to the Franco-Prussian war of 1870-1871 (see p. 163), with its consequent acquisition of Alsace-Lorraine by Germany and Germany's fear (a mistaken one) that France intended a war of revenge if it became strong enough. The hostility between Russia and Austro-Hungary grew out of Russia's claim to leadership of the Slav peoples of eastern Europe and the Balkans (Slavs made up more than half of the nationally mixed population of Austro-Hungary) and out of the two empires' ambitions in the Balkans.

These relations had led to a series of alliances, originally defensive in character. The most important of these were: 1) the Dual Alliance of Germany and Austro-Hungary (signed in 1879 and renewed up to 1918), which became the Triple Alliance when Italy joined in 1882; 2) the Franco-Russian alliance of 1893 which united these very different countries because of the fear each had of the Dual Alliance. In the early years of the 20th century the membership of these two *blocs* was modified. Italy, though remaining a member of the Triple Alliance, made a secret agreement with France (1902) and later with Russia (1909), for co-operation in North Africa and the Balkans respectively. In the event Italy stayed neutral on the outbreak of war and then came in (1915) on the side of Britain and France.

France, because of its greater fear of Germany, had backed out of a military confrontation with Britain (in 1898, at Fashoda, on the Upper Nile) and in 1904 settled the outstanding imperial disputes in the *Anglo-French Entente*. Russia, badly defeated in the Far East by Japan in 1904-5 (see pp. 168-9 and 194-5), turned its attention to south-east Europe, and settled its more important disputes with Britain in Persia, Afghanistan and Tibet in the *Anglo-Russian Entente* (1907). Britain's own willingness to make these new friendly arrangements with France and Russia was due to its sense of isolation and insecurity at the time of the *Boer War* (1899-1902) and to its growing apprehension of German policy. Although trade rivalry and Germany's imperial policy contributed to this, Britain's chief fear was caused by Germany's growing naval power. Germany had the most powerful army on the continent but Britain did not feel threatened by this, even though its own army was relatively small and scattered throughout the empire, because it had much the most powerful navy in the world.

The development of a German High Seas Fleet from 1898 and the decision by the British government to build enough ships to keep ahead was a major cause of Anglo-German mistrust. Then Germany's attempts in the Moroccan crises of 1905 and 1911 to challenge the Anglo-French Entente served only to bind the two countries more closely together.

Thus at the time of the assassination at Sarajevo, Europe was divided into two camps each fearing and arming against the other. The multi-national empire of Austro-Hungary was threatened from within by nationalism, encouraged, its rulers realized,

Above: Map of Europe as it looked before the First World War. The war, which began in 1914, ended in 1918 and left in its wake 35 million dead and injured and the seeds of an even more terrible war which started 21 years later.

by Slav Serbia on its southern border. Believing, probably correctly, that leading Serbs were implicated in the murder of the Archduke Franz-Ferdinand, they were determined to crush Serbia. The Russian government felt that it had to back Serbia, or lose its status as a great power, and mobilized its forces. The allies in both alliances followed suit (see pp. 172-7) and soon war was declared in a nearly unanimous upsurge of patriotic nationalism. On both sides, governments and most of the people were convinced of the rightness and justice of their cause and that it would triumph in a short and glorious war.

The First World War

The Beginnings: 1914

At the outbreak of the war the *Central Powers* had the advantage. The German Army, a uniquely efficient machine, had been born in the *Napoleonic Wars,* and had been developed and enlarged by the military genius of Gneisenau, Scharnhorst and Moltke. Supporting the army were the mighty industries of the Ruhr and a population in excess of 65,000,000. Germany's principal ally, Austria-Hungary, was neither so well endowed nor so prepared for war. She had a tradition of defeat rather than of victory in war and was obliged, however reluctantly, to take direction from her more powerful partner.

France, the principal military power on the *Allied* side, possessed only 60% of Germany's manpower and still remembered the humiliating defeat she suffered in 1870. Her strategy was initially conceived in the belief that this war would be over by Christmas—a miscalculation that was to have the gravest consequences. Russia, cut off from her allies by enormous distances and ice-bound seas, was on the verge of internal revolution (see pp. 178-9). She lacked the manufacturing resources for equipment and munitions which were to prove vital for war on so great a scale, and had to rely on her virtually limitless manpower (the Russian "steamroller") to compensate for these defects. Great Britain could at first supply only a small force and one which, although highly experienced in limited conflicts, had not been manoeuvred in massive formations since the time of Napoleon (see p. 241). She was, however, undisputed mistress of the seas, the one fact which was ultimately to frustrate Germany's ambitions.

Thus, the forces of the Allies and the *Central Powers* became locked in mortal struggle. Few realized on that August morning, when the Germans invaded Belgium, that it was going to be of such carnage and duration, and that European civilization would be entirely engulfed.

The Germans, adopting the *Schlieffen Plan,* launched a massive lightning blow in an attempt to crush the French. Field-Marshall von Schlieffen, who had died in 1913, had finalized this plan in 1905 before he retired as Chief of the German General Staff. In brief, the plan was based on a wide attacking movement which could be likened to the operation of a swing door. German troops would attack heavily on the French army's left flank, as if pushing the door open; at the same time, at the other end of the axis or "door", German troops would actually fall back to encourage the French to push ahead—and thus aid the broad strategic plan by committing their forces in the wrong place. The offensive was frustrated, however, partly by the fact that German commanders, who were supposed to fall back, did not relish the apparent stigma of defeat and began to resist the French army's efforts. Nevertheless, the main German thrust advanced rapidly and threatened the Channel ports, which were vital for the Allies as entry points for British troops and supplies.

The German attack was first made through Belgium, but Belgian forces were more resolute than the Germans had supposed and delayed the advance long enough

Below: Allied infantry going over the top in one of the last battles of the First World War. The war of attrition, with its grim trenches, barbed wire and shell-holes, began in the autumn of 1914. During an Allied push against the flank of the retreating German army, the British general, Sir John French, suddenly halted the advance and ordered his men to dig in. By October a long system of trenches had been built, stretching across Europe from the sea to Switzerland. The war had become a static exchange of artillery barrages and infantry frontal assaults against machine-gun emplacements. This mistaken tactic cost the Allied nations many millions of lives.

the section of the front opposite him, no Germans. He moved his forces forward cautiously, unaware of his advantage, for the bulk of the German western army was heavily engaged with the French on either flank of him. A general German retreat was ordered; everywhere they began to roll back until, on the 14th September, they reached the river Aisne. There, exhausted by long, forced marches, the infantry dug holes in the ground and set up machine gun positions. To everyone's amazement, the Allied counter-attack was halted—for one man with a machine gun in a protected position could repulse the advance of hordes. Now the Allies, to protect themselves from shell fire, started to dig trenches. Soon a complex system of dug-outs, with approach roads and sheltered dumps for supplies, stretched across Europe from Belgium to the neutral Swiss border. The familiar wars of rapid movement gave way to the static warfare of fixed positions; the terrible *war of attrition* had begun.

Meanwhile, on the eastern front, Russian forces had invaded East Prussia, many people on the Allied side were expecting that the weight of the Russian "steamroller" would overwhelm the Germans and force them to sue for peace. The Russian army, however, was entirely lacking in co-ordination and direction and, after some early successes, was decisively defeated at the Battle of Tannenberg by German forces under the command of Generals von Hindenburg and Ludendorff. This crucial success for the Germans enabled them to concentrate yet heavier forces against the west, the area where they sought decisive victory. Despite Russian gains against the Austria-Hungarian forces farther south, this was insufficient to relieve pressure on the Allies in the west. Largely due to the apparent German domination of the war, Turkey came in on the side of the Central Powers in October 1914.

During the last months of the first year of the war, however, British sea power made an overwhelming contribution to the future of the struggle by driving German naval forces from their bases and virtually clearing the seas of German merchant ships. At the battle of the Falkland Islands, in December 1914, German naval forces were soundly defeated. Thereafter, the British could move troops and supplies virtually anywhere in the world. Germany lost her colonies in Africa, for she was unable to support them, and Britain, free to concentrate her naval power in the North Sea and the Atlantic, ensured the safe transport of supplies across the Atlantic from the neutral but friendly United States.

to make the landing of British troops possible. At the mining town of Mons the *British Expeditionary Force,* small in number but tenacious of spirit, halted the German onslaught. However, because of German superiority in numbers, the British were shortly obliged to retreat, to prevent being cut off from their French allies.

Within a few weeks the renewed German offensive brought them within 30 kilometers of Paris, near enough for them to bombard the city. French forces, at this critical moment, organized a courageous counter-attack (sometimes known as the "taxi charge") in which they employed every available vehicle—taxis, 'buses, private cars—to rush troops to endangered points.

On the 5th September the Germans crossed the Marne. Sir John French, the British commander, at last stopped his retreat and returned to the offensive—only to find, in

Above: British infantry soldiers relax in their trench after dinner, 1914. In many ways the first year of the war was more bearable for those in the front line than in later years, when the war deteriorated to little more than the opposing armies trying to smash each other into the ground with the biggest shells and bombs they could find. After the barrage 'it was over the top and attack the enemy trench'. This sometimes resulted in the deaths of hundreds of thousands of men for the sake of a few kilometres of ground.

Efforts to Break the Deadlock

Early in 1915 it became apparent that neither the *Allies* nor the *Central Powers* were capable of winning the war in one swift, decisive campaign. The massive and heavily armoured armies facing each other in Flanders were bogged down in a hopeless, static confrontation.

The central problem facing the rival military commands was essentially the same. To attack enemy positions meant that one's forces were exposed to the accurate fire of modern weapons, while the defenders remained in the relative safety of their trenches. An advance, therefore, could only be made at enormous cost in life. But there was another, and seemingly insoluble, problem for the attacking side. The moment an offensive was launched the troops moved beyond their *railhead* and therefore supplies had to be brought up to them, through the mud and shell holes, by laborious horse-drawn vehicles. Meanwhile, the defenders, retreating on their own supply lines, could at any moment rush reinforcements to endangered positions by rail. Thus, not only was an attack costly in life but it was unlikely to achieve more than a limited territorial gain. Yet how was the war to be won without attacking the enemy?

For the time being futile assaults were all that was attempted. In March 1915 the British tried to break through the German lines at Neuve Chapelle, wave after wave of infantry soldiers hurling themselves against the enemy. The assault was concentrated on a narrow front of some six kilometres; British troops managed to penetrate about one and a half kilometres into German-held territory and were then forced back by counter-attacks. Casualties reached unheard-of figures, but the effect was negligible: the *impasse* remained, the front stood where it had.

The Germans attempted the same tactics. In April 1915 they tried to force their way through the French line at Ypres, using poison gas as an additional weapon. Again, initial success was followed by stalemate. This futile trench warfare was soon to resolve itself into an almost conscious policy of trading lives for lives in the vain and inglorious hope that one side or the other would eventually find it impossible to make good their losses.

On the Allied side one solution presented itself. Rather than attack Germany direct, it was argued, they should knock Turkey out of the war and then, systematically, the other Balkan countries fighting on the same

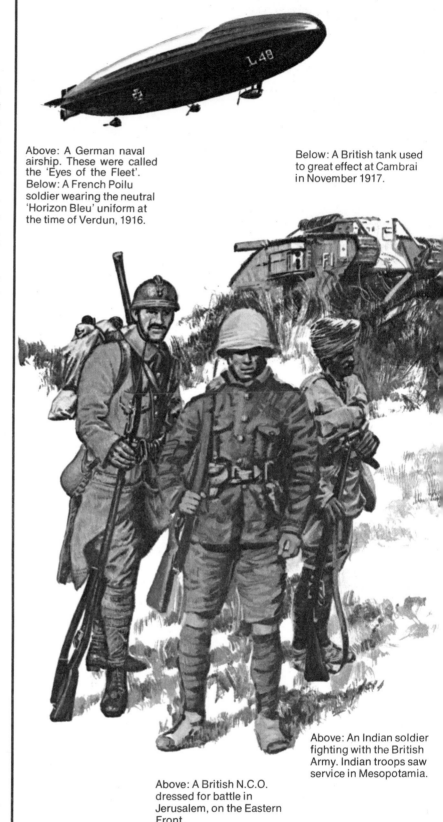

Above: A German naval airship. These were called the 'Eyes of the Fleet'.
Below: A French Poilu soldier wearing the neutral 'Horizon Bleu' uniform at the time of Verdun, 1916.

Below: A British tank used to great effect at Cambrai in November 1917.

Above: An Indian soldier fighting with the British Army. Indian troops saw service in Mesopotamia.

Above: A British N.C.O. dressed for battle in Jerusalem, on the Eastern Front.

The illustration above shows some of the protagonists of the First World War and the equipment they used in battle.

side. Winston Churchill (see p. 233), with his unique understanding of strategy on an enormous scale, at once grasped the significance of this theory and, despite sustained opposition from less imaginative men, forcefully advocated an assault on the Gallipoli peninsula. Tragically, however, the campaign was not under his personal direction; the fighting units took too long to assemble and were not launched with the energy and

Left: A British DH4
fighter plane.
Below: An Italian
Bersaglieri soldier carrying
his own folding bicycle.

Above: A German 10-cm
gun in use during the First
World War.

Left: A German soldier of
1916 wearing the
distinctive 'coalscuttle'
helmet.

of the following year David Lloyd George had succeeded H. H. Asquith as Prime Minister. Lloyd George's vigorous reorganization of all aspects of the war effort, particularly in the production of munitions, brought renewed drive and hope.

However, neither side could see any course other than to persist in greater and greater efforts to break through the enemy lines. It was the Germans who made the next move with their massive and unparalleled assault on the great fortress of Verdun, key to the French defensive system. If they could smash this central point the Allied front must crumble and they could then sweep on to Paris. Accordingly, in February 1916, the greatest artillery bombardment the world had ever known opened up on the *citadel*. General Henri Pétain, commanding the French forces in the area, well knew that this could be the turning point in the war. "They shall not pass", he determined, and concentrated every available man. The German attack was maintained for six months with unrelenting intensity. The slaughter was appalling—at times during those brief months no less than 115 divisions were crammed in by one or other side on a front less than eight kilometres wide; the result, as always, was inconclusive. Eventually, the Germans abandoned the attack.

To help bring about this withdrawal, British troops launched an attack in the area of the Somme. Tanks were used in this action for the first time, and initially their effect was overwhelming. Rain, however, soon bogged down the tanks and yet again the situation remained as before.

Further desperate and fore-doomed attempts to break the deadlock on the western front followed during 1917. An assault under the French commander, Robert Nivelle, resulted in such appalling slaughter that it had to be stopped. The High Commands of both British and French forces began to realize that sections of the French army were in danger of rebelling against the senseless massacre of tens of thousands of men. Pressures on the home fronts, particularly in Germany where the British blockade was beginning to take its full effect, brought the first murmurings that were to lead to *mutiny* and revolution.

In 1917, revolution took place in Russia and, under the *Bolsheviks,* she withdrew from the war and her vast reserves of manpower were lost to the Allied cause (see pp. 178-9). The gloom of that terrible year was only lightened by the small but significant fact that in the Middle East British troops had finally succeeded in capturing Baghdad and Jerusalem.

resolve necessary for success; the Turks, forewarned by Allied delays, lay in wait. This confusion inevitably led, despite great heroism displayed by Allied forces, to failure and eventual withdrawal.

The generally disastrous outlook made changes in the conduct of the war, and the government in Britain, inevitable. Sir John French was replaced as British commander in the west by Sir Douglas Haig; by the end

The Final Phases

While the frightful carnage of the land war in the west continued unabated, Britain also fought a desperate struggle for survival at sea. The country was utterly dependent on shipping for the bulk of her supplies. Although the German navy was still blockaded and her main fleet weakened after the battle of Jutland in 1916, Germany had developed the submarine and by the spring of 1917 sinkings of British shipping in the Atlantic Ocean and North Sea reached alarming proportions. More British ships were being sunk than were being built. Unless these rates could be reversed, disaster loomed. At one point there was a real danger of starvation and therefore collapse. It was calculated that there were only some two weeks' supply of food and essential materials in the British Isles.

In 1917 this perilous situation presented further hazards. Early in that year the United States had entered the war on the *Allies* side, mainly as a result of the German *U-boats'* indiscriminate sinking of neutral

shipping, including American. The entry of that country into the war placed at the Allies disposal virtually limitless resources and considerable additional manpower. However, the soldiers would take time to train and the *munitions* to produce; thus, the American impact on the struggle would not be immediate. To transport such men and material as were at once available, the British organized, in face of the U-boat menace, the convoy system in which ships could cross the Atlantic with considerable naval protection.

For the *Central Powers* the problems were different: Russia was no longer a *combatant,*

but sooner or later the Central Powers would have to face an enormous American contribution. For Germany the situation, if speedily and effectively exploited, offered better prospects than at any time since her initial successes in 1914. Indeed, the problem appeared to be merely one of *logistics*. All she need do, it seemed, was to rush to the western front the many crack divisions which had hitherto been tied down in Russia and inflict a decisive blow upon the Allies before American forces could be brought to their assistance. For a few brief weeks it looked to some as if 1918 might be the year of final German victory. To this end the Germans launched a ferocious attack in the west in March 1918. By the end of the month the attack extended the length of the front; ultimately it brought the Germans to the river Aisne once more and then farther on to within 60 kilometres of Paris. Casualties reached new and more terrible heights.

It seemed as if the Germans were on the verge of complete victory. Had the Allies but realized it, however, their salvation lay in the fact that the German High Command,

even after four years of slaughter, still did not comprehend the dangers inherent in attack. Paradoxically, because their last attack was initially so successful in reality it lost them the war, for the cost of the attack to Germany was more than half a million men. Moreover, at home Germany was suffering acutely from the shortages imposed on her by the wastage of war and the British blockade. Germany's best troops had been sacrificed; its last attack was losing its *momentum*. Already, too, American troops were arriving in Europe and doing so in steadily growing numbers.

The end came quicker than many sup-

Left: American troops going out on patrol in the trenches in France, 1918. Until 1917 the United States had remained neutral, but repeated German attacks on American shipping provoked the Americans into entering the war on the Allies' side.

Above: Armistice Day celebration in France, where street parades and spontaneous celebrations broke out. On 11th November 1918, the day the war ended, the peoples of the Allied countries burst into rejoicing.

posed. An Allied counter-attack began, using tanks in far greater numbers than before. Soon the Allied forces were smashing through the German defences. Bulgaria, Austria-Hungary and Turkey collapsed in the east. German troops began to mutiny and discipline broke in the heart of Germany itself with revolutionary movements demanding an end to the conflict. The German emperor was forced to abdicate and took refuge in Holland. Humiliated and overwhelmed, the German commanders were obliged to surrender and, six hours later, at eleven o'clock on the morning of the 11th November, 1918, fighting ceased on all fronts. The world could at last take stock of what those four terrible years of conflict had cost in life and property.

So massive were the casualty figures on both sides that no wholly accurate figures will ever be available. However, in due course the United States War Department assembled figures which are as detailed and reliable as any. They make appalling reading. The total number of casualties for both sides, including wounded and missing, was an awesome 37,494,186. The total number of killed, including death from all causes, was 8,538,315. Of these, the Allies lost 5,152,115 and the Central Powers 3,386,200. The figure for the British Empire alone, killed, injured and missing, was actually in excess of one million.

Perhaps worst of all was the bitterness of the Germans who felt they had not been truly defeated in the field. The folly and injustice of the treaty imposed on them, provided, even in the moment of returned peace, the ingredients which were, only 21 years later, to bring about a repetition of the war, one in some ways more terrible and costly than the first (see pp. 184-9).

177

EH–M

The Russian Revolution

At the outbreak of the First World War in 1914 Russia was under the autocratic rule of the Tsar, Nicholas II, of the Romanov family, which had ruled for many centuries. He was a weak, superstitious and obstinate man, but as much a prisoner of circumstances as other people in Russia. All power was centred in the Tsar, although some attempts had been made to liberalize the *regime* (see pp. 168-9). The effects of the industrial revolution were being felt but scarcely understood. Many intellectuals and writers realized the need for change, but their works largely reflected a sense of futility and impotence in the face of a rigid system that was years behind social and political developments in the rest of Europe.

All protest was ruthlessly suppressed. A young student named Ulianov was hanged for his part in a plot against the life of the Tsar. His brother, Vladimir, began a systematic study of politics and believed that he had found the 'scientific' answer in the works of Karl Marx, a German philosopher.

Marx considered the whole *capitalist-imperialist* system doomed. It was destined, in his view, to be overthrown by a world revolutionary movement of workers and replaced by a dictatorship of the workers.

Young Vladimir Ulianov joined others in an underground movement to propagate these theories of *socialism*. Ulianov adopted the conspiratorial name of Nikolai Lenin (see p. 238) and with others he was driven into exile. Lenin lived in Poland, Britain and Switzerland, writing books, editing underground newspapers and maintaining close contact with revolutionary elements in Russia. He argued that revolution was a process of historical change which could not be brought about by any individual act of rebellion but only by being directed by dedicated revolutionaries. He also maintained that workers and peasants owed no loyalty to kings and nations but only to the world-wide working-class movement.

The First World War was the historical force which broke the ailing Russian system. Russia suffered disastrous defeats at the hands of the Germans, as much through its own incompetence as through the superior military skill of the German armies (see pp. 172-7). Supplies of food and munitions broke down. The Tsar had no grasp of the strategic situation and was under the influence of the Empress, incompetent generals and ministers and a fanatical monk, Rasputin. Millions of Russian soldiers, often unfed and unarmed, were flung against the Germans, to die without hope. By 1917 the food-producing areas of Russia were overrun and famine spread through the land. Rasputin was assassinated.

In February 1917 riots broke out in Petrograd, culminating in a *General Strike*. People were starving; the military position was hopeless. Even the most loyal Tsarist troops, the *Cossacks*, refused to suppress the rioters. Lenin kept a close watch on the situation, advising revolutionary elements inside Russia. He had long insisted that a war would produce the pressures needed to bring about revolution.

A new government, with the liberal-minded Prince Lvov as Premier, persuaded the Tsar to abdicate and promise to work out a democratic system of government. However, the Russian workers in Petrograd had already organized a *Soviet*, or council (the model of future Russian government), and were only prepared to support the provisional government if its policies met with their approval. Prince Lvov's government attempted to carry on the war and organized a last desperate counter-offensive. The results were disastrous. Mass desertions of soldiers followed and troops organized them-

selves into revolutionary groups. Only the members of the Bolshevik (meaning majority in Russian) party realized that the key to popular support lay in advocating peace on any terms.

In April 1917, the Germans transported Lenin across Germany to Finland in a sealed train. Arriving in Russia, Lenin immediately attacked all attempts at piecemeal liberalization and called for a revolution on Marxist principles. World revolution, he declared, was imminent. A first rising of workers in July failed and Lenin fled to Finland. A Liberal, Kerensky, took over the government and tried to continue the war. General Kornilov tried to crush the Bolshevik revolution. He was defeated by the workers and in November 1917 the Bolsheviks seized power in the so-called October Revolution. Though compelled to make a disastrous peace with Germany at Brest-Litovsk, the Bolsheviks, calling themselves *Communists*, created a basis for reconstructing Russia along social-

ist lines. In a desperate attempt to keep Russia in the war and to defeat the socialist revolution, Allied forces were landed, but Trotsky, a brilliant associate of Lenin, organized a new army which became known as the *Red Army*.

Civil war raged for more than three years and the Communists won. The Tsar and his family were held prisoners at first and were finally brought before a firing squad and executed.

Previous upheavals in Europe had aimed to overthrow, or limit, the powers of monarchs and nobles, often bringing sweeping land reforms but not attacking the basis of the private ownership of wealth and the freedom to exploit it.

The great significance of the Russian revolution is that it turned a *bourgeois*, or middle-class, revolution into a working-class revolution and put an end to the possibility of establishing a liberal, capitalist regime based on private ownership and uncontrolled enterprise.

Wilson and Versailles

In January, 1919, leaders from 32 nations met in Paris to arrange the peace settlement which would end the First World War. The task before them was awesome. The old empires of Austria-Hungary, Russia and Turkey had been destroyed. New countries must be created in their place and their boundaries decided. Germany had been defeated. Her conquerors had to decide what advantage, if any, they should take from their victory. The war had cost huge sums of money. Over ten million lives had been lost. The peacemakers had somehow to try to prevent any similar war occurring again.

The peace talks were dominated by three men: President Woodrow Wilson of the U.S.A., David Lloyd George, the British Prime Minister, and Georges Clemenceau, Premier of France. They looked at the problems from different viewpoints and did not always agree on what should be done. President Wilson was an idealist. He hated war and had kept America neutral for as long as possible. In a speech to the American Congress in 1918 he put forward the famous *Fourteen Points,* which he hoped would bring a just and lasting peace. Wilson suggested that nations should keep only small armed forces and should avoid making secret treaties among themselves. He wished peoples of one race and language to be free to set up their own governments. He declared that 'the world must be a safe place for democracy', and proposed that nations should create an international organization, the *League of Nations,* which would keep the world at peace.

When President Wilson came to Paris in 1919 he found that there was little support for his views among the other leaders. They felt it was easy for Wilson to hold such high ideals, because the U.S.A. had suffered far less than other nations in the war. Clemenceau, like many Frenchmen, also remembered the German defeat of France (1870-71). He knew that his fellow countrymen wanted revenge and would not be satisfied unless Germany was humbled and made weak. Lloyd George arrived in Paris from Britain with the knowledge that his people wanted 'Germany to pay'. Lloyd George did not hold such views himself but he could not ignore them. Some leaders hoped to gain more territory for their countries. Nobody was willing to accept Wilson's ideas on disarmament. However, he insisted that his proposals about a League of Nations must be carried out.

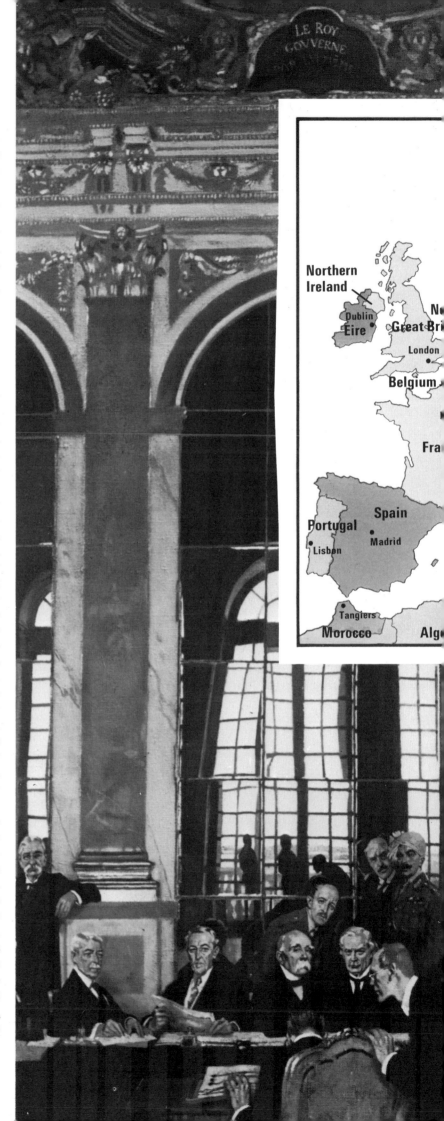

At last on 28th June, 1919, in the famous hall of Mirrors in the Palace at Versailles, a treaty between Germany and the victorious powers was signed. This was the first of five treaties which together make up the *Peace of Paris.* Its terms altered the map of Europe and the Middle East. New countries, such as Estonia, Latvia, Lithuania and Czechoslovakia, were created in Eastern Europe. Poland once again became independent. Austria and Hungary became separate countries. Greece and Serbia (now to be called Yugoslavia) were made larger. Turkey lost control of the Middle East, where the Arab lands of Syria, Palestine and Iraq were now to be looked after by Britain and France.

Germany was harshly punished. Its leaders had to sign the 'War Guilt' clause, admitting that the actions of German ministers had caused the war. They also had to agree to pay a sum of money to their conquerors to make good the losses caused by the war. These 'reparations' were later fixed at the enormous sum of £6,200 million. Alsace and Lorraine were returned to France. Land in eastern Germany was taken away so that Poland should have a coastline on the Baltic Sea. Germany lost its colonies, while the Rhineland was to be occupied by foreign troops. The size of the German armed forces was strictly limited.

There were faults in these arrangements. The defeated countries were not represented at the peace talks. The wishes of Russia were also ignored. The German people did not believe that their leaders alone should be blamed for the war, and they disliked paying reparations. The newly-created countries often contained people of several races within their borders.

However, the Peace of Paris had included among its terms the setting up of a League of Nations. As he sailed back to America, President Wilson believed that the faults of the peace treaties could gradually be removed by the league, and he hoped that the world was moving towards a new age of international co-operation. Unfortunately the United States government, wishing to avoid involvement in the affairs of Europe, refused to join the league. Wilson travelled 12,870 kilometres around the United States in a campaign to change the minds of his fellow countrymen. Disappointment and over-work broke his health.

The Peace of Paris was not always just, yet it was fairer than it would have been without President Wilson's influence. The League of Nations was hardly successful, but Woodrow Wilson's ideas have endured in the work carried out today by the *United Nations Organization.*

Left: Signing the Peace Treaty at Versailles, a painting by Sir W. Orpen. The fighting over, the Allied statesmen hoped to create a lasting peace. But their harsh treatment of Germany, including a demand for reparations which could not possibly be met, helped to sow bitterness which led inexorably to the Second World War, while their redrawing of the map of Europe left many minorities under alien rule, creating tension and resentment.

Above: Europe as it looked after the First World War.

The Gathering Storm

The First World War was a terrible experience for those nations involved. Once the fighting ended, people looked forward to a return to normal life and hoped that the *League of Nations* would prove strong enough to make peace last (see pp. 180-1).

Unfortunately, most countries that had fought in the war had been impoverished and owed money to the U.S.A. In Germany, the government tried to solve its financial problems by printing more money. This caused the *mark* to lose value. By the end of 1923 millions of marks were needed to buy a newspaper or post a letter. Thousands of Germans had lost their savings by the time matters were put right. There was also great unemployment, particularly in Germany, Britain and Italy. Such difficulties caused strikes and riots in many European cities.

In these circumstances governments feared the spread of *Communism*, inspired by the successful Russian Revolution (see pp. 178-9). Lenin had established Communist rule in the *Union of Soviet Socialist Republics* (U.S.S.R.) by the time of his death in 1924 (see p. 238). A five-year struggle for leadership followed. The new leader, Joseph Stalin (see p. 242), wished to strengthen Communist control over the U.S.S.R., and to spread similar ideas elsewhere. In Europe this fear of Communism led to the rise of

Below: Fascist rebel troops, using their dead horses as barricades, firing at loyal Republican soldiers in a Madrid street in 1936. From the beginning of the 1920s, Spanish army chiefs had encountered very little resistance whenever they decided to ignore the will of parliament and to act as they saw fit. Despite the fact that the Republican Popular Front had won a major electoral victory, the right-wing military forces staged an uprising against the elected government, and this marked the beginning of the Spanish Civil War. It lasted for three years and, more than anything else, became a contest between two opposing ideologies, Fascism and Communism. While the Communists' cause attracted young men from all over the world, they had very little weapons and supplies. The Fascists were given all they needed and the German airforce even helped by bombing Barcelona and other cities for them.

Fascism. Its founder was Benito Mussolini, who seized power in Italy in 1922. He was a dictator who believed in absolute power and displays of military strength. He banned all political parties but his own and forbade strikes and *trade unions*. His ideas were supported because he put down the Communists and spoke of creating an Italian empire. He had marshes drained and built new cities and roads. Leaders in other countries, such as Germany and Spain, were soon copying his ideas and methods.

Meanwhile, in the U.S.A., business prospered (see pp. 192-3). Factories turned out goods by *mass-production* and *hire-purchase schemes* enabled ordinary people to buy cars and other luxury goods. Men and women from all walks of life bought shares on the *Wall Street* stock exchange, and watched as the value of their shares rose. In 1929 signs that this prosperity was ending brought a rush to sell shares, which rapidly became worthless. This 'Wall Street Crash' ruined many Americans and caused a business depression throughout the world. Millions of men, particularly in the U.S.A., Germany, Britain and Japan, became unemployed. Millions starved. A crisis of confidence which turned into what became known as the *Great Depression*. One solution to the crisis was shown in America under the wise and courageous leadership of President Franklin D. Roosevelt. His famous 'New Deal' gave the eleven million unemployed

Americans work building dams, roads and schools. These government schemes, such as the *Tennessee River Valley Authority*, were of great public benefit and, at the same time, helped the country out of the Depression. A similar but more brutal answer was found in Germany, where people listened to the voice of Adolf Hitler (see p. 237).

Hitler believed in the superiority of the German race. For years he had been declaring that Germany's defeat in the war was caused by treacherous Jews and Communists. He wanted to change the Versailles Settlement and to build up a German empire that would include the Germans living in Austria, Czechoslovakia and Poland. These ideas appealed to German pride, while Hitler's need for strong armed forces and large supplies of weapons created jobs for the unemployed and prosperity for the industrialists. By 1933 Hitler and the *Nazi Party* had been voted into power, and the German people gave themselves up to the brutality of Fascist rule.

The Depression was not the only problem of the 1930s. World peace was threatened when Japan seized Manchuria from China (1931) (see pp. 194-5 and 198-9) and when Italy attacked Ethiopia (1935-36). The League of Nations showed its disapproval of such aggression but was powerless to stop it. Freedom seemed threatened by the spread of Fascism to Spain, where Hitler and Mussolini gave help to their fellow-Fascists in the *Spanish Civil War* (1936-39). The greatest threat to peace lay in the policy of Hitler, to enlarge Germany and gain living space (*lebensraum*) in Europe. In a series of bold moves Hitler sent his troops into the Rhineland (1936), annexed Austria (1938) and demanded land from Czechoslovakia. Britain and France had at first failed to stop German aggression because they wished to avoid war and could not agree on what action to take. British leaders felt that some of Hitler's demands were fair and tried to appease them. In pursuit of this policy Neville Chamberlain, the British Prime Minister, signed the *Munich Pact* (September 1938) granting part of Czechoslovakia to Germany. Chamberlain returned to Britain convinced that he had brought 'peace for our time'. Hitler was certain that Britain and France would never go to war against Germany. Both men had miscalculated. In 1939 Hitler seized the rest of Czechoslovakia and attacked Poland. As the German tanks and dive bombers went about their work of destruction, Britain and France prepared to honour an agreement they had made to help Poland. For the second time within a generation the opening shots of a world war had been fired.

Above: Hitler youth rally in 1938. Within 18 months of this rally, Germany was at war with Britain and France and in occupation of almost the entire continent of Europe. Below: Clerks in a stockbroker's office in New York check the ticker tape of stock exchange purchases and sales on the night of 25 October 1929, one of the busiest days in the history of the exchange and only a short while before the Great Depression.

The Second World War
1939-1941

The Second World War was shorter than many other great wars but it caused more deaths, particularly among civilians, and greater destruction than any previous conflict. The causes of the war were several—German resentment at the harsh terms of the *Versailles Treaty* which ended the First World War (see pp. 180-1), the weakness of the *League of Nations*, nationalism which prompted expansionist policies and territorial demands and the failure of attempts to secure a general limitation of arms. When Adolf Hitler's *National Socialist Party* came to power in Germany it demanded the restoration of German military prestige. Hitler (see p. 237) gained control of Austria and Czecho-

Above: Troops of the British Expeditionary Force returning to Britain from Dunkirk in 1940. The British army, which had valiantly fought its way back to the French beaches in the face of overwhelming German attacks, was rescued by an armada of warships, merchantmen and even pleasure-boats which were normally ferrying sightseers about the river Thames.

slovakia while Italy under Benito Mussolini seized Ethiopia and Albania. Britain and France guaranteed Poland's independence and, when Germany did invade, they declared war, on 3rd September, 1939. On one side were ranged the *Axis* powers, Germany, Italy and Japan; on the other the *Allies,* Britain, France and the countries of the Commonwealth.

Germany quickly overran Poland but then followed for a few months the 'phoney war', during which the only important activity occurred at sea. Russia entered the conflict independently and had overrun the eastern part of Poland and some of Finland, after desperate resistance. The Allies could not help Finland and were occupied by threats to Norway. But when the attack came Ger-

many occupied Norway with little difficulty, installing Vidkun Quisling as head of a *puppet government.* As a result of this *débâcle* Neville Chamberlain resigned as Britain's prime minister and was succeeded by Winston Churchill (see p. 233).

Hitler's armies now launched a massive offensive in the west. They cut through Belgium and Holland, encountering only feeble resistance, and forced the Allied forces to retreat to Dunkirk. Only the efforts of the small ships that flocked from England's south coast ports prevented total disaster. Almost 350,000 troops were ferried across the Channel as *dog fights* raged above.

The Germans pressed home their invasion of France and entered Paris on 14th June, 1940. France surrendered and Marshal Pétain established a government at Vichy in southern France, which for the moment remained unoccupied. But many Frenchmen continued the fight either in North Africa or

in the *Free French Movement* headed by Charles de Gaulle in London.

Only Britain remained in Hitler's path and he proceeded to make preparations for its invasion. First he ordered the *Luftwaffe* under Hermann Goering to soften up his intended victim by raids, first on ports and airfields and then on London and other cities. The Germans rained down bombs on the capital almost every night in an eight-month *blitz*. But during the Battle of Britain the R.A.F. and ground defences took an enormous toll of German aircraft and kept command of Britain's airspace. Hitler was forced to shelve his invasion plans.

The Balkans were the next target for German expansion. Hungary, Romania and Bulgaria joined the Axis pact, and Greece and Yugoslavia were defeated although *guerrilla* resistance continued. Russia up to now had remained neutral but conflict between the proponents of Fascism and Communism was inevitable, particularly as Russia had expansionist ambitions in Europe. In June 1941 Hitler made what turned out to be his greatest mistake when he sent a huge army into Russia. By late autumn the Germans were threatening both Moscow and Leningrad: three million troops were bogged down in the Russian winter.

At least as important as the Battle of Britain was the Battle of the Atlantic. German submarines, known as *U-boats,* sank enormous numbers of Allied ships and it was only the invention of *radar* that preserved Britain's sea supplies, and protected its cities from surprise air attacks. For more than two years the United States maintained its neutrality, though under the *Lend-Lease* plan it sent generous supplies and armaments. On 7th December, 1941 Japanese aircraft destroyed most of the United States Pacific Fleet at Pearl Harbor.

By the end of 1941 most of the continent of Europe was under Axis control and Britain was virtually under siege.

Above: Battle of Britain. Throughout the autumn of 1940, the Royal Air Force was called upon daily to repulse the constantly arriving waves of German bombers and fighters which were trying to prepare the way for a Nazi invasion of Britain. But the German *Luftwaffe* (air force) lost so many bombers in daylight raids that it had to switch its attacks to night raids on British cities. The attempt to bomb Britain into submission ended unsuccessfully in mid-1941.

The Turn of the Tide

The end of 1941 was the turning point of the war. The *Allies'* fortunes were at their lowest ebb but on the other hand the German front was desperately stretched. From 1942 the Allies won major successes in Russia, North Africa, Italy and France. In Russia the battle hinged on the city of Stalingrad. After months of attrition the German Sixth Army was either destroyed or captured and the Russians began a relentless advance westwards.

In North Africa at El Alamein British and Commonwealth forces succeeded in halting a brilliant attack by Erwin Rommel's *Afrika Korps.* After a steady build-up of supplies and forces the British Eighth Army, com-

manded by Bernard Montgomery, launched a massive offensive in October and forced Rommel's army back across Africa to Tunisia. To cut off the German escape route Dwight D. Eisenhower led a surprise Allied landing on the coasts of Morocco and Algeria in November. In May 1943 the war in North Africa ended with the surrender of all the remaining Axis troops there.

The Eighth Army went on to take the island of Sicily without much difficulty and then landed on the mainland of Italy, while Mark Clark's U.S. Fifth Army fought its way ashore at Salerno. By October 1943 the Allied forces had taken Naples but they became bogged down at the town of Cassino. Rome was not captured until June 1944, and further progress northwards remained slow.

From 1942 onwards the Allied air forces flew a growing number of missions over Europe, many of them involving more than

Above: The German army reached Stalingrad on 12th September 1942 and for six months besieged the city. Stalingrad successfully defended itself and forced the Germans to evacuate the Caucasus and Rostov-on-Don.

Right: General Montgomery, commander of the Eighth Army, observes the progress of the Battle of El Alamein which finally routed Rommel's Afrika Korps.

a thousand bombers. Most of the raids were on military and strategic targets such as dams in the Ruhr valley and aircraft factories, but there was also some saturation bombing indiscriminately covering a wide area. These raids caused great damage and many casualties but may well have strengthened Germany's determination to resist, as did the decision at the *Casablanca Conference* between Churchill and U.S. President Roosevelt that the Allies would accept only unconditional surrender.

On 6th June 1944 General Eisenhower, as supreme commander of the Allied Expeditionary Force, authorised the launching of *Operation Overlord,* the opening of the Western Front for which the Russians had long been pressing. The invasion force included 3,000,000 men, about 10,000 ships of various sizes, more than 11,000 aircraft and prefabricated harbours known by the code name *Mulberry.* This huge force landed on the coast of Normandy, in France. After initial confusion the German defenders resisted strongly but eventually Cherbourg fell, providing an excellent harbour through which supplies could flow. In August Allied troops landed near Cannes on the southern coast of France and later that month de Gaulle made a triumphant return to Paris.

At this point Eisenhower opted for an advance on a broad front rather than a swift drive to the Rhine through Belgium and Holland, which Montgomery favoured. The Allied advance continued steadily in spite of a disastrous airborne landing at Arnhem in an attempt to capture strategic bridges. Hitler took advantage of the stretched resources of the Allies by launching a fierce counter-attack in the Ardennes in December 1944. The aim was to capture Antwerp but after considerable German gains the attack was repulsed and the so-called Battle of the Bulge ended in a successful Allied counter-attack and heavy German losses.

In March 1945 Allied troops crossed the Rhine and advanced into Germany. Meanwhile the Russians had driven the German armies from their soil and had overrun Bulgaria, Hungary, Romania and eastern Austria, including Vienna. Poland followed and by February, when the Big Three, Roosevelt, Stalin (see p. 242) and Churchill (see p. 233), held a summit conference at Yalta, Russian troops were within 160 kilometres of Berlin and the city was threatened on all sides. On 1st May it was reported that Hitler had died and had been succeeded by Grand-Admiral Doenitz. The following day Russian forces entered Berlin and on 7th May General Alfred Jodl put his signature to Germany's unconditional surrender.

The War in Asia

After the attack on Pearl Harbor in December 1941 Japan quickly capitalized on its uniquely strong position in the western Pacific. Hong Kong, Guam and Wake soon fell to Japanese forces and then followed the serious blow of the ignominious fall of Singapore. The Solomons and other island groups suffered the same fate. General Douglas Macarthur was compelled to withdraw US troops from the Philippines but for a time he succeeded in beating off attacks on the Bataan Peninsula. But soon after he had taken over command of the entire *Allied* force in the south-western Pacific the garrison on Bataan surrendered. Only half the men survived the inhuman treatment they received from the Japanese.

The fight for Burma was more prolonged because the British were anxious to keep open the Burma Road which was the only land link with China. Nevertheless by May 1942 British and Indian forces under the command of General Alexander had been forced out of Burma into India, and Chinese reinforcements were unable to hold Man-dalay. Those that escaped death or capture were driven back into China.

By this time the Japanese controlled the southern and western areas of the Pacific, but they wished to secure what they had gained by further territorial expansion. As the threat to Port Moresby in New Guinea became more obvious there were fears that if it fell Japan might use it as a springboard from which to invade Australia. But a Japanese *taskforce* was intercepted by American ships and aerial battles ended with the defeat of the invasion force.

The next threat was far north of this area, aimed at Midway Island north of Hawaii and the Aleutians west of Alaska. In June 1942 a Japanese fleet attacking Midway was severely beaten by American carrier-based aircraft, and any threat there might have been to Hawaii or the United States itself evaporated. The Japanese did succeed in occupying part of the Aleutians but they withdrew the following year.

Just as the tide turned in the European theatre of operations in 1942, so the Allies now began to push the Japanese back although conditions were often appalling for

Right: British jungle patrol probe a native 'basha' where Japanese troops are dug in.

Far right: Raising the American flag on Iwo Jima. Marines of the 3rd, 4th and 5th Divisions spent a month storming this island in the Pacific in 1945 and over 19,000 men were killed and wounded before they finally took it.

Below: The surprise attack on Pearl Harbor which stunned the American public and led to the U.S. declaration of war on Japan. In the picture, the U.S.S. *West Virginia* is burning fiercely after being bombed by Japanese warplanes. Behind is the battleship *Tennessee*.

the troops of both sides and new fighting techniques had to be learned. American marines fought long campaigns in the Solomons and in New Guinea, both aimed at eliminating the vital Japanese base at Rabaul in New Britain Island.

In the central Pacific, American strategy was to attack one island at a time, using each island as a base for attacking the next. By this island-hopping method the Americans advanced from the Gilbert Islands to the Marshalls and to the Marianas, which formed ideal bases for B-29 Superfortress bombers. In October 1944 American forces landed on Leyte in the Philippines. A crushing sea victory gave the Americans control of the waters round the Philippines and by early 1945 Manila and the remainder of the islands were largely under US control.

Pressure was next applied in Burma. It was important to keep supplies flowing to the Chinese, who kept large numbers of Japanese troops pinned down.

American command of the air and the sea was followed by enormously destructive bombing raids on Japanese cities and the decimation of Japanese shipping. Meanwhile island-hopping continued with the occupation of Iwo Jima and Okinawa, in spite of heavy casualties and the depredations of the *Kamikaze* suicide pilots. Okinawa was only 560 kilometres from the Japanese island of Kyushu and the plan to invade this island was given the code name Operation Olympic. The end of the war was approaching. At the Potsdam Conference held in July President Harry Truman, the British Prime Minister Winston Churchill (later Clement Attlee), and Joseph Stalin met to discuss peace terms the Allies would put to the Axis powers.

In fact the war came to a sudden and cataclysmic end when, on 6th August, an

American B-29 aircraft dropped the first atomic bomb on the Japanese city of Hiroshima, followed three days later by a second bomb dropped on Nagasaki. More than 100,000 people died and Japan surrendered almost immediately, the agreement being signed on 2nd September 1946.

The Second World War had cost the lives of up to 35 million people, the majority of them, for the first time in war, civilians.

Above: On 6th August 1945 a single American bomber passed over the city of Hiroshima and dropped one bomb, the first atom bomb. That bomb caused the death of 66,000 people, the severe injury of another 69,000 and the complete destruction of one and a half square kilometres of the city.

DATA DIGEST

Many of the words which are italicized in the previous section are explained more fully in the following data digest. They will help to expand your knowledge of history.

Allies. At the beginning of the First World War the Allies comprised Britain, France, Russia and Belgium. At the beginning of the Second World War the Allies were Britain and France. In both wars the entry of the United States turned the scales.

Anglo-French Entente. Also known as the Entente Cordiale, this agreement signed in 1904 settled a number of disputes between Britain and France. In particular, Britain received a free hand in Egypt and France a free hand in Morocco with certain provisions for the preservation of Spanish rights.

Anglo-Russian Entente. An agreement signed in 1907 in which Britain and Russia settled disputes in Afghanistan, Persia and Tibet.

Bastille. The fortress of the Bastille in Paris was used for 400 years to house political prisoners. The day of its storming by the mob, 14th July, is celebrated in France as Bastille Day.

Blitz. Heavy bombing attacks. The word comes from the German *blitzkrieg* meaning lightning war.

Blocs. Alliances or combinations of parties or countries to achieve some common aim.

Boer War. There were two wars between the British and the Boers, or Dutch settlers in South Africa. In the first, in 1881, the Boers secured the independence of the Transvaal. In the second (1899-1902) the British were victorious and the Transvaal and Orange Free State became British colonies.

Bolsheviks. In 1903 the Russian social democratic party split into Bolsheviks, under Lenin, and the more moderate Mensheviks.

Boston Tea Party. The name given to a protest by American colonists against the Tea Act of 1773 which discriminated in favour of imported British Tea. A group of colonists, dressed as American Indians, threw cargoes of tea from British ships into Boston harbour.

British Expeditionary Force. A British force that landed in France on 7th August 1914.

Central Powers. Germany, Austria-Hungary and Turkey during the First World War.

Citadel. Central fortified point.

Coalition government. Government composed of more than one party.

Combatant. Participant in war.

Congress of Vienna. Conference held between 1814 and 1815 to work out a settlement of Europe after Napoleon's defeat. The main participants were Austria, Britain, Prussia and Russia. Talleyrand of France also played an important part.

Crimean War. A war fought between Russia and Britain and France. In 1854 the Allies landed in the Crimea, fought battles at Balaklava and Inkerman and besieged Sebastopol. Cavour sent Piedmontese troops to aid his own plans for Italy. Russia sued for peace in 1856 and terms were finally agreed at the Congress of Paris.

Crusade. Struggle to further some idealistic cause.

Customs duties. Taxes levied on imports and, less commonly, on some types of exports.

D-Day. The first day of the Allied invasion of Europe, 6th June 1944.

Decembrists. In December 1825 a group of army officers in St Petersburg led a conspiracy against Tsar Nicholas I supported by some nobles. Some conspirators wanted to establish a republic and free the serfs, while others had less radical aims. The conspiracy was betrayed and leaders executed or exiled.

Delegates. Representatives.

Dictator. Absolute ruler of a country. The best-known modern examples are Hitler and Mussolini, but originally a dictator was a Roman magistrate given complete power at a time of extreme emergency.

Duma. The elected parliament set up by Tsar Nicolas II following the uprising of 1905. There were four Dumas, each more radical than the previous one.

Enlightenment. The scientific and philosophical ideas current in the 18th century. Rationalists such as Descartes and Diderot attacked accepted ideas and established authority and tried to adopt a scientific approach to all issues.

Free French Movement. In June 1940 Charles de Gaulle flew to London and called on Frenchmen to continue the fight against Germany. He organized the movement as a political and military rallying point for Frenchmen in Britain and North Africa.

General Strike. Strike of all union-organized workers.

Girondins. A moderate mainly middle-class group, so-called because its leaders came from the Gironde department of France. They opposed the more radical Jacobins and in 1793 attempted to stage an uprising against the National Convention. Several of its leaders were executed.

Golden Horde. The Mongol ruler Batu Khan and his successors were known as the Golden Horde because of the splendour of their tents. This Tartar empire controlled most of Russia for more than 200 years.

Guerilla resistance. Tactics of harassing a superior enemy by small and frequent hit-and-run raids.

Guillotine. A device for execution by beheading in which a heavy blade falls down a slide. It was named after its inventor Joseph Ignace Guillotin.

Holy Alliance. An agreement between Russia, Austria and Prussia in 1815 to act at all times in accordance with Christian principles. Most of the other European countries later signed this vague agreement. This term is often applied to the reactionary policies of the three original signatories.

Jacobins. A radical political club founded in Paris in 1789. The Jacobins urged the trial and execution of Louis XVI and were mainly responsible for the Reign of Terror. They lost their power after the execution of their leader Robespierre in 1794.

Janissaries. Christians and prisoners of war who were forcibly converted to the Muslim religion and trained as an elite corps to serve the sultans of the Ottoman empire. After about 1600 Muslims were admitted to the corps which lasted until 1826.

Khan. A Mongol prince or chief.

Ku Klux Klan. The original Klan founded in 1866 was a southern secret society directed against Negroes and northerners. Its members wore white robes and masks and used terrorist tactics. The Klan was suppressed in 1871 but was revived in 1915 and achieved tremendous notoriety during the late 1950s and 1960s in its conflicts with Civil Rights workers.

Kuiprili. A Turkish family originating in Albania which provided a number of Grand Viziers during the Ottoman empire.

League of Nations. An international organization set up in 1920 with its headquarters in Geneva to enable disputes between nations to be settled peaceably. It had no armed forces at its command and was unable to prevent glaring examples of aggression. The United States was never a member and Germany and the Soviet Union only for short periods.

Lend-Lease. Under the Lend-Lease Act in 1941 the American Congress empowered President Roosevelt to sell, lend or lease war supplies to countries whose defence was vital to the interests of the United States.

Logistics. The science of the movement and supply of troops.

Marseillaise. France's national anthem composed by Claude Rouget de Lisle in the year 1792.

Militiamen. Volunteer forces consisting of citizens specially trained for military service in case of national emergency.

Mosque. Muslim place of worship.

Muslims. Followers of the Islamic religion founded in the seventh century by the prophet Muhammad. Also known as Moslems.

National anthem. Patriotic national song delivered on official occasions.

Peace Conference. The Crimean War was settled by the Congress of Paris in 1856. Russia made a number of concessions including the neutralization of the Black Sea area. Later Peace Conferences took place after the First World War and the Vietnam War in the 1970s.

Praetorian Guard. The personal guard of the emperors of ancient Rome. The praetorians became extremely influential and were able to create or depose emperors.

Puppet government. A government controlled by an outside authority such as a victorious foreign country.

Radar. An electronic means of locating objects over long distances. It was developed in Britain in the 1930s and used by the Allies during the Second World War.

Railhead. Point to which supplies can easily be brought, by rail and road.

Reformation. The religious revolution during the 16th century which was responsible for the eventual rise of Protestantism.

Republic. A system of government in which the head of state is not a hereditary position. In most republics the head of state is an elected president and the legislative body is an elected assembly.

Republican Party. The original Republican Party of the United States was founded in 1792 by Thomas Jefferson. It later split into Whigs and Democrats. In 1854 the Whigs and the Democrats of the north formed a new Republican Party with an anti-slavery programme.

Risorgimento. This term applies to the movement for Italian unification. Cavour founded a newspaper with this name in 1847.

Rurik. Traditionally the founder of Russia. He is said to have been invited by Slavs to be their ruler and to have settled in Novgorod in 862 A.D.

Serfdom. A feudal institution which lasted until the 19th century in Russia. A serf was half-freeman and half-slave. He worked his master's land and also had a smallholding of his own for which he paid rent and gave certain services. His master had certain obligations towards him including his physical protection.

Slavs. Indo-European people who lived in south-eastern Poland and northern Ukraine and migrated into other parts of eastern Europe, including Russia, between 200 and 500 A.D.

Snipers. Sharp-shooters who fire from cover and pick off single men.

Stamp Act. A measure introduced by the British government in 1765. According to its terms the American colonists had to pay stamp duty on newspapers and legal documents. Following violent protests the act was withdrawn after less than a year.

States-general. A French assembly, similar in some ways to a parliament, which was first convened in 1302. It consisted of members from the three estates: clergy, nobles and commons. In 1789 the third estate, joined by some of the clergy, proclaimed the first National Assembly and precipitated the French Revolution.

Tennessee Valley Authority. Federal authority established to exploit the resources of the Tennessee Valley, particularly by a vast hydro-electric scheme involving the building of 20 dams, and to improve the economic status of the poor farmers of the Tennessee Valley.

Teutonic Knights. German military order founded during the Third Crusade (1189-92). It gained great power and privilege and subdued Prussia and other lands to the east.

Treaty of Olmütz Agreement between Prussia and Austria signed in 1850. Prussia gave up its attempt to form a union with other leading German states and acquiesced in the restoration of the German Confederation.

U-Boats. German submarines used in the First and Second World Wars.

United Nations Organization. An international organization set up in 1945 with 51 members to ensure peace and settle disputes between nations. There are now well over 100 members. The two main organs are the General Assembly and the Security Council and there are also a number of specialized agencies.

Vatican. The French protected Rome against the triumphal progress of Garibaldi until 1870 when Rome became the capital of a united Italy. The popes remained in the Vatican in protest until the Lateran Treaty of 1929 made the Vatican an independent state.

Young Turks. A reform movement founded by Turkish exiles and supported by discontented minority peoples. It demanded some liberalization of the Turkish regime and the restoration of the constitution of 1876. A revolution in 1908 brought about the desired changes and two of the leaders, Enver and Talaat, dominated Turkish politics for ten years.

Zollverein. A German customs union dominated by Prussia. Almost all the German states had joined it by the middle of the 19th century.

PRESIDENTS OF THE UNITED STATES	
George Washington	1789-1797
John Adams	1797-1801
Thomas Jefferson	1801-1809
James Madison	1809-1817
James Monroe	1817-1825
John Quincy Adams	1825-1829
Andrew Jackson	1829-1837
Martin van Buren	1837-1841
William Henry Harrison	1841
John Tyler	1841-1845
James Knox Polk	1845-1849
Zachary Taylor	1849-1850
Millard Fillmore	1850-1853
Franklin Pierce	1853-1857
James Buchanan	1857-1861
Abraham Lincoln	1861-1865
Andrew Johnson	1865-1869
Ulysses Simpson Grant	1869-1877
Rutherford Birchard Hayes	1877-1881
James Abram Garfield	1881
Chester Alan Arthur	1881-1885
Grover Cleveland	1885-1889
Benjamin Harrison	1889-1893
Grover Cleveland	1893-1897
William McKinley	1897-1901
Theodore Roosevelt	1901-1909
William Howard Taft	1909-1913
Woodrow Wilson	1913-1921
Warren Gamaliel Harding	1921-1923
Calvin Coolidge	1923-1929
Herbert Clark Hoover	1929-1933
Franklin Delano Roosevelt	1933-1945
Harry S. Truman	1945-1953
Dwight D. Eisenhower	1953-1961
John F. Kennedy	1961-1963
Lyndon B. Johnson	1963-1969
Richard M. Nixon	1969-1974
Gerald R. Ford	1974-1977
Jimmy Carter	1977-

THE SHAPING OF THE CONTEMPORARY WORLD

America's Rise to World Power

The United States did not become an active great power until late in its development. Long after its population and industrial strength had brought it to the front it continued to play a limited role in world affairs. There were two reasons for this: first, its remoteness from Europe, the main scene of action and, secondly, its deliberate policy of isolation. This desire to avoid foreign entanglements went back to the beginnings of America's independent history; it was one of its strongest traditions (see pp. 156-7).

Isolationism as a policy was mainly concerned with Europe. United States' relations with the rest of the American continent were governed by the *Monroe Doctrine* (1832). This was a warning to the European powers not to try to impose their political systems on, or to annexe fresh territory in, the *New World* (see pp. 202-3). In the last years of the 19th and the early years of the 20th century it was used by the United States as an excuse to interfere in the affairs of its neighbours to the south. In the Far East, too, American policy became interventionist. The Far East (as Europeans call it) is to Americans the far western shore of the Pacific Ocean, and it was in this area that the United States definitely became a great power for the first time. In 1898 the Spanish-American war was fought: American intervention to help Cuba in its struggle to free itself from the Spanish empire led to Spain's defeat, not only in the Caribbean but also in the Far East where the Spanish fleet was destroyed and the Philippines annexed. Hawaii, too, was annexed and so the United States, resolute opponent of *imperialism*, itself became an imperial power, at least temporarily. America's activity in the 'Open Door' notes of 1899 and 1900, to prevent the carve-up of China, was another indication of the great power role of the United States.

The opening years of the 20th century saw the continuance of a vigorous policy under President Theodore Roosevelt (1901-1909), who laid especial emphasis on American naval strength, sending the United States fleet on a 'show the flag' mission round the world. He supported the revolution in Colombia setting up the Republic of Panama—which promptly granted the United States rights to build the Panama Canal. His diplomatic intervention in the Russo-Japanese war led to the *Treaty of*

Above: The insurrection in Cuba, 1896. A view of a rebel camp deep in the Cuban jungle. In their fight to free themselves from the Spanish empire, the Cubans enlisted the support of the U.S.A. Two years later, the Americans were at war with the Spaniards and, eventually, displaced them in the Caribbean area. This war, along with other actions in South America, marked the end of Spanish influence in Central and South America.

Right and far right: The Panama Canal, which links the Atlantic Ocean with the Pacific Ocean. The rights to build the canal were granted to the United States as a reward for its support of the revolution in Colombia which led to the establishment of the state of Panama.

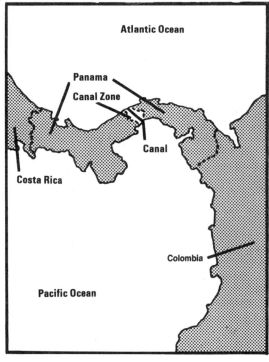

Portsmouth (New Hampshire) of 1905, for which he was later awarded the *Nobel Peace Prize*.

But after striding on to the world stage and making its presence felt the United States left it again, unwilling to abandon its isolationism. On the outbreak of the First World War (1914-1918) America proclaimed its neutrality and only declared war (April 1917) when Germany's unrestricted submarine warfare threatened its shipping, its citizens travelling on the high seas and, hence, its neutral rights (see pp. 172-7). At the Peace Conference the American President, Woodrow Wilson, took a leading part (see pp. 180-1), but the Senate failed to ratify the Peace Treaty.

United States policy was not completely isolationist in the 1920s: the Washington Conference (1922) under American initiative led to naval disarmament and treaties to maintain peace in the Pacific area. But when Japan conquered Manchuria in 1931 the United States merely propounded the doctrine of non-recognition of forcible changes of territory. As the threat of war grew in Europe in the 1930s, the United States became even more isolationist: the Neutrality Laws of 1935, 1936 and 1937 were attempts to avoid war by renouncing the neutral rights which Germany had violated in 1917.

But when the Second World War began in 1939 the United States changed these laws to help Britain and France, and when Britain stood alone after the fall of France, the United States, in President Franklin D. Roosevelt's words, made itself the 'arsenal of democracy'. The Japanese attack at Pearl Harbor (7th December 1941) brought

Above: The two presidents who perhaps more than any others were responsible for America's new role in world affairs as a power to be reckoned with: Theodore Roosevelt (top) 1901-1909, and Woodrow Wilson (below) 1913-1921.

America into the war as a full belligerent. The shock of that attack stimulated the American people into extraordinary levels of production; the U.S.A. was able to equip its own 16 million forces and to provide huge quantities of arms and supplies to its allies under *Lend-Lease*. It also meant that America would not relapse into isolation when the war was over. The United States was a founder member of the *United Nations Organization* and, despite disappointment with its achievement, continued to work within it while seeking other ways of fulfilling its policy.

193

The Rise of Japan: (1850-1950)

During the last quarter of the 18th century the growth of trade in the Pacific had brought about considerable interest in Japan—a country until then largely ignored by foreigners. Since the relaxation of the ban upon western learning and languages after 1716, the Japanese were themselves becoming interested in the outside world. The more intelligent Japanese appreciated the advantages which scientific invention had given the western nations and sought to emulate it. From this sprang the rapid development and modernization of Japan.

The Japanese policy of seclusion was moderated in 1842 when foreign ships were permitted to enter certain specified harbours for fuel and supplies. Thus, when the American Commodore Perry requested a treaty of trade and friendship with Japan in 1853 he was able, a year later, to sign an agreement between Japan and the United States. Influential Japanese opinion had reconciled itself to the inevitability of ending forever Japan's seclusion from the rest of the world. Interest in the west was reawakened and some Japanese even defied the laws, at the risk of death, and travelled to Europe.

The industrialization of Japan is often said to begin with the restoration of power to the monarchy in 1868, although some development had occurred earlier. Gunsmith shops had been built as long ago as 1845 and furnaces and iron foundries were built in Satsuma in 1854. The industrial expansion of Japan was rapid, brought about in large measure by the high concentration of population in cities and the natural skills, application and industry of the Japanese people. During this crucial phase of Japanese development they were fortunate to be spared economic domination by foreign countries.

Politically, too, Japan made advances at this time. Since 1603 the country had been ruled by a *shogun*, or general. In 1867 the reigning shogun was forced to resign and, with the return of absolute powers to the emperor, the government of the country was reorganized on *bureaucratic lines*. However, it was evident that further changes were essential to achieve a rapid modernization of the country, particularly the abolition of *feudal institutions* and their replacement by a central government. This meant the surrender of all power by the feudal clans —such as the *Satsuma, Choshu, Tosa* and *Hizen*—which had been chiefly responsible for the overthrow of the Shogun. In 1869 the heads of the clans, through patriotic motives, willingly surrendered their *fiefs* to the emperor. The *Samurai* (a military class

Above: The Samurai, a Japanese military class dedicated to achieving mastery in the martial arts. They flourished during the 17th and 18th centuries and were generally feared by the ordinary Japanese because of their bullying attitude and brutality.

Right: The Emperor Mutsuhito who, in 1867, ascended the throne and ended almost seven hundred years of feudal military rule.

under the feudal regime) rose in revolt in 1877 but, after a struggle of eight months' duration, were defeated by a national army of *conscripted* soldiers. This was an important contribution to the destruction of feudalism, for it showed that military prowess was not a *monopoly* of the Samurai. The way was becoming clear for the establishment of government on western lines.

The *Meiji* period, or 'enlightenment', opened with the Emperor Mutsuhito. He was fortunate in having, as advisers and ministers, a number of outstanding statesmen, such as Kido, Ito and Yamagata. In these early phases of modernization the Japanese people displayed a lively but wholly undiscriminating enthusiasm for western ideas. The rulers, however, although themselves *reformers,* were opposed to a too rapid adoption of *parliamentary government*. Political struggles for power developed between different factions, and were only abated when war broke out (for control of Formosa and Korea) between Japan and China in 1894. Japanese successes made it difficult for even the strongest critics of the government to challenge the established regime. This situation was strengthened by spectacular Japanese victories against Russia during the war of 1904-5.

Japan had defeated two major powers —China and Russia—within a few short years, partly because of a treaty it had signed with Britain in 1902 in which both parties guaranteed each other assistance if either were attacked by more than one power. This had given Japan military freedom, but the two wars had left it economically impoverished.

To restore economic prosperity to Japan

Above: Assembly line for the manufacture of automobiles in Japan. With American financial aid and technology, the hard-working Japanese soon forged ahead to become one of the world's major industrial powers. Today, Japanese technology is highly respected, and the automated methods of manufacture are studied by experts from all over the world. Japanese goods can be found everywhere —visible evidence of the strength of the Japanese economy.

the government promoted industry and foreign investment to the greatest possible extent and with the outbreak of the First World War, the Japanese economy entered a boom period. Japan joined in on the side of the *Allies*, but was careful to keep its military and naval commitments to a minimum, while nevertheless greatly benefiting from the Allies' need for *munitions*. Thus Japan, from being a buyer on world markets, became an exporter of arms and munitions in a market where there was little competition but great demand. By the end of the war Japan was a dominant force in Asia and it took its part in the peace conference as an undisputed world power.

Opposition to liberal policies, however, rapidly developed after the war, for Japan, in common with most industrialized countries, was overwhelmed by an economic depression. By 1930 it was suffering from unemployment and unrest, and in 1931 Japanese forces in south Manchuria attacked Chinese forces in Mukden and rapidly occupied the whole of Manchuria. Efforts by the League of Nations (see pp. 180-1) to restore peace were unsuccessful and Manchuria was virtually *annexed.* Japan's campaign soon degenerated into an undeclared war against China. By the end of 1938 the Japanese had captured most of the great cities and ports of China. The Chinese government was forced to take refuge in Chungking, from where they continued the war, badly handicapped by a shortage of materials but safe from total defeat by the size and virtually limitless population of their country (see pp. 198-9).

Japan was strengthened by these victories; opposition to war became feeble and the economy was directed towards the manufacture of munitions and the training of troops. By 1938 Japan had become a *totalitarian state*, in alliance (having signed the *anti-Comintern pact*) with Germany and Italy. The conditions were therefore ripe for Japan's entry into the Second World War, which took place with its surprise attack on Pearl Harbor on the 7th December 1941 (see pp. 188-9).

At the end of the war Japan was occupied by British Commonwealth and American troops under General Douglas Macarthur, and an Allied commission was established for the purpose of democratizing the political, judicial and social systems. On the 3rd November 1946 a new constitution came into force which, while retaining the emperor as head of state, provided for government by a parliament elected by the people. Japan, by a hard and often costly effort, had finally entered upon the path of true democracy.

China

The rise of the *Mongols* brought about the end of the *Sung* dynasty. In 1201 the Mongol leader Temujin was proclaimed Genghis Khan (emperor within the seas), unquestioned ruler of the Mongol tribes. China, in spite of brave resistance, could not withstand his military genius (see pp. 84-5). Under the *Yuan* dynasty, as the Mongol rulers were known, roads and canals were built and an efficient postal system was established. The greatest of the Yuan emperors was Kublai Khan whose court, as Marco Polo reported, was rich, cultured and enlightened (pp. 90-1).

The Yuan dynasty was overthrown in the 14th century and was followed by the *Ming* dynasty. Its founder was a monk called Chu Yuan-chang, who took Nanking in 1356 and drove the Mongols out of China by 1371. Many neighbouring states acknowledged China's suzerainty and all attempts by the Mongols to regain their position failed. Perhaps the greatest of the Ming emperors was *Yung-Lo* (1403-24). Scholars and philosophers were encouraged and a number of naval expeditions sailed to places as far away as the South Seas, India and the Persian Gulf. But later China became completely *isolationist* and its subjects were forbidden to leave the country. The Ming period saw vast building projects and also the most delicate of paintings and finest of porcelain workmanship.

The Ming regime began to collapse because of administrative incompetence and a succession of internal rebellions. At the end of the 16th century the *Manchu*, a people of Manchuria, began to exert increasing influence. Allied with the Koreans and Mongols, they harried China, breaking through the *Great Wall* in 1629. The Chinese tried to make peace terms but in 1644 the Manchu took Peking and made it their capital. Within 25 years they controlled most of the country. The new ruling dynasty, known as the *Ch'ing,* reigned until 1911. The emperors made many important social and economic changes; in fact the Manchu to some extent became assimilated with the Chinese, even adopting their language. But at least they brought peace to China for about 150 years and during this early period they encouraged the development of commerce, both at home and abroad.

Many valuable agricultural innovations were introduced under the Ch'ing but one disastrous crop was the *opium poppy*. Merchants grew rich on the proceeds of its sale but millions of Chinese people became completely addicted to opium, until eventually the government prohibited the drug. In 1840

war broke out with Britain when a Manchu official burnt a consignment of opium carried on a British ship. By the *Treaty of Nanking* the defeated Chinese paid Britain reparations, gave it the island of Hong Kong and opened five ports to its ships when previously an isolationist policy had kept open only Canton as a trading port.

The door once forced was soon wide open. Russia, France and the United States demanded similar trading concessions. More ports were opened and trading rights granted. The position of the Ch'ing dynasty was threatened from within as well as from without during the 19th century. Six serious revolts were put down in which millions of people died and irreparable damage was done to buildings and works of art. Japanese troops invaded China in 1894 when the Ch'ing sent forces to suppress a rebellion in Korea, where Japan had important interests. Japan made several gains and in the ensuing peace treaty received Formosa and the Pescadores Islands, while Korea became independent.

Left: German cavalry arrive in Peking after the collapse of the Boxer rebellion in 1900.

Top right: The British Royal Navy steamship *Nemesis* destroying Chinese junks in the Opium War between China and Britain in the early 1840s.

Below: Battalion of the regular Chinese army on the march during the Boxer rebellion.

As the foreign influence and pressure increased so also did national resentment and this was fomented by secret societies, in particular the *Society of Harmonious Fists*, better known as the *Boxers*. In 1900 the Boxers massacred missionaries and other foreigners and murdered the German minister and the Japanese ambassador in Peking. Many westerners took refuge in embassies, where they remained under siege until an international force, including troops from the leading European countries and from Russia and the United States, crushed the uprising. China was compelled to pay large amounts in compensation and to grant generous trading rights. The indemnities were later waived.

In 1911 Chinese army units carried out a *coup* against the government. Sun Yat-sen became president of a republic set up in Nanking, which quickly gained control of the south (see pp. 198-9). In the north Yuan Shih-kai co-operated with the republicans, forced the six-year-old emperor to abdicate and took over the presidency himself.

EH-N'

China 1911-1948

In 1900 China was ruled by emperors of the *Manchu* dynasty (see pp. 196-7), who lived in splendour in the walled city of Peking. Their rule had grown weak, corrupt and unpopular. The past 50 years had been particularly troublesome. The population had increased rapidly, but farming had not improved. Peasants faced a life of starvation, poverty and high rents. Bandits and armies of *warlords* terrorized the countryside. Foreigners from Britain, France, Germany, Russia and Japan had seized parts of China in search of trade and empire. They built railways and factories and modernized ports such as Shanghai and Canton, but the Chinese did not profit from this and felt their way of life was threatened. They wanted reforms and the expulsion of the 'foreign devils'. The rebellions which took place, like the *Boxer Rising* (1900), were often crushed by foreign armies employed by the emperor (see pp. 196-7).

Among the revolutionary leaders was Sun Yat-sen, a farmer's son who had travelled abroad and trained as a doctor. He believed the Manchus must be replaced by democratic rulers. He disliked foreign influence, but knew China would remain backward until old customs were abandoned and schools, hospitals and railways built. The Chinese Revolution came in 1911-12, beginning with disturbances in Hankow. The young Manchu Emperor abdicated and Sun Yat-sen returned from long years of exile to be elected President of the *Kuomintang* (Nationalist) government. Sun had little chance to fulfil his three principles, 'Democracy, Nationalism, and Socialism', in the years which followed. The Kuomintang was only strong in southern China. It was opposed by rival landowners and warlords, like Yuan Shih-kai who died in 1916. Matters were further confused by the intervention of Japan, eager to take advantage of China's troubles. Sun was forced to fight and eventually to seek help from Russia. The Kuomintang was organized along Communist lines and Russians helped to train its armies. Sun died in 1925. His inspiration and sincerity had kept the revolution alive, and he was rightly honoured as the 'Father of the Chinese Republic'.

Chiang Kai-shek, commander of the Kuomintang armies, became the new leader. In 1926 people in the north flocked to his support as he crushed the local warlords. It seemed as though strong government would at last be possible. Unfortunately, a split now occurred in the Kuomintang between the *Communists* and the supporters of Chiang. A visit to Russia in 1923 had turned

Above: Chiang Kai-shek and his wife, Madam Chiang Mei-ling, in 1936. Despite an agreement between the Nationalists and the Communists to put their differences aside in order to resist the Japanese, they failed to achieve any deep measure of understanding. As soon as the Japanese were defeated in 1945, the Communists began an offensive against Chiang Kai-shek and his army and eventually drove them off the mainland and over to Taiwan. There Chiang Kai-shek ruled with the official support of the United States until he died in April 1975.

Chiang against Communism. He hoped for help from rich businessmen and landowners, who were likewise anti-Communist. In 1927, therefore, Chiang began a massive purge of the Communists. Many were brutally executed, while others escaped to remote regions of China. By 1928 Chiang was a *dictator*, protected by secret police, the 'Blue-shirts'. To the survivors of the banned Communist party it seemed he had betrayed the principles behind the revolution.

Among the Communist groups which now emerged was that led by Mao Tse-tung (see p. 240) in Kiangsi province. Having survived five assaults by Kuomintang forces, Mao decided to move the whole community to the safety of the remote northern province of Shensi. The *Long March* (1934-1935) was an amazing journey. Men, women and children faced the hazards of starvation, frostbite, poison arrows, bombs and bullets. They crossed 18 mountain ranges and 24 rivers on the 9,650 kilometre journey. Mao's words, 'The weak will die, but will die bravely. There is no going back', proved true; about one in ten survived the journey. Nevertheless Communism survived, with Mao as its undisputed leader.

Civil war was not the only problem facing China in the 1930s. The government of Japan was controlled by generals eager for military conquest (see pp. 194-5). They

seized Manchuria in 1931 and used this as a base for further minor attacks. Chiang wished to crush the Communists and unite China ('unification before resistance') before dealing with Japan. Mao and the Communists declared a policy of 'resistance above civil war', to which Chiang agreed in 1936, after being kidnapped and released on condition that he cease attacks on the Communists. Full-scale war with Japan began in 1937. The coastal and industrial areas of China were soon overcome by Japanese forces vastly superior in ships and planes. This struggle became merged with the Second World War, and Japan's defeat in 1945 finally freed China from Japanese control (see pp. 188-9).

The struggle between Communists and Kuomintang was resumed in 1946, despite peace moves by the U.S.A. However, Chiang's armies were undisciplined and his officials corrupt. He had improved factories and schools but done nothing for the millions of poor peasants. Their prospect of a better life lay with the Communists, for Mao had adopted the ideas of the 'Father of Communism', Karl Marx, to suit the needs of a farming society. As Mao's armies marched south they were welcomed by the peasants. Chiang was defeated and fled to the island of Formosa with his Kuomintang supporters.

Above: An early photograph of Mao Tse-tung (seated far left) and another Chinese Communist leader, Chu Teh (seated right, facing camera), taken in 1930. Mao's simple peasant background and his innate understanding of the forces that move the Chinese people gained his Communist party a tremendous following during the early years between the two world wars.

Right: 1949 poster proclaiming the way forward under Mao Tse-tung. In this same year, Chiang Kai-shek and the Nationalist army fled the China mainland and Mao Tse-tung became Chairman of the new People's Republic of China.

The Communist Split

Communism used to be noted for its monolithic unity. One-party rule was established in Russia by Lenin (see p. 238); his successor Stalin rid the Communist party of all who did not accept his leadership and policy (see p. 242). Trotsky, a famous leader of the 1917 revolution, was exiled from the Soviet Union and later murdered; other leading 'old Bolsheviks' were condemned to death or imprisoned: millions of people spent years living in concentration camps in Siberia. Foreign Communists were kept to a strict discipline through the *Communist International* (Comintern), until it was disbanded in deference to the Soviet Union's wartime alliance with the United States.

After the Second World War the same discipline was exercised over the east European countries where Communism had come to power with the aid of the *Red Army*. There was one significant exception. Marshal Tito and his Yugoslav comrades had won power, largely by their own efforts, in a partisan war against the Germans. In 1948 quarrels over practical problems and ideological issues led to an open split between Stalin and the Yugoslav Communists. Stalin's efforts to remove Tito were unsuccessful, for they stopped short of armed intervention. Yugoslavia followed its own road to *Socialism*. After Stalin's death in 1953 normal relations were resumed between the Soviet Union and Yugoslavia.

Other changes followed Stalin's death. One was the 'thaw': a softening of the rigour of Stalin's rule, marked by a greater, though limited and widely fluctuating, freedom in literary and cultural life. Nevertheless, this 'freedom' was permitted only within the strict limits of Communist ideology. Another change was a serious split between the Soviet Union and China.

In China, Communists had come to power independently of Russian help, and even against Stalin's advice, which had been that they should co-operate with Chiang Kaishek. At first their relations with the USSR were friendly. A treaty of alliance was signed (1950) and the USSR helped China with arms during China's participation in the Korean War (1950-1953). Economic and technical aid was provided to help China to industrialize and the Soviet Union even promised assistance in developing *nuclear weapons* (1957).

However, a split was already beginning though it was not to become public until 1960. Khrushchev's denunciation of Stalin in 1956 was the starting point, for the difficulties which followed in eastern Europe caused the USSR to cut down its aid to

Above: Joseph Stalin, general secretary of the Soviet Communist party and dictatorial ruler of the Soviet people until his death in 1953.
Below: Nikita Khrushchev, Soviet leader, meeting President Tito of Yugoslavia in Belgrade in an attempt to strengthen relations between the two countries.

China. At the same time the new interpretation of Marxist-Leninist theory which accompanied 'deStalinization' was attacked as 'revisionism' by the Chinese. Khrushchev argued that general war was no longer inevitable and that the strength of world Communism made possible a peaceful transition to Socialism. The Chinese disagreed and were denounced as 'dogmatists' by the Russians.

At the *Moscow Conference* of Communist parties (November 1957) a compromise document was agreed which attacked both 'revisionists' and 'dogmatists', but this did not stop the split from widening. Soviet attempts to achieve a reduction of tension with the United States were resented by China; while China's attempts in 1958 to speed the building of full Communism through the 'Great Leap Forward' and the setting up of huge *agricultural communes* were ridiculed by the USSR. In 1959 the

USSR cancelled the agreement on nuclear arms development and in 1960 suddenly withdrew all technical aid, at a time when China was suffering from great agricultural difficulties.

Behind the ideological arguments were conflicts of interest. Resentment of Soviet policy towards the United States was the result of China's own serious differences with America, for example over Formosa and admission to the *United Nations*. There were direct clashes between China and the Soviet Union on their common border, between Sinkiang and Kazakhstan and between the Far Eastern province and Manchuria. Tsarist Russia's expansion (see pp. 168-9), the 'unequal treaties' of 1858 and 1860 in particular, had given Russia large areas on the Amur River. In 1963 China tried to get acknowledgement of the unjust nature of the treaties and to have adjustments made in the actual frontier at certain places, but the negotiations floundered.

The Sino-Soviet split set up two centres of Communist orthodoxy. This enabled foreign Communists to enjoy a greater freedom than was possible under Stalin's domination. Pro-Soviet and pro-Maoist groups appeared. Western European Communist parties have supported the Soviet policy of peaceful co-existence and proclaimed that the way to Communism must be through democratic elections. Some Communist parties, like the Cuban, have continued to be Soviet allies while supporting a Maoist policy of encouraging revolution and *guerrilla war*. The Cuban leader, Castro, and the late Che Guevara, have joined Mao (see p. 240) as idols of romantic revolutionaries. The Communist split has led to a flowering of Marxist ideas among the young and to many new Marxist 'prophets'. At the same time, small countries in many parts of the world, for example, Algeria, Chile, Guinea, and some states in India, have experimented with their own adaptations of Communism.

Soviet and Chinese Communism do not present a complete contrast of opposites. Soviet forces intervened militarily to halt a liberal trend in Czechoslovakia in 1968 among Czech Communists. The Chinese denounced them for 'social-imperialism'. The Chinese, while talking of promoting revolution, act with caution. They have avoided a head-on clash with America over Formosa, nor have they intervened directly in the Vietnam War. Their 'aid' to the Yemen and Tanzania, for example, has not been used to put political pressures on those countries, as has been the case with Soviet and American aid. Whatever ideological arguments are used, national interest decides the actual policy of each country.

Above: Prague, 1968. In the summer of that year, Czechoslovakia enjoyed a new sense of liberation under Premier Alexander Dubček. But to Russia's leaders this seemed to be a breakaway from Soviet control and Moscow sent in soldiers and tanks to occupy the country.

Right: A map of the border between the Soviet Union and China. During the late 1960s there were several serious military clashes over disputed territory.

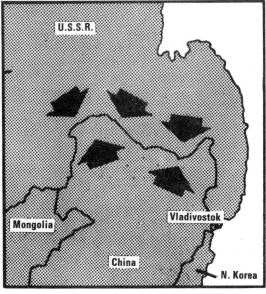

Latin America

By the end of the 16th century Spanish and Portuguese settlers had colonized nearly all Latin America, and Spain and Portugal continued to profit from the richness of the natural resources and the abundance of cheap labour for a further 200 years. By about 1800 discontent was widespread in the continent. The *mestizos* (people of mixed Spanish and Indian blood) and the *creoles* (people of Spanish blood born in the New World) had little or no say in their countries' government even though they might be rich and influential in many other ways. Moreover, the colonies were not allowed to trade with each other but only with their *mother countries*. Nationalistic fervour was encouraged by the French Revolution and by the successful war of independence waged by Britain's North American colonies (see pp. 156-7 and 158-9).

When the people eventually rose, independence came remarkably quickly—in the period 1810 to 1826. The example was set by Haiti, which became independent of France in 1804. The struggle against Spanish domination was sparked off when Napoleon (see p. 241) overthrew Ferdinand VII and replaced him on the throne of Spain by his brother Joseph. Uprisings followed in Mexico, Chile and Venezuela, but these were quickly put down by Spanish forces. Simón Bolívar led the struggle in Venezuela (see p. 233). After his initial failure he gathered a force in Haiti, landed at Angostura, now Ciudad Bolívar, in Venezuela, and marched across the Andes to liberate New Granada, now Colombia. He went on in 1821 to add Venezuela and Ecuador to the republic he had formed under the name Gran Colombia. In 1822 Bolívar completed the task of liberating Peru begun by José de San Martín.

All the northern half of South America was now free of Spanish rule, but Bolívar's republic soon broke up into its component parts and by 1828 he was ruler only of Colombia. Central America won its independence in 1821 after a ten-year struggle. For some years it remained united as the Central American Union, but in 1839 it too collapsed leaving the separate republics of Costa Rica, El Salvador, Honduras, Guatemala and Nicaragua.

Buenos Aires became independent in 1816 and with it what is now Argentina. Brazil won its independence without a fight when the Portuguese regent, Pedro, espoused the nationalist cause and declared himself Pedro I, king of an independent Brazil, in 1822. Two years earlier Brazil had annexed Uruguay which had risen against Spain, but later Uruguay regained its independence

Above: Emiliano Zapata, one of several Mexican revolutionary leaders who ruled large regions of the country after the downfall of President Diaz in 1911. Each leader, such as Pancho Villa or General Obregon, controlled his own area, appointed his own president, fought other leaders and often carried out raids against the territory of other countries.

Right: Fidel Castro, Marxist leader of Cuba since the overthrow of Fulgencio Batista in 1959. Two years later, President Kennedy of the U.S.A. supported the invasion of Cuba by a force of 1600 Cuban exiles then living in Florida. The so-called Bay of Pigs invasion was a complete failure and was the last serious attempt by the United States to use military force to overthrow the Cuban government.

Above: The elegant and ultra-modern business district of São Paulo, in Brazil, visible proof of the economic miracle which has swept over the country.

Inset: But that same miracle has done little to change the way of life for the thousands of people who still live in the shanty towns dotted about the cities and rivers of the coastal region of Brazil.

acting as a buffer state between Brazil and Argentina.

The creoles in Chile rose against Spain in 1810, led by Bernardo O'Higgins. This revolt was put down but San Martín masterminded a brilliant campaign which won Chile its independence in 1818. The first Mexican uprising, led by a priest named Miguel Hidalgo, was also unsuccessful.

The independence movements were encouraged by the attitudes of the United States and Britain. In 1823 the United States formulated the *Monroe Doctrine* guaranteeing Latin America against future colonizing attempts (see pp. 192-3). Britain won a special place in the affections of the Latin American states by putting her navy at readiness to prevent any move by European powers to crush nationalist uprisings.

Many of the new states suffered from a succession of weak governments inter-

spersed with military or popular dictatorships. In general, the armies have taken the decision on who should rule although a form of democracy has often succeeded, particularly in Argentina and Chile. The United States has an especial interest in the area as many of the main companies are American-owned. In 1890 the United States and the Latin American countries formed an organization which in 1910 became the *Pan American Union*. This is now the executive body of the *Organization of American States* (OAS). The OAS expelled Cuba in 1962 after Fidel Castro had established a Communist government there. Relations between the United States and Cuba remained strained into the 1970's. The influence of the United States in the form of the *Central Intelligence Agency* could also be seen in the overthrow of the freely elected Chilean Marxist regime in 1973.

Emergent Africa

European colonization and settlement brought more than railways and ports to the *Dark Continent*, as Africa was once called. The development of nationalism in Europe was reflected by a slow growth of nationalism among Africans. The spur to the growth of African political consciousness came during the Second World War (1939-45).

Prior to 1939 the only black Africans who had travelled and studied abroad were the tribal chiefs or their sons. But the recruitment of large numbers of men for the army, and the development of new industries for war needs, opened the world to thousands of Africans for the first time. They began to see for themselves what the advantages of independence could be, and the soldiers heard from their comrades-in-arms of the early struggles of the European nations to free themselves from foreign oppression. From 1945 onwards, tribal and regional differences were gradually, although only in part, set aside in the fight to be free of white domination. When the old Indian empire was dissolved and two new independent states created, India and Pakistan, this massive withdrawal from a whole continent caused the Africans to consider their own position. The result was the growth of politi-

Below: African leaders gathering in front of Marlborough House in London for a meeting of Commonwealth prime ministers in 1965. From left to right: Sir Albert Margai (former Premier of Sierra Leone), President Nkrumah (former Ghanaian head of state), Dr Hastings Banda of Malawi and Sir Abubakar Tafawa Balewa, former Premier of Nigeria.

cal parties dedicated to the creation of independent states for their people. In Nigeria Dr. Azikwe led a federal group which included *Yoruba, Ibo* and *Hausa* elements. In the Gold Coast Kwame Nkrumah and the paramount chief of the *Ashanti* combined their followers in what became the *Convention People's Party.*

However, not all the colonies reacted in this non-violent manner. There were revolts in the French colonies of Madagascar and Senegal which were suppressed with ruthless ferocity. Sierra Leone, Chad and Mauritania began to rise against their French overlords. In East Africa there were armed risings in Kenya, Southern Rhodesia and Mozambique. The colonial powers' reaction was a two-way approach; first to suppress armed risings and then to talk seriously about granting independence. What actually occurred was that after the leaders of the *nationalist movements* had been imprisoned there was no one with whom to talk. Where the European powers failed to realise this, the political movements went underground (something they had learned during the Second World War from the Europeans) and became *guerilla movements* working for independence.

In 1945, there were only four independent countries in the whole of Africa: Egypt,

Ethiopia, Liberia and South Africa. The first colony to be granted independence was Libya, by Italy in 1951. By 1955, Africa was a patchwork of independent states and nationalist movements. In the white-dominated *Federation of Rhodesia and Nyasaland*, which was made up of Northern Rhodesia, Southern Rhodesia and Nyasaland, the nationalists were trying to end the Federation and move on to independence. In the French North African colonies there was virtually open warfare. Egypt and the Sudan had had their revolutions; in Kenya the *Kikuyu* had abandoned political methods and had become terrorists (*Mau-Mau*), and in the West African colonies it was obvious that only progress towards independence could restore friendship between Africans and their white masters. Even in Boer-dominated South Africa, the *Pan-African Congress*, led by Nelson Mandela, had begun to agitate for civil and political rights for the black and coloured native population. From 1950 onwards successive commissions of enquiry, both from the colonial powers and the *United Nations*, had made it abundantly clear that there was no workable alternative for African development to free, democratic, multi-racial states.

The Sudan, which had been an Anglo-Egyptian dependency since 1885, was granted independence in 1956, and a military-led revolt took over the government soon afterwards. The Sudanese allied themselves with Egypt, and from then on regarded themselves as more Arab than African. In 1957 the former colony of the Gold Coast gained its independence as the state of Ghana. Kwame Nkrumah, who had become the Gold Coast's colonial prime minister in 1952, was premier of the new country. In 1960 Nkrumah proclaimed Ghana a republic, with himself as president; but he ruled badly, and in 1966 he was overthrown.

In East Africa the British had tried to promote an alliance of the colonies of Kenya, Uganda and Tanganyika, but it failed to work. Tanganyika was the first to achieve independence, which it did in 1961, with Julius Nyerere, leader of the Tanganyika African National Union, as the first prime minister. Nyerere, after a spell out of office, became the country's first president when Tanganyika became a republic in 1962. Two years later Tanganyika and Zanzibar merged to form Tanzania. In Kenya the leader of the Mau Mau movement, Jomo Kenyatta, was liberated in 1961 after nine years in prison and two years later he became the first prime minister of Kenya. Uganda achieved independence in 1962.

Above: During the Kenya Emergency in the early 1950s, African Mau-Mau terrorists carried out a campaign of systematic brutality in order to scare the British government and colonial landowners into giving Kenya its independence and then leaving the country.

Below: Jomo Kenyatta, the leader of the Kenyan African Union. The British accused him of being associated with the Mau-Mau terrorists and held him in prison for nine years.

205

In February 1958 the first shipment of oil left the shores of Nigeria; the Nigerians now had an alternative source of income to cocoa and palm, thus making a federal state the practical solution to their twin problems of poverty and tribal and regional differences. The constitutional talks, which had been abandoned in 1957, were resumed and in 1960 the Federation of Nigeria came into being as an independent state within the *Commonwealth*.

The year 1958 was important for the French colonies; the French government, led by Charles de Gaulle, disclosed that their African colonies would be granted independence, with a 'special relationship to France'. This French copy of the Commonwealth had started with Tunisia, under President Bourguiba, becoming a 'Republic within the French community' in 1955, with the Kingdom of Morocco following soon after. However, Algeria did not achieve independence until 1962 after five years of bitter warfare fought in the towns and villages against the French army. The former colony of Guinea, on the West Coast, gained her independence in 1958 and thereby separated from France to become a socialist-oriented centre for the other French West African Colonies in their struggle for self-government.

The French 'commonwealth' experiment did not last long and in 1960 fourteen former French African countries achieved full independence. Senegal and French Soudan formed the independent Federation of Mali, which soon split into Mali (Soudan) and Senegal; Chad, Togo, Dahomey, Niger, the Voltaic Republic (Upper Volta), Mauritania, and Ivory Coast, all in French West Africa, followed suit and proclaimed their independence. In Central and Equatorial Africa Cameroun, Gabon, Congo (Brazzaville), the Central African Republic (formerly Ubangi Shari) all became fully independent. In the east, the island colony of Madagascar became the Malagasy Republic.

Of Britain's remaining West African colonies, Sierra Leone became independent in 1961 and Gambia in 1965. The trust territory of Togoland joined Ghana, and the British Cameroons was split between Cameroun and Nigeria. In southern Africa the Federation of Rhodesia and Nyasaland split up in 1964. Nyasaland became a multiracial state as Malawi and Northern Rhodesia achieved independence as Zambia, with Kenneth Kaunda, leader of the National Independence Party, as its prime minister. Southern Rhodesia took the name of Rhodesia, but remained a colony because its white-dominated government refused to propose a multi-racial constitution. In 1965

its prime minister, Ian Smith, proclaimed his country's independence, but his action was not recognized internationally.

One area in Africa where excessive trouble and violence followed independence was the Belgian Congo (now Zaire). Belgian rule had been harsh and the people of the Congo were never educated towards self-government. When independence was granted in June 1960 there was a series of mutinies and the Congo police attacked Europeans. The government itself could not achieve stability due to inter-tribal hostilities and the efforts of the Belgian mining company to incite one area (Katanga) to break away, which it succeeded in doing. The President of the Republic, Patrice Lumumba, was murdered and chaos ensued, causing extreme hardship and suffering to thousands of Congolese. After a United Nations force had been in the country for several months Katanga was re-united with the Congo and calm was restored.

Similarly, civil war followed independence in neighbouring Angola. When the Portuguese army left, the African liberation movements started fighting among themselves until the Marxist-orientated MPLA, supported by Cuban tanks and Soviet weapons, defeated the other movements and proclaimed itself the government.

Many African states maintain some sort of association with the country which used to rule them. Few are truly democratic; most of them have some form of one-party rule and some have military rule, although with a commitment to introduce *parliamentary democracy* some time in the future. There have been *putsches*, military take-overs and changes of government by force in several countries. Nigeria has experienced a terrible civil war, when one province, the Ibo area of 'Biafra', tried to break away and form an independent state. But the independent states of Africa are still poor and with largely uneducated populations; a country has to be advanced to afford a multi-party system of democratic government and regular, free elections. However, the most significant result of African independence has been the refusal of the new African states to take sides in the struggles between *socialists* and *capitalists* in world affairs.

Top, right: Belgian paratroops on patrol in the Congo (now Zaire) during the civil war which erupted in 1961. The Congo, which had been part of the Belgian empire in Africa, achieved its independence in 1960 and within a year was in the throes of violent war.

Left: Celebration by followers of the MPLA (Marxist popular liberation army) movement in Luanda, capital of Angola, following the news of victory in 1976.

Above: Soviet military transport in use with MPLA units during the 1975 Angolan war.

Right: Ian Smith, the first prime minister of the white minority regime in Rhodesia.

DATA DIGEST

Many of the words which are italicized in the previous section are explained more fully in the following data digest. They will help to expand your knowledge of history.

Agricultural communes. Chinese collective farms larger than those in Russia were set up after the Communist revolution. In both countries virtually all land is collectivized and the state decrees what and how much is to be grown.

Allies. At the beginning of the First World War the Allies comprised Britain, France, Russia and Belgium, but the term was first used during the Crimean War of the 1850s.

Annexe. Take permanent possession.

Ashanti. People of Ghana who formed a powerful state during the 18th century. They fought a number of wars against the British in the 19th century before their defeat and annexation in 1901.

Bureaucracy. A system relying on a centralized administration manned by an excessive number of officials.

Capitalists. A capitalist system is one in which private business trades freely with a minimum of state intervention.

Central Intelligence Agency (CIA). The United States intelligence agency established in 1947. It operates only abroad, collecting intelligence reports and trying to safeguard American interests. It has no function within the United States where the Federal Bureau of Investigation carries out investigations.

Comintern. The Communist International, sometimes called the Third International. Founded in 1919 by the Russian Communist party, it was intended to do away with the moderate policies of the second International. It encouraged revolution throughout the world but was dissolved in 1943.

Commonwealth. The Commonwealth is an association entered into voluntarily by countries which once formed part of the British empire. Its head is the British monarch. Meetings take place every two or three years between the prime ministers of the member countries and much more frequently between officials dealing with specific problems.

Conscripted. Soldiers who are called up by the state to take up arms for a period of time, usually in war, are conscripts. Regular professional soldiers are volunteers.

Convention People's Party (CPP). Political party in Ghana founded by Kwane Nkrumah in 1949. It played the major part in the fight for Ghana's independence.

Coup. Seizure of power, generally by an uprising of the armed services.

Dictator. Absolute ruler of a country. The best known modern examples are Hitler and Mussolini, but originally a dictator was a Roman magistrate given complete power at a time of extreme emergency.

Federation of East Africa. In 1953 Britain formed the three colonies of Southern Rhodesia, Northern Rhodesia and Nyasaland into the Federation of East Africa. In 1963 it was dissolved following pressure by the African nationalist movements.

Feudal institutions. Under the feudal system of the Middle Ages the king granted land and privileges to his vassal lords in return for loyalty and service. Similarly the lords granted land to their vassals on the same terms. There was little centralized government.

Fiefs. Under a feudal system a lord granted land known as a fief to his vassals in return for an oath of loyalty and a promise of various services.

Great Wall. The Great Wall of China was begun about 300 B.C. and completed 100 years later, though it was repaired and extended over the centuries. It runs for about 2,700 kilometres across northern China and was built to protect China from invading nomadic tribes in the north-west.

Guerilla War. Tactics of harassing a superior enemy by small-scale but frequent hit-and-run raids.

Hausa. People of northern Nigeria most of whom are Muslims.

Ibo. People of north-eastern Nigeria.

Imperialism. The expansion of a developed country into other, under-developed areas by founding colonies and dependencies. The main imperialist countries in recent times have been Britain, France, Holland, Portugal, Spain, Germany, the Soviet Union and the United States.

Isolationist. Opposed to political and sometimes economic involvement with other countries.

Kikuyu. Bantu-speaking people of Kenya. Once dominant in the area, they formed the Mau-Mau terrorist movement against the British in protest against losing their tribal lands.

Kuomintang. The Chinese nationalist party founded in 1891 by Sun Yatsen. After the Second World War the Communists defeated the Kuomintang government, forcing its leader Chiang Kaishek to flee to Formosa (Taiwan).

Lend-Lease. A mutual aid plan whereby the United States under President Franklin Roosevelt supplied enormous amounts of supplies and arms to the Allies at the beginning of the Second World War on loan or sale or in exchange for leases on naval bases.

Mau-Mau. Terrorist movement in Kenya in the early 1950s led mainly by the Kikuyu tribe. The object was to drive the white settlers from Kenya and make the country independent.

Monopoly. Something over which a company or country has sole power, command or privileges.

Monroe Doctrine. In 1823 President James Monroe issued this doctrine, which has formed the basis of United States policy in the American continents. The United States announced its intention of resisting any interference in the area by European powers and particularly any attempt to found colonies there. America would not act against existing colonies and would in general not interfere in purely European affairs.

Munitions. Military supplies and equipment used in war.

Nationalist movements. Movements striving for independence, inspired by patriotism and pride in the country's history and racial makeup.

New World. The American continents, or western hemisphere.

Nobel Peace Prize. One of the five prizes awarded each year from the trust fund bequeathed in the will of the Swedish chemist Alfred Nobel. The Peace Prize is given to the person who has done most for international peace.

Nuclear weapons. Weapons such as the atom and hydrogen bombs which are based on the reaction caused by the splitting of the atom. They have vast destructive capacity.

Opium poppy. Opium, a narcotic drug, is obtained by drying the juice of the opium poppy. The dangerous addictive drugs morphine and heroin are derived from opium, which is itself addictive.

Organization of American States (OAS). An organization including the United States and the Latin American countries. The most important point of policy is that aggression against one of the members is regarded as aggression against all of them. The OAS was formed in 1948, developed from the Pan American Union, which has now become its administrative organ. Basically it is a means of settling disputes peaceably.

Pan-African Congress. A political organization representing black and coloured people in South Africa which was banned by the government in 1960.

Pan American Union. The central and permanent executive organ of the Organization of American States (OAS) which has its headquarters in Washington, D.C.

Parliamentary democracy. System of government in which authority derives from a parliament or assembly elected by all the people.

Putsch. A sudden, surprise rebellion aimed at taking over power in a country.

Red Army. The army of the Soviet Union.

Reformers. People anxious to make improvements in a country's institutions and social conditions.

Samurai. Warriors of feudal Japan who served their lord with unswerving loyalty and unquestioning obedience. They prized honour above all and were expected to commit *hara-kiri* (suicide) if they fell into dishonour.

Shogun. Between about 1600 and 1867 the shogun was the effective ruler of Japan, the emperor having little power. The shogunate was held at different periods by the three great aristocratic families, the Minaoto, the Ashikaga and the Tokugawa.

Socialism. A political and economic theory whose supporters advocate that the means of production and all property should be controlled and owned by all the people. Most socialists unlike Communists accept the continuance of some private enterprise and would not claim that all distinctions between individuals should disappear.

Totalitarian state. A country with a dictatorial system of government in which generally only one party is allowed. The state has many more functions than in a democratic country, influencing the whole of the people's lives. Power and authority are centralized. Fascist and Communist states have often been termed absolute totalitarian regimes.

Treaty of Nanking. The treaty, signed in 1842, that ended the Opium War between Britain and China. China ceded Hong Kong to Britain and agreed to open the ports of Amoy, Canton, Foochow, Ningpo and Shanghai.

Treaty of Portsmouth. The treaty that ended the Russo-Japanese war. The United States, Britain and Germany forced Russia to make concessions. Russia recognized Japan's dominant interests in Korea and agreed that Manchuria should come under China's sovereignty and that foreign troops should not remain there. Japan received some disputed territory and extended fishing rights.

United Nations Organization (UNO). International organization created for the peaceful settlement of world problems. Established in New York in 1945, its original membership of 51 countries has more than doubled. It is responsible for various specialized agencies such as the World Health Organization and the Food and Agriculture Organization.

Below: Queue of destitute unemployed waiting for the relief kitchen to arrive in Broadway, New York. It was scenes like this that the Socialists attacked during the American depression of the 1930s.

THE WORLD TODAY
The Cold War

The Cold War, the term used to describe the hostile relationship which has endured between the United States and its allies and the Soviet Union and its *satellites*, began a considerable time before World War II had ended. Winston Churchill (see p. 233) had even wanted Germany to retain some arms in case—as seemed likely—they were needed to resist Soviet aggression. The Allied strategy of a slow advance on a wide front had ensured that the Soviet Union occupied most of eastern Europe, including the eastern part of Germany. Some Western leaders feared that from this position of strength the Soviet Union would try to mastermind a world-wide Communist revolution. The *Potsdam Conference* held in July 1945 deepened the distrust between the two *blocs* and mutual suspicion dictated the decision to perpetuate the military occupation of Germany (see pp. 184-9). In 1946 Winston Churchill spoke of an 'iron curtain' descending across Europe. President Truman of the United States determined on a tough approach, remarking, 'I'm tired of babying the *Soviets*'.

In early 1948 Western misgivings were intensified when the minority Communist party in Czechoslovakia took over the government of the country by a bloodless *coup*. But Germany, and particularly Berlin, was the focus of the Cold War at this time. In June 1948 USSR cut communications between Berlin and West Germany. For the best part of a year an American and British *airlift* defied the blockade, until Stalin (see

Above: United States Senator Joseph McCarthy, chairman of the Senate Unamerican Activities Committee in the late 1940s. He led the public attacks on many people in America on charges of being Communists. Most of these charges were found to be untrue but the damage to people's reputations and careers had already been done.

Below left: A tragic consequence of the Korean war. Homeless children grouped around an open fire in a railway yard in Seoul, the capital of South Korea.

Below right: The Berlin Wall, the enduring symbol of a world divided by two opposing ideologies— Capitalism and Communism.

p. 242) conceded defeat by ending it in May 1949. Later in the year US, Britain and ten other Western countries, determined to halt what they regarded as Communist expansionist ambitions, formed the *North Atlantic Treaty Organization* (NATO). By the terms of the treaty an armed attack against any member was to be regarded as an attack against them all.

The centre of attention moved to Asia when, in October 1949, the inauguration of the People's Republic of China was proclaimed under Mao Tse-Tung. Ex-President Chiang Kai-shek's withdrawal to Formosa was a severe blow to the United States, which had supplied vast amounts of aid to the *Kuomintang*. US Senator Joseph McCarthy claimed that the Chinese fiasco had been brought about by traitors at the *State Department* and a nationwide *witch-hunt* against Communists ensued.

There was an ever-present danger that, perhaps by accident, the Cold War might develop into a shooting war, which again might precipitate a third world war. This danger became far from remote in 1950 when troops of Communist North Korea invaded South Korea, which had a strongly anti-Communist government headed by Syngman Rhee. It is unlikely that Russia had backed the invasion because it had just walked out of the *United Nations* (UN) and so was not in a position to *veto* international intervention. The United States persuaded the UN to vote for such intervention and pledged itself to resist the spread of Communism throughout the continent of Asia.

After initial sweeping successes the North Koreans were pushed back to the border along the *38th Parallel*. The United Nations'

contingents and South Korean army penetrated into North Korea. As a result the
Chinese came into the war on the side of
North Korea. Only narrowly was open conflict between the United States and China
avoided. Some American politicians urged
the invasion of Manchuria, but neither President Truman nor the Chinese leaders
wanted a disastrous collision and the war
remained confined to Korea. In November
1950 a Chinese counter-attack forced a full-
scale withdrawal from North Korea by UN
forces and within two months Seoul itself,
the capital of South Korea, was in Commun-

ist hands. The UN forces soon retook Seoul
and pushed north once more but a stalemate
gradually developed. Chinese involvement
meant that the world was divided not
only by an iron curtain but also by a 'bamboo
curtain'.

In 1953 Stalin died but President
Eisenhower's Secretary of State, John Fos-
ter Dulles, soon became known as a Cold
War warrior. He promised to support any
risings among Russia's East European satel-
lites and relied to a dangerous degree—since
Russia now had the hydrogen bomb—on
America's nuclear capacity.

Above: U.S. Sabre jets in
action against Mig 15s of
the Chinese Communist
airforce over the infamous
'Mig Alley'. At the peak of
the war some 800,000
United Nations and South
Korean soldiers were
forcing an offensive
against 200,000 North
Koreans and one million
Chinese Communist
troops.

The Thaw Begins

Stalin was succeeded in the *Kremlin* by a *duumvirate* of Gorgi Malenkov and Nikita Khrushchev and a more favourable approach to co-existence was soon evident on the Soviet side. One of the first signs was the signing of an armistice in Korea in July 1953 after two years of inconclusive talks.

In 1955 a *summit conference* was held at Geneva which, though it achieved nothing remarkable, brought the leaders together and may perhaps be regarded as the first real evidence of a thaw in the Cold War and a willingness to accept the *status quo*, at least in Europe. In 1956 Khrushchev's denunciation of Stalin's regime gave full articulation to the new Soviet policy of peaceful co-existence with the West. This policy seemed to be confirmed when the USSR acquiesced in some liberalizing policies following riots in Poland. Gomulka, an anti-Stalinist Communist, came to power and leading Stalinists were purged.

The iron fist inside the velvet glove was revealed by the ruthless repression of the Hungarian uprising in the same year. After riots in Budapest and other cities and the release of political prisoners, the Premier, Imre Nagy, abolished the one-party system and announced Hungary's withdrawal from the *Warsaw Pact*, the East's equivalent of *NATO*. *Red Army* tanks rolled in to reverse this liberalizing process and about 30,000 Hungarians died in the hopeless struggle against Communist *imperialism*. The Western powers took no action, partly because at the time they were hamstrung by the ill-conceived Anglo-French adventure to stop Egypt from nationalizing Suez.

In 1958 Khrushchev emerged as the undisputed leader of the USSR. He took no action when Lebanon invited United States marines to protect its regime against Communist opponents nor when King Hussein of Jordan similarly welcomed British parachute troops. But he came near to precipitating another crisis over Berlin when he stated his intention of handing over control of the city to East Germany. In fact Khrushchev was anxious to come to some form of *detente* with the West in view of the Soviet Union's deteriorating relations with China. A summit meeting was arranged in

Above: In 1956, in a courageous attempt to free themselves from the Soviet bloc, the population of Hungary rose up in arms. Despite the fact that they received no material help from the West, Hungarians valiantly attacked heavily-armed Soviet soldiers and the tanks that stormed through the streets of Budapest. With extreme ruthlessness, the Soviet Union suppressed the revolt. Many thousands of Hungarians died in the street battles.

Left: The trial of Major Gary Powers of the U.S. Air Force, who was shot down in a spy plane while flying over the Soviet Union in 1960.

Paris in 1960 but just before the start an American spy plane was shot down over the USSR and Khrushchev, after a violent attack on President Eisenhower, refused adamantly to attend the meeting.

The decade following this *debacle* saw a completely new situation. Great as the antipathy was between the Russians and the Americans, that between the Russians and the Chinese became ever greater. The result was a search for some form of *rapprochement* between East and West. At this time all three *blocs* began to pay special attention to the *Third World*—the uncommitted, developing countries of Africa and Asia.

By 1960 a shared fear of the growing power of China had led the USSR and the USA towards detente. America's increasing involvement in Asia incurred the suspicion of China rather than the Soviet Union, which was most concerned with raising the standard of living of its own people and also with guarding its borders from China.

It seemed somehow out of context with the prevailing trend when, in 1962, American intelligence discovered that the USSR had established missile bases on the island of Cuba capable of launching a nuclear attack

on the United States. President John Kennedy demanded the withdrawal of the bases with the threat of military action. The world waited but Khrushchev backed down and dismantled the missile sites, thus avoiding the gravest threat of a new world war for some years.

The final defrosting of the Cold War, at least in the western hemisphere, was confirmed the following year by the Nuclear Test Ban Treaty. In October 1964 Khrushchev was removed from office and a duumvirate again took over in the shape of Leonid Brezhnev, as leader of the Communist party, and Alexei Kosygin, as Premier. Although a war was to rage for many years in Vietnam (see pp. 214-15), at least the preliminaries to a genuine agreement with the West could be distinguished.

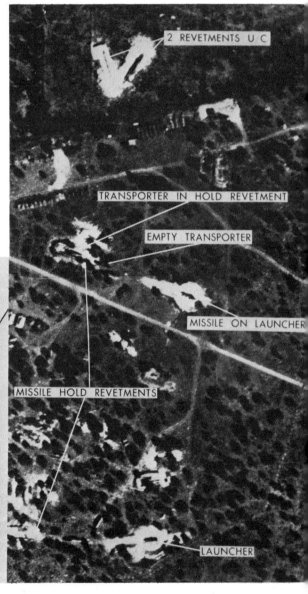

Above: Aerial photograph of Soviet missile sites and bases in Cuba. When Soviet ships were reported to be heading for the island with nuclear warheads, U.S. President Kennedy ordered them to return.

War in Indo-China

America's policy in south-east Asia has been based either explicitly or tacitly on the 'domino' theory. According to this theory the states in the area were like a row of dominoes. If one country fell to the Communists, the next in line would follow. Thus, in Eisenhower's view expressed in 1954, if Indo-China fell, Thailand and Burma would go next, followed by India and Japan. On this view Indo-China had to be kept at best pro-West, at worst neutral.

A war had gone on since 1946 in Indo-China between the nationalist *Vietminh* under the command of the Communist Ho Chi Minh and the French, who were anxious to retain the colony they had held before the war. After the Communist take-over in China President Truman gave large quantities of aid to the French and their *puppet* Emperor, Bao Dai. At the 1954 Geneva Conference Secretary of State Dulles supported US intervention but the question became academic within a month when the *Vietminh* won a decisive victory at Dien Bien Phu. Vietnam was divided into North and South, with America backing Ngo Dinh Diem's *regime* in the South.

When Diem refused to hold the elections that had been promised, a Communist rising took place in 1957. After many changes of government a military regime took over in South Vietnam, but by 1965 the country was close to collapse as the Communist *National Liberation Front* (NLF) controlled increasingly large areas. The NLF troops, known as the *Vietcong*, were supplied with weapons and advisers from the North. America was alarmed at the prospect of the fall of the first domino and President Lyndon Johnson, who became president when John Kennedy was assassinated in 1963, ordered the bombing of targets in the North. America already had about 20,000 advisers in the South, but in March 1965 a force of marines landed at DaNang, the vanguard of a huge American presence which was to reach more than half a million.

After three years of heavy bombing in the North and of desperate fighting, typical of civil wars, in the South, it was obvious that America could not achieve a military victory. Talks began in Paris between the US, representatives of the North and South governments and envoys of the NLF. America withdrew more than 100,000 troops but on the other hand extended the war into Cambodia, which began to suffer the same miseries that had become part of life in Vietnam. In January 1973 a peace agreement was signed by all the four negotiating parties providing for withdrawal of foreign

Above: French paratroops inspect the Vietminh (Communist independence movement) casualties and prisoners after the Communist attack on the French-held hilltop at Na Samh, in North Vietnam. The French garrison was supplied from the air and this successfully enabled them to repulse the Vietminh attack. The French tried to repeat the formula at Dien Bien Phu, but here the Vietminh were more determined, and the resulting French defeat led to their eventual withdrawal from Vietnam.

Right: Ho Chi Minh, the revolutionary and North Vietnam leader whose vision of a unified Communist Vietnam was finally realized six years after his death in 1969.

Below: A North Vietnamese town devastated and gutted after a U.S. bombing raid.

troops and for elections to be arranged by the two Vietnams and the NLF. An *International Commission of Control and Supervision* was established to monitor the ceasefire. Predictably, the Paris peace agreement broke down almost immediately. The Americans began to withdraw their forces but the fighting and killing continued virtually unabated.

The end of the war came, with almost unbelievable speed, in 1975. On 17th April forces of the *Khmer Rouge*, the counterpart in Cambodia of the Vietcong, occupied the capital, Phnom Penh. In South Vietnam an irresistible Communist offensive culminated in a decisive victory at Xuan Loc and on 30th April the Vietcong entered Saigon unopposed.

As yet the domino theory has been neither substantiated nor discredited, though Thailand understandably showed signs of nervousness and a desire to dissociate itself from America as far as possible. But America was unlikely to prop up any more tottering regimes after what had been a politically unpopular and militarily disastrous involvement. By the mid-1970s serious confrontation between the Soviet Union and America appeared unlikely and peaceful co-existence was the order of the day.

In November 1974 President Gerald Ford, who took office in 1974 after the resignation of Richard Nixon, met Leonid Brezhnev of the Soviet Union at Vladivostok in the USSR and agreed that relations would remain on a basis of peaceful co-existence. As if to confirm that the world was perhaps safer from a conflagration than it had been since the end of the Second World War, delegations from 59 governments attended the *Nuclear Non-Proliferation Conference* held in Helsinki, Finland in May 1975.

Above: The Domino Theory. A doctrine formulated in the United States during the 1950s to describe the manner in which individual regimes would come under the sway of Communism. As each country fell, the next in line would follow, until the whole south-east Asian region would become Communist. In turn, according to the theory, India and Australia would be threatened, and so on until the whole world would come under the sway of the Communists.

Problems of Race Relations

The problem of relations between people of different races has come to be considered one of the most difficult facing the world. Among the reasons for its recent growth are: 1) the end of domination of the greater part of the world by Europeans; 2) the democratic spirit of the modern world, with its emphasis on the basic human equality of all men and women regardless of individual differences of ability and achievement; and 3) the discrediting of the theories of racial superiority advocated by the German dictator Adolf Hitler and the *Nazis* (which led to the deaths of six million people of Jewish descent).

In some parts of the world white people have refused to recognize these claims to equality by coloured people. In others they have formally accepted them while continuing in practice to discriminate against coloured people over jobs, housing and education. It is important to note, however, that relations between people of different races are not inevitably hostile. In Hawaii, Brazil and the West Indies, for example, different racial groups live and work in harmony. Nor are difficulties always between whites and non-whites. In Malaysia conflicts have occurred between Malays and people of Chinese descent, and people of Indian descent in Kenya, Tanzania and Uganda are suffering hardship from the policy of *Africanization*—putting the commerce and administration into the hands of Africans. This has resulted in large-scale unemployment and even loss of citizenship among the Indian populations of east African nations..

But the most dramatic cases are between white and black, in the United States, Britain, South Africa and Rhodesia. In the United States 11.3% of the population is of Negro descent, and in Britain between two and three per cent of the population is non-white, most of them West Indian, Indian and Pakistani immigrants and their British-born children. Originally slaves, the black population of America were given constitutional guarantees of equality after the Civil War (1861-1865) (see pp. 164-5). Most of the Negroes lived in the South and local laws and customs backed up by intimidation effectively prevented them from enjoying their supposed equality. In the 20th century, especially during and since the Second World War, millions of blacks have moved to the cities of the North, where they have been discriminated against. A 1954 decision of the *Supreme Court* ruled out the doctrine of 'separate but equal', hitherto used to

Right: The racial laws of the Nazis began with such simple measures as this sign (which reads: 'Jews not desired here') and ended with the calculated murder of six million men, women and children.

Centre: During the summer of 1975, Boston, Massachusetts, became the focal-point of intense confrontation between blacks and whites. This was over a court order to transport children in the city to public schools distant from their homes to achieve a better racial balance. White parents, especially, resented this, demonstrated in the streets and even beat up Negroes when they could catch them.

Below: A street scene in New York during the racial riots which erupted in 1966.

Left: An Indian man of 70 sits on his luggage at Victoria Station in London. He is the oldest member of a party of 30 immigrants who were allowed to settle in the United Kingdom. In the 1930s, at a conference of countries belonging to the British Commonwealth, it was agreed that many would become Dominions and that their people would be considered British subjects. In the 1960s, due to the more difficult conditions which existed then, the British government decided to change the rules of entry so that Commonwealth immigrants would be able to come to Britain only on a strict quota system.

Below: Children of many different races playing together happily in Hawaii. It is possible the adult world has much to learn from the way children relate to each other.

justify a *segregation* that was very unequal in its consequences. Court decisions like this, new *Federal* laws and the work of the *civil rights movement,* supported by blacks and whites, have ended legal segregation and have done much to reduce discrimination. But progress has been slow; the growing concentration of blacks in city *ghettos* has increased discrimination in practice, and urban riots have worsened racial tension. The growth of more militant groups, advocating 'black power', like the *Black Panthers*, shows the dissatisfaction of many Negroes with the non-violent but slow progress of the older civil rights movement.

In Britain the problems are not so serious. Misunderstanding and even fear exist, but racial violence is rare. As a result of the restrictions on immigration imposed by *Conservative* and *Labour* governments, the numbers of new coloured immigrants are dropping sharply. The *Race Relations Acts* of 1965 and 1968 outlaw most forms of discrimination. Immigrants make an important contribution to the nation's economy. There are at present very few old people among the immigrants: this more than makes up for their extra use of maternity services and schools. But the concentration of coloured immigrants in some areas, especially parts of London and the West Midlands, has caused difficulties. If discrimination in housing and jobs ends and if immigrants and their grown-up children settle freely anywhere in the country, these problems may be overcome in time.

In southern Africa the problems are very different. In the Republic of South Africa, a dominant white population of less than one-fifth of the whole is determined to maintain its position. *Apartheid*, they claim, means separate but equal development for all races. Opponents of the policy allege that the areas allocated as 'homelands' to the Africans (13% of the area of the country at present) are too small and too poor to permit adequate development. The hostility of almost the whole of the rest of the world to apartheid has not resulted in any change in this policy, and none seems likely.

In Rhodesia the ruling white population is about one-twenty-fifth of the whole. Failing to get Britain's agreement to their independence, the Rhodesian government unilaterally declared independence in 1965 (U.D.I.) (see pp. 204-7). Since then a constitution has been approved which, while giving Africans some share in government, effectively guarantees white rule as far ahead as can be predicted. Economic sanctions against U.D.I. have so far not altered the government's policy, but the growth of guerilla warfare might change this situation.

217

The Developing Countries

The vast majority of the world's population, now estimated to be approaching 4,000 million, live in *developing countries*. A line may be drawn round the globe north of the equator: to the north of the line lie most of the *developed countries* (North America, Europe, the U.S.S.R. and Japan), to the south the developing countries (South America, Africa, the Middle East, India, China and south-east Asia). The greater part of the world is poor. Furthermore, some of the developed countries are far from rich and are only termed 'developed' because they began to industrialize their economies a long time before those of Africa and Asia.

The contrast between the rich and poor nations is great. To measure the wealth of a country economists calculate the *Gross National Product* (G.N.P.)—that is, the total value of all goods and services added together which are produced by a country. When this is divided by the country's total population, the resulting figure represents the G.N.P. per head, or average income. Figures (1975) show, at one end, a G.N.P. per head for the U.S.A. of £3,938, for the United Kingdom, £2,142 and the U.S.S.R., £1,461; at the other, poorer end, India has a G.N.P. per head of £83 and Malawi has the same.

The problems facing the under-developed or newly-developing countries are many. First the massive and accelerating increase (about 65 million every year) in world population. In 1850 there were some 1,094 million people in the world; in 1930 there were 2,070 million; in 1974, 4,100 million. It is estimated that by the year 2000 the figure could be 7,000 million. This has in large measure been brought about by the spread of skilled medicine (fewer babies die at birth and people live longer), while the process —especially in poor countries—has not been counterbalanced by the use, on a significant scale, of *birth-control methods*.

Secondly, the poor countries are chronically short of educational facilities. It is, to give but one small example, relatively pointless for the government of a poor country to produce cans of, say, fertilizer if the farmers, because they have never been to school, cannot understand the label instructions on the cans.

This lack of education among the farming communities is the root cause of a vicious circle: agricultural methods are primitive

Above: A man and his family preparing to leave their home on a raft during the floods which devastated Bangladesh in 1974. For many millions of people throughout the world, life is nothing more than a continuing succession of crises over the lack of food and shelter and, occasionally, additional catastrophes such as floods, earthquakes and war. In the floods which struck Bangladesh, some 1,300 people died and 27 million were left homeless. This was only two years after a bitter rebellion which brought Bangladesh independence from Pakistan.

and wasteful; the food available for the population is thus poor in quality and inadequate in quantity; *malnutrition* and disease consequently occur.

Moreover, the situation of the poor countries is aggravated by their economic position in relation to the rich. A country's economy is based on selling goods which it produces and buying other goods made by other countries. There are two kinds of goods: *primary goods* (such as coffee, cotton and sugar) and manufactured goods (such as cars and washing machines). Unhappily, nearly half of the poor countries depend on only one primary product for over half of their exports. Ghana, for example, relies heavily on cocoa, Zambia on copper. The poor countries are therefore in an especially vulnerable position. A rich country may have been buying its tea from a certain poor country and then, for economic reasons of its own, decides to buy it elsewhere in future. The poor country's entire economy is immediately endangered.

Again, industrialized countries now manufacture more goods than ever before —for example nylon, whereas in the past they bought cotton from India and Egypt.

Left: Nigerian student-farmers being given instruction on how to use a tractor. The one in the picture was specially developed for use by farmers with limited education and is very simple to operate and maintain. In fact, it is so simple that if it breaks down, the farmer himself would be able to repair it without needing to call in outside assistance.

Rubber provides another example. Until about 15 years ago almost all the rubber used to come from Far Eastern countries; today the world consumes over 60% of the synthetic product.

Among many other difficulties, the poor countries are faced with the problem of rising prices, for, while the primary products which they produce have risen only slowly in price, that of the manufactured goods which they have to import has risen far faster. They are therefore having to pay more while not being able to earn more. In the long run this imbalance benefits neither the rich nor the poor countries.

Much has already been undertaken to rectify the situation. Aid from the rich countries and from international organizations enables the recipients to embark on projects which they could not otherwise afford. The *Food and Agriculture Organization*, for example, advises and assists countries on the improvement of their agricultural and fishing methods; the *World Food Programme* endeavours to utilize surpluses of food in rich countries for projects in poor countries; the *International Labour Organization* helps the poor countries by training

Above: A Chinese experimental farm in Tanzania. Chinese farming experts have long been working in Tanzania and other developing countries, trying to help the local farmers to help themselves. This means making use of local materials and native workers instead of having to depend on expensive foreign agricultural machinery and costly fertilizers. In this way, developing countries learn to evolve local solutions for local problems, and to achieve a high level of economic independence as well as a sense of pride in their own capabilities.

and providing experts for a wide variety of development projects, while the *World Health Organization* is active in training health workers and in fighting disease. There are, in addition, many voluntary agencies, such as *Oxfam*.

Furthermore, the poor countries are now beginning to help themselves. Among other things, they are entering into trade agreements, such as the *Treaty of East African Co-operation*.

The process of stabilizing the world's population, of providing education and industrial development for the poor countries is slow and, some think, inadequate. However, despite the appalling situation (some 60% of the world's population do not get enough to eat, for example) the problem is at last being tackled. Perhaps the most encouraging sign that it will eventually be overcome is that the human race is now concerned about poverty, hunger and illiteracy in a way it has never been before.

Finally, the developing countries are no longer willing to have solutions imposed on them. They want to be involved in the planning stage and they want the solution to be related to their specific problems.

Welfare Services

Government responsibility for the welfare of every individual within the state was limited to times of war, and feeding the hungry in times of famine, until the rise of modern industry. At first industrialization only gave wealth and plenty to the few (see pp. 144-53). It brought misery and grinding poverty to the many who operated the machines and worked in the mines and factories. The result of riches alongside poverty was the growth of *socialism*—the idea that those who created the wealth should have a fair share of its benefits. By 1848, the *Year of the Revolutions*, both *democracy* and socialism were included in the aims of many of the revolutionaries. With the spread of political power to larger numbers of people and the increasing spread of education, by the latter half of the 19th century the socialist demand for a better life for the masses was finally being heard in the Parliaments of Europe.

In the 1880s Bismarck (see p. 233), in Germany, made it more difficult for socialists to get elected to the *Reichstag*. But at the same time he introduced laws which gave sickness and accident insurance to industrial workers and old age pensions to all people over 70. These benefits had been part of the socialist programme and Bismarck admitted his aim was to reconcile the working man to existing society.

In Britain, the first country to be industrialized, a *Royal Commission* in 1902 shocked the nation's leaders when it showed that a large proportion of young men from industry were unfit for military service. The reaction to this was a series of *Acts* between 1906 and 1911 whose purpose was to protect the ordinary people from the worst evils of the *capitalist* industrial system. Old age pensions were introduced, *Labour Exchanges* set up and payments made during unemployment. This was recognition by the Government that if a man had no work it was not his own fault but the fault of the system. In 1911 the *National Health Insurance* Act provided a minimum medical service for workers and their families. By 1914, the Germans had pensions and sickness insurance, as did the British, while the Swedes had old age pensions (1913) and a workmen's compensation scheme.

In 1929-31 there was a world crisis in the capitalist system: modern industry was over-producing and unable to sell its goods, while Russian Five Year Plans functioned quite well (see pp. 152-3). In Europe and parts of America there was widespread unemployment and millions were hungry in the midst of plenty. Out of the *depression* came the concept that the state should take responsibility for the health and welfare of its people, financed from taxes upon the wealthier sections of the population. In Sweden the result was the election of a Social Democratic Government (1932), which remained in power until 1970. A separate Ministry of Social Affairs built up a state system of social welfare.

In Britain, a lead was given by progressive local authorities, such as the London County Council, with school meals and school doctors. There were health and housing Acts, but it was not until the Second World War that advances became general on a national scale. During the war food rationing, which ensured a fairer distribution, and special foods for infants and mothers, produced a really healthy nation for the first time since the *Industrial Revolution* (see pp. 144-5). The *Beveridge Report* (1943) proposed a scheme whereby everybody would receive enough food, clothing and shelter whatever they did or whoever they were. After the war, under the Labour government of 1945-51, these plans were put into action. The welfare food service was continued, a *Family Allowance Act* of 1945 gave money payments for children to assist large families, and a maternity allowance provided the means for working mothers to remain at home for a period before and after childbirth. In 1948 the *National Health Service*, which provided free medical, dental and hospital services for all, came into being. By the 1950s Britain led the world as the first truly *Welfare State*.

France, which had some pension schemes before the war, introduced a generous family allowance system soon after the Second World War to encourage population growth, but its medical aid schemes were still not entirely free and in housing assistance France had one of the worst records in Europe. West Germany, although leaving most of the social services to be administered by the *Länder* (the states), provided government support for insurance, medical care and housing, but was not at that time up to the British and Swedish standards. A national health service also existed in Denmark, Norway, Israel, New Zealand and all the socialist states of Europe. By the late 1960s Britain's Welfare State had steadily fallen behind the progress made in the rest of Western Europe.

Whether welfare services were introduced as a measure of socialism, or 'to reconcile the working man to existing society', the result has been a healthier and better cared-for working class.

Right: The benefits of the welfare state have become an important part of a country's obligations to its citizens. The illustration shows examples of many different sorts of welfare schemes, including maternity care, surgery, caring for deprived or backward children and looking after invalids and the aged.

221

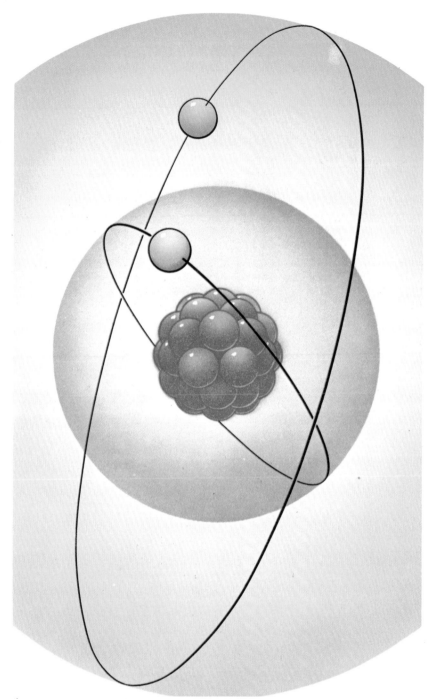

Instant Technology

Those of us fortunate enough to live in the more developed countries of the world enjoy a life of great convenience (see pp. 218-19). We can make quick communication with anyone by *telephone*; darkness is instantly banished at the touch of a light switch; a pill may soothe a headache, prevent unwanted children or ensure a correct *vitamin* intake; a document can be photographed in seconds and a *pocket calculator* may save a great deal of difficult and possibly incorrect arithmetic. Modern science removes the drudgery of unrewarding tasks and gives us the opportunity to live our lives to the full; while modern medicine enables us to live much longer and healthier lives.

Today's instant technology with its brand new inventions may seem to be the product of just a few years' work, but it has its roots in discoveries made a long time ago. From about 1800, scientists began to investigate the internal nature of the things around them instead of just observing how they behaved. *Chemists* realized that all substances are made up of *atoms* of several basic elements combined in many different proportions. New elements were discovered as *electricity* was used to break down substances into their *constituent elements*. The elements included new important metals, particularly *aluminium,* which was found to be light but strong. However, it was an expensive luxury for many years and was not produced in quantity until a cheap way of making electricity, which was needed to refine the metal, was found.

As well as obtaining new elements, chemists began to combine the elements in fresh ways and produced new substances. The first were *synthetic dyes* that not only had different shades from existing

Above: An interior view of an atom, showing the nucleus and the electrons revolving around the nucleus. Causing an atom of Uranium-235 to split into its components by bombarding it with another atom is the basic mechanism of the atomic bomb.

Right: A scientist investigates the effects of a laser beam. Scientists have found many uses for the laser today, such as in navigation, medicine, engineering, surveying and weapons systems.

natural dyes but were more resistant to fading. Then came *plastics*, made by reacting simple chemicals together to produce materials completely unlike those found in nature. Plastics have replaced traditional materials for many uses, often because they are cheap to manufacture and easy to shape into objects, such as buckets and bowls. But plastics also have particular qualities that make them valuable in their own right: a *gramophone record* or *cassette tape* could only be made of plastic and the man-made fibres that give strength to modern fabrics are composed of plastics. Other synthetic products developed by the chemical industry include *detergents* to clean objects and paints or polishes to brighten their appearance, photographic materials to take their pictures, *adhesives* to stick them firmly together and explosives to blow them apart. Modern chemistry can virtually design a new material to fill a particular purpose.

The chemical industry obtains the basic chemicals that it needs to manufacture its products from natural resources, principally *minerals*, timber, coal, oil, water and air. Minerals are also important as sources of metals, which can be mixed together to form all kinds of *alloys* with all kinds of uses, and crude oil is vital to us as a source of *fuel* and *lubricants*.

Having found that everything is made up of atoms and having begun to explore the endless ways in which atoms can be combined to form new products, scientists in the closing years of the 19th century also turned their attention to the interior of the atom. They found that it is not a solid body but composed of particles—tiny *electrons* orbiting a central *nucleus*. Moving electrons are very interesting; if they change their *orbits* in an atom, the atom gives out *electromagnetic radiation*—light, heat or *X-rays* as well as many other rays in the electromagnetic spectrum. And if electrons move among the atoms of a material, an electric current flows in the material and produces a *magnetic field* as it does so. Similarly, a moving magnetic field will cause an electric current to flow in a *conducting material*.

These effects have had enormous consequences. The *interconversion* of electricity and magnetism enables motion to be turned into electricity and vice-versa. This allows electric current to be generated and electric motors to work, giving us our electricity supply and all kinds of electric machines, from shavers to underground trains as well as the *microphone* and *loudspeaker*. Connect these two latter instruments by a wire and we have the telephone; connect them by electromagnetic waves and we have the *radio set*. Radio waves are reflected by the

Above: An integrated circuit board attached to its pocket calculator. Modern technology has so effectively miniaturized electronic systems today that a single integrated circuit (which is responsible, along with many others, for the millions of calculations the machine must perform) is no larger than a ball-pen tip.

ground and by the upper layers of the *atmosphere* and therefore bounce around the world, giving long-distance communication. In *radar*, radio waves are reflected from distant objects, enabling them to be located beyond the limit of human sight. X-rays enable doctors to see through our bodies, helping medical diagnosis.

The development of radio and *television* was not only dependent on the production of electromagnetic waves to carry signals, but also on the motion of electrons within objects and spaces. An electric signal is a varying motion of electrons and the components of an electronic machine—*resistors, capacitors, transistors*—modify the signal as it passes through them. The signal may be made to represent a sound, as in radio, or an image, as in television. Or it may represent a number or quantity, as in the *computer*. Integrated *circuits* have been devised to pack thousands of components into tiny instruments, as in the pocket calculator.

The *laser* triggers exact motion of electrons within atoms to produce an intense beam of very pure light. This exciting new device can drill holes in diamonds, cut out patterns, perform painless surgery, power a *gyrocompass* with no moving parts and produce three-dimensional images that change *perspective* as you walk around them. Its potential is enormous.

223

Future Technology

However soulless it may sometimes seem, science and technology deeply affect people, whether individuals or whole societies.

The investigations of *biologists* into the secrets of life have possibly benefited us more than the advances in the *physical sciences*. The discovery in the mid-19th century of the role that *microbes* play in disease soon led to *antiseptics* and, in this century, to powerful *antibiotics* to combat infection. New products thrown up by the *chemical industry* turned out to be good pain-killers, and an understanding of body chemistry has given us specific drugs, such as *insulin*. New surgical techniques and drugs have made organ transplants a practical proposition. Investigations into *heredity* have improved plant and animal breeding—producing new hardy strains and better yields. Again the chemical industry has been involved, producing *fertilizers* and *pesticides* to improve agriculture.

All new developments need to be provided with *energy*, and the expansion of *technology* has demanded new and powerful sources of energy. Coal has long provided heat and continues to do so, aided by oil and natural gas. Heat engines—*internal combustion engines* and *turbines*—turn heat energy into motion, either powering machines directly or powering *generators* to produce *electricity*. Electricity is a clean and highly flexible source of energy, and technology is now very dependent on it. The probing of 20th-century physicists into the *nucleus* of the *atom* has given us *nuclear power* in addition to other forms of energy. Nuclear reactors produce heat, but are large and complex and therefore mainly suitable for electric power generation. However, they also produce *radiations* that convert substances into *radio-isotopes*, which have many uses as detectors of various kinds.

New sources of power are being investigated: *solar collectors* can utilize the Sun's energy, *nuclear fusion* holds a distant prospect of vast amounts of energy; and tapping the energy in ocean waves or tides could usefully supplement existing sources. Today's power supplies are limited and energy research is vital if we are to find sufficient quantities of power to sustain life in the future.

Power production has been the major factor in the development of transport. The steam engine made possible the growth of mass public transport in the form of railways (see pp. 144-54), while the invention of a compact means of power production in the *petrol engine* brought private transport in the shape of the motorcar within the reach of many and made fast air travel commonplace. The *jet engine* later raised air speeds, and the *hovercraft* and *hydrofoil* skimmed over the waves to make fast sea travel feasible. Nuclear power may prove advantageous to the ship and it has developed the submarine into a true undersea craft that can make an undersea voyage right around the world. On land, the railway train will eventually achieve vast speeds by employing *magnetic levitation* instead of wheels and *linear induction*—a form of *magnetic propulsion*.

Technology is often hailed as a saviour of mankind, but increasingly those who benefit from it are disenchanted with its progress. It cannot be denied that technology has conferred immense gifts, but it does present disadvantages as well.

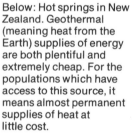

Below: Hot springs in New Zealand. Geothermal (meaning heat from the Earth) supplies of energy are both plentiful and extremely cheap. For the populations which have access to this source, it means almost permanent supplies of heat at little cost.

One of the main benefits of technology is the *automation* of production processes. By freeing workers from jobs that can be done by machines, production becomes more efficient and the real cost of goods—the number of man-hours needed to produce them—falls. Living standards consequently rise. The improvement in health and life expectancy conferred by modern medicine is a real benefit. The opening-up of communications, both in the wider techniques available for education and the greater opportunities for travel, gives people a greater awareness of the world around them.

The disadvantages are not really a consequence of technology itself but rather the way in which people organize themselves. The many benefits listed above are restricted mostly to the western world, and most people still lead primitive, and often short, lives. Technology seems to widen the gap between those who enjoy a good standard of living and those who do not, a situation that is immoral and ultimately unstable (see pp. 218-19).

But disadvantages are evident among the affluent societies of the world. Automation can cause *redundancy* and corresponding hardship. Rising standards of living only

Above left: Billowing clouds of smoke from chimneys at the Welsh coal-fields, one of the unwanted by-products of modern technology.

Top right: The Concorde supersonic passenger plane, a symbol of the most advanced aeronautical technology available today.

Above right: One consequence of automation is unemployment. Here, a queue of unemployed people wait to receive their state welfare pay.

follow from more and more efficient means of production, which consume greater amounts of energy and resources. The environment suffers as *minerals* and forests are torn from the land and factories, power stations and roads proliferate, and *pollution* takes its toll as industry pours out more and more wastes into the environment.

Pressures for *recycling* and *conservation* must eventually grow sufficiently strong to halt the trend of technology towards devastation, but only at a point from which recovery could be slow. The widening of communications could result in a loss of cultural identity and greater conformity, and perhaps lead to a more peaceful but infinitely duller world.

But the greatest danger of technology lies in the impetus it gives to weapons development. This is no accident, for technological breakthroughs often occur in wartime under the threat of enemy progress. The jet engine, radar and nuclear power were all developed during the Second World War, for example. Nuclear weapons are the gravest threat that man has ever faced and are ultimately a greater test of his responsibility and maturity than the most elegant feat of technology.

H–P

New Exploration

Above: Roald Amundsen, the Norwegian explorer, who, in 1911, became the first man to reach the South Pole. He got there just one month before the British explorer, Robert Scott. Scott's own expedition to the Pole was a tale of terrible suffering. Scott reached the Pole in 1912. On the return journey, tired and hampered by blizzards, he and his companions died—only 18 kilometres from his base.

Below: The United States nuclear submarine *Nautilus*. Built to remain below the surface of the sea for many months on end, the *Nautilus* made the first under-the-ice crossing of the North Pole in 1958.

By the turn of this century, intrepid explorers had penetrated the remote regions of Africa and Australia and had completed the basic exploration of all the habitable land masses of the world. Before them lay vast regions, hostile to man and less easily conquered: the polar regions, the ocean depths, the upper atmosphere and outer space. But these finally gave up many of their secrets as new forms of transport were developed to enable men to travel and survive in a variety of environments.

The two *polar regions* are very different from each other, the Arctic consisting of a floating layer of ice on the Arctic Ocean, and the Antarctic consisting of an ice-covered continent called Antarctica. As a result, the exploration of both regions has proceeded very differently. However, in the early years of this century there were expeditions to both poles. In 1909 Robert Peary claimed to have crossed the Arctic ice and reached the *North Pole*. The claim of this American explorer was disputed when later expeditions found that the rates of travel claimed by Peary were unattainable on the Arctic *pack ice*. However, no such argument surrounds the *South Pole*, which was first reached by the Norwegian explorer Roald Amundsen in 1911. He used sleds and a dog team, beating a British team led by Robert Scott by a month. Scott's party had to haul their own sleds. The suffering on the return journey was terrible and Scott and his party died only 18 kilometres from their camp.

An expedition led by the British explorer Sir Vivian Fuchs in 1958 was the first to cross Antarctica. It used mechanical vehicles, but this time scientific bases supplied by air had been set up at the South Pole and in several other parts of the continent. Seven countries lay claim to Antarctica but its value in scientific research is open to the whole world. However, this position may well change if, as seems likely, oil lies beneath the continent and can be profitably extracted on a commercial scale.

No permanent installations can be built on the drifting pack ice of the Arctic Ocean, although bases and oil fields exist in the surrounding lands. A journey to the North Pole was made by a four-man American expedition led by Ralph Plaisted in 1968, and a British team led by Wally Herbert made a crossing of the Arctic Ocean during a 15-month trip in 1968 and 1969. The United States *nuclear submarine Nautilus* travelled under the polar ice and had already reached the pole in 1958.

In 1900, the ocean depths had scarcely been plumbed. *Diving bells* could descend to some 250 metres, about twice the limit to which man can dive without protection. In 1960, the *bathyscaphe Trieste*, manned by the Swiss *oceanographer* Jacques Piccard and the American Donald Walsh, descended nearly 11 kilometres to the deepest point of the Pacific Ocean. Small manned *submersibles* regularly work in offshore waters, attending to undersea cables and drilling rigs. Teams of *aquanauts* are learning to spend weeks at a time in undersea laboratories, so that men may one day work fulltime beneath the sea instead of visiting it in submersibles. The seabed has been surveyed for the rich deposits of minerals which are known to be present there. In addition to mining, undersea fish farming will one day be possible.

Manned balloons have ascended as far as 22 kilometres and *rocket planes* have reached a height of 51 kilometres, but such ascents are more record-breakers than exploration and as such were overtaken by manned spacecraft in 1961. We know a lot about the upper atmosphere, such studies being of importance to *meteorologists*, but this sort of information comes from auto-

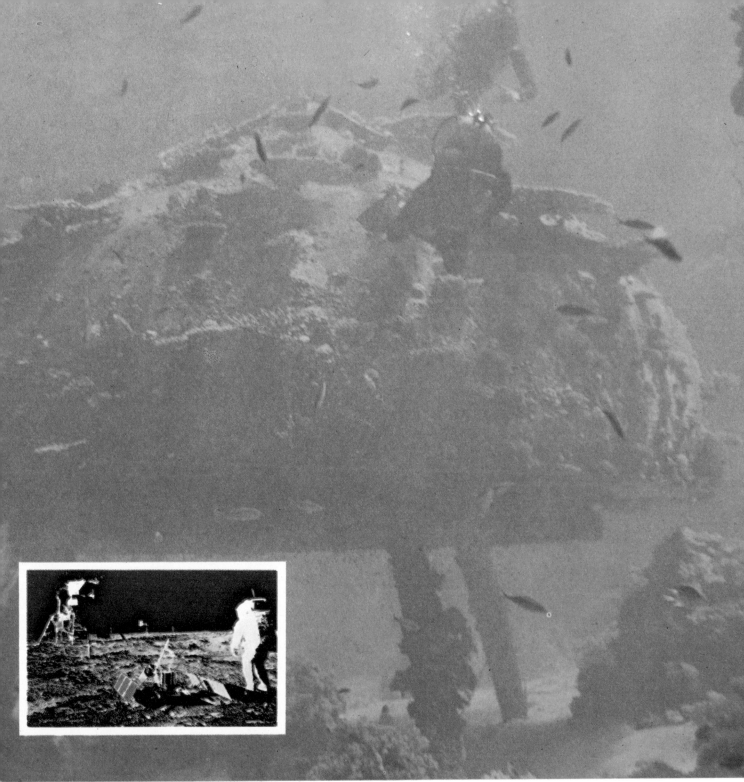

matic instruments and not manned vehicles.

The launching of the first *satellite*, Russia's *Sputnik 1*, in October 1957 ushered in a new era of exploration. From space, satellites orbiting the Earth can look down and offer a new view of our planet, providing meteorologists with an instant picture of the world's weather, as well as helping to map the agricultural land and mineral resource areas below. Other satellites measure conditions in space and some provide television and telephone links between continents. *Space probes* leave the Earth's gravity and travel outwards to other planets. Already they have landed on the Moon and orbited Mars, photographing their surfaces in detail, while other probes have flown past

Above: Precontinental II, Jacques Cousteau's underwater laboratory project located at the Sha'ab Romi Reef at Port Sudan, North Africa.

Inset: A view of the American astronauts on the Moon as they return to the lunar module during the Moon landing of 1972. The first landing, in 1969, symbolized to millions of people on Earth man's eternal curiosity about the Universe. His unsatisfied desire to discover new worlds has perhaps only just begun.

Venus, Jupiter and Mercury and provided us with close-up views of these planets. After leaving Jupiter, another probe is now speeding on its way to take a look at Saturn.

Man first entered space on 12th April 1961 when the Russian *cosmonaut* Yuri Gagarin orbited the Earth. This success spurred a space race between the United States and Russia that culminated in the American Moon landings of 1969 to 1972. The *astronauts* who landed on the Moon were able to set up instruments, gather rock samples and make observations to a far greater degree than automatic Moon probes could have done. Further journeys to the Moon and manned missions to the planets are planned.

The Troubled World

The early 1970s were far from being a time of optimism, and the world and its governments had good reason to feel troubled as *nationalism* and self-interest continued to be the basis on which decisions were generally taken. It may well be argued, however, that it is only a sharpened social conscience and increased means of communication and publicity that make the world seem so much more troubled than in past eras. On the other hand it cannot be denied that never before has mankind had the capacity to destroy itself, so that international collisions are far more serious.

The more serious problems will be with us for the foreseeable future. Drought, floods, famine are endemic to those unfortunate enough to live in certain areas of Africa and the Indian sub-continent. Relief efforts have been only piecemeal and sadly insufficient (see pp. 218-19). Meanwhile large quantities of food in developed countries are destroyed in order to maintain high prices for farmers. *Pollution* of the environment by overpopulation, insensitive planning and chemical waste continues to occur but at least the problem is now recognized.

We may reasonably hope to solve specific political problems in the comparatively short term. At any given time there might be situations that seem incapable of being resolved—during the Korean War and the Vietnam War there seemed to be no end in sight at the time (see pp. 214-15). Yet they are now nightmares of the past, even though their effects may still be reverberating. There were similar problems in the mid-1970s. The most potentially dangerous situation existed in the Middle East. The Arab-Israeli conflict, which had simmered since the Arab states tried unsuccessfully to crush Israel after it received its independence in 1948, burst into violence in 1967. Within six days Israeli forces overran the Sinai Peninsula and reached the Suez Canal. War broke out again in October 1973 and this time Egypt met with some success, regained its pride and so, paradoxically, became more willing to make concessions at the conference table. A disengagement between the two sides was arranged on the Suez-Sinai front and also on the Golan Heights on the frontier of Israel and Syria. But meanwhile *terrorist* attacks by *Palestinian* organizations and Israeli reprisals continued. Huge increases in oil prices levied by the Arab and other oil-rich powers in late 1973 and 1974 caused chaos in the economy of many countries which were already suffering from

Right: The despairing faces of two tribal women as they sit in a United Nations refugee camp in Upper Volta, in the Sahara belt. Several years of very little rainfall brought this area to the level of a desert. The drought caused the deaths of many thousands of head of cattle, the only source of wealth and food of the tribespeople who live here. There are six countries in the Sahara belt, which runs across North Africa, and all of them have suffered tragically from the drought.

Below: Israeli soldiers inspect the remains of a Syrian tank knocked out during the fighting around the town of Kuneitra in the Golan Heights in 1967. The war fought between Israel and Egypt, Syria, Jordan and other Arab states lasted barely six days, yet, in that time, it practically changed the map of the Middle East and almost led to a confrontation between the U.S.A. and the U.S.S.R.

Far right: United Nations observation post outside the town of Nicosia in Cyprus. After the Turkish invasion of the island in 1974, the U.N. arranged a cease-fire and brought in some 3,000 soldiers from seven countries to prevent further fighting and to patrol the area between the Turkish and Greek Cypriot forces.

serious *inflationary problems*, but the huge price increases brought vast wealth to the fortunate producers.

Bangladesh found the world unable to alleviate to any appreciable extent the sufferings caused by a succession of natural disasters made worse by inefficiency and corruption. Having headed the successful struggle for independence from Pakistan in 1971, the Prime Minister Sheik Mujibur Rahman was killed in an *army coup* in 1975. India seemed to be overcoming some of the vast problems raised by an ever-growing and ever hungrier population. But many people were troubled when in 1975 the then Prime Minister, Indira Gandhi, imprisoned members of her political opposition and imposed severe press censorship.

No solution seemed on the horizon after six years of *sectarian strife* in Northern Ireland, during which more than 1,100 troops and civilians were killed. A ceasefire was arranged with the provisional wing of the *Irish Republican Army* (IRA) at Christmas 1974 but the shootings and bombings by both sides continued.

Peace came to Cyprus after the Turkish invasion of the island and its *de facto* partition in 1974. At least the coup against President Makarios, which precipitated the Turkish action, resulted in the downfall of the *colonels' government* in Greece and with the return of Constantine Karamanlis as Prime Minister *democracy* returned to Greece, the country of its origin. The *authoritarian regime* of Marcelo Caetano in Portugal was also overthrown, but the new government was unable to bring stability to the country. The retreat of Portugal from its African colonies left one of them, Angola, torn by warring factions and the scene of full-scale war.

These were some of the problems that plagued the world in the 1970s. No doubt they will be history to the next generation.

Below: Constantin Karamanlis, who became Greek premier in 1974 after the first parliamentary elections in the country for 10 years. During the regime of the Colonels' Junta, many people who opposed it were imprisoned and tortured.

In the end the pressure of world opinion and the growing resistance of the Greek people forced the colonels to surrender their power and to leave office.

DATA DIGEST

Many of the words which are italicized in the previous section are explained more fully in the following data digest. They will help to expand your knowledge of history.

Africanization. The policy in some African countries of reserving jobs for people of African descent rather than for Asians or Europeans.

Alloys. Mixtures of metals, also sometimes of metals with non-metals.

Aluminium. Silvery-white metal obtained by extraction from bauxite ore.

Antibiotics. Drug substances such as penicillin which inhibit or destroy the growth of bacteria.

Antiseptics. Substances that are used externally to destroy bacteria.

Aquanauts. Pioneers of underwater investigations.

Astronauts. American space explorers.

Atmosphere. The air surrounding the Earth, composed of the troposphere, the stratosphere, the ionosphere and, farthest away, the exosphere.

Atoms. Extremely small particles of matter of which all things are made.

Authoritarian regime. Strict government in which the will of the people has little or no influence.

Automation. Extreme degree of mechanization in manufacturing, many of the processes being automatic. Automation often leads to a tremendous increase in efficiency but may also cause widespread unemployment.

Bathyscaphe. Submersible observation chamber developed by Auguste Piccard.

Beveridge Report. Report published in 1942 by a committee chaired by William Beveridge. It recommended a scheme of social insurance to cover the whole population of Britain.

Biologists. Scientists who study living things.

Birth-control methods. Methods of preventing conception and so reducing increase in population.

Capacitors. Devices in electric circuits which store an electric charge.

Chemists. Scientists specializing in chemistry and the new inter-disciplinary fields such as physical-chemistry and bio-chemistry.

Civil rights movement. Movement that aims to give complete legal and social equality to all races.

Colonels' government. The government established in Greece following a coup by a number of army officers in 1967, sometimes also known as the Colonels' Junta.

Computer. Apparatus for carrying out complex calculations and storing information. The computer works at incredible speeds and is now a vital part of almost all industrial operations, space programmes, electronics, mining and increasingly in the medical field.

Conducting material. Material which allows an electric current to flow through it, such as copper and the new generation of special alloys.

Conservation. Keeping from destruction useful features of the environment, such as rural areas, forests and ancient buildings.

Constituent elements. The chemical components which make up all known substances.

Cosmonaut. Russian space explorer.

Débâcle. Disastrous failure.

Detente. Improvement in strained political relations.

Developed countries. Highly industrialized countries, as opposed to the less-industrialized countries of the so-called Third and Fourth Worlds.

Diving bells. Bells made of steel into which air is pumped from the surface to keep water out. They are used for making deep explorations beneath the world's oceans.

Duumvirate. Rule by two men.

Electromagnetic radiation. Waves of energy resulting from the acceleration of an electric charge and associated with an electric or magnetic field.

Electrons. Tiny particles charged with electricity.

Federal. Applied to laws passed by Congress rather than by the various state governments.

Fertilizer. Chemical compound to improve the soil's fertility. Fertilizers may be either man-made or natural.

Fuel. A material that when burned produces heat or power. Among important fuels are oil, coal and natural gas.

Generators. For turning mechanical energy into electrical energy.

Gyrocompass. Compass which does not depend on magnetism but on a rapidly spinning wheel.

Heredity. The transmission of characteristics from generation to generation.

Hovercraft. Vehicle which travels over sea or land supported by a down-driven blast of air.

Hydrofoil. Device which raises a boat from the surface as speed increases. Also applied to the actual boat.

Imperialism. Policy of expansion to gain or maintain an empire.

Inflationary problems. Problems resulting from a rapid rise in prices and a corresponding fall in productivity. This leads to a situation in which the value of money declines and people are forced to pay more for the same quantity of things they need.

Insulin. A hormone which controls the sugar balance in the body. It is produced in the pancreas. People who cannot produce insulin in their bodies suffer from a disease called diabetes.

Interconversion. Ability to convert from one physical state to another.

Internal combustion engines. The type of petrol engines used in motor-cars.

Irish Republican Army (I.R.A.). Military wing of Sinn Fein, the Irish Republican party, which is dedicated to realizing the unification of Ireland.

Jet engine. An engine that provides propulsion by exhaust gases 'pushing' against the air. Turbo-jet engines are the type commonly used in aircraft.

Kremlin. The citadel of Moscow, once the tsar's and now the Soviet government's headquarters. Often used to mean the government.

Kuomintang. Chinese nationalist party founded in 1891 by Sun Yat-sen. Under Chiang Kai-shek it established a government in 1928 and resisted the Japanese. Later it became extremely corrupt, fought a civil war with the Communists and then retreated from mainland China to the island of Taiwan (Formosa).

Labour exchanges. Government offices which help to provide jobs for the unemployed and at which unemployment benefit is paid.

Laser. Made up from the initial letters of Light Amplification by Stimulated Emission of Radiation. It produces a powerful, highly directional beam of light and is now used in a wide variety of applications such as in weaponry, surgery, navigational aids and in precision engineering.

Loudspeaker. Device which, when connected to an amplifier, increases the volume of sound.

Lubricants. Substances, such as oil, which reduce the effect of friction.

Magnetic field. A field of force resulting from the presence of a magnet or of an electric current.

Magnetic levitation. Method of raising a vehicle off the ground by magnetic force rather than by a cushion of air as in the hovercraft.

Magnetic propulsion. The use of magnetic force for driving vehicles.

Malnutrition. Faulty nutrition leading to a number of diseases.

Medical diagnosis. The identification of a disease by its medical symptoms.

Meteorologists. Scientists who study weather and climate.

Microbes. Microscopic organisms, especially bacteria that carry disease.

Microphone. A device which changes soundwaves into electrical energy.

Minerals. Inorganic substances, especially those obtained by mining.

Nationalism. Predominant concern about a person's own country, its political and economic health and its racial makeup.

Nazis. Members of the National Socialist German Workers' Party which Adolf Hitler joined in 1919 and made the instrument of his rise to power. The word 'Nazi' is a shortened form in German of National Socialist.

Nuclear fusion. When a nuclear reaction occurs between light atomic nuclei, a heavier nucleus is formed and there is a release of a huge amount of nuclear energy. This reaction is known as a fusion reaction.

Nuclear power. Power produced by means of a nuclear reactor, using radioactive materials.

Nucleus. The core of an atom in which most of the mass is concentrated.

Oceanographer. Scientist who studies and charts the ocean.

Orbits. Paths of electrons around the nuclei of atoms. It also refers to the orbits of moons round planets, planets round stars and even, in the political

sphere, of satellite countries relationships' to the mother country.

Perspective. Technique a painter uses to give an effect of distance and three-dimensional depth to a picture.

Pesticides. Chemicals used to destroy agricultural pests.

Physical sciences. Sciences concerned with the study of the physical nature of the Earth and universe. The main physical sciences are chemistry, physics, astronomy, geology and meteorology.

Physicists. Experts in physics or natural sciences.

Plastics. Materials manufactured from hydro-carbon compounds and which have a wide variety of applications.

Pocket calculator. Miniature electronic calculating machine which can handle complex calculations, store information and provide data in the fields of mathematics, physics and engineering.

Polar regions. Areas of the North Pole and South Pole.

Pollution. Contamination of the environment, particularly through inefficient methods of processing waste material.

Potsdam Conference. Conference held in 1945 at Potsdam near Berlin. Britain, Soviet Union and the United States agreed that Germany should be kept disarmed and also decided the western frontier of Poland.

Primary goods. Products derived directly from natural or raw material.

Radar. Abbreviation of RAdio Detection And Ranging. The use of microwaves to locate or navigate moving objects such as aircraft or ships.

Radioisotopes. An isotope is an atom of an element with a different atomic weight from other atoms of the element. Some isotopes, such as those of uranium and radium, are radioactive.

Rapprochement. Establishment of good relations.

Recycling. Using again.

Redundancy. Loss of employment through economic contraction.

Reichstag. The German parliament.

Resistors. Devices in electric circuits which resist the flow of current to a fixed degree.

Revolutions. In the Age of Revolutions these were major uprisings occurring in France, Italy, Austria-Hungary and the

German states. There was also unrest in Britain, Ireland, Switzerland and Wallachia. This term also refers to the important uprisings which have occurred in the 20th century in Russia, eastern Europe, Africa and South America.

Royal Commission. A body of inquiry into a particular problem appointed by the British monarch. It presents its findings in a report.

Segregation. A keeping apart of two peoples, usually at the expense of one.

Solar collectors. To use solar energy the sun's rays must be 'captured' in collectors which may be bowl shaped or flat plates.

Space probes. Unmanned spacecraft launched beyond the Earth's atmosphere for exploration of other planets.

Space shuttle. Space vehicle that can travel between the Earth and a space station.

Submersibles. Diving vessels which can be submerged beneath the sea for observation and exploration.

Summit conference. Conference between heads of government.

Supreme Court. The final court of appeal in the United States. It also decides whether laws are constitutionally valid.

Synthetic dyes. Artificially made colouring agents.

Technology. Technical methods; also branches of science that have both a practical value and an industrial application.

Turbines. Motors in which steam, water or expanding hot air drives a wheel or drum.

Transistors. Miniaturized electronic devices which amplify changes in electric currents. Transistors marked a great advance over the older valves, but today transistors themselves are being replaced by semi-conductors which are many times more efficient.

Undeveloped countries. Countries that have not yet fully exploited their natural resources and have a low level of industrialization.

Vitamin. Substance necessary for bodily health. The most important vitamins are A, B, C and D.

Warsaw Pact. Albania, Bulgaria, Czechoslovakia, East Germany, Hungary, Poland, Romania and the Soviet Union signed the Warsaw Pact in 1955.

X-rays. Electromagnetic radiations of a shorter wavelength than light.

Great Names in History

History is about people and in this section of the book we have included biographical details of a few of the famous figures who have made history. It is about the people who have changed the course of events—either by force, or by the peaceful propagation of ideas—or the people whose lives were directly affected, by the actions of others, either at the time or even many generations later.

ALEXANDER III THE GREAT (356-323 B.C.).

King of Macedon and ruler of an empire which at its height stretched from Greece to India. He succeeded his father Philip of Macedon in 336 and quickly regained control of some restless Greek cities, including Thebes. In 334 he began a march of conquest, during which he defeated Persia, took Tyre and Gaza and was welcomed in Egypt where he founded Alexandria. In 331 he routed a large Persian force at Arbela in Mesopotamia and went on to occupy Babylon, Susa and Persepolis. Further conquests south of the Caspian took him into Afghanistan and the Punjab. In 327 he sailed down to the mouth of the Indus and crossed the desert of Gedrosia through Pakistan and Iran. Alexander introduced Greek ideas and laws and ensured fair administration. He died of a fever at the age of nearly 33.

ATATURK, KEMAL (A.D. 1881-1938).

Turkish statesman who revolutionized the political, economic and social life of Turkey. He was born at Salonika and named Mustafa. The name Kemal means perfection, and Ataturk means father of the Turks. As a young man he supported the Young Turk Movement. In the First World War he was chiefly responsible for the Allied defeat at Gallipoli. After the war he resisted the dismemberment of Turkey and set up at Ankara a rival government to that of Sultan Mohammed VI. Ignoring the Treaty of Sèvres, which split up the Ottoman Empire, he retained control of Asia Minor and expelled the Greeks from Anatolia. In 1922 he abolished the sultanate and the next year the Treaty of Lausanne recognized Turkey as an independent republic. Kemal, as president, ruthlessly westernized the country, abolishing such traditions as the wearing of the veil for women, stamping out corruption, encouraging industrialization and introducing modern educational methods and the Roman alphabet.

AUGUSTUS (63 B.C.-A.D. 14).

Generally regarded as the first Roman emperor though technically he was only the *princeps* (first citizen). As a child he was named Gaius Octavius. He was the heir of his uncle Julius Caesar and after his murder he claimed his inheritance. He defeated Mark Antony at Mutina and was elected consul. Then he formed a ruthless three-man dictatorship with Antony and Aemilius Lepidus. Together Octavian and Antony defeated the forces of Brutus and Cassius, the chief conspirators against Caesar, and Octavian took control of the western empire and Antony the eastern. The alliance fell apart when Antony began an intrigue with Cleopatra, queen of Egypt, and at the Battle of Actium in 31 B.C. Octavian defeated Antony's fleet and became virtually sole ruler of Rome, receiving the title Augustus. Augustus secured the empire's boundaries, pacifying Egypt, Gaul, Spain and most of the Balkans though he suffered a serious defeat by the Germans in A.D. 9. At home he ensured honest administration and patronized the arts.

Kemal Ataturk, father of modern Turkey and the country's first president.

BISMARCK, OTTO VON (A.D. 1815-1898).

Creator of a united Germany and sometimes known as the Iron Chancellor. Born in Schönhausen of an upper-class family, he served for a while in the civil service and in 1847 was elected to the Prussian parliament. Four years later he became the Prussian delegate to the German Diet at Frankfurt. After serving as ambassador to Russia and France, he was appointed Prime Minister of Prussia in 1862. In less than ten years he achieved his aim of a united Germany under the leadership of Prussia, winning wars against Denmark, Austria and France. William of Prussia was crowned Emperor of Germany and Bismarck was made Chancellor. Through his diplomatic genius he made a succession of treaties which kept a balance of power in Europe, the most important being the Triple Alliance with Italy and Austria. At home he introduced social reforms although not in sympathy with the socialist viewpoint. In 1890 after a number of clashes William II dismissed him.

BOLÍVAR, SIMÓN (A.D. 1783-1830).

Liberator of Latin America. Born in Caracas, Venezuela, he came into a fortune and for a while toured Europe where he was influenced by revolutionary ideas. Back in Venezuela he took part in an unsuccessful uprising against the Spanish. In 1813 he captured Caracas and when forced out went to New Granada (now Colombia), where he helped to capture Bogotá. Again forced out, he gathered together a force in Haiti and landed at Angostura (now Ciudad Bolívar). He crossed the Andes and liberated New Granada in 1819. Two years later by his defeat of the Spanish at Carabobo he liberated Venezuela and the following year Ecuador fell. He then took over from San Martín the task of freeing Peru, which he accomplished in 1825. The Colombian Union which he established did not last long as the South American countries seceded one by one, and Bolívar died disillusioned.

THE BUDDHA (c. 550-c. 480 B.C.).

Religious teacher who founded Buddhism. The details of his life are shrouded in legend. He was born Siddhartha Gautama at Lumbini in Nepal of rich parents. He married and had a son and lived in extreme luxury. At the age of 29 on a journey he was disturbed by seeing an old man, a sick man and a corpse, all symbols of suffering. He renounced riches, left his family and wandered as a hermit for six years, inflicting severe hardships and mortifications on himself. Eventually he sat under a bo tree and on the 49th day he found Enlightenment and became the Buddha, the Enlightened One. He preached his first sermon at Sarnath near Benares and for the next 45 years travelled, preached and converted people to his ideas.

CAESAR, JULIUS (c. 100-44 B.C.).

Roman general and statesman. When he married Cornelia, the daughter of Cinna, the leader of the popular party, the dictator Sulla drove him out of Rome. He returned in 78 B.C. and made his name as a champion of the great general Pompey. In 60 B.C. they and Crassus formed the First Triumvirate (council of three); Caesar became consul the following year. Later, as proconsul, he showed his brilliant generalship, conquering Gaul, defeating the Germans and twice invading Britain. Pompey, jealous of his success, persuaded the Senate to order Caesar to disband his army. Caesar thereupon crossed the Rubicon, the river dividing his provinces from Italy, and easily took Rome and Italy. He then defeated Pompey at Pharsalus

Sir Winston Churchill, statesman, soldier and writer.

in Greece in 48 B.C. The following year he defeated King Pharnaces of Pontus, his famous report to the senate reading, *Veni, vidi, vici,* I came, I saw, I conquered. He refused the crown but a group of conservatives led by Brutus and Cassius stabbed him to death on the Ides of March (the 15th of March).

CHARLEMAGNE (A.D. 742-814).

King of the Franks and Emperor of the Romans. The son of Pepin the Short, Charlemagne at first shared the Frankish kingdom with his brother Carloman, but on Carloman's death he became sole king. He sealed his friendship with the Church by defeating the Lombards who were at war with the pope. He crushed the Saxons and won victories over the Avars and Slavs. He expanded his kingdom to include Bavaria and much of northern Spain. He made administrative reforms and tried to improve the position of the ordinary people and reduce the power of the nobles. He was a generous patron of the arts; his capital Aachen was notable for the scholars who worked there, led by the Englishman Alcuin. On Christmas Day 800 Pope Leo III crowned Charlemagne Emperor of the West. Charlemagne was later canonized.

CHURCHILL, SIR WINSTON (A.D. 1874-1965).

Britain's prime minister in the Second World War. Born at Blenheim Palace the son of Lord Randolph Churchill and grandson of the seventh Duke of Marlborough, Churchill went to Sandhurst and later served with the Spanish in Cuba and with the British army in India and the Sudan. As a journalist he reported the events of the Boer War, was captured but escaped. In 1900 he was elected Conservative member of Parliament but later crossed to the Liberal party. He became successively Colonial Under-Secretary, President of the Board of Trade and Home Secretary. During the First World War he was First Lord of the Admiralty. He served as a soldier in France for a time, then became minister of munitions. He became Colonial Secretary in 1921, but lost his seat in Parliament the following year. He returned to Parliament in 1924. After a long period out of office he succeeded Neville Chamberlain as prime minister in 1940 and inspired Britain during the rigours of the Second World War with determination and brilliant oratory. In 1945 he was defeated in the first general election after the war, but was prime minister again from 1951 until his resignation in 1955.

COLUMBUS, CHRISTOPHER (A.D. 1451-1506).

Discoverer of the New World. Born in Genoa, he was named Cristoforo Colombo. In 1476 he was shipwrecked off Lagos in Portugal and went to Lisbon and later to the Azores where he developed the ambition to reach the Indies by sailing westward. Since the Portuguese would not sponsor him, he went to the Spanish court of Ferdinand and Isabella. After six years' frustration the queen agreed to finance him. On 3rd August, 1492, Columbus sailed from Palos in the *Santa Mariá* together with the *Pinta* and the *Niña*. On 12th October they reached an island in the Bahamas, continued to Cuba and then to Hispaniola where the *Santa María* was wrecked. Columbus returned in the *Niña*. He made three further voyages to the New World before he died, almost forgotten, in Vallodolid in Spain.

Above: Christopher Columbus, discoverer of the New World.
Below: Captain James Cook, navigator and world explorer.

Confucius, Chinese moral philosopher.

CONFUCIUS (c. 551-479 B.C.).

Chinese moral teacher and philosopher. Most of the details of his life are found in the *Analects*, a collection of his sayings. Born in Tsou in the former state of Lu, he belonged to the class of *Shih* (knights) but was not rich. He became a teacher but in order to reach a larger audience with his theories on how to eradicate the moral evils that were prevalent he needed an influential position. He visited a number of Chinese states trying to find a ruler who would act as his patron, but he was too outspoken and uncompromising and eventually he returned to Lu. There he received a position at court but it was only a minor post. The teachings of Confucius about the proper way to behave later had enormous influence in China.

COOK, JAMES (A.D. 1728-1779).

English navigator and explorer. Born at Marton in Yorkshire, he joined the navy and took part in surveys of the St Lawrence River and the coasts of Labrador and Newfoundland. He led three expeditions to the South Pacific. In 1768 he explored the coasts of New Zealand on board the *Endeavour*. In 1772, with the *Resolution* and *Adventure*, he explored the Antarctic Ocean and discovered New Caledonia. In 1776, with the *Resolution* and *Discovery*, he sailed to New Zealand and the Sandwich Islands (now Hawaii) and showed there was no sea passage from the north-west of North America to the Atlantic. Cook was killed by islanders in Hawaii during a skirmish.

CORTÉS, HERNANDO (A.D. 1485-1547).

Spanish conquistador who conquered Mexico. Born in Estremadura province, he helped in Spain's seizure of Cuba in 1511. In 1518 he led an expedition to Mexico, sailing up the coast and founding Veracruz. He sank his ships to prevent desertions and then led his small force to Tenochtitlán, the site of Mexico City. He took Montezuma, ruler of the Aztecs, prisoner and ruled the country through him. In 1520 the Aztecs attacked the Spanish, who were forced to withdraw in spite of their superiority in arms. The Spanish won a decisive victory at Otumba and in 1521 Cortés, in alliance with Indian tribes hostile to the Aztecs, captured Tenochtitlán and brought about the end of the Aztec empire. Cortés as governor of Mexico sent out a number of expeditions to extend Spanish power. In 1540 he returned to Spain but criticism had lost him the king's favour.

Queen Elizabeth I, the 'virgin queen' who ruled during one of the most glorious periods of English history.

Above: Oliver Cromwell, Lord Protector of England. Below: Charles Darwin, 'Father of Evolution'.

CROMWELL, OLIVER (A.D. 1599-1658).

Lord Protector of England, Scotland and Ireland and fervent republican and Puritan. Born at Huntingdon of a leading local family, he became member of Parliament for that town in 1628. He was extremely active in the Puritan movement, which opposed ceremonial practices in church services. After eleven years, during which the king refused to summon Parliament, Cromwell was re-elected, representing Cambridge. In 1642 civil war broke out between the parliamentarians and the royalists. Cromwell commanded a regiment under Thomas Fairfax, and then in 1648 led the army that defeated the Scots at Preston. After Charles I's execution in 1649 Cromwell ruthlessly suppressed opposition in Ireland. He led the armies that defeated the Scots at Dunbar and Charles II at Worcester. In 1653 he agreed to become Lord Protector but he refused the crown.

DARWIN, CHARLES (A.D. 1809-1882).

Originator of the theory of evolution by natural selection. Born at Shrewsbury, he studied medicine at Edinburgh and theology at Cambridge. He was interested in natural history and acted as official naturalist on a five-year voyage round the world in the *Beagle*. His study of the similarities and differences between various plants and animals led him to the belief, now generally accepted, that all living things have evolved over the ages by what may be termed the survival of the fittest. He worked on his theories in the village of Downe and published his masterpiece, *On the Origin of Species*, in 1859. In *The Descent of Man* (1871) he showed that man has undergone a similar process of evolution to that of other animals. His views caused tremendous controversy for many years.

ELIZABETH I (A.D. 1533-1603).

The 'Virgin Queen', ruler of England during one of its most glorious periods. The daughter of Henry VIII and Anne Boleyn, Elizabeth received a good education. Her half-sister Mary I imprisoned her for a short time for alleged treason, but on Mary's death in 1558 Elizabeth became queen. Because of religious and economic differences Philip II of Spain sent an armada to invade England in 1588 but the skill of the English seamen aided by storms scattered the fleet. Elizabeth was wisely advised for much of her reign by her chief minister, Lord Burghley. Although she never married she had favourites, such as Robert Dudley, Earl of Leicester, and the Earl of Essex, who was executed for treason in 1601. She encouraged enterprise and exploration by men like Sir Francis Drake and Sir Walter Raleigh. At home Roman Catholics were persecuted as the Church of England was the state religion. But the arts flourished, with William Shakespeare later becoming the most famous literary figure of the age.

GALILEO (A.D. 1564-1642).

Astronomer and physicist. Born Galileo Galilei in Pisa, he studied medicine and philosophy. At the age of 25 he became professor of mathematics at Pisa. According to tradition he dropped two objects of widely differing weights from the Leaning Tower of Pisa to demonstrate that gravity pulls with the same acceleration. Certainly he relied on experiment rather than theory to develop general principles. As professor of physics at Padua he built many telescopes and made important astronomical observations, such as the four moons of Jupiter. But he roused the hostility of the Roman Catholic Church when he supported Copernicus's theory that the Earth revolves round the Sun rather than the reverse.

GANDHI, MOHANDAS (A.D. 1869-1948).

Pioneer of India's independence and advocate of non-violence. Born in the state of Porbandar, he was married at 13. He studied law in England and went to South Africa in 1893 as a barrister. He joined the struggle against discriminatory legislation and founded the Natal India Congress. He organized a campaign of non-violent resistance on behalf of the Indian community and won most of his demands. He returned to India in 1915 and after the First World War became a leader of the independence movement. He twice served prison sentences but continued to demand not only a free India but also an end to untouchability, an extreme instance of the caste system. He himself lived extremely simply, wearing only a loin-cloth and a coarse robe and frequently fasting. He was interned for his advocacy of non-violence during the Second World War but took a major part in the negotiations that led to independence in 1947. He was assassinated by a fanatical Hindu and afterwards was known to his followers as *Mahatma*— 'Great Soul'.

Top: Galileo, Italian scientist.
Below and right: Gandhi, pioneer
of India's independence.

Adolf Hitler, dictator of Germany.

Above: Jesus, the Man of Galilee.

HITLER, ADOLF (A.D. 1889-1945).

Dictator of Germany during the Second World War. Born at Braunau in Austria, the son of a customs official, he failed in his ambition to be an artist. He developed a hatred of the Jews and of socialism and became a strong nationalist. He was a corporal in the First World War and afterwards became a demagogic politician building up the National Socialist German Workers' Party, known as the Nazi party. An attempted putsch in Munich failed in 1923 and Hitler was imprisoned. During the economic depression of the late 1920s and early 1930s the Nazis gained vast support. Hitler was defeated for the Presidency but became Chancellor in 1933. He suppressed all opposition, persecuted the Jews and rearmed Germany. His armies invaded Czechoslovakia and Poland and this led to the beginning of the Second World War. By the time Allied armies had entered Germany, and defeat was only a matter of time, Hitler, who by now was completely insane, committed suicide at his Berlin headquarters shortly before the Russians arrived.

GENGHIS KHAN (c. A.D. 1162-1227).

Founder of the Mongol empire and brilliant general. At 13 he succeeded his father as a tribal chief. He built up a Mongol confederacy, subjugating where he could

Above: Genghis Khan.

not persuade, and in 1206 took the title of Genghis (or Jenghiz) Khan in place of his original name, Temujin. He issued a code of laws and reorganized his vast army for a campaign of conquest. First he occupied northern China, taking Peking in 1215. Then he overran Turkestan and Afghanistan and made inroads into Persia and southern Russia. He gained a reputation for ferocity in war but he succeeded in maintaining the unity of a mass of different peoples.

JESUS (c. 5 B.C.-c. A.D. 28).

Founder of the Christian religion and a great moral teacher. His life is told mainly in the four gospels and in the book of Acts. Born in Bethlehem in Palestine, the son of a carpenter, he lived his early life in Nazareth. At the age of 30 he began his mission of proclaiming the kingdom of God and calling on men to repent. He chose twelve apostles as his close companions. The gospels ascribe many miracles to him, mainly instances of healing. After three years he went to Jerusalem. The Jewish authorities arrested him and accused him of blasphemy in claiming to be the son of God and king of the Jews. At their request the Roman governor, Pontius Pilate, reluctantly agreed that Jesus should be crucified. The gospels state that Jesus rose from the dead and talked with his disciples and then went up to heaven.

LENIN, VLADIMIR ILYICH (A.D. 1870-1924).

Revolutionary leader and founder of the Soviet state. Born Vladimir Ulyanov at Simbirsk (now Ulyanovsk), the son of a school inspector, he was expelled from university because of demonstrations against the Tsarist government. In 1895 he was banished to Siberia, after which he lived abroad, continuing to work towards a revolution in Russia. In 1903 Lenin became leader of the newly-formed Bolshevik party. When a revolution broke out in 1905 he returned to Russia but when the revolution failed he went abroad again. In 1917 the February Revolution brought about the deposition of the Tsar, and a moderate provisional government was established. Lenin returned to Russia, won the support of the troops and workers and overturned the government. Lenin introduced sweeping changes, including nationalization of the banks, distribution of land to the peasants and workers' control in factories.

Above: Ilyich Lenin.
Left: King Louis XIV of France.
Right: Abraham Lincoln.

LINCOLN, ABRAHAM (A.D. 1809-1865).

President of the United States during the Civil War. Born in a log cabin in Kentucky, he was storekeeper and postmaster at New Salem, Illinois, to which his family moved. He became a barrister and after serving with distinction in the Illinois legislature was elected to the House of Representatives in 1847. After the Kansas-Nebraska Act allowed slavery in those states Lincoln joined the Republicans, who opposed slavery. In 1860 he was elected president but before he took office seven southern states seceded from the Union. Lincoln, by taking a moderate attitude towards slavery, kept the Union intact though the Civil War could not be avoided. After the Northern victory at Gettysburg in 1863 he made his famous speech about 'the government of the people, by the people, for the people . . .' He was re-elected in 1864 and the war ended the following year, but on 14th April he was shot in Ford's Theatre, Washington, by John Wilkes.

LOUIS XIV (A.D. 1638-1715).

King of France for 72 years from 1643. His mother Anne of Austria was regent until 1661. Louis was determined to be an absolute monarch as is exemplified by the statement attributed to him: 'l'état c'est moi' (I am the state). He also wished to make France supreme in Europe. His territorial ambitions were opposed by various coalitions and seriously depleted the treasury, particularly the War of Spanish Succession (1701-14). At home, aided by the shrewd advice of his minister Jean Colbert, Louis reorganized trade and industry and centralized the administration to some extent. At his brilliant court at Versailles artists of all kinds were encouraged and French culture flourished.

Left: The statue of *David* by Michelangelo.
Above: Michelangelo, painter and sculptor.

MAO TSE-TUNG (A.D. 1893-1976)

Chairman of the Central Committee of the Communist party of China. Born at Changsha in Hunan province, the son of a peasant farmer, he was inspired by the writings of Marx and other revolutionary writers and by the obvious plight of the poor in China to found the Chinese Communist party in 1921. For a while the party was allied to Chiang Kai-shek's Nationalists, but after a split in 1927 Mao lost some influence in his party and devoted himself to organizing the peasants and building up an army. Chiang made several attempts to crush him and he was forced to go on the 'Long March' to Yenan in the north. Mao led guerrilla forces against the Japanese during the Second World War. After the war he advanced inexorably southwards, eventually driving the Nationalists off the mainland. Subsequently, his revolutionary fervour resulted in serious ideological clashes with the Soviet Union.

MICHELANGELO (A.D. 1475-1564).

Sculptor, painter and poet, perhaps the greatest figure of the Renaissance period. Born Michelangelo Buonarroti at Caprese near Florence, he served a year's apprenticeship with Domenico and David Ghirlandaio and then studied under Bertoldo di Giovanni. His earliest works derive from other artists but his genius began to flourish when he went to Rome in 1496 and sculpted *Bacchus*, and the *Pietà* (St Peter's). Back in Florence he sculpted *David* (Florence Academy). In 1508 Pope Julius II persuaded him to paint the magnificent frescoes on the Sistine Chapel ceiling. Michelangelo took four years to complete them, lying on his back most of the time. His next commission was the Medici Chapel in Florence. From 1534 he worked in Rome, his greatest achievement being the *Last Judgment* in the Sistine Chapel. Towards the end of his life he concentrated on architecture. The great dome of St Peter's in Rome is based on his designs.

NAPOLEON I (A.D. 1769-1821).

Emperor of France and one of the world's great military geniuses. Born Napoleon Buonaparte at Ajaccio in Corsica, he went to military schools at Brienne and Paris. He gained quick promotion under the republican governments that followed the French Revolution and made his reputation in northern Italy where he won a decisive victory over the occupying Austrians. After a comparatively unsuccessful campaign against the Turks in Egypt he returned to France, overthrew the government and became first consul of France, the start of a 15-year dictatorship. At home he reorganized the local government and education systems and codified the laws. In 1804 he was crowned emperor. A coalition of Austria, Britain, Russia and Sweden united against France. Napoleon won victories at Ulm and Austerlitz, but the British admiral Horatio Nelson destroyed the French and Spanish navies at the Battle of Trafalgar in 1805. From 1808 France's resources were stretched by the Peninsular War, and the disastrous Russian campaign in 1812 led to Napoleon's abdication and exile in Elba in 1814. The following year he escaped and returned to power but at the end of the 'Hundred Days' he was decisively defeated by the British and Prussians at Waterloo. Napoleon was imprisoned on the island of St Helena in the south Atlantic, where he died.

Above: Napoleon I, emperor of France.
Below: Mao Tse-tung, Chinese leader.

Left: George Washington,
first U.S. president.
Above: Joseph Stalin, Soviet leader.

PERICLES (c. 495-429 B.C.).

Leader of Athens during its Golden Age. Born in Athens into an important political family, he became a leader of the democrats and the dominant figure in the popular assembly. He reduced the power of the aristocracy and the Areopagus, the highest court in Athens, opened up almost all public offices to the whole native-born population and paid salaries for public service. Though known as the founder of democracy, he was an imperialist in foreign affairs. He moved the treasury of the Delian League, Athens' confederacy of allies, to Athens and treated the members as subjects. He used the contributions to construct great buildings, such as the Parthenon and the Odeon. Although Athens and Sparta had concluded a 30-years' truce in 445 B.C., the Peloponnesian War broke out in 431 B.C. Pericles was accused of corruption and deposed, but he was re-elected general in 429 B.C. and died a short while later of the plague.

PETER I, THE GREAT (A.D. 1672-1725).

The father of modern Russia. Born in Moscow, he became sole ruler of Russia in 1689. He was eager to introduce western ideas and make his country a world power. To obtain access to the sea he captured Riga and other Baltic ports and also acquired outlets in the Black Sea. He emphasized ability rather than nobility in his choice of men for high office, but he did nothing to improve the condition of the peasants and forced many to work in the new industries and mining projects that were developed. Peter greatly increased the level of taxation to pay for an improved army and navy, for educational reforms and for a large-scale construction programme of roads and canals. He founded St Petersburg (modern Leningrad) and made it the capital. He died from a cold contracted in an attempt to rescue some soldiers from drowning.

STALIN, JOSEPH (A.D. 1879-1953).

Bolshevik leader and ruler of the Soviet Union for nearly 30 years. Born in Georgia the son of a shoemaker, his original name was Dzhugashvili but he adopted Stalin (man of steel) as his revolutionary name. He was expelled from the theological seminary at Tiflis and worked for the Social Democrats, twice being exiled to Siberia. When the party split Stalin joined Lenin's Bolsheviks. After the overthrow of the Tsar, Stalin edited the newspaper *Pravda* and when the Bolsheviks took power became Commissar for Nationalities. In 1922 he was elected secretary-general of the Communist party. After Lenin's death in 1924 Stalin soon became absolute dictator of Russia. He introduced radical programmes for developing industry and for the *collectivization* of agriculture. He carried out ruthless purges to eliminate all opposition, setting up an extensive secret police network and a vast system of concentration camps to which millions of people were sent for many years. He led the Soviet Union's stubborn resistance, followed by an inexorable advance, in the Second World War. Afterwards he kept a tight hold over the USSR's East European satellites.

WASHINGTON, GEORGE (A.D. 1732-1799).

First President of the United States. Born in Westmoreland County, Virginia, of an old colonial family, his first job was as a surveyor. After five years' service in the army against the French he joined in the movement against British taxation and was a delegate to the Continental Congress in 1774. He was placed in command of the colonial forces and won an outstanding success when he trapped Lord Cornwallis's army at Yorktown, thus ending the war. He presided over the Constitutional Congress in 1787, and in 1789 he was unanimously elected the first President of the United States. In economic affairs Washington favoured a greater degree of centralization than his secretary of state Thomas Jefferson. In his second term he kept America neutral in the conflict between France and other European countries.

Index

PHOTO CREDITS

'To be ignorant of what occurred
before you were born is to remain
always a child. For what is the
worth of human life, unless it is
woven into the Life of our Ancestors
by the records of History.'
Cicero